M.

The Sino-Japanese War, 1937-41

From Marco Polo Bridge to Pearl Harbor

ΛΛΛΛΛΛ
˙·˙·˙·˙·
WVWVV

FRANK DORN

MACMILLAN PUBLISHING CO., INC.

NEW YORK

Library of Congress Cataloging in Publication Data

Dorn, Frank.
    The Sino-Japanese War, 1937-41.

    Bibliography: p.
    1. Sino-Japanese Conflict, 1937-1945—
Campaigns—China. I. Title.
DS777.55.D67   951.04'2   74-10828
ISBN 0-02-532200-1

Macmillan Publishing Co., Inc.
866 Third Avenue, New York, N. Y. 10022
Collier-Macmillan Canada Ltd.

FIRST PRINTING 1974

Printed in the United States of America

Contents

Maps

ACKNOWLEDGMENTS AND SINCERE THANKS ARE OWED TO:

Mr. John E. Taylor, chief of the Military Records Division, National Archives, Washington, D.C., for his cooperation and assistance in making available numerous attaché reports and source materials relating to the Sino-Japanese Incident, 1937–41.

Brigadier General James L. Collins, chief of military history, Department of the Army, Washington, D.C., and Mr. Ditmar Finker and Mrs. Hannah M. Zeidlik of the Records Division, office of the chief of military history, Department of the Army, for their cooperation and assistance in making available extensive Japanese studies and manuscripts dealing with the Sino-Japanese Incident and World War II in the Pacific.

Major Edward Kaprielian and Mr. Stephen Hardyman of the Map Division, Department of Military History, Department of the Army, for their assistance in obtaining large-scale maps of China of the period 1937–41.

Rear Admiral Earl E. Stone, U.S. Navy, retired, now director of the Allen Knight Maritime Museum, Monterey, California, for his personal observations and for making available extensive and authoritative material on the Japanese attack at Pearl Harbor on December 7, 1941.

Rear Admiral Howard S. Moore, U.S. Navy, retired, Camarillo, California, and Brigadier General Frederick P. Munson, U.S. Army, retired, Washington, D.C., for providing copies of the official Chinese · history of the Sino-Japanese War, 1937–45, compiled under the direction of the government of the Republic of China, Taiwan.

General Paul L. Freeman, U.S. Army, retired, and Mrs. Freeman, Carmel, California, for permitting the use of photographs from their private collection of action in China from 1938 to 1941.

Mr. H. Royce Greatwood of Carmel, California, for permitting the use of photographs he collected during his long service as an executive of the Union Oil Company in China and of the British Government.

Miss Charlotte Palmer of the Audiovisual Archives Division, National Archives, Washington, D.C., for her cooperation and assistance in the selection of action photographs of the Sino-Japanese War.

Mrs. Phyllis Moore Dorn, my wife, for her encouragement, advice, countless suggestions, invaluable assistance in editing, and patience during the preparation of this book.

In war, the only sure defense is offense; and the efficiency of the offense depends on the warlike souls of those conducting it.

GENERAL GEORGE S. PATTON, JR.

Those who cannot remember the past are condemned to repeat it.

GEORGE SANTAYANA

The Sino-Japanese War,
1937-41

1

Peking, July 7, 1937

As SUMMER TWILIGHT faded into darkness, the sixteen massive, iron-studded gates in the towering walls of Peking ground in protest on their ancient stone rollers. Each set of slowly closing panels was pushed by straining groups of gray-clad soldiers, until with a final clang they were shut tight. The men dropped heavy wooden locking bars in place and were finished with that nightly task. Wiping sweating faces on dirty towels and retrieving their long-handled swords and ancient rifles, they shuffled off toward the nearest tea shops. A few late-arriving carters, cameleers, and travelers outside the gates shouted in vain for entrance. Their cries attracted the attention of small groups of bystanders who listened with curiosity until the frustration and rage of the protesters began to subside. Then they, too, quietly padded away from the *enceintes* into nearby dark alleys. The Chinese citizens of this former capital of three empires had felt secure in their ancient defenses for nearly 700 years. They still did, as they settled down for the night behind locked doors and gates and shuttered shops.

Not so the majority of the foreign population: diplomats, attachés, embassy guards, educators, and owners of expensive shops, with convenient lapses of memory, or lacking a sense of history or prescience, rested their security on an abiding faith in the unchallenged might of the white man in the Far East. Within their world of power, intimidation, and great wealth, they believed implicitly in the ability of their governments to keep any danger or unpleasantness at a respectable distance—certainly beyond the walls of the Legation Quarter, their converted palaces and their schools.

As was usual, many lesser gates and doors in Peking were swung wide open on that hot July night. In high spirits, fashionably clad guests swept into high-ceilinged dining rooms and reception halls; silent Chinese servants moved among them, around glittering candle-lit tables, through moon gates in lantern-lit courtyards, past still pools in flower gardens under the summer moon. Others, confident that nothing would ever disturb the serenity of their lives in the old city, rode in chauffeur-driven cars through the narrow alleyways. They were off to lavish Russian-style dinners, to centuries-old restaurants for Chinese dinners of many courses, to the cool roof of the French-owned Grand Hotel de Pékin for dancing, or merely to an evening of bridge—continuing along the social treadmill they daily traveled like so many smiling, impeccably groomed marionettes.

In all that great city of walls and towers, temples and yellow-roofed palaces, tree-shaded parks and lakes, great avenues and muddy alleys, haughty embassies and gray mud houses of the poor, only Japanese lights burned late for neither pleasure nor relaxation. Behind the closed, guarded gates of their huge embassy and barracks compound, Japanese military officers pondered over maps, bowed ceremoniously to each other, and gave and took harsh, guttural commands with the solemnity of men undertaking a mission of high purpose. Field exercises of the Japanese army were taking place that night: near Lukouchiao, at the junction of the railway from Tientsin and the Peking-Hankow line, the Tanake Brigade of three infantry regiments, one tank company, and one field-artillery regiment would be operating in the darkness only 12 miles from the old city.

Outside the city, near where the Japanese night exercises were taking place, many of the peasants living in the open villages had been unable to find refuge in the small walled town of Wanping. The commander of the Chinese garrison had ordered the gates closed until the hated troops of the "dwarf people" returned to their barracks in Tientsin and Peking. So the villagers huddled in their mud houses and shuddered with fear at each tread of marching boots. They prayed to the spirits of their grandfathers to spare pigs, chickens, and meager crops of corn and sorghum from the ravages of the foreign troops.

The Wanping commander's orders had come from General Sung Che-yuan, commander of the Chinese 29th Army (actually a corps by western military standards), and had been specific: under no circumstances permit an incident of any kind. Despite the forceful tone of that directive, the general's command of the Peking area was unsteady at best. Many of his troops would be forced to rely on the bravado of swinging their big, long-handled swords if ordered to resist the modern firepower of the ever-threatening Japanese army.

But despite all caution, the incident that had been dreaded occurred. During the night, rifle and mortar fire awakened the terrified villagers of Lukouchiao, the railway workers at Fengtai, the townspeople of Wanping, and Sung Che-yuan's guards at the south and southwest gates of the Outer City. A Japanese soldier had been shot and killed—by whom, no one could, or would, say (not then or later). Had it been an accident in the darkness? Had it been on orders from hot-headed Japanese officers deliberately creating a pretext for further demands on China? In any case, the victim's outraged battalion commander immediately accused a detachment of Chinese troops guarding the railway junction near the Lukouchiao bridge of firing on his men. A brief skirmish followed, and the 29th Army's 38th Division troops withdrew inside Wanping's gates to rejoin their regiment under Colonel Chi Hsing-wen.

Early the next morning, the American ambassador and his staff heard distant artillery and mortar fire as they were handed reports of the night's events near Lukouchiao: Colonel Chi had refused to surrender the Chinese officers charged with responsibility for the death of the Japanese soldier, whereupon the Japanese had surrounded and attacked the town. As he studied the scanty information, Colonel Joseph W. Stilwell, the American military attaché, looked grim. When he glanced out his office window, he saw a flight of Japanese aircraft overhead.

The city grew silent and tense. Worried citizens began to send their women and children through the northerly gates of the old capital into the supposed safety of the country—toward the emperor's summer palace and the Western Hills, Nankow Pass, and

Kupeikou. Reports and conjecture flew wildly about the city. A United Press report stated that the famous Marco Polo Bridge over the Hun River at Lukouchiao had been destroyed. Later that day, it was learned that this beautiful bridge, originally built in 1194, had been only slightly damaged.

When the assistant U.S. military attaché, Major David D. Barrett, drove out to investigate the situation in his office's touring car, a 1929 Dodge, tempers had cooled somewhat. Japanese and Chinese were shouting at each other from the parapets of the town walls and from the road before the main gate of Wanping; they agreed to discuss terms for a settlement. The garrison commander nevertheless refused to open the gate. Instead, he seated himself in a wooden armchair on top of the wall, and dangling at the ends of two ropes, he was lowered to the ground where the discussions were continued in lower tones. It was at once made clear to Barrett that his presence was neither needed nor wanted. As he quit the scene, he saw the dead Japanese soldier lying sprawled on the ground surrounded by a grim platoon of guards.

The next day, July 9, Colonel Stilwell drove to Wanping to talk to the Chinese commander, but was forced back by heavy rifle and machine-gun fire from both sides. The town was attacked that day, but the Chinese garrison held; with the arrival of Japanese reinforcements two days later, Wanping again was assaulted and was taken. From the beginning the Japanese maintained that the Chinese had fired first. They also insisted that a truce had been agreed upon—both sides to withdraw from the Wanping-Lukouchiao area—but that the Chinese had opened fire for a third time and had thus forced the attack on the town. During the brief siege, the Japanese commander, General Tashiro, died suddenly of a heart attack; he was succeded by General Kyogi Katsuki.

In the meantime, disturbing reports began to pour in: the Sakai and Suzuki brigades from the Kwantung Army of Manchuria were moving through the Great Wall at Kupeikou into Hopei province; 10,000 Japanese soldiers had moved into Chinese territory; troop trains headed toward Tientsin were passing through Shanhaikuan at half-hour intervals; trucks loaded with men and matériel of the Japanese 5th and 20th divisions were clogging the Shanhaikuan-Tongshan-Tientsin road. Only two days after the incident at Lukouchiao, the long-expected Japanese invasion of north China was underway. After such a display of logistic efficiency by the Japanese, one must wonder how the killing of a single soldier could have set in motion such a large operation on such short notice—unless, of course, the incident had been deliberately planned as an excuse for aggression.

On July 11 Prince Fuminaro Konoye, the Japanese premier, officially sanctioned military deployments already set in motion. He approved sending into China two brigades of the Kwantung Army, one division from Korea, and three divisions from Japan. With supporting troops and air units, the Japanese invasion forces would number close to 150,000 men.

Foreign troops in Peking and Tientsin, including the embassy guard of U.S. Marines and the U.S. 15th Infantry, were ordered on 24-hour alert. Both Chinese and foreign residents of the port city crowded into the concession areas. Streams of Peking residents surged in panic through the city gates into the country; other streams of country people, equally panicked, poured through the same gates into the protection of the city walls. . . .

There was still little information, not even on the location of most units of the Chinese 29th Army; no word of any possible troop deployments to counteract the perilous situation in the Peking area; no indication of the Chinese government's plans or intentions. Members of Stilwell's staff, hastily augmented by a few officers from Tientsin, were sent off in all directions to seek reliable information. In most cases they returned to report little or nothing about Chinese military movements, but brought back vivid descriptions of the shelling, burning, and seizing of one undefended village after another. I was sent to find out what I could at Fengtai and Wanping. At the Fengtai rail marshaling yards two trigger-happy Chinese soldiers poked their bayonets against my stomach and ordered me back to the city. After much bluffing on my part and shouting on theirs, a young officer resignedly waved me on toward Wanping. The main gate of the town had been blasted open by artillery fire. Houses and shops had either been burned out or blown out. The streets were cluttered with debris and rubble. The townspeople had fled, leaving the wreckage of their homes and shops to skinny stray dogs.

The Japanese issued an ultimatum that if accepted would surrender all of Hopei and Chahar provinces to their control. The Chinese government was given until July 18 to answer—meaning in Japanese eyes to accede to their demands. Meanwhile, the Japanese militarists in Tokyo constantly reassured Prince Konoye, who was opposed to the Kwantung Army's planned venture into China, that the operation now under way was intended merely to protect Japanese lives and property. The whole problem, they insisted, would be solved in three months. At the time, as well as after the war, the general staff of the Japanese army asserted that it had done its utmost to forestall aggressive operations in China. Perhaps it had, publicly; but it had made little or no effort to prevent the actions of its expansionist generals.

Goaded into action by his more bellicose generals, Chiang Kai-shek at last issued a statement: China was forced to accept the necessity of military resistance to Japanese aggression; no further territory in north China would be surrendered; the sovereign rights and integrity of China could not be usurped and invaded. Nevertheless, with good reason Chiang did not rule out the possibility of a settlement with the Japanese. For years, all of his thoughts and plans had been focused on the destruction of his internal enemies, the Chinese Communists; he had no plan to combat an invasion by his external enemies, the Japanese.

But plan or not, the war was on—an undeclared war that was to cause the deaths of tens of millions of people, one of the greatest migrations in history, incalculable destruction of cities, the utter prostration of the most populous nation on earth, and the overthrow of a system of life and thought that had existed with little change for over 2,000 years.

In July, 1937, the Japanese army had 21 regular divisions of 462,000 well-trained, well-equipped, and well-supplied officers and men; about 1.5 million trained reserves; and a replacement pool of nearly 2.5 million partly trained men. The Kwantung Army's additional Manchurian, Mongolian, and Chinese puppet troops were neither dependable nor effective and gradually disappeared from the fields of battle.

The Chinese army had 182 infantry divisions and 46 separate brigades, 9 cavalry divisions, and 28 artillery regiments, with a paper strength of over 2 million officers and men. There were no trained reserves of any kind, but there existed a huge pool of unskilled and semiliterate peasants from which to draft recruits. With the exception of 10 fairly well-trained divisions, Chinese training could be characterized as unsatisfactory to nonexistent for practical military purposes. In general, equipment and weapons, which had been acquired from various unrelated sources, were obsolete and in relatively poor condition. Ammunition was scarce and was usually hoarded by commanders who knew they could not expect a resupply, and without which they would lose all political clout. Large quantities of small-arms ammunition were wasted by poorly fed soldiers who removed bullets from cartridge cases to satisfy their craving for salt with the taste of gunpowder. The central government under Chiang Kai-shek had been able to gain direct control over no more than one-fourth of the total number of troops, partial control of probably one-half by means of tenuous agreements and deals with powerful regional commanders, and little or no control of the remaining one-fourth, who were commanded by virtually independent commanders of the warlord type. On his first contact with the Chinese army in the field, a shocked American officer referred to what he saw as a "goddam medieval mob"—a not too inaccurate description.

At full strength, a Japanese infantry division had 21,945 officers and men and 5,849 horses. It was organized in two brigades of two regiments each, one artillery regiment, one cavalry regiment, one engineer regiment, one quartermaster regiment, one tank company, and miscellaneous headquarters and supporting units. Its armament consisted of 9,476 rifles, carbines, and pistols; 576 grenade launchers and mortars; 541 light machine guns; 104 heavy machine guns; 64 pack howitzers; 44 light artillery guns; and 24 tanks. It was assigned 266 light trucks and 555 horse-drawn vehicles. The supply of ammunition was adequate, though artillery shells and aerial bombs were not always dependable because of the use of cheap, unstable picric acid in explosives.

Theoretically and for pay purposes the Chinese infantry division had 10,923 officers and men; however, only 10 divisions in the entire army came close to that strength, and even their strengths varied. The remainder averaged about one-half of the prescribed number—4,000 to 6,000 men. Many had no more than 3,000 in their ranks. The reason for this seeming neglect in obtaining replacements was intentional. The pay and subsistence allowances for all troops were paid in lump sums to commanders for distribution. Since a military career in China was considered a means of self-enrichment—as were all government and commercial positions—commanders parceled out monies received as they saw fit and pocketed the rest. By falsely reporting nearly full strength for their units, honest commanders—and there were a very few—were able to accumulate extra funds, not to pocket but to provide better rations for their men. The Chinese infantry division was organized in two brigades of two regiments each, one artillery battalion, one engineer battalion, one quartermaster battalion, and usually an oversized collection of headquarters and supporting units. Its armament consisted on paper of 3,821 rifles, carbines, and pistols of obsolete international vintage; 243 grenade launchers and mortars, which were seldom up to full strength; 274 light and 54 heavy machine guns from assorted purchases in the arms market; 16 pack howitzers; and 30 obsolete German, Russian, or Italian light artillery pieces, which usually were not available to most units. A few divisions were armed with the equivalent of six-inch guns and howitzers, for which there was an inadequate supply of ammunition, as was the case in all other categories. But the medium artillery pieces made a fine show and created an illusion of power almost as good as the real thing. The Chinese Ordnance Department had started to manufacture its own 7.92-millimeter small arms and two classes of mortars, but at the time of the attack limited production had permitted only a partial issue of the new weapons to a few selected units. A few divisions had been assigned trucks in inadequate numbers, but the great majority were forced to depend on horse-drawn vehicles and impressed farm carts, pack animals where available, and t'iao-tzes ("human carriers").

The Japanese navy was the third largest and most powerful in the world; the Chinese navy consisted of a negligible number of small vessels, some almost antique, and 12 obsolete torpedo boats, none of which were combat-ready or seaworthy. Nor were the officers and crews ready. One of the torpedo boats had gone about its business for 13 years with an armed torpedo stuck fast in one of its tubes. The mishap had occurred on a rare practice firing, and since removal had been too difficult at the time, the torpedo was left to rust in place.

Between them, the Japanese army and navy had about 2,800 bomber and fighter aircraft, but compared to the more sophisticated combat planes of other countries, Japanese aircraft were sadly lacking in electronic equipment. The Japanese were of course fully aware that they were preparing to confront only a very poorly prepared enemy. Though the Chinese air force had some 600 aircraft of various types and manufacture—Italian, Russian, German, and American—only 305 were combat planes, the others being trainers and transports.

Command in the highly indoctrinated and dedicated Japanese army was harsh, unimaginative, and effective; however, slavish respect for superiors and literal acceptance of detailed orders often left younger officers confused and indecisive when suddenly faced with unexpected situations. Planning and staff work at the upper echelons were meticulous and often bold, if not highly principled. Individual initiative was not encouraged at any level of command, but readiness to sacrifice one's life in serving the emperor was virtually sanctified.

Command in the poorly indoctrinated, ill-fed Chinese army was harsh, sometimes whimsically childish, and steeped in ancient military conceptions suited to bow-and-arrow times; it ranged between being partially effective and completely ineffective. Courage and a willingness to fight heroically were not lacking among younger officers and enlisted men, but too many officers of general and field rank, many of whom were political appointees, were inept, cowardly, and venal, given to such instruction as a soldier marches into battle standing erect and proud like a man, not crawling on the ground like an animal—and of course presenting an easy target to the enemy. The top ranks of the army were riddled with varied allegiances, prejudices, and personal loyalties. There was no focal leader to whom all could give unquestioned loyalty—though Chiang Kai-shek had done his best to hoist himself to that position of respect. His best had not been good enough. His manner inspired fear, his position cupidity—seldom loyalty. Planning and staff work at all echelons of the Chinese army were either inadequate or nonexistent.

In summation, the average strength in manpower of the Japanese division was about four times that of its Chinese counterpart. In small arms it had two and one-half times the firepower; in light and heavy machine guns twice the firepower; in pack howitzers four times the firepower; in other artillery one and one-half times that of the Chinese division—if the Chinese division was fully equipped. In tanks and in ammunition supply Japanese strength was overwhelming; in mobility the Chinese were not even comparable. Following the Lukouchiao incident, the Chinese were able to deploy no more than 40 percent, about 800,000 troops, of their 2-million-man army against the Japanese. To Generalissimo Chiang Kai-shek it was more important to "maintain internal security"—namely, to keep close watch on the recently reconciled Chinese Communists with their some 400,000 men and on various semi-independent leaders throughout the country. Even the Chinese War Ministry at Nanking was committed to the proposition that one Japanese division was equivalent to five Chinese divisions and that six to eight Chinese divisions would be required to launch an offensive action against one Japanese division. Considering the fumbling inability of the average Chinese commanding general and the deplorable condition of his troops, those ratios or rules of thumb were optimistic.

2

What Was behind It All?

THE NEXT DAY, when news of the Japanese attack at the Marco
Polo Bridge reached the chancelleries of the Western world, reaction in those leisurely offices was more annoyance than alarm.
In Washington, where impatience with Japanese aggressive moves
against China had long been manifest, it was decided to await
further developments before submitting one more protest to the
representative of His Imperial Majesty's government. It would
be simpler to wait than to get into another diplomatic hassle.
As usual, London was concerned with the possible effects on its
commercial interests in China and Hongkong, rather than with
any political aspects of the attack. Both governments were still
deeply preoccupied with the aftermath of the depression of
1929 and were in a constant state of apprehension over the
ramifications of Hitler's rise to power in Germany, not to mention the so-called Anti-Comintern Pact between Germany and
Japan made the year before. Perhaps this flare-up, like so many
others, would prove to be just another incident, one more nibble
at China's northern provinces. No one foresaw—or had the wish
to foresee—the cataclysmic results of the death of an unknown
soldier on a minor military exercise in an obscure Chinese village. Some Western observers in China maintained for months
that if one did not accept this latest incident as the beginning of
a war, it would all blow over in time; if one kept pretending it
wasn't there, it would somehow go away.

Long imbued with sentimentality toward the Chinese people,

the governments and nationals of most Western powers once again experienced the pangs of a nagging guilt that was to grow with ensuing years—never, however, to such an extent as to jeopardize their assumed right to benefit commercially in the Far East. That wispy sense of guilt stemmed from the nineteenth-century mercantile policies of the colonial powers—the British Empire, France, Germany, Russia, Italy, and the United States. They had clawed at the edges of a once-great China, had penetrated its interior by a sort of imperialistic osmosis, and had crippled its shaky economy. They had attacked its ancient Confucian system in the name of Christian teaching, and in the process had done as much harm as good. They had created a supine giant so weak and fragmented that it was always ripe for further aggressions. And in doing so, they had pointed the way along the paths of exploitation and aggrandizement to the militarists of the Japanese Empire.

A late starter in the China sweepstakes, Japan was forced by national pride, over-population, and plain greed to move aggressively if she were to keep abreast of her rivals from Europe and America. In the sixteenth century, Japan had itself been the victim of disruptive religious and trade incursions from the West, notably through the conversion to Christianity of a sizable minority of its people by Francis Xavier and his Spanish Jesuits. The Tokugawa shogun of the time had solved that disturbing situation by the simple expedient of ordering the massacre of all Japanese Christians. As the centuries passed, Dutch and Portuguese merchants, like termites gnawing at an unprotected basement, gained small footholds for trade on the island of Kyushu. Then, in 1853, Commodore Matthew Perry, with a small squadron of the U.S. Navy, persuaded the shogun that it would be to his benefit to open Japanese ports for trade with the West. (Perry was astonished to receive a reply in English to the note he had addressed to "the ruler of Japan." The writer, a shipwrecked sailor named Nakahama Manjiro, had been picked up by a Captain Whitfield, master of the ship "John Howland," and educated in Fairhaven, Massachusetts, for six years before returning to Japan in 1849.)

The feudal Japanese were soon to turn their backs on their own past and emulate the technologically oriented civilization

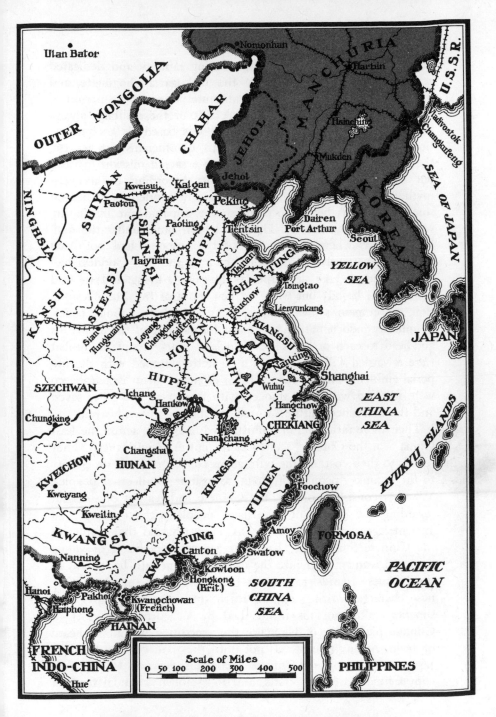

Japanese-occupied Areas in East Asia on July 7, 1937

of the West. They did so with amazing rapidity and dedicated zeal. In 1867, they overthrew the Tokugawa shogunate and restored the emperor to full and absolute power in the person of the vigorous Mutsuhito (Meiji). A cult of the military, always latent in Japan, quickly developed. It was based on a combination of Shinto teaching, Zen Buddhism, Confucianism in reverse, the samurai code, and a blind belief in a sacred mission to carry out the will of their divine emperor. According to accepted mythology the Goddess of the Sun had descended from heaven some 2,500 years before to establish the imperial line by mating with an ambitious mortal. There had been times under the military shoguns when the divinity of the emperor had not been taken very seriously—indeed, one scion of the Sun Goddess had been forced to take up carpentry to earn a living and to feed his imperial brood—but with the new glory of the Meiji restoration, the emperor's divinity became an important, popular belief. In military indoctrination, it imparted a measure of the emperor's god-head to each of his soldiers. In later years, troops in combat were rewarded with the gift of a cigarette stamped with the imperial emblem. These "divine" tubes of cheap, Army-issue tobacco were received with awe, smoked with reverence, the ashes saved and the blackened butts treasured as a blessing from heaven.

Their more rational and sophisticated neighbors across the East China Sea, the Chinese, scoffed at the entire divinity thesis. They relied, to their cost, on the outrageous conceit of their superiority to the "monkey people" of Japan, as well as to all other peoples. Whether consistent or not, the Chinese had reasons of sorts for regarding the origins of the island people with contempt: an ancient legend dating from the sixth century said that a ruler of the Chinese Sui dynasty had sent a great expedition of young men and women to civilize the unlettered, uncouth barbarians of the Japanese islands, to convert their outlandish speech to Chinese character writing, and to teach them the arts, crafts, and superior culture of his realm. Led by an enthusiastic sort of Chinese pied piper of Hamelin, the expedition was never heard of again. At any rate, it was not until the sixth century that the Japanese, by adopting Chinese characters, learned to write, to copy Chinese arts and crafts, and to establish a feudal form of government similar to that of China, which continued with little change until the middle of the nineteenth century.

The Japanese had scarcely begun their relationships with Western powers—somewhat awkwardly to be sure—when they began to realize that they had been duped by a lot of high-flown rhetoric concerning the mutual advantages of trade and the benefits of "civilized" teaching. The big-nosed, red-faced, yellow-haired foreign ruffians talked loudly of democracy and parliaments; yet all the while they continued to prop up the decaying absolutist dynasty in Peking—even as they burned the Chinese emperor's summer palace and looted his capital—because they knew they could manipulate that corrupt regime for their own advantage. The awakening Japanese soon looked on the colonial powers with their great ships and roaring cannons as a threat to themselves as well as to the Chinese.

Since the seventeenth century, the Russians had been pushing steadily eastward across Siberia. In 1860 they had finally managed to wrest from China the Maritime Province with its port of Vladivostok directly across the Sea of Japan from the main Japanese island of Honshu. With tremendous effort the Russians had built the 5,000-mile Trans-Siberian Railway for the purpose, according to the Japanese viewpoint, of transporting troops for further depredations in east Asia. Once they crossed the Amur and Ussuri rivers into Manchuria, the Russians would not only threaten north China, but also check growth of Japan's ambitions for a continental land grab of its own. They had even crossed the Bering Strait and set up trading posts and a government of sorts in Alaska. Since they had sold Alaska in 1867 to the United States, that sale had given the Americans a foothold in the western Aleutians only 500 miles from the northernmost of the Kurile Islands. It was now clear to the Japanese that their empire was threatened from the northwest by Russian land power and from the east by American sea power.

The first British trading ship had put in at the Chinese port of Canton in 1637, less than 20 years after Englishmen had founded Jamestown and the Virginia colony. From the end of the eighteenth century, British, French, and Dutch traders had been permitted by the Chinese government to establish, under stringent regulations, "factories"—actually places of business and trade—outside the walls of Canton. But having little to offer that the Chinese either wanted or needed, this trade was a one-sided affair until the foreigners introduced Indian-grown opium, the sale and use of which had been banned by imperial edict. (The importation of Indian opium continued until 1913, when the Chinese-grown product filled the needs of the people.) When the Viceroy of Canton refused to permit further sale of the drug to his people and ordered part of a British cargo burned at the wharves, British men-of-war attacked the flimsy junks of the Chinese fleet at the mouth of the Pearl River and proceeded upstream to the viceregal capital. The Opium War of 1839–42 had begun. Soon defeated, the humiliated Chinese were forced to cede the island of Hongkong to England and to open six so-called treaty ports between Canton and Shanghai to foreign trade. On the heels of the final settlement, American clipper ships appeared at the ports and, along with the British and French, traded opium for tea and other Chinese goods. The second Opium War of 1856–60 resulted in another resounding defeat by Anglo-French forces of the poorly armed Chinese imperial troops, the opening of 10 more treaty ports, legalization of the sale of opium, the right to navigate the Yangtze River, to own property, to exchange diplomatic representatives, and to establish foreign courts in China. Though not belligerents, Russia and the United States took part in the negotiations leading to the unequal treaty. Such inroads by these foreign vultures, reasoned the Japanese, might occur in their islands, too, if the empire failed to act fast in building a modern army and navy to block them.

In 1885 France moved in troops and took over the tributary kingdoms of Tonkin and Annam (they had already established themselves to the south in Cochin China), the British seized the Chinese tributary states of north Burma, and 10 more treaty ports were more or less forcibly opened to Western trade.

In 1894, in defiance of all the accepted rules of the Far East game as laid down by the Western powers, the Japanese attacked China. This was Japan's first overt act of military aggression against the Chinese since their attempted invasion of Manchuria nearly 500 years before. The war did not last long: not only were

the neglected Chinese armies overwhelmingly defeated in southern Manchuria, but the powerless navy—most of whose funds
had been diverted to construct and embellish the dowager
empress's summer palace—was wiped out. The "dwarf people" of
Japan forced China to abolish the tributary status of the kingdom of Korea and to grant it "independence"; to cede Formosa,
the Pescadores, and the Ryukyu Islands to Japan; to give up the
strategic Liaotung peninsula in southern Manchuria; and to pay
a large indemnity.

Alarmed at the success of the Asian upstarts, Russia and the
other European powers pressured the Japanese into withdrawing
from Liaotung, managing, however, as though they were render-
ing a great service to China, to exact additional special rights and
concessions for themselves. When the dust from the diplomatic
maneuvering had settled, the Russians had been granted a concession to build the Chinese Eastern Railway across the northern
half of Manchuria to connect Vladivostok and Chita, thus short-
ening the rail distance between the two cities by over 800 miles.
Then, in 1898, by means of threats and bribes, the Tsarist government induced China to lease the southern part of Liaotung, the
Kwantung peninsula, where the naval base of Port Arthur and
the commercial port of Dalny (later called Dairen) were constructed. The British grabbed Weihaiwei on the north coast of
the Shantung peninsula and extracted a long-term lease to Kowloon on the mainland across the bay from Hongkong. The
French took Kwangchow Bay near the Indo-China border and
were granted a concession to build a railway linking Haiphong
and Hanoi to Yunnanfu (later called Kunming) in Yunnan
province.

Berlin blatantly used the murder of two German missionaries
as an excuse to demand, and receive, Kiaochow Bay as a naval
base, the port city of Tsingtao, concessions in the hinterland of
Shantung province, and the right to build a railway from Tsingtao to the provincial capital of Tsinan. From that time on, none
of the Western powers ever hesitated to exploit the difficulties of
their missionaries, preferably dead ones because of their bargaining value, to achieve their own ends; the race for prizes between
the predatory foreigners gained momentum. The rich Yangtze
Valley became a British sphere of interest, most of Shantung a

German sphere, and Yunnan a French one. And smarting over the loss of one of the choice fruits of their victory over China, the resentful Japanese determined to regain the Kwantung peninsula, Port Arthur, Dalny, and more. The militarists of Japan did not have long to wait for their first revenge.

The American war with Spain, originally billed as a crusade to liberate Cuba from the harsh yoke of the Spanish government, had scarcely got under way when, on orders from Assistant Secretary of the Navy Theodore Roosevelt, Commodore George Dewey destroyed a decrepit Spanish fleet in Manila Bay. The American leap from the Caribbean to the South China Sea left the Japanese fairly gasping for breath. Not only were American troops now within 200 miles of southern Formosa, but the American navy had established a string of stepping stones all of the way across the Pacific: the Hawaiian Islands, Midway, Wake, Samoa, Guam, and finally the Philippines—within relatively easy striking distance of the China coast. This could only be interpreted as one more threat to the safety of the empire of the Japanese.

But the Boxer uprising in north China in 1899–1900 gave Japan's generals and admirals genuine cause for satisfaction. Though few of their nationals were imperiled, they gladly joined the international force of some 6,000 troops from Britain, the United States, Germany, France, and Russia that slowly bungled its way over the 90 miles from Tientsin to Peking to rescue the besieged legations from the murderous intentions of the dowager empress Tzu Hsi's Boxers. In this operation, largely because its troops were readily available, Japan was at last accepted as a member of the exclusive club of Western powers and, along with the other victorious allies, was allowed to enjoy the right of conquerors—namely to pillage and burn the palaces, temples, and homes of Peking. Japanese chagrin because the Americans were the first to scale the walls of Peking and raise their flag and because the Russians made off with the largest share of the loot was somewhat mitigated by the final protocol imposed on China for its "crimes against civilization." The separately walled Legation Quarter was established in the very heart of Peking, just south of the palaces of the Forbidden City; a huge indemnity was levied; and, best of all, foreign governments were granted the right to station limited troop garrisons in Tientsin, Peking, and the area between the two cities. The Japanese army, even though limited as to strength, was now legally settled not only on the soil of China inside the Great Wall, but also in the capital itself. And who among the international rivals could check to ascertain if and when the prescribed troop limits were exceeded?

Starting in late 1900, Russia used the excesses of the Boxers in China—overlooking their own excesses in Peking—as the excuse to occupy most of Manchuria. Protests from Japan and Britain and repeated reminders from the United States of the nebulous principles of the so-called Open Door policy failed to interest them or to budge them from their positions. But the anger of the Japanese militarists gradually rose to the boiling point. The war with Russia broke out in February, 1904. The new Japanese navy bottled up a Russian fleet in the harbor of its base at Port Arthur; when it attempted to escape, it was virtually destroyed. Both army and navy then laid siege to the strong Russian fortifications, and both sides suffered heavy casualties. For months, fighting raged in other areas of Manchuria—all still officially Chinese territory, a matter of minor importance to the contestants. The Japanese achieved a great victory at the battle of the Yalu River, but eventually action became stalemated. Then on May 27-29, 1905, the Japanese Navy surprised and annihilated the 32 ships of the Russian Baltic fleet in the Tsushima Straits off Korea. Japan and a reluctant Russia finally agreed to President Theodore Roosevelt's repeated overtures for mediation.

The Treaty of Portsmouth, signed in September, 1905, and a subsequent treaty with China in December, 1905, switched the long-term lease of Port Arthur and Dairen from Russia to Japan, granted Japan a concession to complete and operate the South Manchurian Railway linking Dairen and Korea through Mukden to the Chinese Eastern Railway, and awarded extensive rights to Japan in southern Manchuria, but it gave the Japanese no indemnity. The Russians gave up nothing that really belonged to them; they merely withdrew to the north half of Manchuria to await the next act in the play of power politics. But they and the other Western powers had been startled by the military prowess of the fledgling army and navy of Japan. And Japan was firmly ensconced in southern Manchuria, poised for further aggressive moves to the north, west, and south against China.

While the Japanese settled back to digest the latest morsels of aggrandizement, unrest and hatred for the reigning Manchu dynasty seethed throughout China, particularly in the south. The decadent imperial authority had been threatened since the middle of the nineteenth century and had been maintained only through the iron will of the old dowager empress. Her death in 1908 signaled the end of Manchu rule and the loss of the "mandate of heaven"—a recurring condition throughout China's long and bloody history. The latest unrest, fanned to fever heat by inept and inexperienced intellectuals, was symptomatic of the decline and disintegration of an aging Chinese society that had stubbornly continued to look inward on its past.

The explosion of a bomb by revolutionaries in Hankow and a subsequent mutiny of the viceroy's troops led to the seizure on October 10, 1911, of the three cities constituting Wuhan (Hankow, Wuchang, and Hanyang) on the Yangtze River—a success that surprised the revolutionaries as much as it did the court in Peking.

Sporadic uprisings erupted throughout south China, usually in locations where it was convenient to massacre Manchu families and pillage their possessions. Leaderless and bungling, the council of the amateurish revolutionaries in Hankow, always a center of revolution, named Colonel Li Yuan-hung as president of their provisional government, the actual authority of which was practically nil. Now came a bewildering, tragicomic time of maneuvering for power among countless factions as events got out of hand. The Manchu court selected Yuan Shih-kai, who had betrayed a former emperor, to subdue the rebels. But Yuan's alleged illnesses, including "a sickness of the foot," delayed his acceptance of the commission until he was offered the premiership. The new dowager empress was induced to abdicate for herself and her five-year-old son. Sun Yat-sen, father of the Chinese Revolution, having at last returned to his homeland from the United States in order to get in on the ground floor, was elected president by the Nanking council. Then he resigned in a huff when Yuan was elected to the same office by the Peking council. Meanwhile, a completely independent Canton council was free-wheeling in Kwangtung and Kwangsi provinces. In 1913 the southern provinces rose in open revolt against Yuan Shih-kai, but that crafty, unprincipled politician managed to maintain himself in power as the head of the only foreign-recognized government in China. In 1915 he maneuvered his rubber-stamp parliament into reinstituting the monarchy and proffering him the title of emperor. This was too much; putting aside their quite bitter rivalries, for the first time the factions banded together. Uprisings occurred all over China. In the face of this storm Yuan was forced to resign in 1915. He died the following year.

As president, Yuan had appointed military governors in nearly all of the provinces, a sensible procedure in view of the chaotic conditions in China; but forced to rely on his own resources, each governor quickly established his own private base of authority and power. This marked the beginnings of the so-called warlords who dominated all of China with merciless greed from 1916 to 1926. In that year Chiang Kai-shek and his army marched north from Canton to destroy their power and to unite the vast central core of the country, while leaving a periphery of unconquered warlords in the north, west, and southwest. Most of them were illiterate or semiliterate opportunists who had clawed their way to the top through banditry or the military, or both. Some convinced themselves—but few others—that their mission was solely for the good of the people under their iron control. One, Chang Tso-lin, who emerged as the *tuchun* ("warlord") of Manchuria, started as a common soldier, switched to the more lucrative profession of banditry, managed to get himself appointed commander of a garrison outside of Mukden, became fabulously rich by supplying both the Russians and Japanese in their 1904–05 war, and even aspired briefly to don the dragon robes of the emperor of China.

The outbreak of war between the European powers in 1914 presented the Japanese Imperial General Staff with a mouthwatering situation: freedom of action in the Far East. With all of Europe at one another's throats, the Western powers had neither the time nor the means to curb aggressive moves toward China. With no danger of interference from the West, Japan could at last become one of the governing nations of the world, with China, of course, as the prime target for benevolent control from Tokyo. Though not invited to do so nor particularly wanted as an ally, Japan promptly declared war on Germany and thus joined the Allies. Japan attacked and seized the German-leased naval base at Kiaochow Bay and the port of Tsingtao and proceeded to take over the railway and all other German concessions in Shantung province. The Japanese navy then descended on the German possessions in the Pacific and gobbled up the Marshall, Mariana, and Caroline islands, a 3,000-mile string of outposts between the Hawaiian Islands and the Philippines. These operations against a virtually defenseless enemy were Japan's sole military contribution toward the success of the Allied cause. They had no effect on the defeat of Germany, but a great deal of effect on future events in the Far East.

In 1915 Japan bluntly presented the infamous Twenty-one Demands to Yuan Shih-kai's Peking regime: among them, to confirm Japanese assumption of all former German rights in Shantung; to extend their lease to Port Arthur and Dairen to 99 years; to grant numerous railway and other concessions in Manchuria, Mongolia, and the Yangtze Valley; to grant no concessions and negotiate no loans without Japanese approval; to accept Japanese military, political, and financial advisers; and to accept joint control of all Chinese arsenals, police, and schools. In other words, China was to be forced into the position of a semiautonomous Japanese colony—with precious little autonomy.

At the time, Yuan Shih-kai needed strong backing to achieve his ambition to proclaim himself emperor of China. He knew that he would not be able to count on much support from his own people, and none at all from the warring Western powers. The announcement of the Twenty-one Demands in America produced pompous talk about the Open Door policy and a meaningless government statement of nonrecognition. Yuan's only hope was Japan. For form's sake, to save face, he went through the motions of a weak protest, then agreed to all of the Japanese demands except those calling for advisers and joint control of government functions. However, the uproar in China over his attempt to become emperor resulted in Yuan's downfall and unmourned death. He was succeeded as president by Colonel Li Yuan-hung. Warlords quickly moved into regional positions of power amid the chaos created by Li's inability to establish any kind of central governmental control. Sun Yat-sen set up a separate government in Canton with himself as president.

In March, 1917, by threatening to change sides in World War I, Japan won a secret agreement from England, France, and Italy to back up its seizure of German possessions in Shantung and the Pacific when peace talks were eventually held. When the United States entered the war in April, 1917, the Japanese succeeded in obtaining a statement from the American government, the Lansing-Ishii Agreement, recognizing Japan's special interests in China because of "territorial propinquity." This was tantamount to a betrayal of all previous American policies and actions regarding China.

In August, 1917, both the Peking and Canton regimes in China declared war on Germany, a gesture solely intended to give them a voice at the peace table after the war and one that ironically allied China with her enemy Japan. At the quarrelsome Versailles peace conference, President Woodrow Wilson's Fourteen Points raised Chinese hopes of getting out from under the smothering rug of Japanese ambitions. Wilson's tabulation of high principles, amounting to little more than a statement that he was against international sin, ran head-on against the pragmatism of the European Allies, most of whom were very much in favor of any kind of sin if it furthered their hopes of coming out of the war with a good national profit. However, under the conflicting pressures of the huge war settlement and the pragmatism of the European Allies, Wilson, on April 30, 1919, knuckled under to Japanese threats to withdraw from the peace table and agreed to Allied confirmation of Japan's fait accompli in Shantung.

Within a week after the adjournment of the peace conference, Chinese students and intellectuals, none of whom had ever thought of taking up a gun in their country's defense, were on the rampage in the streets of Peking, Shanghai, Nanking, Canton, and Hankow screaming for a boycott of all Japanese goods. May 7, 1919, was declared a national humiliation day, the first of many such popular flagellations that seemed to satisfy some peculiar need in the Chinese character.

In the United States, the "shameless," "damnable" provisions of the peace treaty that applied to Shantung occasioned much wrath and accelerated oratory in the Senate. Senator Borah, in partïcular, trumpeted his outrage over the "revolting injustice" done to China. The Hearst press shrilled over this latest proof of the existence of the "yellow peril," a color and a danger that fascinated William Randolph Hearst for years, and increased the circulation of his newspapers. Most Americans had only the vaguest notion of the location and sudden importance of the distant province of Shantung. Some, evidently out of the mainstream of American political thinking, even had the temerity to wonder what all the fuss in Congress was about and why the Chinese were unwilling to defend themselves against the aggressive Japanese.

As if Japanese ambitions were not enough, in 1919, the Russians' new Bolshevik government unilaterally declared the independence of the Chinese province of Outer Mongolia.

In 1919 President Wilson sent a force of 7,000 men under Major General William S. Graves to Siberia. With a vague mission to assist two groups of Czech troops who did not seem to want American help, this expedition turned out to be one of the most inexplicable wild-goose chases in recent military history, the more so because Wilson invited Japan to collaborate with a force of the same size. Delighted to plant an army anywhere on the mainland of Asia, the Japanese cooperated to the extent of dispatching 70,000 men, not only into eastern Siberia but to northern Sakhalin as well, and managed to keep them there until 1922, long after U.S. troops had gone home.

In the winter of 1921–22, an international conference was called in Washington to reach agreements on limitations in the naval arms race. After three months of discussions, the conference announced a whole series of agreements: a four-power treaty prescribing naval ratios of capital ships; a five-power treaty forbidding fortification of possessions in the Pacific basin; a nine-power treaty guaranteeing the rights of China but failing to mention any means by which those rights might be protected. In a separate document, the Japanese agreed to withdraw their troops from Shantung, but not to give up their economic privileges in that province, nor their military and economic stance in Manchuria. The U.S. Senate ratified the treaties with unusual speed and returned to domestic matters.

During the next 10 years, the nature of events in China can only be described as chaos accentuated by constant Japanese pressure—military, diplomatic and economic—in an attempt to impose control on the tormented land. The armies of rival warlords marched up and down the country pillaging their own people. Large, ill-equipped forces of opposing troops clashed in battles that were often no more than martial confrontations at which the side with the most men, the most artillery, and the most silver for buying off the enemy leader won the day. So-called crushing defeats usually caused relatively light military casualties. Alliances were made and broken, with open rebellions, mutinies, and treachery more common than not. Famine and death stalked the land. The people struggled under crushing burdens of levies and taxes, watched their crops wither and die, and sold their girl children as a last resort to avoid starvation.

Each self-appointed leader became known by the epithet he chose. Among the warlords were Yen Hsi-shan, the "model governor" (it has never been clear what he was a model of); Feng Yu-hsiang, the "Christian general," who baptized his troops with water hoses as they marched past and whose operations were anything but Christian; Wu Pei-fu, the "savior of central China" (for himself); Chang Tso-lin, the "Old Marshal" and lord of Manchuria; Sun Ch'uan-fang, guardian of the lower Yangtze coastal areas and the large financial interests of Shanghai; Han Fu-chu, the "good governor" of Shantung (because he collected taxes only four to five years in advance); Lung Yun, the "dragon cloud," unabashed ex-bandit who plundered his province of Yunnan. There were many other lesser leaders who worked over one area after another for personal aggrandizement.

Sun Yat-sen based his shaky regime in that nursery of revolutions, Canton. There he tried to bolster his pretensions with the aid of Russian Communist advisers. Several times during the frequent ebb and flow of alliances and defections, Sun found it expedient to flee his southern capital to the safety of the well-guarded foreign concessions of Shanghai. However, these visits did not prevent him from frequent denunciations of the foreign enclaves as manifestations of imperialistic colonialism. During his more or less conspiratorial existence, he managed to find time to coalesce his fuzzy political thinking in the Three Principles that for years were regarded as the philosophical keystone of the party he founded, the Kuomintang. In 1924 he appointed Chiang Kai-shek commandant of the Whampoa Military Academy, the training school for young officers, the West Point of China. It soon became the source of the more reliable, but not necessarily most capable, military men of the future. When Sun died in 1925, Chiang Kai-shek, by fair means and foul, assumed his mantle of leadership.

In early 1926 Chiang Kai-shek and the Canton regime felt strong enough to destroy the powerful warlords who had been tearing China apart and who had prevented the establishment of a unified country. Starting his triumphant march from Canton in July, Chiang was welcomed everywhere because he represented a change—any change—from the horrendous conditions under which the people had been forced to exist. City after city fell before the advance of his rapidly growing army—Changsha, Nanchang, Hankow, Shanghai, and finally Nanking in March, 1927. On his approach, the British, French, Americans, and Japanese reinforced their garrisons in Shanghai to a total of 40,000 men to protect the foreign concessions. The seat of government moved to Hankow in February, 1927; to Nanking in 1928. Chiang split with the Russian advisers and the left wing of his party at Hankow, and the new nationalist government broke off all relations with the Soviet Union. Chiang stamped out left-wing opposition in Shanghai with merciless brutality and firmly allied himself with the great financial interests of the city both by marriage and by investments.

In May, 1928, as Chiang continued his march to the north from Hsuchow toward Tsinan, the capital of Shantung, the Japanese landed 7,000 troops at Tsingtao, some 2,000 of whom moved up the railway line to Tsinan to protect their nationals. Fourteen ships of the Japanese navy and 11 supply ships anchored off Tsingtao. Several clashes occurred and men on both sides were killed. Then, by murdering a Chinese official, his wife, and a number of officers, the Japanese deliberately forced the issue into full-scale outbreak of hostilities and an excuse to continue their occupation of Shantung. Blocking his route to the north, they demanded that Chiang and his army turn back. Afraid to risk open warfare with the Japanese, Chiang ignominiously backed down and marched southwest to the Peking-Hankow rail line, thus abandoning Shantung to the Japanese. He then continued on to Peking, which he reached on July 3. A few days after his arrival in the old capital, he and the former warlords Yen Hsi-shan and Feng Yu-hsiang solemnly announced to the spirit of Sun Yat-sen at the Temple of the Azure Clouds that his aim for a united China had succeeded at last.

A month before the Tsinan incident, the Old Marshal, Chang Tso-lin, Warlord of Manchuria, realized that all real resistance to Chiang Kai-shek's advance had crumbled. About the same time he was informed by the Japanese, who feared an alliance between his army and Chiang's nationalist army, that if he did not return to Mukden from Peking at once he would be barred permanently from his satrapy in Manchuria. The Old Marshal wasted no time in following this advice. On the night of June 2, 1928, he departed Peking by train with his almost imperial entourage and all of the rolling stock of the Peking-Mukden rail line he was able to commandeer. The next day, as his private train passed under an overhead railway bridge near Mukden, a perfectly timed unexplained explosion occurred—a Japanese-planted bomb—and the old Tiger of Manchuria, Chang Tso-lin, was killed. His son, Chang Hsueh-liang, known as the Young Marshal, immediately took over his father's domain and 400,000-man army. Within a few months he ordered the nationalist flag of China raised over all Manchuria, a gesture that earned him the enmity of the Japanese and the suspicion of his own people south of the Great Wall.

Since 1927, drawn by promises of land for all and the organization of a soviet-type state, Communist groups in ever-increasing numbers had gravitated to Kiangsi province and the adjacent mountainous areas of Fukien. With Mao Tse-tung as political leader and Chu Teh as military chief, a defense force armed with captured weapons was slowly built up. Land was distributed after driving off or killing landlords, previous owners, and their families by tens of thousands. Between 1930 and 1934, Chiang Kai-shek, who refused to call Mao's state within a state anything but a bandit stronghold, hurled five separate so-called bandit-suppression campaigns against the rugged Red enclave. The results were catastrophic. The first four campaigns were badly trounced, suffering heavy casualties, an enormous loss of weapons, and many thousands of defections from the ranks of the nationalist armies. The greatly superior numbers and equipment of Chiang's armies proved to be no match in combat for Chu Teh's highly indoctrinated troops and their hit-and-run guerrilla tactics. But the 700,000-man nationalist army of the fifth campaign, which was planned and directed by General Hans von Seeckt, chief of Chiang's German military advisers, finally broke the back of Communist resistance in the summer of 1934. In October, Mao and Chu, with about 100,000 followers, slipped through the tightly encircling blockade of the nationalist army and began the famous Long March to the far northwest. After enduring incredible hardships and continual attacks, they reached Shensi province a year later; nearly half of those who had started had died. The remainder established their headquarters in the cave city of Yenan. Then, following that pattern so common among individualistic Chinese leaders of the time, Mao Tse-tung and Chu Teh had a complete falling out. Later they patched up their differences and expunged the story of their break-up from the official history of the Communist rise to power.

A minor quarrel over an irrigation ditch between Chinese farmers and a colony of Korean immigrants to Manchuria in May, 1931, precipitated violent anti-Chinese riots in Korea and the massacre of a number of Chinese residents. China retaliated with a boycott of all Japanese goods. In August, the murder of a Japanese officer, a Captain Nakamura, by Chinese soldiers inflamed public opinion in Japan and raised outraged demands in the rigidly controlled press for vengeance.

Following its penchant for conducting night maneuvers in troubled areas at opportune times, the Japanese Kwantung Army was holding field exercises near Mukden on September 18, 1931. Another unexplained explosion cut the tracks of the South Manchurian Railway at Liutiaokou outside the city. In what could only have been a carefully preplanned operation, the Japanese seized the arsenal, took over a few nearby small towns, and before daylight began to occupy Mukden. Within a matter of days Kirin was occupied, as was Harbin in February; the complete military occupation of Manchuria was accomplished before the following summer. The Japanese justified their action as a matter of self-defense. The Young Marshal was forced to move his army south of the Great Wall. Chinese dependence on the Confucian principles of discussion and compromise, of nonresistance to physical force, lost the three provinces of the northeast in one great Japanese bite. But popular reaction to this piracy caused an intensification of the anti-Japanese boycotts.

Influenced by the strident encouragements of Colonel Kanji Ishihara, many officers of the Kwantung Army sincerely believed they were acting for the good of the emperor and Japan. For years, younger men throughout the army, both in Japan and in Manchuria, had been outraged at corruption and what they considered weakness in the civilian elements of the government, as well as the greed of the great industrialists who controlled the politicians. In their fiery zeal they had convinced themselves that only by acting semi-independently of the War Office in Tokyo could they restore the true greatness of Japan. They had organized into a number of cliques whose so-called principles ranged from extreme conservatism to near radicalism. They were, however, united by one goal: expansion of the empire to make Japan the strongest nation on earth. Only by military expansion could white domination be destroyed and the people of the Far East be given their rightful position as the superior race. The entire philosophy of the young rebels was rooted in color—in this case, a deep resentment toward the white man.

In the spring of 1932 the more aggressive elements of these dedicated idealists assassinated the Japanese premier, several other government officials, and an important industrialist. At the subsequent trials the defendants announced that their purpose had been to sound an alarm to awaken the nation to the danger it faced and to the urgent necessity of sacrifice on the altars of reform—all of which meant that they wanted Japan to accept a policy of expansion under the control of the military. Their high-flown rhetoric was, of course, cloaked in visionary and speculative schemes for leading the farmers and workers out of their grinding poverty—a project for which the young officers cared not a whit.

But their youth and fervor elevated them in the eyes of many Japanese people to the status of self-sacrificing heroes.

In January, 1932, Secretary of State Henry L. Stimson warned the Japanese government that the United States strongly adhered to a policy of nonrecognition of Japanese claims on Manchuria. He threatened economic sanctions and even dug the somewhat frazzled Open Door policy out of mothballs to wave vainly through the halls of diplomacy. These words made but faint noises in the ears of the Japanese militarists. They knew very well that none of Stimson's statements of policy and principles would be followed up by military action. The British government, whose Foreign Office was then headed by Sir John Simon—a great lawyer but naive in world affairs—was more concerned with its commercial investments in the Far East than with the fate of China and would have no part of Stimson's proposals for sanctions. Stimson's prophetic warning to President Herbert Hoover that a war between Japan and China could spread to the entire world created barely a ripple on the murky waters of domestic economic crisis.

In late January the Japanese landed 70,000 troops at Shanghai to compel the Chinese to abandon the boycott of their goods that was proving ruinous to manufacturers and merchants in Japan. This time the sacrificial lamb for the contrived incident that preceded the landing was a murdered Buddhist monk, undoubtedly killed by *ronin* (Korean thugs in the pay of the Japanese army). But unexpectedly, the Chinese 19th Route Army, commanded by a dedicated officer known as the poet general, and the 5th Corps defied Chiang Kai-shek's orders and put up such stiff resistance that the Japanese did not overcome them for five weeks. In this First Battle of Shanghai, the 19th Route Army was left entirely on its own by the Chinese government—no supplies and no support of any kind—and was badly mauled before it was forced to withdraw. After raising the rising-sun flag over the battlefields, the Japanese proceeded to destroy a Chinese section of the city called Chapei by aerial bombing and fire, with the resultant loss of thousands of lives. An agreement was then negotiated to end the boycott, and most of the Japanese troops departed.

Piously quoting the right of self-determination in accordance with the principles of the League of Nations, the Japanese government, having been confronted with a fait accompli by the Kwantung Army, suddenly proclaimed the independence of Manchuria on January 18, 1932. The new nation, to be called Manchukuo, was to consist of the provinces of Heilungkiang, Kirin, Liaoning, and Jehol, though the last was a part of Inner Mongolia and still under Chinese control.

In March the former boy emperor of China, Henry Pu-yi, was installed as regent of Manchukuo at the capital of Changchun. Two years later he was promoted to "emperor"—presumably for good behavior—and docilely went through a second marriage to a Korean princess of his masters' choice. His throne was purely synthetic; his every action was dictated by the Kwantung Army command; his Japanese cabinet and secretaries controlled all government functions. (With the surrender of the Japanese in 1945, Pu-yi was dragged from his throne and made a prisoner of the Russian Red Army; later he was turned over to the Chinese Communists, under whom he led a miserable, degraded existence of rehabilitation, performing menial tasks until his death in 1966.)

In February, 1933, the League of Nations adopted the findings of the Lytton Commission, which condemned the Japanese occupation of Manchuria, and accepted Secretary of State Stimson's nonrecognition formula. The League found no grounds for the Japanese assertion that the occupation had been based on self-defense; the creation of Manchukuo was in no sense a genuine and spontaneous independence movement, and Japanese military pressure on China should cease. The Japanese delegation showed its contempt and defiance of the wordy and powerless proceedings by walking out of the meeting.

On the other side of the world, the Kwantung Army did some walking of its own by marching into China's Jehol province in a well-planned, bloodless occupation. The Chinese warlord governor, Tang Yu-lin, accepting the inevitability of a Japanese seizure, had simply sold his province for a reputed $9 million, a huge supply of opium, and safe conduct to China for himself, his wives and numerous concubines, his children, and his personal possessions. The deal consummated, he left at once for Peking where he lived in great state in an old palace. He was a jovial physical-culture buff; for years after, he delighted in demonstrating his great strength and skill with the old 160-pound-pull Manchu bow, particularly to fascinated foreigners.

The momentum of the Japanese drive into Jehol swept their troops through the Great Wall into Hopei province. One Chinese army and the equivalent of five corps put up a brief, inept resistance against one Japanese division, and afterward referred to this military minuet as the Great Wall War. Following this Japanese seizure, the Tangku Truce (Tangku is at the mouth of the Pei River below Tientsin) was imposed on the Chinese government on May 31, 1933. Its provisions required the Chinese army to evacuate the entire Tientsin area, thus extending the demilitarized zone that had been established two months before. Beyond angrily throwing a few teacups at his helpless negotiators —a long-time habit—Chiang Kai-shek did nothing to prevent this further loss of Chinese territory. Perhaps he could do nothing; at the time he was entirely preoccupied with his fourth bandit-suppression campaign against the Communists south of the Yangtze in Kiangsi province. At the close of 1933, Chiang Kai-shek had lost face with his own people and lost prestige abroad: he was afraid to stand up to the Japanese in the north, and his obsession of destroying the Communists was so intense it had led him into one disastrous venture after another in South China.

During the next two years there was a lull in Japanese pressure while the Kwantung Army attempted to digest the enormous banquet of its Manchurian and Jehol seizures. But plans for pacification and commercial exploitation were wrecked by the activities of large forces of Chinese bandits and guerrillas and the consequent excessive costs of occupation. Manchukuo was on the verge of bankruptcy. The large resources and markets of north China appeared to be the only salvation. Efforts to engineer the secession of the five northern provinces of Shantung, Hopei, Shansi, Chahar, and Suiyuan had failed. As the first step in the next move, General Yoshijiro Umezu forced the Ho-Umezu Agreement of June 9, 1935, on General Ho Ying-chin, the smiling, round-faced representative of Chiang Kai-shek. This time the pretext was the murder of the chief of a Japanese news service in Tientsin. Unusually to the point, the basic provision of the agreement called for the withdrawal from Hopei province of all

Chinese troops "objectionable to the Japanese." Although all Chinese troops were obnoxious to Japanese, an exception was made of General Sung Che-yuan's 29th Army, probably because Sung was clever enough to render lip service, but little else, to their diplomatic and military emissaries. He was also wise enough to disappear from the scene when the pressure became too great, since he could always claim the necessity of returning to his native province to sweep his ancestors' graves.

The next step of the Kwantung Army, in late November, 1935, was to establish in the already demilitarized zone south of the Wall the East Hopei Autonomous Regime between Tungchow, 12 miles east of Peking, and the sea. Japanese goods and great quantities of narcotics were immediately flooded into the area and smuggled into China. In less than a month the Japanese inaugurated the Hopei-Chahar Political Council with Tungchow as its capital and General Sung Che-yuan, the crafty peasant from Shantung, as its chairman.

On February 26, 1936, the momentum of military expansion was furthered by another of those peculiarly Japanese outbursts of sacrifice for a cause—suicidal self-sacrifice as well as sacrifice of reluctant others. A series of assassinations of high officials even bloodier than those of four years before took place in Tokyo. The plot was again engineered by groups of young officers dedicated to the emperor and the nation. In Western eyes, these violent actions constituted nothing less than political murders. Not so in the eyes of the Japanese people, most of whom looked upon this latest uprising as a sincere manifestation of the national spirit.

For days after the assassinations, rebellious officers and their troops held the center of Tokyo; but martial law was declared, and 13 officers and 4 civilian conspirators were tried and executed. Though the Japanese people were still sympathetic to their cause, they realized that discipline had to be enforced in the army. The new premier, Koki Hirota, was a liberal, and all too soon he found himself in the iron grip of the military Control clique—control meaning control of China from Manchuria and eventual expansion into southeast Asia. Bitterly in opposition, the Imperial Way clique argued for productive expansion, avoidance of all international conflicts, and eventual all-out war with Japan's real enemy, Soviet Russia. Meanwhile, General Doihara, the commander of the semi-independent Kwantung Army in Manchuria, went ahead with his scheme to set up an autonomous regime in the five northern provinces of China.

In the meantime, factions all over China were agitating for active armed resistance against Japan, the two loudest being the Kwangtung-Kwangsi group in the far south and the Communists in the northwest. By the spring of 1936 the powerful leaders of the southern clique, General Pai Ch'ung-hsi and General Li Tsung-jen, decided to use demands for action against Japan as an excuse to oust Chiang Kai-shek as generalissimo and leader of the central government. Ostensibly to force Chiang into a war of resistance, rebellion broke out that summer. The revolt was quashed by September, the southern armies proving to be no match for Chiang's planes, artillery, and elite German-trained troops. The brief civil war was settled with an agreement to combine resources in a united front of resistance. The generals Pai and Li were allowed to save face with loud protestations that this was exactly what they had hoped to achieve. Meanwhile, anti-Japanese sentiment in Shantung broke out in riots of serious proportions. Japanese places of business in Tsinan were attacked, and a number of men and women were brutally killed by frenzied Chinese. After order was restored, the Japanese seemed to derive a strange satisfaction in displaying photographs of Japanese women who had been pierced with long metal spikes and impaled to the ground. What better incident could they themselves have devised?

On August 15, 1936, Premier Hirota informally enunciated to the emperor the goals that he and the military proposed as the national and foreign policies of Japan: Philippine independence; expansion into the Netherlands Indies; guidance and assistance to Siam and other underdeveloped nations of southeast Asia; and promotion of growth in Manchuria and close economic ties with China. Having advocated, in effect, the expulsion of the white races from the Far East, Hirota nevertheless concluded that peace and economic cooperation should be maintained with the United States and Great Britain.

The Japanese presented a new series of demands to the Chinese government on October 1, 1936, accompanied by a threat to invade north and central China if the demands were not accepted. The demands were to institute joint Chinese-Japanese military campaigns against the Communists anywhere in China, to place Japanese advisers in all branches of the Chinese government, to grant autonomy to the five northern provinces, and to reduce customs tariffs on Japanese goods. The Chinese government rejected the ultimatum, falling back on its usual practice of triumph via procrastination, and asked for further discussions and time to study the effects of acceptance.

Still determined to annihilate the Communists, Chiang Kai-shek appointed the Young Marshal commander of a mixed force consisting of his own Manchurian troops and those of several local commanders with the mission of eliminating the so-called bandit threat to the internal security of the nation. But the sixth bandit-suppression campaign against the Communists failed even to get started in Shensi province. The Young Marshal, with a number of other dissatisfied generals, had allied himself with the very Communists he had been ordered to suppress. Fully cognizant of what was going on, Chiang Kai-shek decided to go to Sian to correct the situation and to inject a more aggressive spirit in the commanders of his punitive force of 10 divisions with artillery, tanks, and bombers. The Nanking leaders, convinced that some form of compromise with the Reds was inevitable, urged Chiang not to go; but he insisted. His personal prestige, he said—especially since the defeat of the Kwangtung-Kwangsi revolt—was strong enough to enable him to nip the trouble at its source. He flew to Sian and took up residence in a hot-springs hotel outside the city.

On Chiang's arrival a group of senior generals called on him, but he refused to talk to them. However, he agreed to listen to grievances through the Young Marshal as spokesman. After several days of discussions, the generalissimo took it for granted that the situation had been straightened out. He invited all of the disaffected generals to a large dinner at which he announced his intention to depart for Nanking the following morning. At the dinner he took occasion to scold the assembled officers, pointing out that they had been in error. He concluded his speech with a somewhat grudging statement of forgiveness.

Before daylight on December 12, Chiang was startled out of

sleep by the sound of gunfire. Discovering that the hotel was under attack, he climbed out of a window and fled barefoot, wearing only a nightshirt, up a nearby rocky hill, followed by various aides. Pursued by the attacking soldiers—all members of the Young Marshal's trusted bodyguard—Chiang and his followers were soon caught, none too gently, but not before the Generalissimo had lost his false teeth.

As Chiang stepped into his car, surrounded by his captors, the captain of the guard ordered the members of his Chiang's party not to try to recapture their leader or the generalissimo would be killed at once. However, firing did break out, and in the ensuing melee (unsuccessful from Chiang's point of view) the captain and several others were killed on the spot. Also, the vice-president of the legislative Yuan was shot and killed as he tried to escape, and the wife of the governor of Shensi was wounded. Chiang was rushed in his car to the southwest quarter of the inner city and placed under house arrest with heavy guard.

When they met a few hours later, the Young Marshal informed a much discomfited generalissimo that he had been taken prisoner, kidnapped, in order to convince him that he should cancel the campaign against the Reds, that Chinese should not fight Chinese, and that China should resist Japanese incursions by declaring war. One group among the military commanders in the city, all members of the conspiracy, loudly declared for execution of Chiang for betraying China to the Japanese. Chou En-lai, the emissary of Mao Tse-tung, on whose head Chiang Kai-shek had set a price of $80,000, argued for common-sense discussion and compromise. He had obviously won his point with the Young Marshal and General Yang Hu-ch'eng, the two strongest nationalist generals.

Meanwhile, the panicked Nanking leaders seized control of the government. No one knew whether Chiang Kai-shek was alive or dead. They ordered an army to move on Sian to attempt a rescue; they bombed a nearby innocent town and threatened to bomb Sian itself. Stressing the danger to her husband if force were used, Madame Chiang with a few trusted officers flew to Sian to demand the release of the generalissimo. By the time she arrived, however, a compromise had almost been reached; so her main function was to deliver a new set of false teeth to Chiang. On

Christmas Day, the generalissimo and Madame Chiang with the Young Marshal flew to Nanking. (The war lord was tried by the Military Affairs Commission, sentenced to ten years in prison, finally pardoned by Chiang Kai-shek and placed under house arrest for an indefinite period. With the collapse of Chiang's government in 1949, he was moved to Formosa where he is still under house arrest.)

It is hardly surprising that the astonishing picture of a head of state being kidnapped by his own subordinate commanders produced a number of major results. A united front for resistance against Japan was agreed to by all factions. The anti-Communist campaign was cancelled. After weeks of discussions, Mao Tse-tung and Chou En-lai agreed to place their Red Army under nationalist guidance and overall direction. But probably the most important outcome was the overwhelming support for Chiang Kai-shek that swept like wildfire throughout China. This first genuine feeling of national unity alarmed the Kwantung Army and the militarists in Tokyo. It could undermine all their carefully laid plans. The time for direct action had come; the right time and right place awaited only the spark of another incident to ignite the tinder of war.

On April 16, 1937, Premier Hirota's national goals of eight months before, under renewed pressure from the militarist groups, were expanded and clarified as far as they related to China. They now prescribed that close economic links with China could be attained only by the development of north China (Hopei, Shansi, Shantung, Chahar, and Suiyuan) into a pro-Japanese, pro-Manchukuo, anti-Soviet autonomous regime; and considering Japan's claims and investments, special emphasis was to be given to Shantung and the port of Tsingtao.

The spark that ignited war was the rifle shot that killed a Japanese soldier at the Marco Polo Bridge on the night of July 7, 1937. It was the last incident in a long series of contrived justifications for each step of Japanese aggression against China's territory and national integrity.

3

The Occupation of the Peking Area and the Japanese Drive into Inner Mongolia, July 7 to October 17, 1937

CHIANG KAI-SHEK'S announced intention of resisting the Japanese was followed by a lifting of the ban on patriotic songs and slogans. The news triggered wild outbursts of misguided enthusiasm throughout China, particularly in the south, where patriots felt safe from any immediate danger. In Peking, however, as the people of the city waited tensely for the axe to fall, a pall of gloom hung over the *hu-t'ungs*, markets, and entertainment districts. When the great gates were closed at darkness, a furtive silence replaced the chaotic activity that usually swirled about Ch'ien Men and Hata Men, the principal gates between the Inner and Outer Cities.

But for those foreign residents who had not departed for the coast there was little change in the untroubled rounds of their activities. Still firmly believing in the divine right of white skin, they "just knew in their bones" that this latest nuisance would be smoothed over, as had so many others. Cloudless nights found them dancing under the stars on the roof of the Grand Hotel de Pékin; rainy nights in the grand ballroom below, the walls of which, now tinted a bland cream color, had until recently pictured cavorting nude and seminude nymphs. Painted by a French artist who had been snubbed socially, the murals had revengefully memorialized the stuffy matrons of the early 1900s, for he had painted their faces on the prancing figures. English and American tourists still filled the hotels and pensions. Shoppers still prowled from one store to another for bargains in antiques, which were seldom either bargains or antiques.

Under Colonel Stilwell's direction, the office of the American military attaché in San Kuan Miao, an old temple taken over after the Boxer uprising, was busy with coded cables, telephone calls, and visits of other attachés seeking reliable information about the military situation. Reliable information was scarce, and most of the visitors ended up in the paneled English bar of the Wagon Lits Hotel across Canal Street.

Outside the city the occasional sound of exploding aerial bombs, the sharp crack of artillery fire, and the dull boom of bursting mortar shells were constant reminders of the tense, dangerous situation. While surrounding villages were being shattered and their survivors put to flight, a strange quiet existed within the walls of Peking, except at the Japanese embassy and barracks. There, businesslike, sand-bagged machine-gun emplacements had been set up at each gate. And it was there that the sister-in-law of a Lieutenant Cornell, a member of the embassy guard of U.S. Marines, learned that the divine right of white skin was no longer what it had once been. With more curiosity than sense, she climbed up the sandbags to see what was inside, only to be slapped in the face and kicked in the stomach by a Japanese sentry.

One night, panicky Chinese troops guarding the *enceinte* of P'ing Tze Men, a gate in the west wall of the Inner City, got into a firefight with nothing and plunged the neighboring area into terror. False rumors of an impending Japanese attack had set off the two-hour fusillade, which wrecked shops and homes in the vicinity. The soldiers ended their jamboree by looting vacated premises along the street leading to the gate.

Japanese troops continued to pour into the Tientsin area by rail, then fanned out to occupy or patrol the lower sections of the Peking plain. Lightly armored trains, their wheels equipped with hard rubber treads, edged along the Peking-Tientsin rail line and silently swooped down on unsuspecting villages just south of Fengtai and the port city. Most of the Chinese 29th Army seemed to have withdrawn from contact with the Japanese. This lent credence to reports that the commander of the 29th, General Sung Che-yuan, had sold out to the enemy—a pattern of

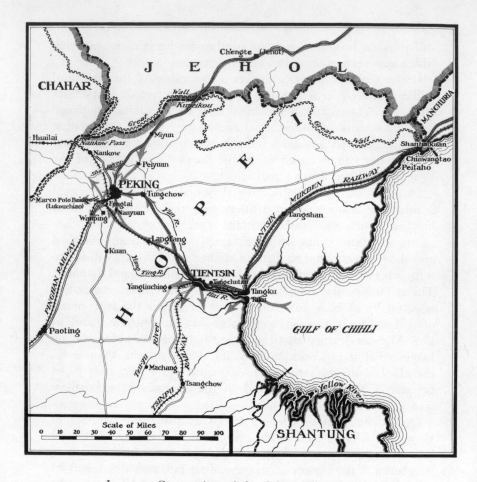

Japanese Occupation of the Peking-Tientsin Area

conduct not uncommon in the past—although in fact Sung had
only moved his army headquarters to Nanyuan, about 10 miles
south of Peking. His 38th Division, less two brigades, was near
Tientsin, with one detached brigade at Taku at the mouth of the
Pei River and the other at Langfang, half way between Peking
and Tientsin. The 132nd Division was just south of Nanyuan.
One brigade of the 143rd Division was 14 miles northwest of
Peking, while the rest of the Division was sitting tight at Kalgan,
nearly 120 miles away, where it could be of no possible use in
the Peking area.

On July 25 advance troops of the Japanese 20th Division on a march along the rail line and road toward Peking made a probing attack on Langfang. When they encountered resistance they pulled back. The next day the town was bombed. The skirmish of the previous afternoon developed into a full-scale battle; Langfang was captured and the road to Peking was cleared for the passage of Japanese troops.

On July 27, as units of the Japanese 20th Division approached Tungchow, the Chinese garrison fled in panic to Nanyuan. On July 28 General Katsuki announced that he intended to launch a punitive expedition against the Chinese troops "who have been taking acts derogatory to the prestige of the empire of Japan."

On the same day, the Sakai and Suzuki brigades, having arrived in the vicinity of Kupeikou, attacked Peiyuan, about 15 miles northeast of Peking. Also on that day, the 20th Division under General Kawakishi and the Tanake Brigade, supported by air strikes, attacked Nanyuan. Caught by surprise, the headquarters units of the Chinese 29th Army and the 132nd Division suffered heavy casualties, among them the deputy army commander and the division commander. The Chinese had yet to learn the value of vigilant patrolling over wide areas, as well as that their "big sword" units were utterly useless against machine guns firing from several hundred yards. During a one-sided engagement, a brigade of the Chinese 53rd Corps from the south occupied the railway station and yards at Fengtai. The commander claimed a great victory, but whom he vanquished is not known since no Japanese units were within 10 miles. Before the end of the day this "victorious" brigade, the battered 132nd Division and the headquarters troops of the 29th Army were in a hasty, disorderly retreat toward Kuan, 30 miles to the south. A brigade of the 143rd Division, now designated the 29th Separate Brigade, and several other lesser units were ordered to look after the military interests of Peking, now at a very low ebb.

Complete disaster struck one unit of the Chinese 132nd Division as it withdrew from Nan T'ai airfield toward the south gate of the Outer City. Moving north on a road that cut through flooded fields, the progress of Chinese trucks and mounted men was unexpectedly blocked by a large Japanese patrol backed up by more troops hidden among the dense, six-foot-high stalks of kaoliang, a form of sorghum not unlike corn in appearance. When ordered to give up their arms and surrender, a number of Chinese soldiers leaped from their trucks and tried to hide in the fields, only to run head-on into heavy Japanese rifle fire. Machine guns opened up from both sides of the road; grenades were hurled among the trucks. Caught in the cross fire, the Chinese were slaughtered, their bodies ripped to pieces by metal fragments. When the carnage was over, nearly 600 Chinese lay sprawled on the ground or hung grotesquely from the sides of bullet-riddled trucks. To finish off the butchery the Japanese withdrew to a safe distance and called in an air strike; exploding bombs blasted the wounded remnants of the column.

On July 29, false rumors of victories spread among the Chinese puppet garrison of the Hopei-Chahar Political Council at Tungchow. With wild, hysterical cries of "Sha! Sha!" ("Kill! Kill!"), the gendarme-type troops rushed from their barracks swinging their big swords and firing old German-made rifles. They coursed like wild animals through the walled town hunting down Japanese and Chinese officials of the puppet regime and massacring them brutally. Over 300 Japanese civilians, both men and women, were slaughtered. Heads were hung in wicker baskets from the parapets above the closed town gates. Mutilated bodies were left where victims fell in the muddy streets for hungry dogs and flies. Only a small detachment of 120 Japanese regular troops equipped with one light machine gun managed to hold out behind the stone walls of the old *yamen* ("headquarters"). The Chinese nationalist flag was raised above cheering —and looting—crowds. But the celebration was brief.

The next day the wrath of the Kwantung Army descended on the small city in overwhelming force: bombing, strafing, artillery and mortar fire. Japanese troops battered down the gates, poured into the town, and wreaked a terrible vengeance. Every man of the garrison they caught was killed and beheaded. Hundreds of women were raped. The place was sacked and then set afire. A vast column of heavy black smoke rose high in the sky. In a single day, Tungchow, the former terminus of the Grand Canal, was reduced to blackened ruins, battered walls, death.

Ninety miles away in the commercial port of Tientsin—often referred to as being over-sexed and under-cultured compared to

Peking—the Japanese military presence had been abundant since the day after the incident at the Marco Polo Bridge. In the British and French concessions and in the foreign barracks areas, Japanese troops, having the same treaty rights as American, British, French, and Italian military units, moved about at will. At the time, about 9,000 foreigners of various nationalities, about 5,000 foreign troops, and about 180,000 Chinese lived in the concessions. Still sensible to foreign opinion—except that of the English, whom they held in low esteem if not contempt—Japanese troops, although truculent, caused remarkably few incidents. However, several British men and one young woman were publicly stripped to the buff at the railway station as soldiers searched them for "articles dangerous to the safety of the Japanese army." Although the Japanese erected barricades and virtually took over the railway station to handle the influx of their troops and equipment, they neither entered nor threatened the sprawling Chinese city of nearly 1.5 million people on both sides of the Pei River. The ancient walls of Tientsin had been demolished as one of the humiliations imposed by the invading allies after the Boxer uprising of 1900, so the city's boundaries were ill-defined. Claiming that outlying suburbs infringed on areas necessary for troop housing and training, Japanese units constantly nibbled at the edges of the city as they concentrated their ground organizations and air squadrons.

On July 29 Japanese planes staged a leisurely, four-hour raid on the Chinese city, concentrating particularly on Nankai University with a steady rain of incendiary bombs. According to Japanese headquarters, the attack was necessary in order to disperse or destroy anti-Japanese elements—students and faculty— who menaced the good intentions of the Kwantung Army to bring peace and prosperity to the Chinese people. Meanwhile, the Japanese 5th Division commanded by General Seichiro Itagaki attacked units of the Chinese 38th Division on the outskirts of the city. Japanese marines made an assault landing against the Taku forts at the mouth of the river. These forts were picturesque old stone relics of imperial days whose rust-encrusted cannons had been emplaced in cement to point only toward the sea. Avoiding the fixed lines of fire presented no difficulty, and the attackers took the forts with ease. While this action was taking place, one

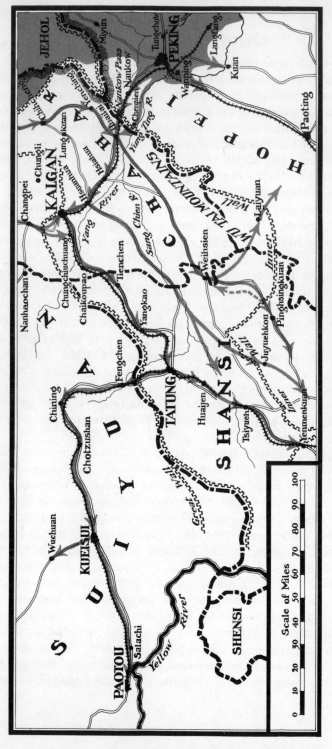

The Japanese Drive into Inner Mongolia

Chinese unit staged an unusually bold raid on the Japanese-held airfield at Tungchutzu outside of Tientsin and destroyed a number of enemy aircraft. This minor triumph was as short-lived as the token defense put up by the bulk of the 38th Division troops. During the night, the entire Chinese division retreated toward Machang, 55 miles south of Tientsin. On July 30 the city was occupied by the Japanese 5th Division.

During the afternoon of July 29 the last of Sung Che-yuan's 29th Army began its withdrawal through Peking. The long single files of infantry troops, tired, dirty, sullen, and wild-eyed with fear, trudged north on each side of the broad, ceremonial Ch'ien Men Ta Chieh (Front Gate Avenue). Many wore bandages darkened with dirt and encrusted with blood; others hobbled along on crude canes and crutches. They knew that if they faltered they would be abandoned, as had hundreds of their comrades too badly wounded to keep up. All doors were barred, all shop fronts tightly shuttered. Carriers who had been impressed into service at gunpoint bore each company's meager baggage suspended from long poles balanced on their shoulders: a few cooking pots, sacks of rice, officers' equipment, a scanty supply of ammunition. But for the padding of rubber-soled shoes, the faint rasp of straw sandals, and an occasional rattle of equipment, an ominous silence hung in the hot afternoon air.

As the shadows lengthened, the clatter of iron-wheeled carts, the hooves of shaggy, jug-headed Mongolian ponies echoing against the pavement, and the rumble of outworn artillery pieces entering the distant Yung Ting Men shattered the tense silence. The crack of whips on the backs of tired, hungry animals, a harshly barked command, and a few foul curses brought momentary life to the almost ghostly passage of defeated men. Their only hope of escape from the driving scourge of their enemies led through the north gates of the city and down the stony road to Nankow. There, with luck, they might be able to board a train and climb the steep pass to safety. There was no other way out of the trap. The Japanese had surrounded Peking on three sides. Why they had not tightened and drawn the noose on the north, no one knew. Some time during the night the acting mayor of Peking, having found that Japanese arrogance and overbearing made it impossible for him to carry out his duties (meaning the jig was up), decamped into the darkness for the safety of Kalgan.

Before dawn on July 30 the last Chinese troops had cleared the city and were well on their way to the crossing of the Sha River and the town of Nankow. Miraculously there had been no looting or burning on the march-through. The 1.5 million residents of Peking trembled for what next lay in store for them. The apprehensive city police were now their only remaining protection against either the Japanese or hysterical outbreaks of violence by the poor, the hungry, and the lawless elements. The black-uniformed police remained at their posts throughout the day, maintaining a tenuous form of order. For 24 hours the people of Peking waited numbly for time to raise the curtain on the next act in the long and bloody drama. They had seen the pall of smoke over Tungchow and were well aware of its fate. Now they watched Japanese planes crisscross the sky above their roofs.

After his pell-mell retreat to the south on July 28th, General Sung and his army troops had not stopped at Kuan, but had continued on to Paoting, on the Peking-Hankow railway line, where he had set up his headquarters a safe distance from the sounds of battle. His 37th and 132nd Divisions followed as rapidly as their lack of transportation would permit. Unlike other armies, when the Chinese gave ground they usually did so in great retreating leaps of 50 miles or more. Although the commanders professed to believe that such "tactical" moves would lure an enemy to eventual defeat, the real rationale behind their thinking was that the loss of an army meant the loss of the commander's job.

As the last wounded stragglers from Peking stumbled along the road beyond the Yellow Temple to the north of the city, the stocky troops of His Imperial Majesty rushed forward determined to close the final gap in the encirclement. Peking was surrounded. All that day the city gates remained closed. But some time during the early morning hours of July 31 the Japanese marched in. They paraded up Ch'ien Men Ta Chieh, through the shadowed tunnel of the great front gate, and into the Legation Quarter; they swarmed along the broad avenues. Shouts of "Banzai!"

accompanied the raising of the rising-sun flag on city walls and gate towers, over government buildings and palaces.

There was no looting or burning in Peking, no drunken soldiers rampaging through the streets. Generals Kotouki and Kawakishi held firm control of their troops. Occasionally, Chinese were shoved into the gutters by passing Japanese soldiers, but that was no worse than the treatment that had been accorded them by their own 29th Army. With a vast collective sigh of relief the people of Peking began to make adjustments and to scheme for profit as they always had in the past.

North Hopei was in Japanese hands and the flow of information on Chinese military movements had ceased. Someone from the military attaché's office was needed to make his way through Japanese lines to the other side. Demanding cables and radio messages from Washington were piling up on Colonel Stilwell's desk; something had to be done. Stilwell called me into his office.

"I've an idea," he began. "It may not work, but it might be worth a try if you're willing. If the Chinese are really serious about putting up a scrap, they should be moving troops into the area around Paoting on the Pinghan line. Think you could get there by car?"

I thought I could.

I was wrong, however. At a roadblock outside a small village about 10 miles south of Peking, a Japanese patrol stopped my car. They waved their arms wildly, pointing north. I waved mine just as wildly, pointing south. Since my recalcitrance was not according to the rule book for such a situation, the Japanese sergeant motioned me back into the car, climbed in himself, and pointed toward a town a few miles ahead. On arrival in the town I was turned over to the commanding officer, a grinning major who politely informed me in fair English that I should not be in the combat area. It was dangerous. I might be shot by the Chinese. He then said that he and his advance battalion had just occupied the town and were now preparing for the entrance of the colonel and the rest of the regiment. Would I like to see how the grateful Chinese people welcomed the troops of His Imperial Majesty?

Indeed I would, and did: the main street was lined with sad-eyed little children waving small paper Japanese flags. A large supply of these flags had hastily been distributed by the first troops, the children had been herded to their positions along the street, and now all was in readiness for the colonel and the photographers.

"See how happy they are to receive the liberation we bring," my major hissed through his buck teeth. "When I enter the town, all peoples wave flags of welcome. American and Japanese peoples good friends. Yes? You will now report happy situation to embassy of U.S.A. Yes?"

"I sure as hell will."

"So sorry, sir. Now necessary you return to Peking before colonel arrives. He not like to find you here."

Having no other choice, I took off at once to report my failure to Colonel Stilwell. I suggested to him that I try to get through the Nankow Pass the next morning. If that failed, I'd try the long way around—train to Tientsin, ship to Tsingtao or Shanghai, and train to Paoting and Taiyuan.

All Stilwell said was, "If you do get through, contact all Americans along the way and tell them to go south as fast as they can."

On August 3, accompanied by Jack Belden, a United Press stringer who had asked to come along, I took off in the old office touring car. Stooped, dark-eyed, and rather gloomy by nature, Belden wore a faded khaki shirt and shorts, low shoes, and an old pith helmet. I had on a pair of old trousers and an open-necked shirt, but no hat. Not long after we crossed the Sha River about 25 miles northwest of Peking, the road ended abruptly at an arched stone bridge that had been collapsed by explosives. I sent the car back to town by my driver, and carrying only light knapsacks on our backs, Belden and I started off on foot across the rock-strewn, sandy country toward Nankow, about 15 miles ahead. I knew that large Japanese patrols were moving about the area, but had no idea if we might encounter the more friendly Chinese. This made for a distinctly uncomfortable feeling. The low foothills encircling Nankow and the higher ridges toward the pass loomed ahead. It looked as if we were in for a long walk, but a double line of trenches suddenly appeared directly in our path. At the same time we spotted a Japanese infantry patrol between us and Peking. We had landed in a sort of no-man's-land.

As we hurried forward, the roar of approaching Japanese bombers speeded our pace into a fast run toward the shelter of the earthworks. When we reached the parapet and were about to jump into the excavation, Chinese bayonets held us at bay. The low-flying bombers were now almost directly overhead. Finally a boyish-looking lieutenant agreed to take my calling card—skewered on the point of a bayonet—to his company commander. The captain appeared just as the bombers zoomed off. He stated somewhat pompously that he would have to get authority from his battalion commander for us to pass and that final authority for us to pass through the defensive positions would have to come from the regimental commander. Eventually the tangle of red tape, or protocol, was cleared and we were escorted to the colonel in command of the sector. Not knowing just what to do with us, he decided to pass the buck by sending us to Nankow. There we would be placed on the first train and passed on—under escort, or arrest—to the commander of the 89th Division at Huailai.

Since Nankow had been bombed the day before, no trains were allowed to move during daylight hours. It was dark as our train chugged up the steep zigzag through Chuyungkwan and Kanchuang to the pass. As we moved slowly through the bombed-out station area of Kanchuang, fires were still raging from the air attack of only a few hours before. A sergeant closed the window blinds with a jerk—his idea of security, no doubt. We saw no more until we reached Huailai about midnight. There we were marched to division headquarters and shown into the office of the chief of staff, General Hsiao I-hsu. He had a fiery temper and flashing brown eyes; he had lost a thumb scaling a city wall in one of the campaigns against the Reds in Kiangsi province. As we entered the room, he was chewing out a young officer. The loudness of his voice increased in proportion to his rising fury.

Having reduced the victim of his wrath to a trembling wreck, he asked politely why we had come. I told him it was impossible to return to Peking and that we wanted to go to Kalgan and on to Taiyuan as quickly as we could. He had no objections, but since the railway line was closed because of heavy bombings, a train trip was out of the question that night or the next day. Perhaps the day after. We would have to wait. When the division commander entered the room, I proposed that we go forward by mule or on foot. He flatly vetoed that idea, saying that refugees, military patrols, and *lao pai hsing* ("local peasants") on the road made any such plan too dangerous. In the meantime we were to remain at an inn he designated. To be certain we did not stray off, an officer and a squad of soldiers would accompany us.

The inn was comfortable enough. The rooms were clean, but its walled courtyard was inhabited by at least 20 hungry pigs whose favorite foraging spot was the noisome outdoor toilet in a corner off the gate. The food was scanty. The innkeeper apologized profusely for the shortage as if it were entirely his fault and continued to do so for the two nights and days we remained in the walled mountain town. Huailai was a place of stone watchtowers and a forbidding castle-like fort that topped a high hill. The town seemed to be bursting at its seams with troops from five or six divisions.

Could I send a telegram to Peking? No, I was told, the lines had been cut. But my guards saw no harm in mailing a letter at the post office. They had heard that there was no delay in mail deliveries, and this proved to be correct; strangely enough, the Japanese permitted the postal and telegraph services and the foreign-controlled customs service to operate without interference. I sent a letter at once to Stilwell. To avoid arousing suspicion, it was addressed to Mr. J.W. Stilwell at his house in Magpie Lane. In it I reported all of the divisions and other troops I had seen and drew the obvious conclusion that the Chinese were actually deploying for a fight. Twelve days later in Tsinan I learned that my letter had been the first word from outside the Japanese lines around Peking and that it reached its destination in close to normal time.

Late at night on our second day I was notified that space in a boxcar was being held and that Belden and I were free to leave within the hour. But the train only got as far as Hsiahuayuan, where the station and tracks had been completely wrecked by big bombs. Craters were 15 feet across in the hard-packed station platform. In the darkness the still-burning ruins and dim silhouettes of men moving through clouds of smoke in the flickering light of crackling fires created an eerie Dante-esque picture of infernal destruction. At 13th Corps headquarters the chief of staff told us he had no idea when there might be another train to Kalgan; so he sent us on our way by road in the commanding general's car.

We pulled up to the undamaged station at Kalgan at daylight. The first order of business was to set up a base of operations at the inn where I had stayed two years before on the last lap of a rugged trip through Inner Mongolia. The place was run by a solicitous, fat Chinese man who promptly provided us with guides to the American missions on the outskirts of the city.

That morning I had my first experience with the classic stubborn determination to proclaim the word of God, come hell or high water. A stern-faced woman ran the first mission I visited—a woman whose attitude and appearance gave every indication that she had been cast of iron. When I explained the military situation and told her that once the Japanese took Kalgan banks would close and money would be scarce, her chin closed like a vise on her uncompromising mouth. In a voice that sounded like an accusation of sin, she asked how long I had been in China.

"Only two and a half years!" she exclaimed. "Young man, I was *born* in China. When you've been here as long as I have, you'll realize these flare-ups come and go. They always have. But the voice of God is heard above them all."

"But madam, the embassy is warning all Americans to evacuate north China."

She tossed her gray head.

"They always do," she said. "That's all they have to do, except to lead sinful lives surrounded by women and alcohol."

"Then you refuse?"

"Indeed I do. I intend to remain right here, to harvest more souls in the garden of the Lord."

That afternoon I tried another mission with equal lack of success. The next morning I made a third try. As I was talking with the missionary, black wicker warning balls were hoisted on high poles and wheezy sirens wailed to announce an approaching air raid. Within minutes the long whistle of falling bombs, explosions, screams, and the crackle of roaring flames rent the air. The center of the town around the railway station was taking a terrific plastering.

"See, I told you," I pointed out hopefully.

"Thank you for your concern, captain," the missionary said, "but we will remain at our posts."

It was hopeless, so I hurried back to town. The inn was gone! A heavy bomb had landed in the courtyard and demolished the U-shaped building. Belden and I ran to the station, which miraculously has been spared. The exodus of frightened people had already begun. By fighting, pushing, and gouging through the crowd clamoring around the passenger cars we managed to squeeze into a tiny space on the slatted board seats. By the time the train finally lurched away from the station on the 90-mile trip to Tatung, it was jammed with people, crying children, chickens, dogs, pigs, bundles, blankets, and baskets.

On arrival at Tatung about three hours later, we saw the last southbound train for the day disappearing down the tracks on its way to Taiyuan. But across the square an ancient bus, already taking on passengers, held out hope of continuing to the south. We fought and clawed through the yelling crowd to a seat in the midst of another cargo of chickens, dogs, bundles, and wailing children. The rickety old vehicle eventually took off in a series of backfires, and again we were on our uncertain way.

The overloaded bus ground its way up the winding gravel road to the pass at a spur of the Great Wall, stopped to cool its steaming radiator, and like an overexerted mule, wheezed and sputtered into silence. The driver announced that the remainder of the trip through Yinghsin would be all downhill. Now he could save precious gasoline—and cheat the bus company—by cutting off the motor and coasting down to the floor of the Shansi Valley. The passengers, not knowing a spark plug from a brake band, grinned approval and settled themselves, so closely and happily wedged together they seemed to breath as one. Once under way, the bus tore down the mountainside spraying loose gravel and careening from side to side. As we sped around hairpin turns, the rear wheels skidded wildly to the edge of steep slopes. The Chinese yelled with delight at the speed. We screamed "Huang chia!" ("Get in gear!") with no effect other than to make the driver and his happy flock stare at us as if we wanted to spoil the fun.

At last the road began to level off, and we soon reached the flat farmlands of the valley. Wiping our perspiring faces, Belden and I sighed with relief. During the late afternoon the bus wallowed through villages and small towns, past mile after mile of cultivated fields where farmers and their families seemed unaware of the holocaust being loosed in the north. As the sun sank in red splendor behind a low ridge of hills, our bus roared through the tunnel of a city gate and the driver frantically honked his way along the streets of Taiyuan crowded with carts, mules, camels, a few herds of pigs, and seething mobs of people. Eventually we reached the bus station across the main square from the Grand Hotel de Taiyuan, a somewhat run-down establishment that had long since lost all pretensions to grandeur. But its high-ceilinged rooms were cool and the bath a much-needed haven of soap and water.

The next morning we left on the first train to Shihkiachuang on the Pinghan Railway, hoping to go north from there to Paoting. Our trip across the forested slopes of the Heng Mountains was a scenic wonder; our destination, a dirty, bustling rail junction. But there were no trains going north. No buses. No carts. No horses. No anything. Everything was headed south. But thousands of troops were marching toward Paoting, 50 miles to the north. Belden and I discussed the problem; there was only one thing left to do: go south to Chengchow on the Yellow River, east on the Lunghai Railway through Kaifeng to Hsuchow, then north on the Tsinpu line through Tsinan as far as possible. Another battle of elbows, kicks, and shoves finally enabled us to climb through an open window on a southbound train. We made it aboard, but we were trailed by curses of resentment, unflattering references to our ancestry, and consignment to all the tortures of the eighteen hells.

At Chengchow, although the train was fairly crowded, we managed to establish squatters' rights in a clean first-class compartment. As we fought off would-be intruders at the Kaifeng station, I recalled my last visit of two years earlier. Then I had been a guest of General Shang Chen on his rather elegant private train. He had invited Captain Roberts and me to observe the maneuvers of his 20th Army Group and 32nd Corps with General P'ang Ping-hsun's 40th Corps. The exercises had not been too impressive, but General P'ang had been. He was a huge, jovial man with an enormous belly appropriate to his name, which, with a play on words, means fat. One afternoon after the somewhat formal military exercises, we had hunted ducks around a small lake with General Shang. Having posted ourselves across the water from our host, our wild shots scared all the ducks and geese to his side, thus ensuring he brought home a big bag. Home was his comfortable house in town where it took hours for the three of us to bathe in the single tub. The delay between our ablutions, I learned at dinner that night, was due to the servants. Instead of draining the tub after each bath, they had bottled and sold the used soapy water in quart containers to beggars and poor people. Having been used, our bath water cost the impoverished street people less than the price demanded by professional water carriers.

At Hsuchow, the only difficulty in buying a ticket to Ts'angchow, the most northern station to which any trains were running, was in convincing the stationmaster that I was not crazy. No one was going that far north! Didn't I realize the dangers I might encounter? But with a shrug he finally gave in and sold me a ticket. Like most Chinese at the time he had grave doubts about the sanity of all foreigners anyway. After all, compared to the people of the Middle Kingdom, they were little more than subhuman. During the nine-hour wait for train departure, I had a much-needed two-hour sleep on a bale of hay sitting on the bustling station platform.

Belden left for Shanghai where bigger events were beginning to shape up, so I went on alone. On arrival at the Ts'angchow station, I was immediately arrested by an officer and a squad of eight men. They marched me down the street in a hollow square to an inn where I was assigned two rooms. A guard of four soldiers armed with Luger pistols was posted with instructions to remain in the rooms at all times. Requests to see my fat friend, General P'ang Ping-hsun, who was in command of the area, were brushed aside. I was told that my diplomatic passport was a forgery, that I was a White Russian spy in the pay of the Japanese. Why a Russian? I asked. The answer was simple and irrefutable—because I had blue eyes. And it was well known that all Russians had blue eyes. Who could dispute that? I could and did, but to no avail.

During my four days of incarceration, Ts'angchow was bombed four times—twice quite heavily. Not being a large place, most of the town was either wiped out or left in flames. Luckily the Japanese bombers missed the inn that was my jail, though the area around it was reduced to shambles. Adding to the discomfort of wondering when a 500-pounder might blow up the inn, the place was full of bedbugs. On the fourth day, with no explanation of any kind, I was ordered to take the southbound train for Tsinan at two that afternoon. Skipping the legal questions involved in the imprisonment of a member of the staff of the American embassy, I wasted no time in accepting my release and boarded an ancient coach.

In about two hours the train rattled and chugged into the station at the provincial capital. It was a huge German–Victorian architectural monstrosity that had been erected at the turn of the century when Shantung was a German sphere of interest. I made a beeline across a wide cobbled square to the two-story Stein Hotel. It was clean and comfortable and served excellent food. The German owner and his blond son seemed relieved to learn that I was not British. They despised everything about the British, who had bombed out their home city of Mannheim during the Great War. Walter Bosshard, an old friend from Peking, was also staying at the hotel. A Swiss photographer of international renown who supplied news photos and other pictures to a number of European and American agencies, he had devised an ingenious camera to allay the suspicions of the military in the Far East. Apparently aimed in one direction at a harmless landscape or temple, at a 90-degree angle it photographed the news or military scene he wanted. He always carried two cameras slung from his neck. When his undeveloped film was demanded, he obligingly handed over the blank roll in the decoy camera.

That afternoon I bought a suit and a few shirts and threw away the filthy things I had been wearing. Having been tailored to fit a Chinese model, everything was too tight, although they were a big improvement on my soiled shirt and trousers.

When I reported to the American consul John Allison, he

handed me a telegram. It instructed me to remain in Tsinan until further orders and to send daily reports on the situation, even if negative. Coded reports would be sent as letter mail to Sam Sokobin, the American consul at Tsingtao. He would deliver them to the commander of the U.S.S. *Marblehead* anchored in Tsingtao Bay, who in turn would radio them to Peking, Nanking, Manila, and San Francisco, and thence to Washington. (Some of these reports turned up in 1947–48 as part of the so-called pumpkin papers during the Alger Hiss–Whittaker Chambers controversy and trial.)

After settling down in Tsinan, I summed up my 1,000-mile trek in a long letter to Colonel Stilwell: "Speaking in general, I have seen numerous cases of the chronic incompetence of the Chinese Army. But they have accomplished a great deal with troop movements. How it's done God alone knows. We would go nutty, but somehow or other they seem to get things done. The current expression to cover all ills is '*pu i-ting*' ('not certain, or not definite'), and it sure as hell hits the mark."

Through the consulate's Chinese secretary, H.T. Ch'en, I was soon able to establish good relations with Han Fu-chu, the intriguing warlord governor of Shantung. At our first meeting, Han asserted that he was only a soldier and would abide by all decisions of the central government. In the next breath, however, he stated that defeated Chinese armies from the north, whether of the central government or otherwise, would be allowed to pass through his province only if their retreat was orderly. If they were in a rout, they would be stopped at the provincial border, and thus be squeezed between Han's troops and the Japanese. When I asked about the possibility of a declaration of war, he laughed and said: "What difference does a declaration make? We are at war already."

Other contacts were added to my list, and a steady flow of reports on the military and political situations as I saw them crackled from the *Marblehead*'s radio. Before long a blunt message from the Nanking embassy set my adrenalin flowing. Most of my reports had plainly indicated my belief that a major war was developing, that the term incident merely referred to the fact that there had been no declaration. The ambassador's message stated that my personal conclusions were not in accordance with

State Department policy and should be changed forthwith. Henceforth my reports were to reflect the official attitude of the United States government and no longer contain such terms as the Sino-Japanese War. A copy of these instructions had also been sent to my boss, Colonel Stilwell. He quickly straightened out the clash between policy and fact. As was usual with him, his message was brief and to the point: "You're doing a great job. Continue reporting things as you see them. I will handle the big boys."

On August 1 Generalissimo Chiang Kai-shek ordered a deployment of troops to counteract the Japanese threat from north Hopei, Jehol, and Chahar provinces. If the Pingsui Railway (Peking-Suiyuan line) should fall into Japanese hands, all of Suiyuan, Chahar, and north Shansi would be lost. As usual, the chain of command for the expected operations was one of those complicated puzzles of authority so dear to the heart of the Chinese military mind—a yang and yin political balance between doubtful generals, overlapping command, and provision for Chiang to bypass commanders when his intuitive sense of tactics inspired him to issue orders directly to subordinate units. Always distrustful, and in many cases rightly so, he named a former enemy, General Yen Hsi-shan, pacification director for Taiyuan, an office theoretically equal in authority to his own as commanding general of the 1st War Area. Under this dichotomy of command he placed five senior generals: one the commanding general of the 14th Army Group consisting of three divisions; two with the 7th Army Group of two corps with a total of two divisions and four brigades; a fourth in command of the 1st Cavalry Corps, a jumble of four cavalry divisions and four independent brigades hastily thrown together into a new organization whose units were then widely separated; and a fifth with the prestigious title of front-line commander-in-chief in command of the 13th and 17th Corps of five divisions. This was an imposing force on paper, but actually a poorly armed and indifferently trained aggregate of overstaffed units numbering less than 90,000 men, of whom no more than 60,000 could be considered combat troops. An illusion of strength was created by the sonorous tones of impressive titles and lengthy rosters of army groups, armies, corps, divisions, and brigades. As a defensive force, its inherent weakness lay in a lack of cohesion—the result of too hasty a mobilization. Its basic impotence was further aggravated by mutual distrust between commanders and between units from central China and those from north China. Indeed, on more than one occasion gray-clad northern troops opened fire on khaki-clad men from the south, the color of whose uniforms was similar to that of the Japanese. And for their part, southern troops returned the compliment on the assumption that the northerners were an invading foreign army. To meet the Japanese threat, units were deployed in depth—meaning that they were strung out for some 240 miles from Nankow to Kalgan and along the Suiyuan-Chahar border.

Meanwhile, in the interest of national defense, Chiang Kai-shek was going through the motions of cleaning house politically. When General Pai Ch'ung-hsi, whose Kwangsi-Kwangtung clique had been in open rebellion the year before, flew to Nanking to offer his services, he was appointed the generalissimo's chief of staff, an empty title that continued to be empty for the next eight years. Offers of support by the warlord governors of Yunnan and Szechwan were welcomed, though few of their untrustworthy troops were to be utilized for over a year. The Chinese Red Army under Chu Teh was redesignated the 8th Route Army, but for all practical purposes remained the Red Army.

The attacking Japanese forces were organized in two separate commands: the Japanese garrison forces on the Nankow front (5th Division, 11th Composite Brigade, a tank unit, and supporting air squadrons) and the Chahar Expeditionary Force on the Kalgan front (three composite brigades from the Kwantung Army and nine Mongolian cavalry divisions). Of varied size, the cavalry units consisted mainly of the semifeudal mounted retainers of Mongolian princes who had been bought off by the Japanese. "More divisive than divisions" and of little military value, each of the Mongolian units operated more or less independently.

On August 8, advance elements of the Japanese 5th Division and 11th Composite Brigade engaged the Chinese 13th Corps[1] of two divisions, which had deployed around Nankow. The Chinese 17th Corps[2] of two divisions and one separate brigade had sprawled itself over 50 miles "in depth" from Huailai on the rail line to north of Chihcheng. The Chinese dispositions failed completely to take advantage of the narrow, precipitous defiles leading up to Nankow Pass. Commanders made no use whatsoever of demolitions that could easily have destroyed the railway line and blocked the pass. Elements of the Chinese 1st Cavalry Corps "attacked in north Chahar" by moving up to the Suiyuan border and grazing their animals. Advance elements of the 14th Army Group[3] of three divisions under General Wei Li-huang started to cross the Wu Tai Mountains from Shansi into the north Hopei plain to reinforce the 13th Corps at Nankow. They arrived too late to do anything more than contact the Japanese at Chenpien, 20 miles west of Nankow, on August 23 and were never able to establish contact with the 13th Corps.

Though temporarily checked, the Japanese 11th Brigade succeeded in taking Nankow on August 11 and immediately pushed on toward Nankow Pass.

In May, 1938, in a letter to me, Colonel Stilwell recounted the report of an English-speaking Chinese colonel, Yao Ts'an-mou, concerning the latter's slightly inaccurate and highly subjective description of the loss of Nankow. Finally able to break out of his office in the spring of 1938, Stilwell was at the Lunghai Railway front near Hsuchow, from where he sent the letter. Headed "How We Lost Nankow—A Comedy by Yao Ts'an-mou," Stilwell's recounting follows:

That son of a bitch in Kalgan [General Li Hsien-chou, commander of the 21st Division] beat us. We had the Japs on ice, and suddenly without any warning he ran away and left the back door open. How could we stay in Nankow after that? It was terrible. I could not take any food for a week, and everybody was weeping very bitter tears. The general [T'ang En-po, commander of the 13th Corps] tried to kill himself, and we had to restrain him.

Just think, we were right within striking distance of Peking and Tientsin, and that bastard traitor, Liu Ju-ming [commander of the 7th Army Group consisting of the 143rd Division and three brigades] spoiled it all. When we retired, everybody was very sad. We had lost 10,000 men.

When the Japs came around the flank, they got to a place called Hunlinch'en, where we held them. Then we sent a regiment around their left flank to attack their rear, but that bandit, Liu Ju-ming, was there, and a part of his force turned and attacked *our regiment*. If he had not done this, we could have ruined the Japs. This Liu Ju-ming is a bastard. He prevented Wei Li-huang [commander of the 14th Army Group of three divisions] from joining us. Wei was moving up with the 10th and 85th Divisions, and Liu moved in *between* us, so we could not effect a junction. If it had not been for him, Wei Li-huang could have joined us, we could have held off the Jap flank attack, and we could have held on. It was that son of a bitch Liu who spoiled it all.

Stilwell's letter continued:

Yao claims that the 4th and 89th Divisions were in the Nankow fight complete; that a lot of the 21st Division was dribbled in here and there; that at least part of the 84th Division went in on the east of the 89th; that they knew nothing of the capture of Kalgan until one day in trying to get Fu Tso-vi on the phone, the Japs answered the call; that the total losses were 10,000; that 1,300 were killed at the little temple on the first hill out of Nankow town just west of the railway, practically all by artillery; that the Japs had one hundred 75's and thirty 150's. Further the deponent saveth not— at least not anything very coherent.

Station B-U-N-K now signing off—Cheerio, J.W.S.

At Nankow Pass the Japanese were confronted by the Chinese 21st, 94th, and 72nd divisions, but the defense melted away when threatened on its flank by the approach of the Japanese 5th Division near Chenpien. Meanwhile, the Chinese 1st Cavalry Corps occupied four undefended Chahar border towns. The Chinese 143rd Division occupied Changpei, about 40 miles north of Kalgan, and a second town about 30 miles to the northeast. When attacked by a Japanese force of three brigades[4] from southern Chahar on August 18, the 143rd Division fell back on Kalgan. On August 20 the Chinese 7th Army Group[5] of one division and three brigades arrived in the Huailai area to reinforce the 17th Corps. But on reaching a town 40 miles west of Huailai, the 200th and 211th brigades turned back, ostensibly to aid in the defense of Kalgan, actually to continue turning back right through Kalgan until they reached Chaikoupao, 40 miles to the west.

Three days later the Japanese 5th Division attacked Huailai

"via Chenpien," as the official Chinese history* of the conflict has it. On August 26 the defending 13th Corps of two divisions was ordered to break out to the southwest, leaving the 17th Corps more or less stranded about 50 miles to the north. However, that situation was soon accommodated by a Japanese column from southern Chahar that struck hard at Chihcheng. "After repelling the enemy," the official history continues, the 17th Corps made a precipitate exit from the scene by breaking out to the southwest where it rejoined its companion force. With the fall of Huailai, the Chinese 72nd Division and 7th Brigade pulled out and, partly by rail, partly by marching, eventually found a haven of safety with the rest of the 7th Army Group at Chaikoupao, 120 miles to the west. The units of this army group had accomplished nothing but to jam the overloaded railway line with their feckless movements and countermovements.

The way was now open to Kalgan from the north and east. The Chinese 143rd Division, left more or less high and dry, withdrew in considerable disorder. It did not stop withdrawing until it had crossed the Hsiangyang River, 30 miles to the south, and then it pushed breathlessly on all the way to southern Hopei. On September 3 the Japanese entered Kalgan, brushed aside light resistance at Chaikoupao, and continued on toward Tai-yuan.

The Chinese 61st Corps from the 2nd War Area, composed of one division and two separate brigades, briefly confronted the advancing Japanese at Tienchen, about 45 miles southwest of Kalgan. On September 11 it pulled back 20 miles to Yangkao, exchanged fire with the enemy from prepared positions, and hastily withdrew another 20 miles to Tatung. The Chinese abandoned Tatung on September 13 and the Japanese marched in. The 61st Corps made another withdrawal of about 20 miles to Huaijen and occupied defensive positions. But by September 15 the Chinese had pulled back an additional 40 miles to Yenmenkuan at the Inner Great Wall. From that town they occupied new defense lines extending along the arc of the Wall through Juyuehkou to Pinghsingkuan, 60 miles due east of Yenmenkuan

* Hsu and Chang. *History of the Sino-Japanese War, 1937–45.*

and 70 miles southeast of Tatung. The extreme right of the line was held by Shansi provincial troops under General Sun Chu.

From Huailai the Japanese 5th Division turned south through Weihsien toward Pinghsingkuan. One of its brigades was in contact with the Chinese provincial troops; the other, the 21st, waited at Weihsien for orders to move into the rugged mountainous area of north Shansi, where it was due for a rude surprise. Early on the morning of September 23 the 21st Brigade started out from Weihsien in one column, followed by its motorized supply and baggage convoy. By this time, the other brigade of the 5th Division had been drawn off toward Laiyuan, 35 miles east of Pinghsingkuan, in a series of continuous actions against General Sun Chu's provincial troops. About 8 miles northeast of Pinghsingkuan, the advance elements of the 21st Brigade were stopped by two battalions of Chinese troops firing from the adjacent hills. After an all-day fight on September 24, the Chinese withdrew; on the following morning the Japanese column resumed its march.

In this particular area the road to Pinghsingkuan ran through deep loess, the yellow loamy soil characteristic of north China. For generations iron-wheeled carts, aided by strong winds, had cut deeper and deeper into the soil until the road had become a perpendicular-walled trench many feet deep with no means of exit for miles.

On September 20, after a 300-mile march from Shensi province, the 115th Division of the Communist 8th Route Army under the command of General Lin Piao had arrived at its destination in the Wu Tai Mountains a few miles south of Pinghsingkuan. The division consisted of three infantry regiments with a strength of about 9,000 men. General Lin had accurate information on the movements of the Japanese 21st Brigade. Having delayed the enemy column for a day and a half with two of his battalions firing from the hills until he had had time to dispose the main body of his troops, General Lin's plan—according to the Communist account—was to block the advance of the enemy force in the deeply sunken road, attack its left flank with the bulk of his division, and by a rapid encirclement to the Japanese rear, seize the motorized transport. Lin's 115th Division troops were in place to implement the plan at 6:00 A.M. on September 25.

The first warning to the Japanese commander of his entrapment in the defile was a sudden outburst of rifle and machine-gun fire, exploding hand grenades, and alarmed shouts from the head of his column. Unable to climb the high walls of the road, he had no idea what was going on. As the main body of his troops continued to press forward in the narrow trench, it jammed into a confused tangle of men and equipment from the advance elements in a desperate stampede to the rear. Meanwhile, the Chinese had lined up on the banks above the road and were happily tossing hand grenades into the struggling mass of Japanese 12 to 15 feet below them. Eventually, by climbing on each other's shoulders, some of the Japanese managed to scramble out of the defile and get a machine gun into action. Facing steady machine-gun fire, the head of the trapped column was now a mass of piled-up dead and wounded. The road behind was strewn with grenade-torn bodies. Caught completely by surprise, the headquarters staff and the personnel of the truck convoy at the rear were all killed; the vehicles with all their ammunition and supplies were captured.

About noon General Lin attacked the flank of the second brigade of the 5th Division. By 3:00 P.M. the entire Japanese division, including its badly mauled 21st Brigade, was in full retreat to the north. The Communist 115th Division, now joined by General Sun Chu's Shansi troops—since the battle was over—continued the pursuit until late afternoon, then halted for the night.

The Japanese had paid dearly for using the sunken road without flank patrols: they lost nearly 3,000 killed, compared with a Chinese loss of about 400 killed and wounded; all of their codes, maps, and records; over 100 trucks loaded with supplies; 2 light field guns; 400,000 yen for payment of the troops; and great quantities of equipment, ammunition, and clothing. No prisoners were taken. The Japanese had not been taking any and expected the same treatment from their enemies.

The unexpected Chinese guerrilla tactics had nonplussed the unimaginative Japanese commander; before he had had a chance to determine what was happening, his brigade was a shambles.

The first Chinese victory of the Sino-Japanese conflict, Pinghsing-kuan demonstrated that smug trust in conventional tactics, hide-bound adherence to orders from distant commands, and assumption that the enemy would do nothing out of the ordinary were no match for surprise, mobility, concealment, and the support of a friendly countryside. Unfortunately this lesson was not absorbed by the rigid Chinese command, and the poorly trained forces of Chiang Kai-shek were to pay for the uncompromising attitudes of their commanders with complete defeat at the hands of the Chinese Communists some 12 years later. Chiang and the National Military Council were so contemptuous of the Reds and their guerrilla tactics that the Communist success in the battle at Pinghsingkuan was recorded in the expurgated official history of the war as having been accomplished by troops under General Yen Hsi-shan.

Although the 5th Division had been temporarily checked, one partly motorized Japanese division and nine Mongolian cavalry units of miscellaneous size turned north at Tatung and headed through Fengchen and Chining for Kueisui, the capital of· Suiyuan. To avoid being cut off and isolated in the northwest, the Chinese 35th Corps of three infantry brigades and the 1st Cavalry Corps of two cavalry divisions were withdrawn into Shansi south of the Great Wall. Two Chinese infantry brigades, four cavalry divisions, and three cavalry brigades were left behind for disposition in depth and sustained resistance. When the Japanese approached Kueisui on October 10, there was very little resistance, sustained or otherwise. And evidently the Chinese commanders interpreted literally the meaning of disposition in depth, for like riders in an old-style western movie, they and their horsemen disappeared in the afterglow of the setting sun as it dropped below the sandy vastness of the Ninghsia plateau. On October 14 the Japanese marched unimpeded into Kueisui and three days later into Paotou at the end of the railway.

During the Peking-Suiyuan campaign, destruction of civilian areas had been relatively light—with the exception of several railway stations bombed into complete ruins, villages located directly between contending armies, the destruction of Tungchow and Huailai, and air raids on Nankai University and Kalgan. But the psychological effect on the Chinese people of a Japanese army occupying their territory was deep and lasting, as any near reign of terror is bound to be. Under the eyes of foreign embassies and consulates in the big cities, Japanese behavior was stern and uncompromising; but in the small towns and villages of the countryside it was oppressively brutal. Hundreds of men, unable to answer questions on military matters, were tortured and executed at the whim of junior and noncommissioned officers. Countless women were raped, often repeatedly by gangs of drunken Japanese soldiers. When the women and girls of one Chahar village were hidden in nearby hills, the Japanese, not to be denied the rights of conquerors, rounded up the youths and boys and raped them. Houses were looted, granaries emptied, men and animals commandeered as carriers, stock driven off and slaughtered.

At times Chinese military casualties had been heavy—on an overall basis as much or more from sickness and desertion as from enemy action. Because of the lack of any medical care worth the name, most of the seriously wounded had died. All stragglers and prisoners had been shot or beheaded by the Japanese. Horrible as such action was, it was no different from what they themselves meted out to Japanese under reverse circumstances. As a matter of fact, the Chinese usually shot their own seriously wounded as an act of mercy, since "they would only die anyway."

Although the strength of Japanese forces had never approached that of their opponents in numbers of men, they had defeated or outmaneuvered the Chinese armies at every confrontation except Pinghsingkuan. This was not entirely due to superior equipment and air support. Feudal in their thinking and strongly influenced by politics of one kind or another, the Chinese looked upon the scene of a campaign as a gigantic military chess board about which pieces were shifted in various confrontations to checkmate an enemy. Unfortunately for them, the more aggressive Japanese met all confrontations head-on and brusquely swept aside the Chinese chessmen, be they kings or rooks or pawns. In addition, Japanese officers and men were highly indoctrinated, dedicated, and honored by their people as representatives carrying out the will of the emperor. Chinese officers and men were neither indoctrinated, dedicated, nor honored by anyone. To the Chinese people, armies were a necessary and expensive evil they would much prefer to do without. In Japan, senior generals had one unquestioned leader, the emperor. In China, most senior generals had only an overriding ambition—to supplant the de facto leader, Chiang Kai-shek.

The Japanese campaign into Suiyuan province resulted in one material benefit for China—a treaty of friendship between the Soviet Union and the Nanking government. Signed on August 29, it opened the way for Russian military aid, large loans, and as time went on, actual support by air units. Stalin had never considered the Chinese Reds as either real Communists or real Marxists and had never made the slightest move to help them. He was obsessed with a fear that the establishment of a strong Marxist state below his Siberian and Outer Mongolian borders would create a far greater danger to his eastern flank than would the maintenance of the existing dissension-torn nationalist government under Chiang Kai-shek. He had repeatedly urged Mao Tse-tung to come to terms with the central government at Nanking. Now, as he saw the long arm of the Japanese army, which had already outflanked him in Manchuria, stretching out to seize Inner Mongolia, he decided to support Chiang Kai-shek, regardless of his conservative political stance.

A second benefit emerged from the military operations in the lower Yangtze Valley in the form of sympathy via the condemnatory processes of the League of Nations. But the declarations of that powerless forum amounted to little more than a clucking of international tongues. Chiang Kai-shek had always clung tenaciously to the belief that eventually foreign intervention, particularly that of the United States and Great Britain, would pull his chestnuts out of the fire. Turning a deaf ear to all contrary advice, his undeviating determination in this fallacious conviction led him into a disastrous trap from which he and his armies never fully recovered. That trap led to the Battle of Shanghai and the loss of Nanking.

4

The Battle of Shanghai and the Fall of Nanking, Mid-July to Mid-December, 1937

THE ORIGINAL GRAND DESIGN of the Kwantung Army and the Tokyo militarists had not gone beyond the seizure of north China and the establishment of an autonomous regime of the five northern provinces. Based on past experience in dealing with the Chinese government, the Japanese had believed that the occupation of north Hopei, north Shansi, and Chahar, and the long thrust into Suiyuan, would accomplish two purposes: first, compel the Nanking government to knuckle under and accept their demands; and second, check any possible Russian plans for future expansion into east Asia by the extension of their border with Outer Mongolia for some 700 miles. But they had neither expected nor wanted their armies to be drawn into the vast morass of central China. Nor had they reckoned with the rising tide of resistance that swirled around Chiang Kai-shek.

For years Chiang had been determined to destroy the Chinese Communists. Meanwhile, he had played a waiting game hoping to counteract and defeat the aggressive aims of the Japanese by foreign pressure or intervention, although he had never been given any more tangible reasons for clinging to that hope than futile League of Nations demarches and high-principled U.S. State Department pomposities. Nonetheless, his unreasoning convictions were as tenacious as his peasant mind was stubborn. So, with the announced purpose of stiffening the resistance, he deliberately embarked on a hopeless campaign that brought the war to the very doorstep of Shanghai, the largest and richest city in Asia.

Shanghai had grown from a small walled town on a mud flat beside the Whangpoo River at the time of the first Opium War in 1840 to a complex city with a population of 3,650,000. The original International Settlement, now under British control, and the French concession had expanded through eight separate treaty arrangements with China to include seven miles of riverfront and areas extending from one to five miles inland. In July, 1937, these two areas of extraterritoriality had a combined population of 1,575,000 Chinese and about 63,000 foreigners, of whom 20,000 were Japanese, 9,000 British, 4,000 American, 2,500 French, 18,500 White Russian, and the remainder smaller groups of European and Indian origin. In addition to the civilian residents, five nations maintained garrisons in the city: the 4th Regiment of U.S. Marines, of 150 officers and 2,600 men; a British force of 90 officers and 2,500 men; the French, 50 officers and 2,000 men; the Italians, 20 officers and 750 men; and the Japanese a mixed unit of 5,000, including a specially trained force of 1,800 men in fortified barracks located in Hongkew, a section of the city straddling the north boundary of the Settlement. The Japanese controlled and operated Hongkew as their own private fief without regard for other governmental or treaty arrangements. As in the north, they had made their presence in Shanghai not only well known but obnoxious. The Japanese held frequent training exercises around Hongkew. Their troops, artillery, and tanks often paraded through the crowded streets of the Settlement and along the Bund, the wide quay that extended parallel to much of the riverfront. Ringing the Settlement and concession areas was the Greater Municipality of Shanghai, usually referred to as the Chinese City. It included the old walled city itself, Chapei, Paoshan, Hongkew, Kiangwan and Kiangnan west of the river, and Pootung on the east bank. The Municipality had a population of over 2,000,000.

In addition to the 20,000 Japanese residents of the International Settlement and French concession, about 6,600 lived in the Hongkew section. There were about 1,700 Japanese civilians and a sizable military guard in Hankow, and 1,700 more residing in the Yangtze River cities of Nanking, Wuhu, Kiukiang, Changsha, Ichang, and Chungking. These 30,000 Japanese citizens, including families, were provided a measure of protection by the 11th Gunboat Squadron under Rear Admiral Tasimoto Umataro. His 13 vessels were stationed at the various ports along the river. By early August, all Japanese, including military units, had been evacuated from upriver towns, and the women and children from Shanghai. An additional 12,000 Japanese resided in the coastal ports of Foochow, Amoy, Swatow, and Canton. They were protected by the 5th Destroyer Squadron of four ships commanded by Rear Admiral Nasakichi Okuma. They, too, had been evacuated by early August.

During the tense situation in mid-July, 1937, the Japanese continued to indulge in their favorite irritant: night military exercises in the Kiangwan-Hongkew area on the outskirts of Shanghai. On August 9 a Japanese sublieutenant, Isao Oyama, enraged because he had been ordered to stop his car at a gate at the Hungjao airfield, shot and killed a Chinese sentry. Other sentries killed Oyama and a Japanese enlisted man on the spot. Two days later, four Japanese cruisers and seven destroyers escorted five transports crammed with troops up the Whangpoo and dropped anchor off the Settlement. This naval force of the Japanese 3rd Fleet brought to 30 the number of warships then concentrated on the river from Wusung at its mouth to Shanghai. On August 13 the better part of two divisions of the Shanghai Expeditionary Force under the command of General Iwane Matsui disembarked at Shanghai.

Two days before, on August 11, the Chinese 36th, 87th, and 88th divisions had moved to positions on the line of siege with orders to attack the Japanese. At the same time, the 55th, 56th, and 57th divisions and the 20th Separate Brigade had been ordered to move on Pootung along the east bank of the river. On August 13, elements of the 88th Division clashed with Japanese troops in the Chapei-Kiangwan area near the North Station. Both sides suffered some casualties, but neither was in a mood to continue the fight at the time. Also on the thirteenth, the 87th Division occupied the east bank of the Whangpoo from Shanghai University to the mouth of the river. House-to-house fighting broke out in Chapei and continued for five days. By August 19 the Chinese had forced the Japanese back to Hongkew, but were not able to break their lines. The Japanese began to pour in reinforcements, supporting their infantry units with bombing attacks and naval gunfire, lobbing shells over the Settlement, and wreaking havoc in the Chinese City. Across the Whangpoo, the Chinese 55th Division attempted to take the river bank, but it was stopped by enemy artillery and naval guns.

Bombs and shells exploded in the Settlement and concession areas on several occasions. Nonetheless, as in Peking before its capture, the luncheon, cocktail, and dinner hours in Shanghai were as gay as ever. The lounges and dining rooms of the Cathay, Metropole, Astor, and Carlton hotels, the long bar at the Shanghai Club, the luxurious French Club, and the Russian restaurants were crowded with milling foreign customers who seemed impervious to what was going on outside. Businessmen, *taipans* ("foreign traders"), elegantly gowned women, even more elegantly gowned White Russian prostitutes on the prowl, military officers and attachés, newsmen in droves—all sought surcease from the battle at their doorstep by the usual means in the Far East: good drink, good food, good service, and good companionship. But the danger to their personal safety was soon brought home by the horror of a battle right in the main streets.

At noon on August 14 a futile and inaccurate attempt by poorly trained Chinese air force pilots to sink the Japanese battleship *Izuma*, tied up at the Bund off the business and hotel district, resulted in a ghastly loss of life on shore. A symbol of past victory to the Japanese, the *Izuma* was an old ship built for the Russian navy in 1898. She had been turned over to the Japanese as part of the settlement of 1905. In attempting to modernize the *Izuma*, the Japanese had stacked every nautical gadget ever heard of on her decks and superstructure, not to mention great slabs of armor plates riveted to her hull. Compared to a modern warship, she was an awkward, top-heavy grab-bag. All of the Chinese bombs missed their target completely, but a 1,000-pounder landed on a great department store on Bubbling Well Road and another struck the roof of a multistoried hotel. Nearly 2,000 people were cut to pieces by shards of falling glass. Another 1,500 were badly injured. When the smoke and dust finally

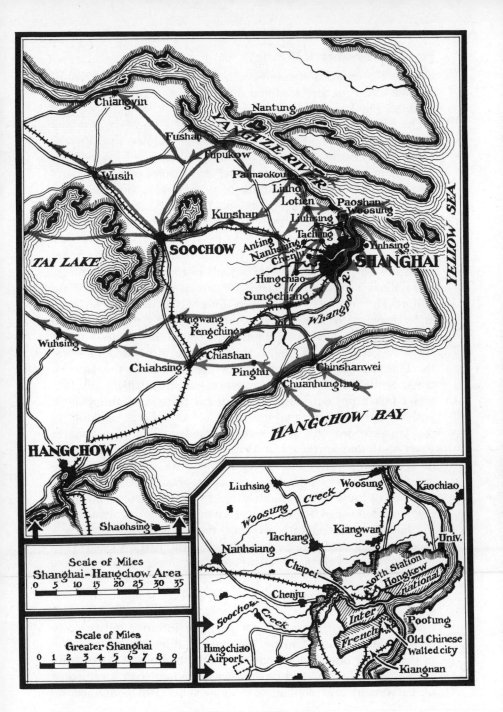

The Battle of Shanghai

cleared, the crowded streets were a shambles of bodies, smashed rickshas and cars, and scattered debris. Most of the victims were Chinese. The *Izuma* was not even scratched.

On August 20 Chiang Kai-shek promulgated the first of a continuing series of "operational guidances, principles, and dispositions." Supposedly an operational order, it was full of hedging expressions such as "attack gradually" and heroics such as "assault regardless of sacrifices." Although it included instructions to destroy the enemy, it contained no tactical plan for doing so. The bulk of the order meticulously prescribed the command structure of the newly designated 3rd War Area, with the generalissimo retaining command from Nanking, over 180 miles away, but not responsibility for actions in the field. This arrangement allowed him to take credit for success and to lay blame for failure. The five sectors that were directed to ring the Japanese in Shanghai with armies were somewhat vaguely prescribed. Details such as boundaries of command responsibility were omitted.

On August 21 the Chinese 36th Division attempted to storm the Huishan wharves directly across the river from the International Settlement. Struck by heavy naval and artillery fire, the attack failed; but not before the Japanese forces had almost been pushed into the river. On the night of August 22, elements of the Japanese 3rd and 11th divisions landed along the Yangtze River north and northwest of Wusung. At Lotien they succeeded in penetrating nearly four miles before three divisions of General Ch'en Ch'eng's 15th Army Group stopped their advance. On October 24 the Chinese counterattacked in this sector, and a see-saw struggle ensued for 14 days. Despite landings of elements of the Japanese 9th and 13th divisions, the Chinese held the seven-mile front essentially as it had been when the battle started. During this period both the Japanese army and foreign observers were astonished at the tenacity of the Chinese throughout the entire Shanghai area. Lacking naval, air, and artillery support, they suffered very heavy losses.

On September 6 a second document of intuitive military wisdom emanated from Chiang Kai-shek. It directed the cessation of the general offensive—a movement that had not yet been initiated by the Chinese—and ordered what amounted to a campaign of harassment and containment. This order still contained no plan of battle other than to make a stand to the last man. The tone of the order and the detailed action prescribed for each senior commander destroyed all individual initiative as surely as if it had been so designed.

Between September 7 and 16, newly arriving Japanese reinforcements pressed the attack without letup. The Chinese resisted against vastly superior fire power, but (quoting their own official history) "the battle line was interspersed." Translated, this military euphemism means that the line caved in. This was followed by a readjustment of positions, meaning a withdrawal to a new line two to two and a half miles back from the Whangpoo and the Yangtze. But in other areas the Chinese lines held.

Meanwhile, the Japanese landed the Formosa Independent Brigade, a large force of marines, and over 200 tanks. In addition, they flew about 100 aircraft into three newly constructed airfields. The inferior, poorly trained Chinese air force had virtually ceased operations in the area—possibly a boon to their own people in view of the *Izuma* catastrophe.

On the eighteenth the lines were more or less stabilized, although attacks and counterattacks were to continue for more than a month: a Chinese force was surrounded near Chapei; when it ran out of ammunition and supplies and had no escape route, it was wiped out.

On September 21 the 3rd War Area was subjected to a third command adjustment and a third set of new designations—the Right Wing, Central Wing, and Left Wing Operational Army Corps. General Chang Fa-kuei commanded the Right Wing Operational Corps consisting of the 8th and 10th Army Groups. Chang Fa-kuei had been commander of the Ironsides Army in 1927 and had earned a great reputation fighting against no opposition worth the name. Now, 10 years later, the iron had become somewhat rusted. General Chu Shao-liang, a run-of-the-mill type whose chief claim to fame was long association with Chiang Kai-shek, commanded the Central Wing Operational Army Corps. General Ch'en Ch'eng (later vice-president of nationalist China on Taiwan) commanded the Left Wing Operational Army Corps. A short, slight man with keen eyes and hair cut *en brosse*, Ch'en Ch'eng was one of the most intelligent and capable officers in the Chinese army. General Lo Cho-ying commanded the

10th Army Group and General Hsueh Yueh the 15th Army Group, the latter a part of Ch'en Ch'eng's Left Wing Corps. Lo Cho-ying was plump, indecisive and more interested in money than in men. In 1942, he was to become General Stilwell's "chief of staff" during the First Burma Campaign, and later, Chiang Kai-shek's representative at the Ramgarh Training Center for Chinese troops in India. Hsueh Yueh later became a protegé of T.V. Soong, Chiang Kai-shek's brother-in-law. In Soong's 1942–43 plan to overthrow the Generalissimo Hsueh Yueh was selected to become the "front man" at the head of a new wartime government.

By this time the Chinese had deployed seven army groups and the equivalent of two more army groups containing 71 divisions, 5 separate brigades, 4 separate artillery regiments, 5 separate artillery battalions, and miscellaneous peace-preservation units and garrison and fortress commands totalling over 500,000 men, less casualties already inflicted. The Japanese had thrown into the battle the entire Shanghai Expeditionary Force under the command of General Matsui, consisting of six divisions[1], four separate brigades, one separate infantry regiment and the Formosa Brigade. The whole force, with supporting air, armored and other units, totalled nearly 200,000 men, less casualties already sustained. The line of battle west of the Whangpoo River ran from the Chapei–North Station area in the Greater Municipality just north of the International Settlement north through Kiangwan to a point on Woosung Creek about 6.5 miles northwest of the Settlement, then west to the Chenhsing-Nanhsiang area about 7 miles northwest of the Settlement, then north to Liuho on the Yangtze River about 18 miles north of Shanghai.

On October 7 the Japanese forced crossings at several points along Woosung Creek north of Tachang where the creek ran through Nanhsiang. The Chinese had dug in along the south bank. Severe fighting for the eight-mile line continued for two weeks, with each side suffering heavy casualties. On the sixteenth, with a great show of outrage, the Japanese complained to British and American consular authorities that the Chinese had resorted to the use of poison gas in the desperate struggle along Woosung Creek. The Chinese insisted that they had used only harmless

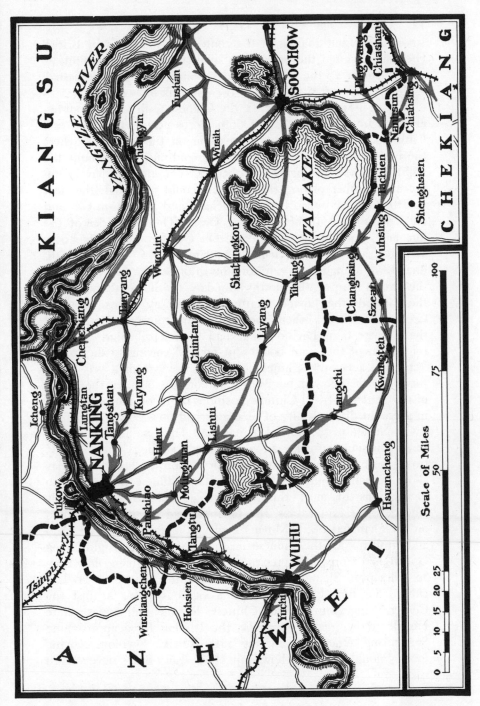

The Fall of Nanking

smoke shells, but analysis of the contents of the shells by British chemists disclosed the presence of phosgene in toxic amounts.

By October 20 the Chinese had sustained over 130,000 casualties on the Shanghai front since the outbreak of hostilities.

At 7:00 P.M. on October 21 the Chinese 48th Corps counterattacked from the south, the 66th Corps attacked on the east flank, and the 98th Division moved in on the left flank where the line ran generally north. Fighting continued throughout the night. On the morning of October 22, supported by naval gunfire and bomber planes, the Japanese counterattacked; the next day the Chinese pulled back to Tachang and Kiangwan, two and one-half miles south of Woosung Creek. The remainder of the line held, but only for two days. On October 25 the Japanese assaulted and took Tachang. Outflanked, the Chinese withdrew from Kiangwan to positions north of Soochow Creek where the stream formed the north boundary of the Settlement. On the thirtieth the Japanese rammed their way across Soochow Creek into Chapei where they came up against a regiment of the Chinese 88th Division that had been left behind to cover the retreat of the main body. Cut off and vowing to die to the last man (a favorite Chinese boast when aware of a way out), this unit was allowed by British authorities to enter the safety of the Settlement. All Chinese positions north of Soochow Creek in the immediate vicinity of Shanghai had now been abandoned.

On November 5 General Yanagawa's Japanese 10th Corps of three divisions[2] made an unopposed landing with 30,000 troops near Chinshanwei on the north shore of Hangchow Bay about 30 miles south of Shanghai. The Chinese had made no preparations to meet this contingency. Including the newly landed 10th Corps troops, the Japanese had about 225,000 men on the Shanghai front. Moving swiftly, the 10th Corps attacked and brushed aside the Chinese 109th Division of the Right Wing Operational Corps and pressed on toward Sungchiang, less than 20 miles from Shanghai. Simultaneously, the Japanese who had crossed Soochow Creek launched a vigorous attack against the Center Wing Corps. Three Chinese divisions and one separate brigade were ordered to attack the landing force approaching Sungchiang. One of them, the 11th Reserve Division, moving south along the Soochow-Hangchow rail line, never even approached the scene of battle. After suffering minor casualties, the other two divisions pulled back. Units of the Chinese 67th Corps, arriving piecemeal, were picked off one by one and quickly rendered useless. The Chinese right flank and rear were now dangerously threatened, and the route to Shanghai along the Shanghai-Hangchow rail line lay virtually wide open.

Meanwhile, the Japanese attacked all along the main lines. Exhausted, half-starved Chinese units, their ranks badly depleted by superior fire from artillery, naval guns, and dive-bombers, began to fall back before the unceasing enemy assaults. The tragedy of retreat had now begun; and once begun, after a three-month defense, there was no stopping it.

On November 5, Chiang formulated the Third Phase Operational Guidance and Objectives. Full of pomposities and orders that crisscrossed both retreating units and command functions, the plan died a well-deserved death within three days. The only practical operational objective suited to the desperate situation would have been an order for a general withdrawal to be carried out as quickly as possible. And indeed, on November 8 Chiang issued the order to move, which in this case meant retreat. On the next morning the Central Wing armies began to fall back to a line extending from Paiho to Chingpu, both over 20 miles west of Shanghai. But at this time, Nanhsiang, only 10 miles west of Shanghai, was still held by 100,000 Chinese troops. The withdrawal of the troops, now near panic, was a nightmare; in haste to save their own skins, commanders deserted their units. Japanese planes constantly harassed the exhausted Chinese with bombing and strafing attacks. The wounded and sick were abandoned where they fell, some crying for help, others crawling or dragging their broken bodies through the rice fields toward the west, anything to escape the rampaging Japanese. But there was no escape from enemy bullets and swords; the victors caught up with them. In the wild disorder and confusion, Chinese units became entangled with other outfits; unable to distinguish friend from foe at night, they opened fire on each other. Weapons and equipment were cast aside, artillery abandoned.

On the same night, after violent street fighting, the Japanese 10th Corps stormed through Sungchiang. They immediately pressed forward to attack the south pivot of the new line before the Chinese had a chance to dig in. On the eleventh, the south end of the line was abandoned by its defenders; now seriously threatened with an envelopment, the defeated Chinese troops of the Central Wing Operational Corps began a mad scramble to escape.

On November 12 the Japanese 16th Division made an assault landing near Fupukow on the Yangtze, knocked aside the Chinese forces in the area, who had put up little resistance, and fanned out to the west and south. In the face of this Japanese move, the main force of the Chinese Left (north) Wing Operational Corps hastily fell back from its positions near the river. At the same time, the Right (south) Wing Operational Corps, after strong Japanese assaults, pulled back to the line of the Soochow-Hangchow rail line, 30 miles west of Sungchiang. Now threatened on both flanks, the remnants of the retreating forces of the Central Wing Corps broke and fled under constant air attacks. By November 14 the three Chinese wings were struggling to establish a new north–south line along the Soochow-Hangchow rail line and north to Fushan on the Yangtze River.

Staggered by a frightful toll of casualties, Chinese forces had by now retreated over 50 miles west of Shanghai. The defense of Nanking, the capital, would be in the hands of a demoralized, disorderly mob—the largely unarmed, poorly led remnants of what had once included the best-trained, best-equipped troops in the entire Chinese army. The unexpected resistance with which they had fought and died in the useless defense of Shanghai had provoked the Japanese to fury. They now combined a determination to avenge their losses with an irrational urge to destroy.

Chiang Kai-shek had sacrificed nearly 240,000 Chinese troops in a ploy calculated to gain world support. He had gambled on the possibility that a serious incident involving foreigners in Shanghai would lead to intervention by the United States and Great Britain. His only battle plan had been to exhort his armies to die before giving ground. With Shanghai's large foreign population and full press coverage, he had given the world a grandstand seat to observe the most bitterly contested struggle protected civilians had ever seen. Chiang had aroused world sympathy for the courageous Chinese will to fight; but the terrible cost in casualties had broken that will, and Chiang's troops had lost confidence in his leadership. His stubborn belief in his own infallibility as a manipulator of international affairs had prolonged a hopeless defense that should never have been undertaken.

During the Battle of Shanghai, Japanese armies in the north had not been idle. Frustrated in their original plan by the struggle on the Yangtze, in September they launched three southward drives from the Tientsin-Peking-Kalgan area, each following railway lines leading to the Yellow River.

On August 25 the Japanese navy established a partial blockade of Chinese shipping. On September 5 this action was extended to include all ports except Tsingtao, British Hongkong, Portuguese Macao, and French Kwangchowan. The blockade was more irritating than effective, since European and American ships continued to ply their usual routes and call at their usually scheduled ports from Tientsin to Canton. However, Japanese authorities insisted on their right of search and their right to enforce their own quarantine regulations on all shipping.

On August 29, a nonaggression treaty of friendship was signed by the Chinese and Soviet governments. Long obsessed by possible threats to the Maritime Province and eastern Siberia, Stalin looked upon the increased Japanese military presence along his southern borders as a considerable danger. As a safeguard, the Soviet Far Eastern Army under General V. K. Bluecher was greatly strengthened. The treaty opened the door for the sale of military equipment, trucks, aircraft, and aviation fuel to China and brought into existence the long supply route from Siberia through Sinkiang, Kansu, and Lanchow to Sian. By rotating Soviet air units, Stalin was later able to provide training in actual combat for his air force.

On October 6, 1937, the assembly of the League of Nations adopted a resolution that was barely more than a slap on the wrist to Japan: "[The assembly] expresses its moral support for China, and recommends that members of the League refrain from taking any action which might have the effect of weakening China's power of resistance and thus of increasing her difficulties in the present conflict, and should consider how far they can individually extend aid to China."

By the middle of November, I was still waiting in Tsinan for the expected Japanese push across the Yellow River. To impede the enemy's progress, three spans of the huge steel railway bridge across the river had been dynamited and dropped at varying angles into the water. Unfortunately, when Chinese army engineers had detonated the explosives, the bridge had not been cleared of hordes of refugees. Troops had tried to hold them back on the north bank, but there was no stopping the terrified mob; so the bridge had been blown up, and many hundreds of men, women, and children tumbled to their deaths in the water below.

During the previous two months, I had been able to send a continuous flow of political as well as military reports to Stilwell in Peking. When informed that Captain Maxwell D. Taylor (later chief of staff of the U.S. Army and ambassador to South Viet Nam) had been ordered from Tokyo to Peking, I had radioed him an invitation to move into my well-staffed house and to use my car, which he accepted. His fluent Japanese had been badly needed by the military attaché's office in order to communicate —reluctantly on Stilwell's part—with the Japanese military command.

Early in October, a month after the Japanese had initiated a leisurely drive south along the route of the Tientsin-Pukow rail line, the consul, John Allison, had been ordered to depart Tsinan and report to the embassy in Nanking as third secretary. The ambassador's instructions had stated that Allison's safety could be endangered as the Japanese advance continued. In the same message I had been directed to take over certain consular functions—but not the seal—in addition to my other duties and to assist Americans attempting to evacuate to the coast. A rather quiet, blond man, Allison had not seemed happy with the prospect of Nanking and departed with regret.

Warning missionaries to get out of the war zone and collecting non-battle information proved to be neither arduous nor exciting. One morning the same cast-iron missionary woman who had assured me in Kalgan that she would never desert her particular garden of the Lord nor the souls she had saved turned up at the consulate. I had barely started to greet her when her grim mouth opened to snap: "Well, young man, you were right. I was wrong." Then it closed like a steel trap as she busied herself with consular clerks preparatory to boarding the train for Tsingtao. She had traveled the same route I had, though under far more difficult conditions, and was now ready to leave her garden for America. The most interesting character in Tsinan was the governor, Han Fu-chu. He was a tall, austere man who, though in command of his own army of 80,000 men and a militia of 20,000, usually wore the long black gown of a Chinese gentleman. Born of a peasant family in Pahsien, Hopei, he had had little aptitude for schooling. Nonetheless, while quite young, he had worked as a clerk in his *hsien* ("county") *yamen* until gambling debts forced him to run away, whereupon he enlisted in the army of General Feng Yu-hsiang, the Christian general. Han rose quickly, from clerk to chief clerk, then to lieutenant, to captain, and after an uprising, to major. During the warlord upheavals of the 1920s he emerged as commander of General Feng's 1st Army Group. In 1928 he was appointed chairman (governor) of Honan province by Feng, and in 1929 he was confirmed in office and concurrently named commanding general of the 11th Division. When the Christian general revolted later in the year, Han declared his allegiance to the central government of Chiang Kai-shek. In a second revolt in 1930, Han fought against the rebel troops of Yen Hsi-shan and his former commander Feng Yu-hsiang in Shantung and was rewarded with appointment as governor of that province.

As governor, Han was a stern disciplinarian with both civil servants and the military; he made his own laws to fit situations as they arose and meted out harsh, sometimes eccentric, punishments. He had virtually wiped out banditry and traffic in narcotics in unrelenting campaigns of suppression. In doing so he had ordered or approved over 500 executions a year since taking office. Through commercial operations, principally in cotton, tobacco, and real estate, he had grown enormously rich; but unlike most warlords, he gave generously to schools, hospitals, and civic improvements—even to Christian missions and the Presbyterian university in Tsinan. Imitating the ancient custom whereby the emperors of China had set up drums of remonstrance at their palace gates, Han Fu-chu established grievance-airing bells before his *yamen*. Thus, in theory, his people could appeal directly for justice by beating on the bronze bells. It is doubtful, however, if many of their complaints got results from the bureaucracy of Han's provincial government, which, with its master, was responsible for most of their grievances in the first place.

Old-fashioned in his personal life, Han had one wife, two concubines, and four sons. A fanatic on the subjects of cleanliness and womanly modesty, he took daily strolls of inspection in the streets of his sprawling capital, always accompanied by guards. If he spied a young woman so immodest as to wear short sleeves, he would descend on her like an avenging angel, slap her face several times, and leave the poor creature trembling and in tears. If his eagle eye spotted a carter leading a horse and wagon, he would follow along with eager anticipation, waiting for the animal to drop a pile of dung. When that happened, he would wait a moment, his gleaming eyes alert; all carters, herders, and cameleers had long been required to carry shovels and sacks while in the city to clean up the droppings of their animals. If no shovel appeared, the old warlord would accost the unfortunate peasant, order his guards to beat the man with their rifle butts, then force him to remove the droppings by hand.

Taking a walk one morning, I ran into the old man in a furious altercation with a protesting carter over a pile of camel dung. The farmer was trying to explain that his two horses could not be guilty, that horse and camel droppings were entirely different; but that did not deter the outraged governor. His streets had been soiled; so, innocent or not, the first drover who had happened along was soundly beaten and forced to clean up.

When Han first received me in the study of his *yamen* (a combination official residence, magisterial complex, and courtyards), he was pleasant and courteous, the complete opposite of the curmudgeon in the streets. From our first meeting, he had been willing to give me any information I asked for, provided it was transmitted only to my government, never to the press. In time I grew to like the old scoundrel. He seemed to like me, too, even to the point of taking me to the main hall to show me the enormous silver-plated coffin that some day would be his last resting place.

When Arch Steele, a correspondent for the *Chicago Daily News*, came to Tsinan looking for a story on Shantung politics, he asked if I could arrange an interview with the old man. This was a challenge I could not resist. That afternoon I asked Han if he would talk to Steele. For a second he glared at me, then smiled frostily. "You say he is your friend?" he asked. "You will vouch for him? He will write nothing for the newspapers unless I approve?" I agreed to be responsible for Steele, and he agreed to meet him the next day if I would be present at the interview. At the confrontation Han was all affability. Since Steele was an intelligent man with a winning personality, the meeting did not seem to be much of a strain on the old man. To our surprise, he was frank and talkative. Steele was probably the first and last foreign newsman to talk to Han Fu-chu.

Having heard through the Chinese staff of the consulate that Han was in communication with the Japanese, I decided to ask flat out if the rumors and a story in the *Tsingtao Times* of September 28 were true. Since I could hardly accuse him of being a traitor by asking a direct question about his activities, I handed him a translation of the newspaper article. After he finished reading it, he raised his head, his black eyes boring into mine. I said quickly that no one in China would give any credence to such a story, but that the outside world, having little knowledge of Chinese affairs, would not understand and would not know what to think. I suggested that for their benefit he issue a statement on his position. For a full minute his narrowed eyes continued to fix mine in cold appraisal. Then he smiled and said that a statement was not necessary. I urged him to think it over, recounting a story of intense interest the article had stirred up in Europe and America. Actually, I doubted if anyone outside of China had ever heard of it or would have been interested. But I was after a statement to clarify his attitude and to indicate probable future actions.

I was about to depart, not sure just where I stood in the old man's eyes, when he called for tea and asked me to remain for a while. He had something he wished to say—as it turned out, something that staggered me. Without preliminary remarks he said that only the day before he had received a long message from the commanding general of the Japanese 2nd Corps. The letter had been dropped in a bamboo tube from a Japanese plane onto a drill field at the edge of town near the barracks of his most trusted troops—doubtless I had heard the alarms and had noticed that no bombs were ever dropped. The sounding of the alert had been to drive people indoors or to the shelters so no one would see the expected Japanese planes circling the drop area and delivering their communication. He had received a number of such messages. Drawing aside a curtain that concealed a recessed cabinet, he showed me perhaps eight bamboo tubes propped against the inner wall, all containing messages from the Japanese. He said that his replies had been transmitted by reliable officers carrying white flags as they approached forewarned enemy outposts. Also, he had representatives in Tientsin. When I asked what all this correspondence was about, he drew the most recent communication from its bamboo tube and read it aloud while his secretary translated for me.

Then Han explained his rather unusual actions. In all probability the Japanese would be content with setting up a controlled autonomous regime in the five provinces north of the Yellow River. Han's army and militia of about 100,000 men dominated Shantung, the northern border of which ran a few miles south of the river, while the southern border ran approximately along the east–west line of the Lunghai Railway. He had refused to allow Chiang's armies to enter his province from the south, and would continue to block their entrance. He intended to preserve his army intact and to save Shantung from the ravages of warring troops. He paused, and then gave his appraisal of the future. The Japanese could keep the north. They had it anyway. Chiang Kai-shek could have everything south of the Lunghai Railway. He, Han Fu-chu, would be the chief of a buffer state between them and thus continue as master of Shantung. This was the plan that had been the subject of his negotiations with the Japanese. When he finished, I wondered if the Japanese had not been playing a cat-and-mouse game with him, and just how long he would be able to resist increasing pressure from them and from Chiang.

A few days later, Han sent a letter to Doctor Stanley, the American president of Cheeloo University in Tsinan, stating his undying loyalty to the central government and asking that the letter be made available to the foreign press. He also let it be known to Stanley and his own staff that this action was due to the advice of an American captain.

After the fall of Shanghai, just before the middle of November, I received orders to join Captain Roberts in Nanking, where we would act as a team to report on the Japanese drive to take the capital. For two days I pushed and fought to board a southbound train at the Tsinan station. It was hopeless. Every car was jammed with yelling, struggling people and their incredible belongings. Two deep, men clung precariously to the sides of coaches and freight cars, some roped to window frames, others depending only on the grip of their clawing fingers to hang on. Hundreds scrambled to the roofs of cars, clutching at ventilators for support, with countless others clinging to them on their perilous perches. But the two daily eastbound trains to Tsingtao were half empty. So I went to the port city, where I was lucky enough to find a Jardine and Mathewson ship in the harbor, and the next day I was on my way to Shanghai. From there I planned to make my way as best I could, either by land through Japanese lines or by some form of river craft up the Yangtze, to Nanking. I realized, of course, that crossing from one side to the other held an element of danger, but I had done it before and figured I could probably do it again.

The next morning, as the ship glided slowly up the Whangpoo past the eastern extension of the Settlement, a heavy layer of dark smoke hung over Chapei and the Greater Municipality. Occasionally bursts of flame splashed a reddish glare on the thick haze of billowing ashes. The next day I learned that the Japanese were systematically removing all iron, copper, and brass from buildings and homes in the city to be sent as scrap metal to Japan. Even nails were collected, with houses either left to collapse in heaps of debris or, if their wreckage blocked a street, set afire. Roofs of warehouses near the riverfront that had been struck by naval gunfire gaped open, their blackened rafters etched against the gray sky. British, French, Italian, and American warships and merchant vessels from ports around the world tugged at their anchors in midstream. Scores of Japanese naval ships of all sizes, their guns leveled at the city, crowded the roadstead already teeming with Chinese sailing junks, sampans, and river craft.

Leaning on the railing, I watched as we passed the Astor House with its great glass dome; the British consulate at the mouth of evil-smelling Soochow Creek set typically in the midst of wide, tree-shaded lawns; the high tower of the Cathay Hotel topped by a three-story pyramidal roof; the lower silhouette of the Custom House. Finally the ship was nudged by tugs to its home berth on the Bund just past the river end of busy Bubbling Well Road. After disembarking, I went straight to the Metropole Hotel, registered, left my one bag in my tower room, and reported to the American consular offices across the street.

Again I was handed a waiting radio message from Stilwell. This time I was instructed to contact the Japanese command in Shanghai and report on their plans and activities for the drive on Nanking. That afternoon a consular officer and a newsman friend introduced me to the chief of Japanese public affairs at his informal daily press conference in the spacious bar-lounge of the Carlton Hotel: an army officer in civilian clothes wearing round tortoise-shell glasses, Captain Asami had been educated in America and spoke perfect English. He had obviously been told to be pleasant and friendly to foreign newsmen and attachés; he ordered a round of drinks and then read the daily communiqué of official pap. With the second round of drinks, I asked if I might visit the front, then a north–south line just east of Soochow. Smiling broadly with a glittering display of piano-key teeth, he informed me that it would be impossible. Too dangerous.

The next afternoon Captain Asami brought along a general, also all smiles, ingratiating bows, and hisses. Since I was supposed to extract all of the military information I could from Japanese authorities, I proceeded to act as friendly as possible. I called a waiter to order drinks and was promptly informed that this was not permitted at Japanese army news conferences. All drinks for American and European friends were at the expense of His Imperial Majesty, who was happy to provide them. The thought of drinking all we wanted "on the emperor" had a certain appeal to the press, and to me. The news conferences soon degenerated into daily cocktail parties characterized by a steady flow of liquor, but little information, other than accounts of the steady and heroic advance of the Japanese army.

On one convivial occasion I asked the general, who like most Japanese had little capacity for whisky or gin, if I might accompany the Japanese commander when he made his entry into Nanking.

"Yes-s-s-s-s," he replied. "That might be possible."

"Riding a white horse?" I asked, knowing full well that only the emperor and imperial princes rode white horses at military formations. He pursed his lips and let out a long hissing sigh.

"So sorry, captain. Afraid that is not possible," he said sadly. Then he brightened and added with a broad smile: "But perhaps a brown horse? Yes? A brown horse."

But white, brown, or any other color, the opportunity to ride into Nanking with the conquerors never materialized. After about a week of drinking "on the emperor," I was ordered to Tsingtao to observe and report on the expected attack and occupation of that city by the Japanese navy.

As the Chinese armies withdrew toward a north–south defense line extending from Fushan on the Yangtze through the ancient city of Soochow to Hangchow, Japanese aircraft bombed and strafed the retreating columns almost without letup. On November 15 the Japanese 16th Division attacked the north end of the line; on the nineteenth the Chinese defense began to give way. On the same day, a Japanese column crossed a small lake, landed on the opposite shore behind the Chinese positions, and pushed rapidly south to Soochow. Meanwhile, Japanese forces that had been driving west on the Shanghai-Nanking rail line against sporadic opposition reached the eastern outskirts of the city. During the night of November 19 the outmaneuvered Chinese abandoned Soochow without a fight, "in order to avoid a decisive battle"—exactly what the Japanese were straining to bring about. On the night of the twentieth the Chinese 15th and 21st army groups began a disorderly retreat of 25 to 30 miles to another indefensible defense line. It ran from Chiangyin on the Yangtze to Wuhsi just north of Tai Lake, and along the west shore of the lake, where the 50th Corps began to dig in. For nearly a week these troops stared pointlessly out from their prepared positions across an empty 40-mile expanse of water. They could have been used to advantage either north or south of the lake.

On November 20 the capital was moved to Chungking, over 1,100 miles upriver from Nanking. However, the executive power (Chiang Kai-shek) and military headquarters—now so intertwined as to be almost indistinguishable—were established at Hankow, about 400 miles up the Yangtze from the capital.

Hundreds of thousands of civilian refugees clogged the inadequate roads leading to the west, seriously hampering the retreat of Chinese troops. Ill-fed and increasingly worn down by unremitting Japanese pressure, under artillery fire and bombing from the air, most Chinese military units were too weak to make a determined stand. At this stage, some had nothing more than their bare hands to make a stand with. Reaching Wuhsi on November 25, the Japanese briskly marched through the town and continued along the railway line to Wuchin. The north pivot of the Chinese defense line was abandoned. On the twenty-seventh, a Japanese column from Soochow crossed Tai Lake, swept through the useless shoreline positions of the Chinese 50th Corps, and turned north, effecting a junction with their main force at Wuchin. In the face of impending assaults from the east and south, the Chinese broke out of Wuchin on November 29 and fled toward Tanyang. Their flight was so precipitate that the Japanese were hard put to maintain contact, except with the abandoned dead and dying. On December 3, they took Tanyang, less than 45 miles from Nanking.

With the fall of Wuchin, the main force of the Chinese 50th Corps was inexplicably ordered to withdraw toward the southwest, a move that if completed would have cut diagonally across the retreating units and increased the confusion in a rapidly worsening situation. When in their own good time the Japanese turned their attention to Chiangyin on the Yangtze (December 1), its defending 103rd and 112th divisions broke in a rout that did not slow until they reached Chenchiang, 50 miles to the west.

To the south the Japanese 10th Corps, which had landed at Hangchow Bay, met only slight resistance from the Chinese 10th Army Group as it moved west from Sungchiang. The towns of Fengching (November 10), Chiashan (November 14), Chiahsing (November 19), and Nanhsun (November 20) fell like ripe plums into Japanese hands on their 50-mile push to the south end of Tai Lake.

In a vain effort to stem the Japanese juggernaut, the Chinese 7th Corps was ordered to take up defensive positions from Tachienchen, east of Wuhsing, to Shenghsienshih, 18 miles west of Nanhsun—a mission impossible to carry out with troops out of control in the face of the furious pace of the Japanese. In an equally futile gesture, the Chinese 23rd Army Group of five poorly trained, poorly equipped, under-strength Szechwan divisions, then concentrated about 30 miles west of Wuhsing in the Kwangteh-Szean-Anchi area, were directed "to respond to the operations of the 7th Corps." (The use of "respond" in military orders is vague at best; in this case it was apparently interpreted as an order to stand in place and do nothing.)

On November 24 the Japanese charged through the incomplete positions at Shenghsienshih, meeting little resistance from the demoralized Chinese forces. Two days later the same thing happened at Wuhsing. On the twenty-seventh the enemy pursuit drove the fleeing Chinese through Changhsing, about 12 miles to the northwest. At Changhsing the Japanese 10th Corps divided. The main force turned north to Yihsing, which they took with no resistance whatever on December 2, then west to Liyang, which they captured on December 4, then northwest to Lishui, only 30 miles from Nanking. Three divisions of the Chinese 23rd Army Group started a move to counterattack the Japanese at Changhsing, but they were struck hard by a column from the Japanese 10th Corps before they even reached their jumping-off positions. The forward Chinese division was chopped to pieces unit by unit; the other two scattered like chaff before the whirlwind of the enemy advance. The Japanese swept through Szean on November 27 and Kwangteh on November 30. From Kwangteh they sent one column to Langchi, which it took with ease on December 4, before turning north toward Lishui. A second column continued driving west against the depleted Chinese 15th Army Group, reaching Hsuancheng on December 6, Wuhu on the Yangtze on December 10, and Tangtu on December 11. Since leaving the main body of the 10th Corps, this column had covered over 110 miles in 14 days of constant deployments and engagements, none of which, however, had amounted to more than large-scale skirmishes. From Tangtu the column crossed the Yangtze and headed for Pukow, directly opposite Nanking, which it seized on December 13.

Still convinced that foreign sympathy could be converted to intervention, Chiang Kai-shek ordered that Nanking be defended "to the last man." Though most of the ambassadors and their senior officials had sailed upriver when the Chinese government departed, junior staff members of the embassies were ordered to remain at their posts. In addition, the commercial, missionary, and educational elements constituted a sizable foreign group in the city. Chiang's hope that foreign residents of Shanghai would become involved had not materialized. Now, in grim, irrational desperation, he transferred that hope to Nanking.

In a hopeless, last-stand effort to save the capital, two defense lines were prepared in feverish haste, each arched around the city and extending to the river banks. The first was located 8 to 12 miles outside the ancient walls; the inner line was from 1 to 3 miles outside the walls—each too close to be of any real defensive value. The outer line was manned by the 88th and 36th divisions and the Training Division, plus units of military police. These positions were quickly reinforced by the 74th Corps of two divisions[3] and the 83rd Corps of two divisions.[4] Seven divisions,[5] all top-heavy with staff, were rushed to man the inner defense line barely outside the walls of the city.

In a forlorn gesture, the National Military Council at Hankow, 400 miles from the scene of battle, asserted its prerogative to meddle in the dispositions and actions of units over which it had no control and with which it could not communicate. General Liu Hsiang was directed "to leave powerful forces behind" in the Anchi area, 100 miles south of Nanking, "to attack the enemy's flanks at the opportune time." He was also directed "to leave [another] powerful force in the mountainous area . . . north of Kwangteh [70 miles south of Nanking], to delay the enemy and destroy the lines of communication in response to the operations at Nanking." These were pitifully absurd chessboard plans, for Liu Hsiang's five divisions had already been put to flight and scattered by the Japanese 10th Corps. They had suffered severe casualties, had lost a large part of their weapons and equipment, and at the time the order was issued were about as powerful as a band of fleeing peasant farmers. The order was probably never received. If it was, it was ignored, which was just as well. General Liu Hsiang's commanders were struggling to extricate and reassemble the remnants of their troops from the isolated pockets in which they had been trapped. In its usual unrealistic flow of words, the official Chinese history of the conflict dismissed the absurdity inherent in the order with the remark: "The fact that all units were on the move precluded the implementation of the plans." All units were indeed on the move, as fast they could run from the Japanese.

By December 6, four columns of the Shanghai Expeditionary Force and the Japanese 10th Corps converged from the east and south on the outer defenses of Nanking. Preceded by heavy bombing attacks and supported by intense artillery fire, Japanese infantry units stormed up to the Chinese lines the same day. At dawn on the seventh, they attacked all along the defensive positions. On the eighth they took the pivotal Chinese strongpoints. Now crowded into an ever-diminishing area around the city and thus offering more concentrated targets, the Chinese suffered terrible casualties from bombing and artillery barrages. Japanese pressure continued to mount. On December 11 the inner defense line began to crumble, forcing the Chinese defenders back against the city walls and through the gates into the city itself. On the twelfth the Japanese broke through three gates in the badly battered walls. Violent street fighting broke out, the Chinese now battling for their lives rather than to save the foredoomed capital. General Tang Sheng-chih, the garrison commander, ordered his defeated forces to break out, a term that more and more had begun to mean every man for himself. As the generalissimo's orders had been to make a death stand, there were no plans for controlled withdrawal; but the 66th Corps of two divisions,[6] which had managed to hold its units intact, succeeded in breaking out to the south and east, battling its way through Japanese lines and eventually reaching safety 100 miles to the south. Only a few other scattered units were able to escape from the city by crossing the river and moving to the northwest. In the words of the official Chinese history: "The bulk of our forces defending Nanking were sacrificed." They were trapped within the city walls, hunted down by the Japanese and slaughtered.

According to General Iwane Matsui's somewhat archaic socio-political viewpoint, the capture of Nanking on December 13, coupled with the Japanese conquests north of the Yellow River, should have ended the growing loss of Japanese lives and removed the danger of their armies becoming overextended in the interior of China. (On December 23, 1948, General Matsui was sentenced by the International Military Tribunal for the Far East to be hanged; the sentence was carried out in Tokyo.) By now the Japanese armies should have brought the Chinese to their knees begging for almost any kind of peace through negotiation. Instead, the Chinese had taken to their heels—there was no one to negotiate with.

Frustrated by this unanticipated situation contrary to all the rule books, or simply enraged at being unable to achieve the quick victory that had been planned, the triumphant Japanese commanders turned their troops loose to pillage the city in the worst holocaust of brutality since the troops of Count Johan Tilly sacked Magdeburg in the Thirty Years' War of 1618–48. For the better part of two weeks General Hashimoto's officers and soldiers, like bullies infuriated by the cringing of a weaker adversary, raged through Nanking in a drunken orgy of looting, raping, burning, and slaughter. Groups of 50 or more Chinese were forced to dig long trenches, then were lined up along the edges and mowed down by machine guns, their bodies toppling into the graves they had just dug. Other groups were lashed together to be drenched with kerosene and set afire, or were machine-gunned and shoved into the Yangtze to be swept downriver toward Shanghai. Many, while still alive, were used for bayonet practice as Japanese officers gleefully directed this form of training. The Red Cross hospital, crowded with wounded, was the scene of some of the bloodiest carnage. Bandages were ripped off screaming men, who were then hacked and bayoneted to death. Broken arms and legs were rebroken with clubs. Between sessions of slashing and beating, nurses who had been unable to escape were repeatedly raped. The shops and homes of not only wealthy Chinese but the poorest coolies were looted and burned. Thousands of women and hundreds of young men and boys were raped, often by dozens of Japanese soldiers while their companions, waiting their turns, passed the time by stabbing the terrified children of their victims with swords and bayonets. All the new government buildings were put to the torch by cheering, drunken troops. By the end of December, according to Japanese reports, more than one-third of the city had been completely destroyed by fire and demolitions. Most of the rest had been badly damaged. Over 20,000 civilian men of military age had been slaughtered. At least 20,000 young women and girls had been raped, murdered, and then gruesomely mutilated. Over 200,000 civilians, and possibly as many as 300,000, had been senselessly massacred.

It is difficult to even begin to understand the insatiable savagery and insane glee that drove the victors on to outdo each other in acts of brutality. All their lives the Japanese had been restricted and guided by restraint in manners, customs, and personal relationships. But once a young man donned a uniform or picked up a sword, he felt 10 feet tall and cast aside the constrictive restraints that had characterized his youth. Partaking of the aura of the emperor's divinity, as most soldiers believed they did, made them immune in their own eyes to censorship by mere humans for slaughtering those whom they considered a lesser order of humanity.

Brainwashed into a pseudoidealistic belief that his mission was essentially a crusade to liberate the Chinese people from oppression, the average Japanese soldier had been shocked at the rejection of his efforts at liberation. Resentment and frustration over Chinese ingratitude and resistance to Japan's high purpose, and the nagging fear that he was being drawn into an endless, ever more perilous morass, were transformed in his mind into a sullen urge for vengeance and violent action. His moral lapse sought expression in blood, fire, and destruction. In his authoritative and understanding book *The Rising Sun,** John Toland has tried to explain the unexplainable: "Within the Japanese, metaphysical intuition and animalistic, instinctive urges lay side by side. Thus philosophy was brutalized and brutality philosophized. Assassination and other bloody acts . . . were inspired by idealism. The soldiers who sailed to China to save the Orient for the Orient ended by slaughtering [hundreds of] thousands of Orientals in

* John Toland, *The Rising Sun: The Rise and Fall of the Japanese Empire, 1936–1945.* (New York, Bantam Books, 1971), pages 65–66.

Nanking. There was no buffer zone in their thinking . . . between the chrysanthemum [ideals] and the sword [blood]."[5]

The entries in a diary found on the body of a young Japanese soldier after the battle of Taierhchuang in May, 1938, underscored the theme of the chrysanthemum and the sword in his mind; it was a theme common to the minds of thousands of others. In one entry he had written in the most minute detail of the gratification and glee he and three of his companions had experienced after gang-raping and brutalizing a 13-year-old Chinese girl they had found in the ruins of a village house. Satiated at last, they had thrown her battered, naked body into a dry drainage ditch and had marched off singing. The next day's entry described picturesquely a branch of pink-white peach blossoms gently swaying in a soft breeze against a bright blue sky as he lay enthralled on a patch of sweet-smelling grass. The simple picture in the midst of war had reminded him of his own village home in the fruit-growing valley of Yonezawa, of the love and respect he had always felt for his parents, of his tender affection for his younger brother and sisters. That was the last entry in the diary. The next day his company had been annihilated and his troubled spirit had been released from the violence of the sword to seek its own chrysanthemums in another world.

Japanese soldiers took countless photographs of their deeds in Nanking and sent them back to relatives and friends in their homeland. Developed and printed in Chinese photography shops —the only ones available—many of the prints fell into Chinese and foreign hands and substantiated the outrages perpetrated on a trapped and helpless population.

John Allison, then third secretary of the American embassy, was slapped in the face by a drunken Japanese soldier while investigating reports of interference with American property and trying to intercede on behalf of Chinese employees. This incident, trivial in the welter of horror, was glossed over by a prompt apology and assurances that the offending soldier would be punished—though in all probability he was not.

In keeping with his position as commander of the Shanghai Expeditionary Force, General Matsui kept personally aloof from the plunder of Nanking; however, as his share of the spoils of war, he accepted an art collection belonging to a wealthy Chinese banker in Shanghai. Valued at over $4 million, the collection was shipped to Matsui's home in Japan.

As an anticlimactic footnote to the thunderous Yangtze River campaign, the Japanese marched unopposed into the beautiful old city of Hangchow on December 24.

A few days before the fall of Nanking, the American gunboat *Panay* pulled away from its berth opposite the city and moved about 28 miles upriver to Hohsien. With Japanese columns closing in on the capital, the ship's captain, Lieutenant Commander James J. Hughes, decided that the constant bombing and artillery fire were endangering the safety of his vessel. Since it was obvious at the time that the city was about to be taken, Captain Frank Roberts, two secretaries from the American embassy, two from the Italian embassy, and several civilians boarded the small ship before its departure from Nanking. On December 12, while acting as escort for three vessels belonging to the Standard Oil Company—all clearly marked with large American flags—the *Panay* was attacked by Japanese bombers. One bomb struck the bridge, wounding Hughes so severely that he was completely incapacitated; other bombs killed two seamen and one steward. Forty-eight members of the crew and several of the passengers were wounded. The three Standard Oil vessels were also bombed and sunk. As the *Panay* began to list badly, Captain Roberts, being the senior military officer present, assumed command. He ordered the stricken gunboat to make for shallow water to be beached on the riverbank. As the *Panay* began to sink, Japanese fighter planes strafed the decks. A battery of artillery on shore opened fire, but missed its target. Roberts ordered the crew to abandon ship and to carry off the dead and severely wounded. He then led the party—still under strafing attacks—through a mass of high, dense reeds and across a muddy flat to solid ground. After a march of several miles, Chinese farmers led the crippled party to safety.

Within a week, United States naval intelligence decoded an intercepted radio message clearly indicating that the attack on the *Panay* had been deliberately planned by staff officers on board the Japanese carrier *Kaga*. The sharp reaction of the American government to the sinking of the *Panay* could have provided

Chiang Kai-shek with his hoped-for intervention. But the Japanese government, with its hands already full and recognizing its navy's error, immediately expressed regret. The apology was accompanied by a lame statement that the Panay was mistaken for a Chinese vessel by the carrier-borne fighters and bombers of the 2nd Combined Air Group. Those responsible for the incident were relieved of duty, and indemnities for loss of life and property were paid. The American claim of $2,214,007.36, of which $1,287,942.00 represented property losses of Standard Oil, was not questioned by the Japanese. It was probably the fastest paid international claim on record.

On the same day the four British gunboats Ladybird, Bee, Scarab, and Cricket, no doubt also mistaken for Chinese river craft, were attacked and damaged by Japanese shore batteries and air force planes. The Japanese government apologized and promised to make amends without even waiting for a British protest. It was apparent that local commanders, overexuberant and heady with success, were responsible for the attacks on both the American and British vessels; neither the Japanese government nor General Matsui were ready to take on additional difficulties, particularly against two nations whose combined navies were over three times the size of their own.

In February, 1938, as an aftermath of the Panay incident, the American 15th Infantry, having long enjoyed the good life at Tientsin, was ordered to depart its cushy post for reassignment in the United States. After 35 years, the tasks of packing up and of breaking off relations with their Chinese and White Russian women were enormous; but eventually the sad-eyed men of the regiment marched through the streets of the city, flags flying and bands playing, and boarded the trains that would take them to Chinwangtao and a transport waiting to return them to the rigors of a discipline and training they had not known for years.

Months before the fall of Nanking, one of the greatest migrations in history had begun. Millions of Chinese in the north had left their homes and farms to march south of the Yellow River. Even more millions had left the lower Yangtze Valley on a long trek to the west. Terrified by the Japanese armies, their only aim was to escape the scenes of a war they could not understand.

The wealthy moved by car until gasoline ran out, then by train, steamer, river junk, and finally on foot. The poor, carrying as many of their belongings as they could, plodded along in carts until their animals died of exhaustion, the aged carried in wheelbarrows until those rickety vehicles fell apart, the very young on their parents' backs until they collapsed by the roadside.

Not the least astonishing aspect of this gigantic move to the west was the dismantling, transportation, and rebuilding, in areas remote from the Japanese advance, of entire ordnance factories, first in the vicinity of Hankow and finally near Chungking. This staggering undertaking was directed by General Yu Ta-wei (later minister of defense on Taiwan), a stocky, soft-spoken, highly intelligent man who had earned a master's degree at the university of Berlin and a doctorate at Harvard. Several years before the outbreak of hostilities, he had been sent to Germany on an arms-buying mission and had astounded Chiang Kai-shek by his unexpected honesty: instead of pocketing the standard buyer's commission—in this case said to have been over $10 million—Yu had turned it back to the treasury as uncommitted funds. This action was so unusual that Chiang had immediately promoted him from colonel to major general and had appointed him chief of ordnance. Now Yu Ta-wei's mission was to ensure that ordnance factories, safe from Japanese destruction, would continue to turn out rifles, machine guns, mortars, ammunition, and even some light artillery pieces. To accomplish this herculean task, hundreds of thousands of men struggled for as much as 1,000 miles with heavy loads on their backs or swung from carrying poles. Loaded to capacity, sailing junks plowed upriver to Ichang. From there they were hauled through the Yangtze rapids by many thousands of coolies straining on heavy straw ropes sometimes hundreds of yards in length. Stacked high with precious factory parts, horse-drawn carts and wagons moved along the roads until the animals neared exhaustion, then rested and pushed on. Under such difficulties, perhaps no people but the Chinese could have accomplished the monumental task of moving the enormous tonnage involved, and even they would probably have failed without the driving spirit of General Yu Ta-wei. (In 1949 a similar effort was undertaken to transport by air and ship the priceless, centuries-old collections of paintings, jade, ivory, porcelain, and bronze from the imperial palaces in Peking to Formosa, where they are now on display in the National Museum.)

Having presided over the deaths of between 600,000 and 800,000 of his troops and people because of his stubborn ineptitude at world politics, Chiang Kai-shek attempted on December 17 to tidy up his colossal military blunder at Shanghai and Nanking with another of his messages. It was directed to "the People upon our withdrawal from Nanking." At that time the "withdrawal" also included the loss of Suiyuan and Chahar provinces, about half of Shansi and Hopei, and the northwest part of Shantung. "Far sighted and determined"—no doubt with eyes fixed on the image of his Confucian–Methodist god—he publicly renewed his vow to the tens of millions of Chinese now under the Japanese yoke "to fight to the last." No mention was made of those who had already fought to their last. He still hoped that somehow the United States and Britain would pull his blackened chestnuts out of the fire. But those two powers, engrossed with the dangerous situation Hitler had created in Europe, were in no position to prevent the Japanese from pursuing their aims in China.

After the Shanghai-Nanking campaign, the Chinese central government "realigned the command agencies" throughout the army. Chiang Kai-shek reappointed himself supreme commander (generalissimo) of the armed forces and chairman of the National Military Council, with General Ho Ying-chin as chief of the general staff. Six war areas and four additional major commands were designated.

The 1st War Area was commanded by General Cheng Chien, who was assigned the corridor of the Peking-Hankow rail line north of the Yangtze River as his operational area, with 25 divisions, 3 separate brigades, and 2 cavalry divisions.

The 2nd War Area was commanded by General Yen Hsi-shan, the model governor of dubious loyalty, who was assigned Shansi province as his operational area, with his own army of 27 divisions, 3 separate brigades, and 3 cavalry divisions.

The 3rd War Area was commanded by General Ku Chu-tung, who was assigned what remained of Chekiang and Kiangsu provinces as his operational area, with 24 divisions and 6 separate brigades.

The 4th War Area was commanded by General Ho Ying-chin, who was assigned Kwangtung and Kwangsi provinces as his operational area, with nine divisions, two separate brigades, and other miscellaneous provincial troops.

The 5th War Area was commanded by General Li Tsung-jen, who was assigned the corridor of the Tientsin-Nanking rail line as his operational area, with 27 divisions and 3 separate brigades. Theoretically, General Li's command included Shantung as well as Anhwei province, but Governor Han Fu-chu still barred the entrance of troops of the central government into what he considered his private domain of Shantung.

The 8th War Area was commanded by Generalissimo Chiang Kai-shek, who was assigned the northwest provinces of Kansu, Ninghsia, and Tsinghai, all west of Japanese-occupied Suiyuan and Communist-controlled north Shensi, with five divisions, four separate infantry brigades, five cavalry divisions, and four separate cavalry brigades. None of these troops were well trained or well equipped, nor were they considered dependable.

The Wuhan (Hankow) Garrison Headquarters was commanded by General Ch'en Ch'eng, who was given Hupei and Hunan provinces, with 14 divisions, 1 separate brigade, and miscellaneous river defense units. The Sian Headquarters was commanded by Generalissimo Chiang Kai-shek, with a director at Sian; he was to cover the southern half of Shensi province with 12 divisions, 4 separate brigades, and 3 cavalry divisions. The Fukien Pacification Headquarters was directed by General Chen Yi, who had the province of Fukien as his operational area, with two divisions and four separate infantry brigades. The National Military Council was chaired by Generalissimo Chiang Kai-shek, who retained a general reserve of four army groups consisting of 17 divisions, each commanded by a general considered to be reliable.

In addition, 26 divisions that had been badly mauled in the Shanghai-Nanking campaign were sent to rear areas for reorganization, training, and reequipment, which they badly needed. Fourteen divisions and seven separate infantry brigades of provincial troops of various warlords remained in their respective areas where they could do the least harm.

The newly designated 8th Route Army and 4th Corps (both Communist) were not included in the realignment. The operational area of the 8th Route Army was in north Shensi and north Shansi; it had three divisions. The 4th Corps in the lower Yangtze River area had the equivalent of about one division.

In theory, this represented a potentially powerful force of 206 divisions, 37 separate infantry brigades, 13 cavalry divisions, and 4 separate cavalry brigades, totaling over 2 million men, with which to continue the war of resistance against Japan. In substance, it was top-heavy with too many chiefs and too few Indians. In many commands the potential for aggressive action was extremely questionable, the will to fight almost nonexistent. The basic weakness lay in Chiang Kai-shek's design: to disorganize political opposition among senior generals and possible rivals rather than to reorganize the structure of the military forces for efficiency. The entire realignment was underscored by inconsistencies and mistrust.

The inherent defects at every level of command were pinpointed by a number of insurmountable and widespread circumstances:

The great majority of senior commanders were determined to preserve their units as nearly intact as possible, for political bargaining value, rather than risk their destruction in battle by offensive action.

Nearly all commanders, whether committed to battle or not, valued equipment and ammunition far more than the lives of their men. One could always conscript men, but it was usually next to impossible to replace lost equipment or expended ammunition.

The majority of the commanders were incompetent and inadequately trained, and many had been appointed to their positions on a purely political or family basis.

Mutual distrust and the knowledge that adjacent units in battle could not be depended on for support poisoned relationships between many senior commanders. This was best exemplified when units suddenly retreated with little or no concern for the exposure of an adjacent unit's flank. This lack of a sense of mutual responsibility in combat often created panic when a flank was even threatened.

Most of these weaknesses had not appeared at the Battle of Shanghai, where the best units in the Chinese army had fought with tenacity and courage, and as a result suffered staggering casualties. Once those elite units were annihilated, the defense of Nanking by run-of-the-mill divisions exhibited all these weaknesses under the fierce assaults of the Japanese forces. In contrast to most senior officers, the majority of battalion commanders, junior officers, and enlisted men were not afraid to fight and not afraid to die. Their only fear was that they might be left wounded and helpless on the field of battle. What they needed most—even more than food and equipment—was courageous leadership from their higher commanders. This they seldom got.

As the realignment was structured, Chiang Kai-shek not only commanded the entire army from his distant headquarters at Wuchang, across the Yangtze from Hankow, but he also retained personal command of 17 divisions, 8 separate infantry brigades, 8 cavalry divisions, and 4 separate cavalry brigades, whose only function in the war against the Japanese was to contain Mao Tse-tung's Communist 8th Route Army on the west and south. Though all five of his bandit-suppression campaigns had failed, Chiang had no intention of relaxing his watch on the Communist presence in China. In addition, General Yen Hsi-shan blocked the Reds on the east with his army of over 175,000 men. In effect, some 300,000 troops were immobilized in guard duty to satisfy Chiang Kai-shek's obsession. (By 1941 this waste of manpower had been augmented by an additional 100,000 men.)

General Ho Ying-chin, who had been named chief of the general staff—though there was no general or any other kind of staff worth the name—concurrently commanded the 4th War Area, where he could keep an eye on the rebellious southern provinces of Kwangtung and Kwangsi.

General Li Tsung-jen, one of the two leaders of the Kwangtung-Kwangsi clique, was assigned to command the 5th War Area north of the Yangtze River, over 600 miles north of his home base where he might have been tempted to make profit of the unrest and dissatisfaction of his followers.

General Pai Ch'ung-hsi, the principal leader of the southern group, who happened to be Mohammedan, was kept in Hankow as Chiang Kai-shek's deputy commander, assistant chief of staff, and adviser, where he commanded nothing and thus was rendered harmless. In his role of adviser, his advice was seldom heeded—a pity, since he had strongly opposed the gamble for foreign intervention at Shanghai. Pai was a more capable tactician than either Chiang Kai-shek or Ho Ying-chin had ever dreamed of being; but even Madame Chiang was gifted with a natural understanding and grasp of military tactics far exceeding that of her husband.

5

The Three-pronged Japanese Drive from the Peking-Tientsin-Kalgan Area toward the Yellow River

In MID-AUGUST, 1937, before the fall of Kalgan and while the Battle of Shanghai was beginning to gather momentum, the Chinese high command recognized the imminent threat of Japa- nese offensive actions from the Peking-Tientsin-Kalgan area. The five northern provinces that Japan had long planned to organize into an autonomous regime (Hopei, Shantung, Shansi, Chahar, and Suiyuan) embraced an area of over 400,000 square miles (almost the size of Texas and California combined) and a popula- tion of about 90 million. Now, with the first steps of conquest a success, that rich region was far too great a prize to escape Japanese military ambitions. Unfortunately for the Chinese, the natural and man-made transportation routes in the area offered the Japanese a relatively easy means of penetration. Three rail- way lines paralleled by roads ran south from Peking, Tientsin, and Kalgan. Just south of the Yellow River, the east-west Lung- hai Railway ran from Lanchow to the newly constructed port of Lienyunkang. It crossed the north-south lines and completed the southern boundary of the transportation grid. Because of the tor- rential summer rains and floods of 1937, particularly in the cor- ridor of the Tientsin-Nanking line, the railways offered the only practicable routes of advance to the Japanese armies.

To meet the expected offensive, the Chinese deployed the 1st Army Group of nine divisions with five infantry and two cavalry divisions in support under General Sung Che-yuan, along the Tientsin-Nanking Railway from Tacheng, approximately 40 miles south of Tientsin, for about 65 miles to Ts'angchow. General Han Fu-chu's 3rd Route Army of between 80,000 and 100,000 men was ordered to remain south of the Yellow River in Shantung as a back-up force.

The 1st War Area command, directly under Chiang Kai-shek, was deployed in depth along the corridor of the Peking-Hankow Railway from the Yung Ting River south of Peking through Paoting to Shihkiachuang, 130 miles south of its forward elements. It consisted of the 2nd Army Group, commanded by General Liu Ch'ih, of twelve divisions, three separate infantry brigades, one cavalry division and one cavalry brigade; the 14th Army Group of three divisions under General Wei Li-huang; the 20th Army Group of three divisions under General Shang Chen; and the 53rd Corps of three divisions. The Generalissimo retained personal over-all command of this sector until October. In early September, his usual inclination to tinker with the order of battle got the best of him. This time his "genius" manifested itself in a military game of chess wherein large units were shifted from one combat area to another. For example, the 14th Army Group, augmented by two additional divisions and one separate infantry brigade, and the 1st Army were ordered to the Shansi sector for no apparent reason.

Early in September, a huge force under General Yan Hsi-shan was deployed along the corridors of the Kalgan-Taiyuan and Taiyuan-Shihkiachuang Railways for the defense of Shansi province and the 2nd War Area. Composed of three army groups, 2nd War Area troops and six other major commands, it consisted of a total of twenty-six divisions, fifteen separate infantry brigades, six cavalry divisions and one cavalry brigade. Under strength, under trained and under equipped, the dubious potency of this command rested on its imposing and complicated organization rather than on its effectiveness as a military unit.

By early September the Japanese had deployed over 200,000 combat troops in North China, consisting of two corps under the command of General Count Hisaichi Terauchi and a composite force made up of Kwantung Army troops and Mongolian cavalry. The 1st Corps under General Kotouki included the 5th, 14th, 6th, 20th and 108th Divisions; the 2nd Corps under General Nishio included the 10th, 16 and 109th Divisions. The Kwantung Army Expeditionary Force was made up of five composite brigades and nine puppet Mongolian cavalry "divisions". The Kawabe Brigade was designated as the reserve for the entire North China Front Army.

Facing this invasion threat were three Chinese armies with a total strength of approximately 515,000 men: 225,000 in Shansi province; 160,000, including Han Fu-chu's uncertain army of 80,000, near the northern sector of the Tientsin-Nanking rail line; and 130,000 in the Peking-Hankow rail corridor. The Chinese preponderance in manpower was more than offset by determined Japanese leadership, well-trained troops, and supporting artillery, armor, and air power. Psychologically, the Japanese had in their favor the conviction, derived from a series of easy victories, that they could defeat any Chinese force regardless of its size. The Chinese were equally convinced they were facing an army so superior that they could only delay it, harass it, or wear it down over a period of time. And, of course, Chiang Kai-shek was convinced that given time he could enlist Great Britain and the United States to save his skin.

Among the better known Chinese commanders, Feng Yu-hsiang, who commanded the 6th War Area along the Tientsin-Nanking rail line, and Yen Hsi-shan, commanding the 2nd War Area in Shansi, were more accustomed to political maneuvering, switching loyalties, and avoiding battle than facing an aggressive enemy. Along with Fu Tso-yi of the 7th Army Group, jovial P'ang Ping-hsun of the 40th Corps and Sung Che-yuan (formerly in command at Peking) of the 1st Army Group represented the warlord type of general who had risen from uneducated peasant stock and whose heyday was past. They had enriched themselves and had driven their troops with a bludgeon rather than led them by any form of motivation. They were opportunists· out for the main chance, old-fashioned and unable or unwilling to face up to the realities of modern warfare. Liu Ch'ih, originally in command of the 2nd Army Group on the Peking-Hankow rail line, was relieved of command on September 30, which was just as well; he was not a leader—with bludgeon or otherwise. In the Chinese equivalent of getting kicked upstairs, he was "promoted to a high ranking staff position" where his talent for doing nothing could be utilized.

Wei Li-huang of the 14th Army Group and Shang Chen of the 20th Army Group represented the more enlightened element among senior Chinese commanders. They were conservative and fully capable of comprehending events beyond the confines of their own local areas. Shang Chen came from a Paoting family with centuries of service in high civil office under both the Ming and Manchu dynasties. He was well educated, wealthy by inheritance of property, and completely adjusted to modern life, even to the point of organizing polo, boxing, and tennis teams among the young officers of his army. From a family of the upper middle class, Wei Li-huang was also well educated; he, too, had learned to accept modern realities and was extremely wealthy from collecting the entire tax revenue of four *hsien* in Hunan province, a reward bestowed upon him by a grateful Chiang Kai-shek for his service against the Communists. Both Shang and Wei were inclined to consider all sides of a question before making a decision—a characteristic usually more suited to philosophers than to forceful military commanders. They were both pro-American and were to become closely associated with the American command in China from 1942 to 1945.

T'ang En-po of the 20th Army was courageous, intelligent, and aggressive. He had volunteered to accompany Madame Chiang Kai-shek when she flew to Sian the year before to demand the release of her husband from the Young Marshal, and in so doing he had put his life on the line, as indeed had she. Sun Lien-chung of the 1st Army was educated and wealthy, but indecisive and a Saturday-night drinker of brandy in large quantities. He was sometimes given to unpredictable actions. Although highly cooperative with the American command in Yunnan during World War II, he failed to measure up in combat in the Salween campaign: he and his army hastily withdrew before the first assault of Japanese reinforcements, thereby delaying the successful conclusion of the campaign for nearly two months.

On the Japanese side, Count Terauchi, commander of the North China Front Army, was descended from an aristocratic family that had served shoguns and emperors for generations. He was tall and dignified, intelligent and forceful, and imbued with the most honorable traditions of the ancient nobility. General Kenji Doihara, commander of the 14th Division, who had long been connected with Japanese aggression in Manchuria, was the exact opposite. A man of common origin, he had worked his way up in the military hierarchy by every trick known. He was ruthless, devious, and cruel, and he was motivated by an unswerving will to expand the Japanese Empire by any means, good or bad. (On December 23, 1948, General Doihara was sentenced by the International Military Tribunal for the Far East to be hanged; the sentence was carried out in Tokyo.) The other Japanese commanders were well trained, aggressive, and determined to destroy China as an independent nation.

Operations in the Peking-Hankow (Pinghan Railway) Sector

AUGUST 31 TO NOVEMBER 12, 1937

After the fall of Kalgan on September 3, 1937, the Chinese 13th Corps of two divisions broke out of the area of the Peking-Kueisui rail line, eventually retreating as far as Anyang in northern Honan province, some 320 miles to the south—a truly monumental withdrawal. (Anyang had been a Shang dynasty capital and in recent years has been the site of extensive excavations yielding ancient bronzes of fine craftsmanship.) The 14th Army Group, having failed to relieve the Japanese attack on Huailai, withdrew to Shihkiachuang, about 175 miles south of the combat area. The routed 143rd Division managed to retreat for over 300 miles to Taming. On August 27 General Sun Lien-chung's 1st Army of four divisions fell back to prepared positions—a euphemism suggesting that this action was exactly as intended, instead of a forced withdrawal—in the Fangshan-Liuliho area about 20 miles south of Peking on the Pinghan Railway. The 3rd Corps of two divisions was astride the rail line, the 47th Division and 10th Cavalry Division to the east just south of Kuan and the 53rd Corps of three divisions at the eastern end of the 60-mile defense line at Yungching.

On September 14 the Japanese 1st Corps attacked the line with three divisions: the 20th Division between Fangshan and Liuliho west of the rail line; the 6th and 14th divisions the east end of the line on the north bank of the Yungting River. After crossing the river against spotty opposition, the 6th and 14th divisions turned west toward Chochow on the rail line about 20 miles behind the Chinese defensive positions. The Chinese 53rd Corps, 10th Cavalry Division, and 47th Division were merely brushed aside in passing. By September 18 "the situation was most unfavorable," according to the official Chinese history, but it would not have been had the 53rd Corps and 10th Cavalry Division counterattacked the Japanese flank and rear. Instead, the 53rd Corps marched some 80 miles to the south and the cavalry division galloped off, eventually slowing to a walk when it reached the Yellow River. The 3rd Corps, with the 47th Division attached, abandoned Chochow without even attempting a delaying action and marched nearly 60 miles south to Paoting. The Chinese 1st Army, with the Japanese 20th Division on its tail, did not halt its hasty withdrawal until it reached Shihkiachuang, 135 miles to the south. The so-called Chinese defense by 11 divisions had simply dissolved at the first Japanese assault. Paoting was now open to attack, its fate dependent on the pace of the Japanese infantry and their supporting units on the 50-mile march from Chochow.

Paoting, the capital of Hopei province, was an old walled city with a population of about 200,000. Its distinction came not from splendid imperial palaces and temples, but from its being the seat of the Hopei Medical College, one of the best in China, and the Hopei Agricultural Institute. For many years the program of the latter for improving antiquated farm methods had been more progressive than any in China. Its records on crop and weather statistics had grown to become an invaluable research source that was widely used.

Chinese troops of the 52nd Corps of two divisions, 3rd Corps of two divisions, and the 17th and 47th Divisions hastily occupied defensive positions extending from Mancheng to Tsaolo, about 10 miles north of Paoting. On September 21, advance elements of the Japanese 6th, 14th and 20th Divisions made a frontal attack on the Chinese positions and, understanding their enemy's fear of flank exposure, proceeded to envelop the eastern end of the line at Tsaolo. At the time, the three divisions of the Chinese 53rd Corps were only 12 miles east of Tsaolo, but the commander apparently did not feel this was his fight and simply sat on his hands. The next day Mancheng and Tsaolo fell, and the entire defense collapsed in a rout that did not slacken until it reached the Hutou River, 60 miles to the south.

The Japanese took Paoting on September 24 and again unleashed their rage on the Chinese for the lack of cooperation with their offers of co-prosperity. A week's drunken frenzy of rape, murder, burning, and looting followed. Thousands of civilians were killed, and much of the city was destroyed. All schools and schoolbooks were burned. The library and laboratories of the medical college went up in roaring flames, into which a number of screaming students and instructors were thrown for good measure. The library of crop and weather statistics and most of the agricultural institute's buildings were destroyed.

The Chinese forces were now backed up against Shihkiachuang on the Hutou River, with its direct rail connection to Taiyuan. General Shang Chen's 20th Army Group of four divisions, one separate infantry brigade and two cavalry divisions was deployed along the north bank of the Hutou River east of the rail line. General Wei Li-huang's 14th Army Group was deployed on the north bank of the river astride the rail line at Chengting, less than 12 miles north of Shihkiachuang, with its positions extending to the west. The 1st Army of five divisions under General Sun Lien-chung was massed about 20 miles southwest of Shihkiachuang "to go on the offensive from the left flank for a decisive battle with the enemy." On October 2, almost before these dispositions had been put into effect, Chiang Kai-shek decided on yet another change in alignments. Because the Japanese had advanced some 65 miles south of Tatung in northern Shansi, he directed Wei Li-huang to detach five divisions and one separate infantry brigade from his 14th Army Group and move them by rail to defensive positions 50 miles north of Taiyuan in order to block the Japanese drive to the south in that sector. At this time, Chiang's compulsion to shift units on the map in his remote office accomplished nothing but to confound field commanders and wear out already weary troops with constant movements.

Finally satiated with their devastation of Paoting, the Japanese 1st Corps, unimpeded by any Chinese defensive action, marched south until it reached Changshou, 15 miles north of Shihkiachuang. On October 6 the Japanese attacked Chinese advance positions and on the next day assaulted the main line along the

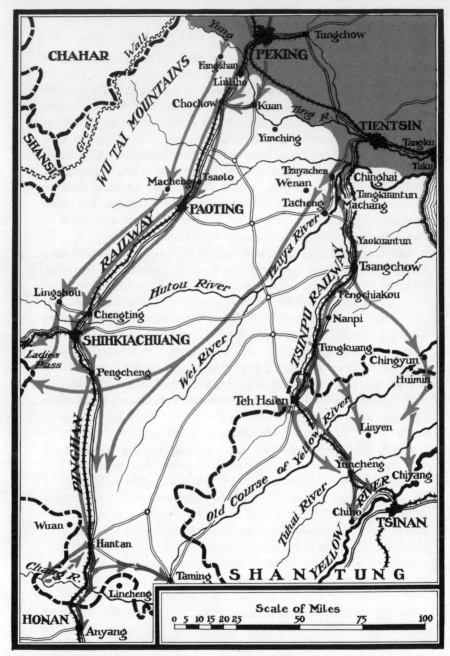

Operations in the Pinghan and Tsinpu Railway
Sectors to November 1937

Hutou River. At the same time, the 16th and 109th Divisions of the Japanese 2nd Corps, moving rapidly from the Tientsin area along the Tzuya River, reached a point 75 miles east of Shihkiachuang from where they continued to the south and southwest. The Chinese 67th Corps, left to guard against just such a Japanese move, made a disorderly retreat that finally ended at Tangyin, over 200 miles south. In the same general area north of the Hutou River, the 53rd Corps floundered around the flooded countryside and eventually bogged down completely without having established contact with the threatening Japanese 109th Division, which continued on its way.

Once again, Chiang Kai-shek—still from a distance of 600 miles—began meddling with subordinate units in the threatened area. Without any reference to his senior field commanders, he ordered the 1st Army, 14th Army, and 3rd Corps, totaling nine divisions, to move into prepared positions "to consolidate the gate to eastern Shansi"—meaning to block the route, known as Ladies Pass, through which the branch rail line from Shihkiachuang led directly to Taiyuan. Once through the pass, the Japanese would have a clear route with few natural barriers into the Shansi Valley. The 32nd Corps of three divisions was left astride the Pinghan Railway, 12 miles north of Shihkiachuang, "for sustained resistance."

The sustained resistance worked for exactly 24 hours. On October 8 the Japanese took Chengting and Lingshou on the main defense line and forced their way across the Hutou River. No match for the Japanese, the 32nd Corps fell apart under their attacks. However, it was able to delay the Japanese briefly a few miles to the rear; it then withdrew in a disorderly manner to a shaky defense position about 20 miles farther south. Meanwhile, the Japanese 109th Division had turned west and was now completing a wide envelopment that was planned to cross the Pinghan Railway 30 miles south of Shihkiachuang.

On October 10 the Japanese 6th, 14th, and 20th divisions walked into Shihkiachuang and raised the rising-sun flag over the empty railway yards—empty because all rolling stock had been moved to the south. The 6th and 14th Divisions continued to the south in pursuit of the routed Chinese 32nd Corps. Two days later, they were joined by the Japanese 2nd Corps' 16th

Division on the southward march. At Shihkiachuang, the Japanese 20th Division turned west toward Ladies Pass to effect a junction with the wide-swinging 109th Division.

With the complete collapse of the defense of Shihkiachuang, the Chinese 32nd Corps withdrew to Pengcheng on the Chang River 100 miles south of its last delaying position. The 53rd Corps finally managed to pull itself out of the flooded fields and mud and reached Wuan on October 15th. The 67th Corps and 10th Cavalry Division rushed pell-mell toward Anyang, which they reached on October 17th. Sung Che-yuan's 1st Army Group of nine divisions and two cavalry divisions was concentrated in the Taming-Neihuang area south and west of the Wei River and about 50 miles east of Anyang. General T'ang En-po, now in command of the 20th Army of four divisions, took up defensive positions astride the railway along the south bank of the Chang River.

The Japanese command had accomplished its objective on the Pinghan Railway, an effort that had been well coordinated with campaigns on the Tsinpu Railway and in Shansi. Its 20th and 109th Divisions now moved into positions to attack the Chinese positions at Ladies Pass. Its 6th and 16th Divisions were moved north to Tientsin and redeployed to the Shanghai area where they were badly needed. On October 19th, the Japanese 14th Division, having pressed on to the south, crossed the Chang River, engaged the Chinese 52nd Corps in a series of sharp, isolated skirmishes over a period of two days, and established its forward elements south of the river about 12 miles north of Anyang.

Now for a week the front was quiet, which General Doihara, the commander of the Japanese 14th Division, intended it should be. Optimistically, the Chinese convinced themselves that at last they had stalemated the enemy advance. They had not. The Japanese had no intention of moving farther south on the Pinghan Railway until the flanking sectors in Shansi and on the Tsinpu Railway had caught up with them. They were overextended at Anyang and knew only too well that any farther advance at this time would be dangerous.

The short lull offered Chiang Kai-shek the opportunity to make another series of confusing and demoralizing rearrangements in the disposition of the 1st War Area. The most direct result of the reshuffling was a lost chance. A determined, coordinated Chinese assault on the one Japanese division, the 14th, now strung out for 130 miles along the Pinghan Railway south of Shihkiachuang, could have forced it to withdraw to the north. The Chinese in the Chang River area had four times the number of troops that the lone Japanese force could muster, even if General Doihara were able to concentrate his total strength. But, split into some 20 separate units, each top-heavy with noncombat elements, the Chinese not only lacked the will for offensive action but did not understand the meaning of coordination or teamwork. Nor were Chinese commanders psychologically capable of moving without orders from Chiang Kai-shek. Though many were afraid to face up to the Japanese, all were even more afraid of the generalissimo. Had the Chinese forces been reorganized in 6 divisions, instead of 20, with effective leadership they could not only have forced the Japanese 14th Division to retire northward but could also have relieved the pressure on the Taiyuan-Shihkiachuang rail line at Ladies Pass. Trading reality for illusion, the Chinese now convinced themselves that they were launching a counteroffensive by initiating a series of piecemeal attacks by small units. The Japanese reacted vigorously to these weak and uncoordinated efforts. On November 4th, a few battalion- and company-size units of the 20th Army Group attacked the forward outposts of the Japanese on the railway. The Japanese promptly counterattacked and drove the Chinese out of their base at Anyang. A small portion of the 52nd Corps crossed the Chang River, advanced about 15 miles toward Hantan, encountered the Japanese in a few skirmishes, and raced back to its position south of the Chang River. On November 6th, troops of the 1st Army Group moved from their base at Taming and cut the railway 40 miles in rear of forward Japanese elements. The Japanese retaliated with a vigorous counterattack that sent the 1st Army Group fleeing out of Taming on November 11th. In the midst of these moves and counter moves, General T'ang En-po led his 13th Corps out of the scene altogether "to save Taiyuan."

The official Chinese history comment on these ineffective pinpricks reads: ". . . the original plans were not fully implemented. Regretfully, our strength . . . was insufficient."

On November 22 the 1st War Area still commanded by Chiang Kai-shek again readjusted its disposition in a further reshuffling of commanders and troop units. But the campaign was over, and the readjustment meant, in effect, that the Chinese forces were to remain inertly in place to await the next Japanese move. The defense of the Pinghan Railway had been a failure in every respect.

From the point of view of the successful Japanese command, however, difficulties were beginning to arise in areas that should have been permanently conquered. They had already learned that it would be impossible to occupy all of China. Even with a million troops, the Japanese could do little more than hold the key points along the railway lines and extend their influence but a few miles on each side of them. Huge pockets of villages and farmlands, undisturbed by contending armies, were reorganizing their existence and looking for new Chinese leadership. Their own central government had abandoned them, but another government within a government—that of the Chinese Communists—was already dispatching organizers and cadre leaders to raise a banner that promised a new life and a new future.

Operations in the Northern Sector of Tientsin-Nanking (Tsinpu Railway)

SEPTEMBER 4 TO NOVEMBER 13, 1937

After the fall of Tientsin and Peking on July 30 and 31, the Japanese established defense perimeters around each city and waited for over a month before moving south in the corridor of the Tsinpu Railway. A number of factors dictated this lull in military operations: the Japanese military expected the Chinese government to negotiate; the Japanese military buildup was not of sufficient strength to launch offensives into the interior; the flat farmland of northern Hopei was mostly under water from unusually heavy summer rains, which would have impeded an offensive; and secret negotiations with Governor Han Fu-chu of Shantung offered the possibility that this rich province might fall into Japanese hands or under their control without a military campaign.

But by late August it was apparent that the Chinese had no

intention of entering into discussions of any kind. Since the floods had now begun to subside, it was decided that a Japanese move southward down the corridor of the Tsinpu Railway might nudge Han Fu-chu into a decision regarding which side he was to join.

At this time, the Japanese 2nd Corps, commanded by General Nishio and consisting of the 10th, 16th, and 109th divisions, was poised to strike from the Tientsin area. With supporting units, this force had a strength of close to 75,000 men.

Facing the Japanese were a number of Chinese units, totaling nearly 150,000 men, hastily thrown together as the 1st Army Group under the command of General Sung Che-yuan. It consisted of General Sung's 29th Corps (three divisions) occupying defensive positions on the railway about 30 miles south of Tientsin and holding Chinghai, 20 miles south of the city; the 53rd corps (three divisions) and the 3rd Cavalry Corps (two cavalry divisions) deployed between the Tsinpu Railway and Pinghan Railway just south of the Yungting River; the 67th Corps (two divisions) between Wenan and Tacheng; the 59th Division in the same area east of the railway; the 59th Corps (three divisions) and the 39th Division of the 40th Corps 60 miles south of Tientsin; the 109th Division of the 49th Corps; the 49th Corps and the 23rd Division at Teh Hsien, 120 miles south of Tientsin; the 77th Corps (three divisions) in the same area west of the railway; and the 12th Corps (two divisions) south and east of Teh Hsien.

The 1st Army Group also included Han Fu-chu's 80,000-man 3rd Route Army and militia of about 20,000 men, but neither group could be depended on for either aggressive action or loyalty. The 1st Army Group was strung out in depth, a chronic tactical failing of the Chinese that enabled the Japanese to pick off one division at a time. In this case the depth of some 150 miles was even farther extended by the placement of Han Fu-chu's army along the northern border of Shantung as a backup force for the army group. Of the 25 infantry divisions and 2 cavalry divisions, only 3 were deployed to meet the first Japanese assault along the railway line, and only 3 more were in secondary defense positions 10 miles to the rear of the forward lines. Units east and west of the railway were designated as mobile forces to attack the flanks of the enemy—presumably after the Japanese had broken through the initial resistance. In the ensuing campaign, the only mobility demonstrated by these units was in hasty retreat.

On September 4 the Japanese 10th Division spearheaded the offensive of the 2nd Corps with an attack on Chinghai. In the face of the first artillery fire, the Chinese 29th Corps withdrew to Tangkuantun, 12 miles to the' south. Two days later, Tangkuantun fell to the Japanese, who then shifted their main effort toward Machang, 8 miles to the southwest. The Japanese 16th and 109th divisions, following closely behind the 10th Division, turned west to Tzuyachen on the Tzuya River. Now under attack by two enemy divisions, the 29th Corps defense of Machang collapsed, the town falling to the Japanese on September 10. Its Chinese defenders fled in considerable disorder to the next in-depth positions, 15 miles to the south and about 10 miles north of Ts'angchow. On arrival, the three 29th Corps divisions were in such deplorable condition they were sent to the rear where they "underwent reorganization"—after only their first combat in over six weeks.

Meanwhile, advance elements of the Japanese 16th Division struck hard at the 67th Corps of two divisions and forced it to withdraw from its prepared defense positions extending from Wenan to Tacheng. The 67th Corps counterattacked on September 15, temporarily compelling the Japanese to withdraw to the east bank of the Tzuya River. Enemy reaction to this setback was a violent assault on Tacheng, which was captured on September 20. Then, with the 109th Division, the 16th marched to the southwest along the Tzuya River. This was the beginning of the end for the Chinese 67th Corps, which was never again able to put up any serious resistance. By November it ended up at Tangyin in the Pinghan Railway sector, nearly 240 miles south of its original positions on the Tsinpu Railway, and was sent to Shanghai.

The new 40-mile defense line north of Ts'angchow was manned by four divisions,[1] each plucked hastily from a different corps organization. A fifth division, the 109th, was placed in reserve south of Ts'angchow. This hodgepodge was dumped into the lap of General P'ang Ping-hsun. Jovial though he may have been, General P'ang was a product of the warlord days of political maneuverings, alliances, and defections. His recent military experience had largely been centered on loud conviviality and heavy drinking. He was not the man to command in a tight situation.

On September 21 the Japanese 10th Division attacked Yao-kuantun in the center of P'ang Ping-hsun's defense line. Despite their disorganized command situation, the four Chinese divisions put up a good fight for two days. Then, as the line crumbled under heavy air attacks and artillery fire, they fell back on Ts'angchow, which was taken by the Japanese on September 25. After the fall of Ts'angchow, the Chinese pulled back to a new defense line running through Fengkiakou and Nanpi, about 15 miles to the south. The quick loss of Ts'angchow led to persistent, although false, rumors that P'ang Ping-hsun had sold out to the Japanese. Actually, the Japanese had no need to buy him, for once they had knocked out his troops he was worth nothing to them.

At this time, Chiang Kai-shek, again frenetic at his military chessboard, designated the sector of the Tsinpu Railway north of Shantung as the 6th War Area under the overall command of the Christian general Feng Yu-hsiang. Feng was directed to conduct sustained defense in the area between Ts'angchow—which had already been lost—and Teh Hsien, then to shift to the offensive upon the arrival of reinforcements from the 5th War Area south of Shantung. Blocked from passage through his province by Han Fu-chu, the reinforcements never arrived. Even had these troops been able to join the defending Chinese north of the Yellow River, it is doubtful if General Feng's brand of Christian prayer—on bended knees—could have injected the will to fight in his faltering command. Feng's days of action had passed.

Between September 26 and 29 the Japanese took Fengkiakou and Tungkuang, 16 miles to the south. With the whole defense withering away and with Feng Yu-hsiang unable to pull either himself or his troops together, the deputy commander of the 6th War Area, General Lu Chung-lin, went to Nanpi on September 29 to light a fire under the vacillating commanders. Using the 49th and 59th Corps and the 23rd Division, a total of five divisions, General Lu struck at the Japanese left flank in the railway zone. By noon the next day he had recaptured Fengkiakou and cut the railway behind the Japanese forward elements. But under strong counterattacks, the Chinese were unable to hold the ground they had regained—though they had more than twice the number of troops—and on October 1 they withdrew hastily toward prepared positions just east of Teh Hsien, 45 miles to the south.

On October 3 the Japanese 10th Division began a frontal assault on Teh Hsien, at the same time sending a flanking column to attack and nail down the Chinese positions 15 to 20 miles east of the city. As the attack developed, General Isoya of the 10th Division detached a second column to follow the old bed of the Yellow River (some 50 miles northwest of the new river) east of Teh Hsien, then cut across the railway 6 miles south of the town. By this move, Isoya surrounded the city on three sides and cut off the possibility of escape for many of the defenders inside the walls. Before Teh Hsien fell on October 5, one Chinese regiment was completely wiped out in a day-long hand-to-hand struggle with enemy troops.

A piecemeal, haphazard defense of the Yuncheng area, 35 miles south of Teh Hsien, fell apart on October 15. The Japanese continued to move south along the railway toward Chiho on the Yellow River against almost no opposition, for general Han Fu-chu had ordered three divisions of his 3rd Route Army to pull back to the south bank of the Tuhai River, which generally marked the northern border of Shantung province. However, one of them, the 23rd Division, delayed its withdrawal to the south, remaining in prepared positions in the Linyen area, about 17 miles north of the Tuhai. On November 5 a small Japanese flank column, having followed a route about 20 miles east of the railway, attacked the Chinese at Linyen. But the 23rd Division made a successful counterattack and took several hundred prisoners—both Japanese and puppet militia—as well as a considerable amount of arms and equipment. The prisoners were herded into Shantung where Han Fu-chu rather inexplicably ordered them all executed by shooting and beheading. A second, parallel Japanese column, over 35 miles east of the first, crossed the old bed of the Yellow River at Chingyun; encountering no opposition of any kind, it moved rapidly south to take Huimin on November 11 and Chiyang on the Yellow River two days

later. The Chinese 1st Army Group, now composed of the remnants of nine battered divisions, had already decamped on a long
march to Taming and Lincheng in northern Honan, completely
out of the Tsinpu Railway sector. Again attacked by the Japanese, the 23rd Division managed to scramble nimbly to safety
across the Yellow River. Except for dead and wounded, the
Chinese command had now completely abandoned the northern
sector of the Tsinpu Railway.

Barring an occasional clash, the Tsinpu Railway sector was
quiet for a full month. During that period the military situation
along the Yellow River can be described by quoting a message I
sent to Colonel Stilwell: "Neither side is doing a thing except
rape, loot and have a swell time off the countryside. They skirmish
and exchange fire, call it a battle, and then settle down for the
night and a good sleep."

In a futile and totally unrealistic attempt to flex some military
muscle—or perhaps to save face—Chiang Kai-shek ordered the
commanding general of the 5th War Area, Li Tsung-jen, to
launch a counterattack with the main force of the 3rd Army
Group (six divisions) to recapture Teh Hsien, operate in
Ts'angchow, and tie down the enemy. At the time, two divisions
of Han Fu-chu's 3rd Army Group (formerly the 3rd Route Army)
of over 80,000 men had not yet completed their withdrawal to
the south bank of the Yellow River. Still in a sort of dream world
over the hoped-for outcome of his negotiations with the Japanese, Governor Han immediately withdrew all his troops to the
south bank of the river, destroyed the huge steel railway bridge,
and concentrated the bulk of his army along the southern border
of Shantung to block the passage by rail or road of General Li's
army to the north. Whether or not Han would have attacked
Li's troops had they attempted to force a passage through the
province is a matter of conjecture. In any case, Li Tsung-jen, an
able military commander, did not choose to risk open combat.
Had he done so, he would have played into Japanese hands and
opened the way for immediate occupation of Shantung. In the
meantime, convinced that he held all the aces, Han Fu-chu maintained an irresolute posture squarely between his own government and the enemy, afraid to jump to either side.

Regardless of the outcome of the political poker game between

Han Fu-chu and the Japanese, it was too late for a Chinese counterattack. Any attack would have been prevented from crossing the Yellow River by enemy air and artillery units and would therefore be forced to make a wide swing to Chengchow, then north and northwest through southern Hopei, to attack the Japanese flank and rear—a march of over 400 miles involving tactics far too bold for the Chinese to carry out.

The failure of the Chinese in the Tsinpu Railway operation can be attributed to poor leadership, untrained and poorly equipped troops, and a chronic reluctance (except in the hopeless defense of Teh Hsien) to come to grips with the enemy. The whole Chinese attitude was defensive rather than offensive. Most of Chiang's commanders apparently refused to believe the axiom that no war has ever been won, or even long resisted, from previously prepared defense positions. Another factor in the Chinese collapse was Han Fu-chu's traitorous refusal to commit his troops to combat or to permit reinforcements from the south to pass through his personal domain of Shantung. As far as the Japanese were concerned, operations came to a standstill at the Yellow River because that was as far as they chose to send their overextended forces at the time.

Operations in the Kalgan-Taiyuan and Shihkiachuang-Taiyuan Sectors

SEPTEMBER 12 TO NOVEMBER 9, 1937

Shansi province (the 2nd War Area) had long been considered a natural barrier to invasion from the north. Rugged mountains extended along its eastern border with Hopei, the principal pass, Ladies Pass, cutting through the barrier west of Shihkiachuang and connecting by rail with Taiyuan, the capital. In the north, three easily defended passes were the only access routes through the mountains, along whose crests ran the outer Great Wall. The railway from Kalgan to Taiyuan cut through one of these passes just north of Tatung, from which junction the Peking-Kueisui line (Pingsui Railway) extended into Mongolia. To the west, high ridges ran parallel to the Yellow River, which formed the border with Shensi province. A long valley running the length of the province from north to south contained prosperous towns and fertile farmlands. Located at the geographical center of the valley was Taiyuan, an old walled city on the Fen River with a population of about 250,000. It had become a symbol of stability and strength, an ancient bulwark against dangers from the north and northwest from where all historical invasions of China had originated. To Chiang Kai-shek, however, Shansi represented an eastern barricade against the Chinese Communists in northern Shensi, just as the 8th War Area, under his personal command, blocked them to the west and northwest and his Sian Headquarters command contained them from the south.

In mid-September, 1937, the command structure of the Japanese forces poised to plunge into Shansi was divided. The North China Front Army under General Terauchi consisted of General Itagaki's 5th Division and the Kwantung Army's Chahar Expeditionary Force of four composite brigades, one of which, the 11th, was known as the Suzuki Brigade, and nine Mongolian cavalry divisions. As the offensives following the route of the Pingsui Railway and through the passes into Shansi progressed, the command organization of the Japanese forces was modified to meet changing developments. But the number of troops remained the same (about 60,000 including the Mongolian cavalry units) until late October, when the 20th Division from the Pinghan Railway sector and the 109th Division from the Tsinpu Railway sector were attached to the North China Front Army. This increased Japanese strength in the main effort to take Taiyuan by about 40,000 men.

The Chinese defending forces, totaling about 225,000 men, were under the overall command of General Yen Hsi-shan, commander of the 2nd War Area, and consisted of 4 army groups with a total of 20 divisions, 13 separate infantry brigades, 2 cavalry divisions, and 1 separate cavalry brigade; 3 independent corps of 5 divisions and 2 separate infantry brigades; 2 cavalry corps of 3 cavalry divisions; 1 separate cavalry division; and the Communist 18th Army Group (formerly the 8th Route) of 3 divisions under the command of General Chu Teh.

No longer young, Yen Hsi-shan had first been appointed military governor of the province of Shansi by Yuan Shih-kai in 1912. He had firmly hung on to his province for 25 years, had built up a large private army of troops who were neither well trained nor well equipped, and had grown enormously rich from the high taxes he levied. Uneducated and a schemer, Yen had coined his own nickname of the model governor. His various projects to benefit the people—roads, bridges, irrigation, schools, and land reclamation—had not been undertaken with any spirit of benevolence on his part, but from his knowledge that higher incomes for the people produced higher rents and taxes for himself. A pragmatist and an opportunist, he had switched through the years from one political side to another. His capabilities as a commander were of a low order, his military reputation existing only because it had never been seriously challenged. Fu Tso-yi, commander of the 7th Army Group, was another overage product of the warlord days. Like Yen, his reputation was based more on his ability to survive changing political situations than on military prowess. Chu Teh, commander-in-chief of the Red Army and the second man in the Communist hierarchy, had a natural instinct for leadership and military tactics. He had masterminded the Communist defense against Chiang Kai-shek's various bandit-suppression campaigns, was revered by his troops, and had led his people on the famous Long March to northern Shensi.

By mid-September, the Japanese Chahar Expeditionary Force had sent columns south from Tatung toward Huaijen, toward Tsoyin, 30 miles west of Tatung, and northwest toward Chining on the Pingsui Railway leading to Kueisui. The 11th Composite Brigade had turned southwest from Hsuahua, 25 miles southeast of Kalgan, had taken Yangyuan, and had broken through one of the three northern passes. The 5th Division had moved southwest from Huailai on the Pingsui Railway, had taken Weihsien where it had detached one regiment to march south toward Paoting, had taken Kuangling and Lingchiu, and had suffered a severe, but temporary, setback near Pinghsingkuan where its advance brigade had been ambushed by the Chinese Communist 115th Division.

Between September 21 and 25, one column of the Chahar Expeditionary Force took Tsoyin and against almost no opposition marched 50 miles south to occupy Suyi. A second column routed the Chinese 61st Corps at Huaijen, took Shanyin, 20 miles to the south, and moved 15 miles farther south to attack Chinese positions at the inner Great Wall near Yenmenkuan.

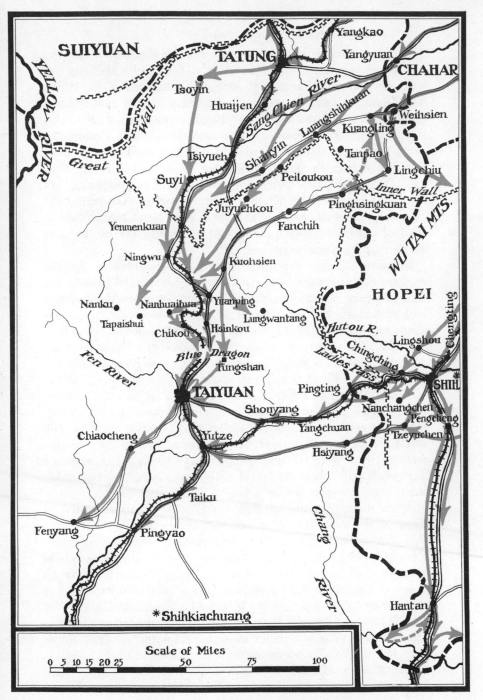

Operations in the Taiyuan and Shihkiachuang
Sectors, September-November, 1937

The Suzuki Brigade battered its way through the Wall at Juyueh-kou on September 29 and forced the Chinese 34th Corps to withdraw through Fanchih to prepared positions in the Wutai Mountains, 20 miles to the south. Reacting sharply to the shame of being caught in an ambush at Pinghsingkuan by what it considered an inferior enemy (in this case the Chinese Communist 115th Division), the 5th Division drove the Chinese out of Lingchiu just outside the inner Wall. Then they crashed through the Wall to assault the Chinese positions at Pinghsingkuan, but found the town and its defenses empty of troops. Alarmed at the capture of Fanchih to their flank and rear, the Chinese defenders had decamped during the night of September 30 to safer positions 25 to 30 miles southwest.

In early October the west column of the Chahar Expeditionary Force approached Ningwu, only 22 miles above the main Chinese defenses north of Taiyuan. Its main column had broken through the inner Great Wall at Yenmenkuan and was about to attack Yuanping, 5 miles north of the defense line. In a forced march of over 60 miles, the Japanese 5th Division linked up with the Suzuki Brigade and was now in position to join the assault. The bulk of the Chinese forces pulled back behind the 60-mile defense line extending from Nanku at its western extremity through Tapaishui, Nanhuaihua, and Hsinkou to Lungwang-tang at its eastern extremity, its center about 50 miles north of the capital. Already alarmed at the streaming hordes of refugees pouring down from the north, the panicky civilian population of Taiyuan hastily began to evacuate the city, using the two roads leading south and southwest.

At this point, Chiang Kai-shek was again up to his old habit of directing the movement of subordinate units without reference to their senior field commanders. Apparently it never occurred to Chiang to assign a mission to the sector commander and hold him responsible for carrying it out. Although his lack of confidence in the ability and judgment of his area commanders was often justified, his own was no better. This time, according to the official Chinese history, "having carefully weighed the situation, Generalissimo Chiang judiciously and resolutely shifted forces from the Pinghan Railway to consolidate Shansi."

On October 2 Chiang ordered General Wei Li-huang to move

his entire 14th Army Group[2] of two corps, one separate division, and one separate brigade by rail from Shihkiachuang to the defense positions north of Taiyuan. So far as is known, he did not specify the speed with which the trains should move, but he omitted few other details. He also directed Yen Hsi-shan to "dispatch powerful forces to mass and provide cover for the defense of Kuohsien and Yuanping."

On October 10, following Chiang's orders, Wei Li-huang's 14th Army Group arrived at its positions behind the western end of the Taiyuan defense lines. With these reinforcements, the 2nd War Area troop units were restructured into the Right Flank Army[3] of five divisions plus two separate infantry brigades, the Central Army[4] of four divisions plus seven separate infantry brigades, and the Left Flank Army[5] with a total of five divisions. Wei Li-huang was named overall commander of this defense force of 14 divisions and 9 separate brigades.

Three days later, on October 13, the Japanese 5th Division, less one regiment, and the Chahar Expeditionary Force, less one infantry brigade and the Mongolian cavalry, stormed the outer defenses of Kuohsien and Yuanping and opened the attack on the main positions at Tapaishui, Nanhuaihua, and Chikou. The Chinese lines held for five days against air attacks, heavy artillery fire, and frequent infantry assaults. Daily hand-to-hand fighting on the parapets of the trenches left thousands of dead on both sides, including the commanders of the Chinese 9th Corps and 54th Division.

Finally, exhausted by the day and night attacks, each side was forced to pause in what the Chinese wishfully interpreted as a stalemate. It was not. Five days later, renewed Japanese attacks cracked the badly battered Chinese positions. As the Japanese stormed through breaks in the lines, the Chinese forces pulled back 25 miles to prepared positions on Blue Dragon Ridge, only 20 miles north of Taiyuan. Again the Chinese lines held for five days against unremitting air, artillery, and tank attacks. But Japanese engineers had been tunneling under Tungshan, a key fort whose height dominated the entire eastern half of the Chinese defenses, and on the morning of November 2 they set off a charge that blew the key bastion and its defenders sky high. On the third the Chinese began withdrawing to their last defensive positions, only 5 miles north of Taiyuan. Most of the Left Flank Army crossed the Fen River in great disorder and headed for the mountains to the west. The Chinese lost nearly 30,000 men in the attempt to hold Blue Dragon Ridge. General Fu Tso-yi was ordered to hold the city at all costs with his depleted command of three divisions and seven separate brigades.

Meanwhile, the Japanese attack from Shihkiachuang against Ladies Pass was beginning to threaten the entire defense of Shansi. On October 8, when they captured Chengting near Shihkiachuang and Lingshou 10 miles to the west, Chiang Kai-shek "judiciously and resolutely" (again) ordered the 1st and 14th armies, 3rd Corps, and 17th Division (a total of eight divisions and one separate infantry brigade) diverted from the Pinghan Railway sector for the defense of Ladies Pass, the gateway on the rail line that led directly to Taiyuan. The Chinese occupied a 35-mile defense line just east of a long spur of the inner Great Wall, with forward positions about 15 miles west of Shihkiachuang. After the fall of Shihkiachuang on October 10, advance elements of the Japanese 20th Division attacked Chingching, a key point in the outer defenses over 20 miles east of the main positions. On October 14 the Japanese broke through the Chinese lines at two places, but pushing recklessly ahead, they found themselves surrounded by troops of the Chinese 3rd Corps and guerrilla-trained units. Though the Japanese were badly mauled, they held their ground, and the Chinese did not follow up their advantage with a full-scale attack. Instead, "unable to destroy the enemy," they pulled back to the main defensive positions at Ladies Pass on October 22.

On October 27 the Japanese 109th Division from the Tsinpu Railway sector met up with the 20th Division just southwest of Shihkiachuang. While the 20th made a frontal attack against the pass, the 109th moved rapidly to Tzeyuchen and Nanchangcheng to outflank the Chinese 3rd Corps, which panicked at this threat to its flank, pulled out of its positions, and withdrew to Pingting, over 20 miles to the northwest. Meanwhile, the 20th Division stormed through the main Chinese positions and the Wall at Ladies Pass, and on October 30th, proceeded toward Pingting and Yangchuan. By this time, the 109th Division had reached Hsiyang, directly south of the 20th Division, and continued its advance to the west. Then, since "the situation was so unfavorable that our [the Chinese] forces were scattered," the Chinese abandoned Pingting and Yangchuan in a near rout to the west. The route to Taiyuan, 50 miles ahead, was now wide open to the advancing Japanese.

On November the Japanese 5th Division and the Chahar Expeditionary Force attacked the defense positions just north of Taiyuan. On the next day, the 20th and 109th Divisions, having marched virtually unopposed through the towns of Shouyang and Yutze, effected a junction with the Japanese forces from the north. Taiyuan was now under attack from the north, east, and southeast. By November 7 most of the Chinese troops had evacuated the city as a disorderly mob. The Japanese demanded the surrender of the city. But having decided to make a last-ditch stand, the remaining Chinese troops ignored the summons. On the morning of the eighth, the Japanese commander began intensive bombing, artillery, and tank attacks. The north, east, and northwest gates were destroyed. The heavy concentration of direct artillery fire breached the massive old city walls. Assault troops of the 5th Division broke through the last outer defenses and crashed into the city through gaping breaks in the walls and gates, but they immediately ran into the Chinese defense forces. Bitter house-to-house fighting slowed their progress as they pushed through rubble-strewn alleys and past burning houses. By evening, the Japanese had taken over half of Taiyuan.

That night, the last defending Chinese troops broke out to the west; in their mad scramble to escape, frenzied troops using gun butts and bayonets shoved carts and people off the one bridge into the Fen River to make room on the roadway for themselves. On the morning of the ninth, more Japanese broke into the wrecked city from the north and east. Chinese troops and refugees still jammed the southwest gate and the sole bridge in a wailing, terrified rabble. With the first light, the Japanese bombed and strafed the crowded bridge. Explosions ripped through the human flood, killing and maiming. By nightfall, Taiyuan, the bulwark of the northwest, was in Japanese hands. In the futile defense effort the Chinese lost 20,000 men and 80 artillery pieces. The civilian inhabitants lost their homes and shops and everything in them.

The next day the enemy pushed through Yutze and Taiku toward Pingyao, about 55 miles to the south, where they knocked out the last Chinese resistance and established a strong defensive position. A second column crossed the Fen River and marched southwest to attack and capture Chiaocheng, about 25 miles from Taiyuan. The defeated Chinese forces broke contact and withdrew to reorganize their badly disarrayed units. The best that the official Chinese history could say of the Shansi campaign was that "this battle came to an end."

Why the disastrous military debacle on three fronts? Why the abandonment in less than five months of some 90,000,000 people living north of the Yellow River? Why the callous attitude of the intellectuals, the wealthy, and the middle class to the deaths of hundreds of thousands, both soldiers and civilians?

Equipped with their Confucian attitude toward the settlement of difficulties by discussion and compromise, the Chinese were unable to match the Japanese attitude that violence, self-sacrifice, and courage on the battlefield could overcome all obstacles. The Japanese were willing to gamble their lives for the stakes involved. Most Chinese commanders were not—though their losses were staggering anyway. Chiang Kai-shek, however, was not only willing to but did gamble his best troops on a stupid and shortsighted campaign at Shanghai and Nanking to win overt foreign intervention—and lost. Forced then to depend on many senior generals of doubtful loyalty, and able to hold them as part of his military team only by alternately releasing and threatening to withhold funds, he had no real army with which to fight off a determined enemy. The Japanese were deeply imbued with a sense of patriotism for their emperor and his cause. The Chinese soldier had no sense of national patriotism. He had been taught from infancy that all loyalty was vested in the family.

Chiang's only solid advantage was the vastness of China. All previous invaders had so overextended their conquests that the very size of the land had eventually absorbed them or rendered them helpless, and in the end overextension undermined a Japan besieged from all sides by powerful enemies in 1945.

The wonder is that the Chinese soldier fought as well as he

did. He was conscripted into service as if into a chain gang and dragged from his native village to join a distant regiment. He was haphazardly trained to fire a rifle but little else, for his officers were untrained, sometimes illiterate, with little idea how to command a unit of any size. Officially, he was paid eight Chinese dollars per month (in 1937 the equivalent of between one and two American dollars), a good part of which was usually withheld by his rapacious commanders. His daily ration—when he could get it—was 22 ounces of rice and one-eighth ounce of salt. Under combat conditions the average soldier was weak from hunger and exhaustion. He was night-blind from deficiencies in his diet—no meat, almost no fats, few vegetables, and no sugar. He was badly clothed, often nearly in rags. More often than not his footgear on long marches consisted of straw sandals he had made himself. Lucky indeed was the infantryman who found an old rubber tire from which he and his companions could fashion durable soles for their sandals. The elite bodyguards and a few reasonably well-equipped units were better shod—usually with cheap, rubber-soled sneakers. If sick or wounded, the Chinese soldier had virtually no field medical service on which to depend. The rare military hospitals were staffed with politically appointed incompetents whose principal interest was to enrich themselves by the sale of the scanty supply of drugs and medicines. The soldier knew from bitter experience that his own people scorned his lot, hated him for foraging to provide himself with the barest necessities, and despised him as a member of the lowest stratum of society, for Confucius had pronounced that good iron went into plowshares, poor iron into swords and spears.

Yet the Chinese soldier was courageous and not afraid to die. When he saw his companions fall around him in combat, he simply believed that fate had been kinder to him than to the others. But all too often his leaders were more determined to save their own skins than to win battles. As summed up by Major David D. Barrett: "The Chinese soldier is excellent material, wasted and betrayed by stupid leadership." In speaking of senior Chinese officers, Colonel Stilwell observed: "The offensive is not in them." After many years of experience in China, Ambassador Nelson T. Johnson pinpointed the attitude of the upper and middle classes with the remark: "Let us fight to the last drop of coolie blood." He was correct, and one of the tragedies of China was that her peasant soldiers knew it only too well. After four months of combat in north China and the Yangtze Valley, the Japanese general Terauchi and his senior commanders agreed with these views of the Chinese military. The Japanese officers told a visiting group of foreign attachés that they had found the Chinese junior officers and enlisted men to be courageous and tenacious fighters, but that their superior officers lacked military training and offensive spirit.

And what of Chiang Kai-shek's abandonment of tens of millions of his people? Steeped in the unwarranted conviction or conceit that they would welcome back his leadership when the time came, he had sown the seeds of his own eventual downfall. Trapped between Japanese-controlled lines of communication, the leaderless villagers and farmers were cut off from the only world they had known. With the desperation of drowning men they were ready to grasp at any straw, any helping hand. Mao Tse-tung's Communist cadres held out that hand and a hope the people could not at first believe or understand, but which slowly won their loyalty and support.

Two months before the Chinese collapse on all three fronts, I sent the following comments to Colonel Stilwell in a letter dated September 10, 1937:

The Chinese are now in a good position to cause the Japanese considerable embarrassment and if the Japs . . . advance down the Pinghan line, they might even achieve some small success—if only they would act with a little more vigor. More likely they will mess around as they have for the past six weeks and accomplish little or nothing. The Chinese allowed two very good opportunities to slip by in August to attack in the area of Tientsin because they felt that their "preparations were not complete." I don't suppose that preparations will ever be complete if that entails facing the music in an honest-to-God battle.

. . . [As to the fact] that I believed in the possibility of a Chinese victory in this war . . . forget it. When I saw the immense movements of troops along the three railway lines, the new and quite good equipment (not enough, but enough to put up a good show) . . . and heard what was apparently an honest ring of determination in the voices of both commanders and men . . . I was impressed. But flabby inertia, almost stupid incompetence, and complete lack of staff work of any kind—one division headquarters did not even have a map of its area—I have lost my former glimmer of optimism. My reaction now is one of disgust. If defensive tactics are employed on the Pinghan and Tsinpu lines and troops stand their ground, it should take months for the Japanese to reach Shihkiachuang and Tsinan. But I have no faith that the resistance will amount to much, once the Japs attack with their usual determination.

I could not help but smile at your request for information on operations maps, orders, staff work, etc. I saw one operations map at 10th Division headquarters at Shihkiachuang, but it was several days out of date and full of lines indicating great offensives which have never even been started. If you graded their staff work with a grade of 100.00 for perfect, I would give them a mark of about .0001. There must have been a little or they could not have got on the trains. Most orders, except telegraphic ones from Nanking, are verbal. . . . There seems to be no attempt to carry out any kind of training (behind the front).

. . . I still believe that Shantung will be safe for some time to come. [It was, for three and a half months.] To begin with, Han Fu-chu unquestionably had an agreement with the Japanese for the protection of the province—and himself. But I don't kid myself into thinking that the Japs would hold to this if it suited their purposes to do otherwise. . . . I think that the Japs, being over occupied elsewhere, do not want to take the chance of large scale destruction in a province they have marked out for their own use . . . the large destruction of Japanese interests in Shanghai has given them a good idea as to what would happen in Tsingtao and Tsinan. The Japanese investment in Tsingtao alone amounts to more than Yen 300,000,000. The Chinese as much as told the Jap consul that at the first sign of a big landing, it would be destroyed. The actual statement was that Chinese authorities would no longer be able to control the mobs.

Though the original plan of the Chinese was to attack on the Tsinpu, Nanking must be withholding the order . . . until they can be certain there will be no dirty work behind their backs in Shantung, which means until they have control of Han's army. The Japs, realizing the internal politics of the province, must find it expedient . . . to withhold their activities until later. Why not allow Shantung to drop as a fat undamaged plum into their laps? . . . *and it will fall to them.*

In November, 1937, a super command agency over both the Japanese army and navy general staffs—the Imperial General

Headquarters—was activated in Tokyo. Though its announced functions were to coordinate and direct combat operations in China and to plan for the future, it was also intended to quash military rivalries between the Kwantung Army, the North China Front Army, the Central China Expeditionary Force, the navy, and the various officer cliques in Japan.

Before the next major phase of combat had time to develop, the Japanese government, on January 3, 1938, made overtures for peace through Doctor Oscar Trautmann, the German ambassador to China. Though appointed to his post by the Hitler government, Doctor Trautmann was neither a member of the Nazi party nor a Nazi sympathizer. An intellectual and an intelligent man, he had managed to steer a difficult personal course through the vagaries of his country's politics.

The four Japanese proposals were: that China abandon attitudes favorable to Communism and unfavorable to Japan and that China collaborate with Japan and Manchukuo against Communism; that China agree to the establishment of certain demilitarized zones and accept a special regime (Japanese-controlled) for such areas; that an economic block be formed between China, Japan, and Manchukuo; that China pay necessary indemnities to Japan.

Acceptance of the terms would have ended China's independence as a nation, but the Chinese government did give the proposals some consideration, though no reply was sent to the Japanese government. On January 16, 1938, the Japanese premier, Prince Konoye, answered the Chinese silence with the announcement that "the Japanese government will cease from henceforward to deal with that [Chinese] government, and will look forward to the establishment of a new Chinese regime . . ." Konoye's declaration was the first of many steps in the ensuing years to establish a puppet government in China.

Following Prince Konoye's statement, the Imperial General Headquarters proposed a national mobilization law designed to direct every aspect of Japanese life toward a war economy. After ineffectual opposition by civilian liberals, the law was passed by the Diet in March, 1938. In so doing, Japanese legislators surrendered the last vestiges of their dwindling authority to the military until the final collapse of the empire in 1945.

6

Operations in the Corridor of the Tsinpu Railway between the Yellow and Yangtze Rivers, December 15, 1937, to May 19, 1938

AFTER THE FALL OF NANKING on December 13, 1937, Chiang Kai-shek assumed personal command of all Chinese forces in the field. Since he had constantly interfered with the command prerogatives of his area commanders and other senior generals, this action merely formalized an existing situation in the chain of command. With Chiang's lack of tactical skill and his predilection to play at war as one would at a game of chess—or Chinese checkers—this did not bode well for future operations. At this point, according to the official Chinese history, Chiang envisioned that the next Japanese objective would be an attempt to move westward up the Yangtze River, or to cross the Yellow River at Chengchow "in a dash toward Wuhan"—a dash of 300 miles. Therefore, in order to delay the enemy forces in either or both of these plans, he decided "to lure the main strength of the enemy forces to the areas along the Tsinpu Railway."

Imperial General Headquarters in Tokyo was well aware that its forces in China—now designated as the North China Front Army of nearly 280,000 men and the Central China Expeditionary Force of about 260,000 men—did not have the capability to carry out either of the plans so gratuitously attributed to its staff. The next logical Japanese move was to link up troops on the Yangtze River with those just north of the Yellow River. This

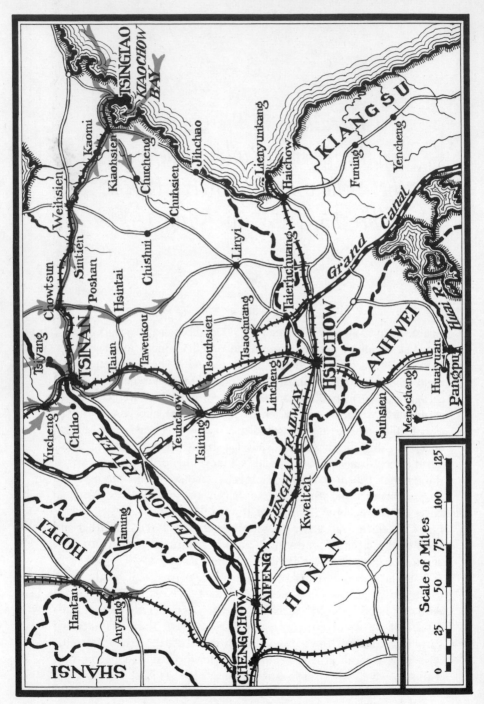

The Loss of Shantung

would eliminate all effective Chinese military opposition in the corridor of the Tsinpu Railway and east to the Yellow Sea.

Chiang Kai-shek's plan to lure the Japanese into an area they obviously intended to seize, either through negotiations with Han Fu-chu or by combat, sounds like an attempt to rationalize the staggering losses in manpower and territory that took place in the next five months. In any case, over 14 divisions were concentrated for the defense of the Hankow area; "powerful forces" (which had just been badly defeated) were deployed just south of Shantung and between the Huai and Yangtze rivers north of Nanking; and reinforcements were sent to southern Shansi and northern Honan to "tie down" the Japanese north of the Yellow River. Since mid-November, as he waited for a firm Japanese commitment to his overtures, Han Fu-chu had maintained two divisions of his 3rd Route Army, now called the 3rd Army Group, on the south banks of the Yellow River just north of Tsinan facing the Japanese 10th Division on the north bank. From trenches and positions dug into the high dikes of the river, the outposts on each side stared at each other across the water for over a month wondering what would happen next.

By mid-December General Nishio's North China Front Army in the northern sector of the Tsinpu Railway had available for further operations to the south five divisions, less one brigade,[1] three separate infantry brigades, and the equivalent in mixed units of about three additional brigades—a total of about 140,000 combat troops. General Hata's Central China Expeditionary Force in the southern sector of the Tsinpu Railway had available for operations north of the Nanking and Yangtze areas two divisions,[2] one separate infantry brigade, and the equivalent of five additional brigades drawn from the 3rd, 11th, 101st, 116th, and 13th divisions—a total of approximately 85,000 troops.

The Chinese 5th War Area under the command of General Li Tsung-jen, which included all territory in the corridor of the Tsinpu Railway between the Yellow and the Yangtze rivers, had available 8 army groups of 30 divisions and 1 pistol brigade, an unusual unit of Han Fu-chu's troops; 4 armies of 12 divisions and 1 cavalry division; 9 corps of 19 divisions; 2 separate divisions; and 5 separate artillery regiments. This imposing force (on paper) of 63 divisions, 1 infantry brigade, 1 cavalry division, and

5 artillery regiments had a strength of nearly 400,000 combatant troops, almost twice the combined strength of the two Japanese armies. It had the additional advantage of operating on interior lines in ostensibly friendly territory. However, it faced the distinct disadvantage of including 80,000 of Han Fu-chu's troops and the possibility of unpredictable actions on his part.

The Loss of Shantung

On December 15, 1937, two days after the fall of Nanking, elements of the Japanese 11th and 13th divisions crossed the Yangtze River at Pukow opposite Nanking and to the east. Against little opposition they occupied Chuhsien, 13 miles to the north on the Tsinpu Railway, and Chiangtu, about 8 miles north of the river. At the time, General Han Fu-chu's 3rd Army Group of five divisions and the pistol brigade and General P'ang Ping-hsun's 3rd Army of one division were ordered to defend key localities along the Yellow River and the Yellow Sea. The only key localities on the sea were Lienyunkang, the eastern terminus of the Lunghai Railway, and Tsingtao in the old German-leased territory of Kiaochow Bay. The Chinese 27th, 11th, and 24th army groups, with a total of nine divisions, were directed to defend Anhwei and Kiangsu provinces east and west of the railway line.

In late November, Mayor Shen Hung-lieh of Tsingtao had received orders from Hankow to destroy his city. On his urgent plea for reconsideration, Chiang Kai-shek had rescinded the order on December 1. Still playing his double game, Han Fu-chu had repeatedly urged Shen to start the work of destruction, claiming that he was in personal communication with the generalissimo. But General Yu Hsueh-chung, commander of the 51st Corps of two divisions, then west of the Tsingtao area, had opposed any action that might cause later drastic retaliation by the Japanese. On December 10 Chiang Kai-shek again changed his mind and ordered the immediate destruction of the city. Again the mayor procrastinated. Finally, after receiving nine messages to destroy the port city, Shen issued orders to begin blowing up all Japanese property in his jurisdiction.

On the same day, December 18, General Yu Hsueh-chung was ordered to withdraw his 51st Corps from the Tsingtao area to the vicinity of Pangpu, about 60 miles north of Nanking on the Huai River. The crossings of the Yangtze River by the Japanese had compelled General Li Tsung-jen, commander of the 5th War Area, to execute an about-face. His former front along the east–west Lunghai Railway had suddenly become the rear of his army, and the front forced to face south. When he learned of Mayor Shen's demolition order, General Yu Hsueh-chung countermanded the directive to move his troops to the new front. His corps remained where it had been at Kaomi, 20 miles west of Tsingtao, despite continued urgent pleas from Han Fu-chu to move south at once. By this time Han had realized that his plans vis-à-vis the Japanese had failed. He wanted to move his own 3rd Army Group to the safety of the south, but as long as the 51st Corps remained in the province, to do so would incur the risk of accusations of cowardice.

Tsingtao, a prosperous port with a population of over 600,000, was unlike any other city in China. German influence had left the permanent stamp of nineteenth-century middle Europe, particularly on the inner harbor. There, ringing a semicircular quay, old-fashioned red-brick buildings with steep gables stood as reminders of a past that saw the fall of an empire and an over-ambitious emperor. Later, Japanese influences had been grafted to the German; then came English and American overtones. Because of two great cash crops of the province (cotton and tobacco), British interests had built cigarette factories and operated large tobacco plantations in the hinterland. The Japanese had constructed enormous walled cotton mills. Great breweries, built by the German overlords, had been confiscated by the Japanese in 1915, but the old brewmasters had remained to ensure a steady flow of excellent beer. The Kiaochow peninsula was encircled by white beaches and was blessed with a climate that drew thousands of foreigners and Chinese to its shores during the summer.

Not long after the outbreak of hostilities, the large Japanese population of Tsingtao had been evacuated to Japan. On December 20 the Japanese cotton mills were destroyed by demolition and fire. On the same day, looting of Japanese shops and business establishments broke out in the city. By this time, all Chinese troops had been withdrawn.

On December 24, at Chowtsun, advance elements of the 51st Corps encountered about 3,000 Japanese-officered irregulars who had crossed the Yellow River between Chingcheng and Tsiyang, 16 miles northeast of Tsinan. 'The Japanese were driven back toward the river. On the same day, Han Fu-chu ordered the destruction of the railway bridge at Weihsien, 65 miles east of Tsinan. Since the bulk of the 51st Corps had not yet entrained, this compelled General Yu Hsueh-chung to march south at once in order to avoid the risk of being cut off and trapped in eastern Shantung. Han had always considered General Yu an interfering outsider who had been sent to the province to block his freedom of action. By destroying the Wei River bridge, Han denied the use of the Tsinpu Railway to the 51st Corps, ensured rapid passage for his own troops from Tsinan to the south, and by forcing the immediate evacuation of eastern Shantung, stole a march on his one rival for military power in the province.

Late that afternoon Han Fu-chu left Tsinan in an armored train for Taian, 30 miles to the south, where he established a temporary headquarters—very temporary, as it proved. In the rush of his departure he did not forget to arrange for the loading of his silver coffin and large sums of cash from the provincial treasury. On the same day the main force of the 51st Corps began the 130-mile march to Hsuchow by way of Chucheng, Linyi, and Taierhchuang.

On December 25 Han's 3rd Army Group headquarters departed Tsinan for Taian; by the next morning its 22nd Division was the only troop unit left in the city, and by evening that, too, had withdrawn to the south. During the day, all communications facilities, except telephone and electric, all government buildings, and most of the Japanese property were destroyed. With the departure of the last troops on the night of December 26, looting broke out on a vast scale. By the next morning a number of warehouses and banks had been burned to the ground.

On the morning of December 26 Mayor Shen of Tsingtao advised all Chinese to leave the city at once, and tens of thousands of residents began to depart. The shuffle of slippers on paved streets and the scratching of straw sandals on gravel roads echoed strangely in the sudden silence, occasionally broken by a pistol or rifle shot and the sharp crackle of flames. Shen also ordered the destruction of all public utilities, the railway station, and all bridges on the Tsingtao-Tsinan railway line. The next day General Ke Kuang-t'ing, chairman of the railway company, departed with the firm's reserve funds amounting to nearly $10 million in his private coffers. Local police, many of whom had already slipped off to the country or had shed their uniforms, were now the only force for the preservation of order in the city; but there was no order—except uniform fear in the minds of those who remained. Like the people of Peking, foreign residents continued to ride in chauffeur-driven cars from one Christmas party to another and plan New Year's Eve parties at the cavernous old German-built Tsingtao Club.

On December 26 troops of the Japanese 10th Division[3] occupied Chowtsun, 30 miles east of Tsinan, without opposition. By this time, the last of the Chinese 51st Corps had departed for the south. The next day about 1,000 Japanese troops entered Tsinan without meeting any resistance. During the following four days the entire 10th and 5th divisions crossed the Yellow River on a temporary wooden bridge erected by Japanese engineer troops beside the wrecked spans of the old steel structure. On December 30 General Nishio, commander of the North China Front Army, arrived to assume command. The 10th Division moved south immediately, and the 5th marched east along the railway toward Chowtsun and Poshan, 10 miles to the south. About 4,000 Japanese troops remained in Tsinan to garrison the city. Troops of the 10th Division clashed with the rear guard of the Chinese 22nd Division 6 miles south of Tsinan. However, the clash was brief as the Chinese were retreating down the railway line as fast as they could move.

Two of Han Fu-chu's division commanders argued for making a stand against the Japanese, but they were overruled. Once before, on November 2, the same pro-Nanking generals, commanders of the 74th and 20th divisions, had got into such a violent argument with the pro-Han commanders of the 81st and 22nd divisions that General Chang Shu-t'ang of the 81st was shot—but not killed.

During the night of December 28 the Tsingtao cable terminals to Japan and Chefoo were cut and the telegraph office destroyed. Tsingtao was now cut off from all communication with the outside world—except by means of the U.S.S. *Marblehead*'s radio. On the following night the newly completed Sino-Japanese main power plant, the arsenal, and the dry-dock installations were blown up, as were all bridges within a radius of 15 miles of the city. Terrified by the all-night explosions, thousands more of the population fled to avoid the expected wrath of the Japanese when they eventually took the doomed city. By the morning of the thirty-first, all police had departed and the city was without organization or control of any kind. Encouraged by the absence of authority, gangs rampaged through the streets smashing shop fronts, looting, and occasionally starting fires. Giving up in the face of the chaotic conditions and trailed by additional thousands of frightened refugees, Mayor Shen departed on January 1. Armed volunteers from the foreign community and about 100 former railway guards patrolled the streets, but they could do little more than prevent the complete sack of the city. Strangely enough, the general appearance of the great port was little changed, beyond occasional fire-blackened shops, ruined mills on the outskirts, and blown-up utility and communications plants. An air of tense expectation of the worst characterized those who remained; Tsingtao was a prostrate city with no means of defense, utterly at the mercy of the conquerors.

By January 2 the last of the Chinese 51st Corps had cleared a point 20 miles south of Weihsien, an important town about 45 miles west of Tsingtao, destroying all road bridges as they passed. On the third, Weihsien civilian authorities blew up all public utilities and began removing both tracks and ties from the railway line for 25 miles east and west of the town. On the same day the Japanese occupied Taian, which had been abandoned by Han Fu-chu's 3rd Army Group. The Chinese high command ordered a new line of resistance at Tawenkou, but General Han had no intention of resisting anything. If he had made a stand, his army of 80,000 troops and some 20,000 militia could have prevented the crossing of the Yellow River by a few thousand Japanese irregulars. Han seemed gripped by terror in the face of the Japanese advance, retaining an almost maniacal urge to keep his army unscathed by combat.

On January 5 a Japanese column moving parallel to the railway from Chowtsun and Poshan marched into Hsintai, 35 miles south of the Tsinan-Tsingtao railway line, then continued its uninterrupted progress toward Linyi, only 30 miles north of the Lunghai Railway defenses. By January 7 Tawenkou and its new line of resistance had been abandoned by Han's fleeing troops; then they fled Tsining and Tsouhsien, each about 25 miles south of Tawenkou and 15 miles apart. As units of the 51st Corps, on the march to Hsuchow, passed through Linyi, they were attacked by local militia and irregulars, or deserters, from Han Fu-chu's militia who were after equipment and arms from what they assumed to be a defeated and demoralized outfit. But Yu Hsueh-chung's troops beat off the attacks and continued their orderly march toward their destination.

On January 6 General Han Fu-chu abandoned his army altogether and flew to Kaifeng, 65 miles west of Hsuchow—still accompanied by the silver coffin and millions in cash. On the same day Mayor Shen of Tsingtao arrived by car at Hsuchow, grimly clutching about $4 million from the city treasury. His motor trip had been interrupted at Chucheng and Linyi by retreating Chinese marines who had tried, but failed, to get the money away from him. General Yu Hsueh-chung finally reached the Lunghai Railway with the bulk of his troops. Thus the three principal military-political figures of Shantung had removed themselves from the scene of their activities—Han because cowardice rendered him unable to face the Japanese; Shen because he feared retaliation by the Japanese for his needless destruction of their property at Tsingtao; Yu because of the acts of the other two.

Moving east from Chowtsun along the Tsinan-Tsingtao rail line, the Japanese 5th Division occupied Sintien on January 7; Weihsien on the tenth; Kaomi, 20 miles west of Tsingtao, on the fourteenth; and Kiaohsien on the west side of Kiaochow Bay (Tsingtao) on January 15. The division had encountered no opposition of any kind on its 80-mile march.

After Han Fu-chu's 3rd Army Group had withdrawn from Tsining and Tsouhsien on the Tsinpu Railway, Chiang Kai-shek ordered two Szechwan divisions and the 22nd Army Group of four divisions to occupy defensive positions just north of both towns and at Lincheng, 10 miles to the south, in order to stop the southward advance of the Japanese. These well-prepared positions had been designed by German advisers under General Hans von Seeckt to hold against attack from the north. The 51st Corps was directed "to respond to the operations of the 3rd Army Group"—a vague and meaningless order since even under a new commander Han Fu-chu's former troops were still in pell-mell retreat from the west bank of the Grand Canal, which ran parallel to and a few miles west of the railway line. General Li Tsung-jen, the overall commander of this sector, knew that if the Tsining-Tsouhsien defenses fell and the Japanese drove toward Kweiteh on the Lunghai Railway, 45 miles west of Hsuchow, the line could be cut and its eastern extension to the port of Lienyunkang seriously endangered. Therefore he ordered the destruction of the harbor works at Lienyunkang and all military installations at Haichow, 15 miles inland. On January 10 the Chinese began to withdraw from their "impregnable" defense positions. On January 12, after five days of intense bombing and artillery fire, the Japanese captured Tsining and forced the two Szechwan divisions to withdraw to the west bank of the Grand Canal. However, the Chinese 22nd Army Group still held its lines just south of Tsouhsien.

Early in January the Japanese 4th Fleet, commanded by Vice-Admiral Toyoda, appeared about 8 miles out at sea off Tsingtao harbor. The arrival of the 29 warships signaled another wild exodus from the city. Each day, as the ships edged closer to land, more refugees fled to the countryside. The foreign community, at last convinced that war threatened even them, patrolled the streets, watched the silent ships, and waited.

On the afternoon of January 8, seven destroyers and mine-sweepers entered the outer harbor, then departed after a brief sojourn and continued to patrol the coastline. That night Chinese gangs attacked the breweries, all of which happened to be situated in the hilly part of the city. The mobs smashed the huge vats of malt, split open hogsheads of beer, and set the buildings afire. Tens of thousands of gallons of malt and beer poured in a sudsy torrent down the sloping streets toward the harbor area. On the ninth, more destroyers, an aircraft carrier and tender, cruisers, and transports entered the outer harbor. Early on the morning of January 10, a market village and an industrial settlement outside the city were bombed. Seven planes flew over the town dropping leaflets in English warning foreigners that the city was about to be occupied and recommending that they seek assured safety at the Edgewater Beach Hotel in case fighting should break out. At the same time, leaflets in Chinese were dropped warning the Chinese to offer no resistance, ordering military forces to repair the docks in the inner harbor and to be prepared to surrender, and directing civilian officials to the Shinto shrine—which had been burned—for the official surrender of Tsingtao to the Japanese naval commander.

At mid-morning about 1,500 Japanese marines with one battery of old 77-millimeter Krupp guns and one company of small infantry cannon landed near Swallow Island, about 15 miles by road northeast of the city. A courageous delegation of British and American businessmen and voluntary police, carrying a white flag, drove out to meet the landing force. They explained to the commander the impossibility of any kind of resistance in Tsingtao—no Chinese troops, no police, and a population reduced from over 600,000 to no more than 50,000—and asked that the city be spared unnecessary destruction. The Japanese commander accepted their word and dispatched a representative to arrange for a formal surrender. At about 1:00 P.M. the landing force reached the outskirts of the city. At 2:35 P.M. the Japanese flag was raised over the municipal administration building. By nightfall, the occupying forces had spread throughout Tsingtao.

By the morning of January 11 the entire 4th Battle Fleet—one battle cruiser, three cruisers, one aircraft carrier and tender, destroyers, and submarines—had anchored in the bay. During the day about 1,500 more marines landed at the inner harbor. More transports arrived on the twelfth, and about 3,000 troops disembarked, immediately moving out to occupy the suburbs. On the thirteenth and fourteenth several thousand additional troops landed at the inner harbor, at the junk harbor, and about 10 miles north on the beach. The occupying force now numbered about 10,000 men. The boom across the inner harbor was cleared and the airfield swept clean of obstacles, and on January 17 the landing forces made a junction with the 5th Division, which had marched along the railway line from Tsinan. Meanwhile, the mayor and the chief of police of Chefoo on the north side of the Shantung peninsula departed that port, leaving it to Chinese mobs and looters. Chefoo was occupied by the Japanese a few days later.

In the late afternoon of January 6 General Han Fu-chu arrived at Kaifeng with only a small personal staff and a few bodyguards. He was visibly shocked at his reception by a low-ranking officer and a company of well-armed troops. Helpless without an army under his command and looking like a beaten giant, Han permitted himself to be taken to living quarters in an official guest house. Once installed within the walled compound, which had immediately been surrounded by troops, he was invited to remain within the premises until orders were received from Hankow. For five days he waited to hear what was in store for him. Finally, on January 11, telegraphic orders arrived. By command of Chiang Kai-shek, Han Fu-chu was to be placed in arrest at once, deprived of all posts and privileges—including his property and the large sums of cash he had with him—and turned over to the jurisdiction of the inspector general for trial at Wuchang on a variety of charges including disobeying the orders of superior commanders and retreating of his own accord, forcing the sale of opium on the people of Shantung, exacting taxes from the people by force, seizing public funds, and depriving the people of Shantung of their firearms.

Han's trial began within a few days. At the beginning, he tried desperately to explain his actions. But in his heart he must have known that there were no acceptable explanations for his cowardly, panicky behavior during the time of grave crisis. As the trial progressed and evidence of his misdeeds accumulated, he gradually lapsed into glum silence. Han was found guilty of repeatedly disobeying orders from his superior commanders and thereby causing the loss of Shantung; of refusing to defend the Yellow River, which caused the loss of Tsinan; of disobeying the order to defend Taian and withdrawing to Yenchow, whence he retreated to Tsining. In addition, he was found guilty of all other charges regarding the forced sale of opium, the exaction of taxes by force, the seizure of public funds, and the taking of firearms from the people. Han Fu-chu stood before his judges on the

Marco Polo Bridge (Lukouchiao) outside of Peking, the scene of the outbreak of Sino-Japanese hostilities on July 7, 1937. The marble balustrades have been damaged and most of the columns removed.

Photograph by the author.

Typical courtyard of north China inn outside of Dolonnor, Jehol province. The car is the one in which the author, Captain Frank Roberts, and James Penfield traveled through Inner Mongolia in April 1935.

From the collection of the author.

Contented, well paid, a Chinese executioner poses with a "big sword" used for beheading condemned malefactors. In July and August, 1937, many of General Sung Che-yuan's 29th Army (Corps) troops were armed with identical "big swords" as their principal weapons.

Entrance to the Palace Hotel, Shanghai, after the Chinese Air Force missed the Japanese battleship *Izuma* and dropped several bombs into Shanghai in August 1937.

National Archives [Domei], Washington, D.C.

Peking, July 31, 1937. A Japanese cavalry unit marching through Tung Tse
Pailou after the fall of Peking.

Shanghai, September 1937. General Iwane Matsui, commander of the Japanese Central China Front Army, inspecting Japanese positions during the Battle of Shanghai.

Chapei District, Shanghai, October 30, 1937. Japanese artillery piece firing into Chinese barricades less than 200 yards to the front in preparation for an infantry assault.

Prince Teh Wang, second from left, and General Li Shou-hsin, the puppet
Mongolian leaders, with Japanese officers at Kueisui, Suiyuan, in October 1937.

General Wei Li-huang, commander of the 14th Army Group and the 1st War Area. During World War II he commanded the Chinese Expeditionary Force in Yunnan province.

General Feng Yu-hsiang, the "Christian general," commander of the Pingham Railway sector, after an inspection of his troops.

The U.S. gunboat *Panay* sunk by Japanese bombing planes in the Yangtze River near Nanking on December 12, 1937.

Bombing of Tientsin on July 30, 1937.

Bombing of the Tientsin Railway station from across the Hai River on July 29, 1937.

Nanking, September 1937. The U.S. gunboat *Luzon*, flagship of the Yangtze Patrol, which later evacuated the American ambassador and his staff to Hankow, and the following year to Chungking.

General view of Tsingtao in 1937, showing the German-built cathedral in the center and smoke stacks of cotton mills in the right distance.

Shansi province, November 1, 1937. Japanese infantry storming Chinese positions near Blue Dragon Ridge.

National Archives [Domei], Washington, D.C.

Taiyuan, Shansi, November 8, 1937. Japanese troops scaling the city wall of Taiyuan in the final assault.

night of January 23 to hear General Ho Ying-chin, the minister of war and chief of the general staff, solemnly pronounce the death sentence, because of the "extreme gravity of his crimes." Erect and dignified now, Han heard himself condemned to be shot at seven o'clock the following evening. There would be no appeal. Han was at once led from the courtroom to a cell in the military prison at Wuchang.

Shortly before seven on the evening of January 24, Han Fu-chu, the deposed governor of Shantung, former commander of an army of nearly 100,000 men, and one of the last of the warlords, marched firmly down the stone corridor to a small courtyard against one wall of which a thick post had been implanted. Having been deprived of all rank, he wore the long dark gown and black skullcap of a Chinese gentleman. Under a cold drizzle he was roped to the post by nervous soldiers. For an instant, as he glanced down at his silver coffin on the ground beside him, a fleeting smile lit up his worn face. Then he raised his eyes, refused a blindfold, and stared straight ahead at the waiting firing squad. An officer barked a command and the squad snapped to attention. Another command and the men raised their rifles to aim at the tall figure only 10 paces before them in the deepening dusk. At seven o'clock sharp the officer raised his arm and with the order to fire let it drop. Eight rifles cracked in the rainy night. The lifeless body of Han Fu-chu slumped grotesquely against the post. The officer stepped forward, pressed the muzzle of his Luger pistol against the dead man's temple, and fired the coup de grace to be certain he had carried out the execution.

The soldiers shuffled off in silence. Four shivering coolies slipped into the dripping courtyard and placed the remains of the once-powerful man in his last and only possession, the silver coffin. Groaning under its weight, they placed it on a two-wheeled cart and trundled it off to an unmarked and unhonored grave.

Han Fu-chu had lost his life, and China had lost his province of Shantung. The loss of both ended my usefulness as an observer between the Yellow River and the Lunghai Railway; so I was ordered back to Peking to await the next assignment in the interior.

The Battle of Taierhchuang

In the latter part of January, 1938, the Japanese were advancing in three columns down the corridor of the Tsinpu Railway in southern Shantung: the first south from Tsining toward Kweiteh and Liupo in northern Honan; the second south from Tsouhsien along the railway line; the third from the vicinity of Linyi south toward Taierhchuang and southeast toward Haichow. On the Yangtze River front the Japanese 13th Division was moving north along the railway in the vicinity of Chuhsien, 14 miles north of the river.

On January 25th, the Japanese attacked the Chinese 31st, 7th and 48th Corps, which had occupied prepared positions at Mingkuang and Chiho, about 30 miles north of the Yangtze. One Japanese column captured Chiho on the 30th and Tingyuan on February 1st. Pressing north on the railway, the second enemy column took Mingkuang, Linhuaikuan, Fengyang, and Pangpu on successive days. On February 9 the Japanese crossed the Huai River at Pangpu and against little opposition took Huaiyuan on the north bank. In addition, the Japanese 11th Division, marching in two parallel columns, cleaned up the area 30 to 50 miles east of the railway for a distance of 75 miles north of the Yangtze. The 11th Division met no opposition of any kind, the relatively few troops and local militia in the area having faded away at the enemy approach. The aggressive action of two Japanese divisions against nine Chinese divisions that failed to put up a fight (except at Mingkuang and Chiho) placed the enemy on the Huai River, roughly parallel to and 65 miles north of the Yangtze. Thus the gap between the North China Front Army and the Central China Expeditionary Force was narrowed to a mere 75 miles—a serious situation that threatened to pinch off the entire Chinese 5th War Area.

Clearly it was again time for Chiang Kai-shek to get out his chessboard and shift around his armies, corps, and divisions. He rose to the occasion, of course, with detailed instructions. "In order to consolidate the defense of Hsuchow, lure the enemy's main forces to the Tsinpu Railway [where they already were] and gain time to achieve combat readiness for Wuhan," nearly

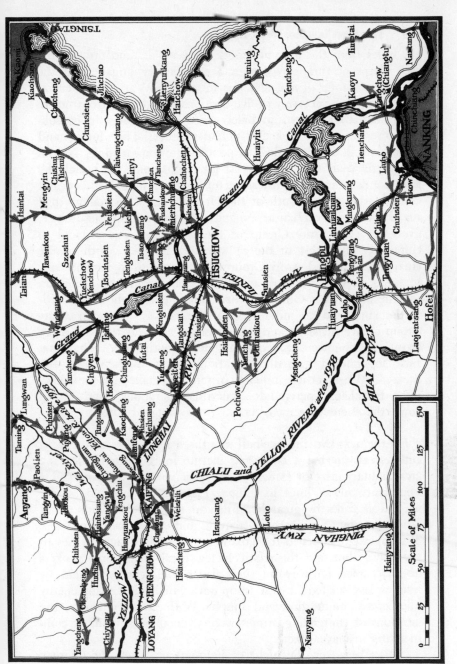

The Battle of Taierhchuang; The Battle for Hsuchow; Operations in East and North Honan to June 1938

250 miles from the fighting front, the generalissimo ordered the 59th Corps of three divisions and one cavalry brigade and the 21st Army Group of five divisions to the 5th War Area. General T'ang En-po's 20th Army of five divisions was shifted from northern Honan to Kweiteh, 40 miles west of Hsuchow, "to consolidate the rear area" of the defense forces. This luring and consolidating was intended to permit the commanding general of the 5th War Area to "readjust his dispositions," to attack the Japanese flank in the southern sector of the Tsinpu Railway, and to "hold the enemy south of the Huai River." (The enemy had already crossed the Huai at Pangpu.) To accomplish these objectives, the 11th Army Group of three divisions was ordered to Hofei, 45 miles west of the railway and 25 miles south of the Huai River; the 21st Army Group of five divisions to Laojentsang, 20 miles west of the railway and 35 miles south of the river; and the 26th Army Group of three divisions to Loho, just north of the Huai and 20 miles west of the railway. The 3rd Army Group of five divisions and the pistol brigade and the 3rd Army of one division were directed to defend southwestern Shantung and "to conduct guerrilla operations so as to tie down the enemy." When other military inspirations failed to emanate, those two hardy perennials, "guerrilla operations" and "tying down the enemy" seemed certain to be dragged forth.

For the next two and one-half months, a series of seesaw attacks and retreats created a confusing picture in the struggle for the great military prize of Hsuchow, the junction of two of the most important railway lines in China. Fighting on both sides was marked at times by great heroism and sacrifice, by boldness; at other times by no more than "alarums and excursions." Since lack of manpower compelled the Japanese to confine their activities to the railway line and the relatively few good roads, large pockets of unoccupied territory on their flanks and rear were held by more or less isolated Chinese troop units capable of cutting enemy lines of communication and supply. With no fixed fronts, the locations of contending armies were likened by a Chinese commentator to a layer cake.

Action began on the night of February 12 when the Chinese 3rd Army Group launched an attack from west of the Grand

Canal to recapture Tsining and Wenchang, 50 and 65 miles north of Hsuchow. Taken by surprise, the Japanese were forced to yield a part of the town of Tsining to the Chinese 22nd Division. Then, strengthened by reinforcements that were rushed to the scene, the Japanese counterattacked and drove the Chinese back to their jump-off lines east of Chuyen, 8 miles west of the canal. On February 14 the Chinese 22nd Army Group of four divisions, which had been isolated east of the railway line, made an abortive attack—actually no more than a feint—on Tsouhsien, 40 miles north of Hsuchow. On the 26th, the Chinese 39th Division, reinforced by Tsingtao marines, moved against the thinly held Hsintai-Szeshui-Mengyin area about 20 miles east of the railway. In effect, a large-scale guerrilla operation, this attack resulted in the temporary recovery of Mengyin.

In the southern sector, the Chinese 51st Corps of two divisions, after suffering 4,000 casualties, was forced to retreat from Huaiyuan just north of the Huai River on February 9. The 59th Corps of three divisions was ordered to "race to the scene" and to force the Japanese back to the south bank. At the same time, the 7th and 31st Corps, totaling six divisions, were ordered to attack the Japanese at Tingyuan, 17 miles south of the Huai River, in order to compel the Japanese 13th Division to pull back to protect its threatened flank. By February 15 the Japanese had beaten off the halfhearted Chinese attacks and had been able to maintain their positions as they had been on February 9. From that time until early May the southern sector of the Tsinpu Railway remained relatively quiet.

By late February, two columns of the Japanese 5th Division, marching southwest from the Tsinan-Tsingtao railway line toward Linyi, had taken Mengyin, Yishui, Chuhsien, and Jihchao on the coast in a 40-mile sweep. General P'ang Ping-hsun's 39th Division offered "piecemeal resistance"—rear-guard action while the main body retreated—and occupied prepared positions northeast of Linyi to make a stand. General Chang Tse-chung's 59th Corps of two divisions[4] was ordered to Linyi to join the 39th Division at the defense positions.

The ensuing action can best be described by quoting Colonel Stilwell's brief account from the battle area:

The japs moved down from Chucheng, strength about 10,000, and on March 14th struck P'ang Ping-hsun's 40th Corps [the 39th Division] about 8 miles north of the city [Linyi]. The 39th was deployed along a north-south line, and the jap attack made progress against P'ang's right center. By night of the 14th, they had made a dent in P'ang, but he held out. The next day, Chang Tse-chung's 59th Corps arrived. He had been north of Pangpu along the Huai on the right of Yu's [Yu Hsueh-chung] 51st Corps, and had been sent direct to Linyi. Chang took over the left of P'ang's line, put in the 38th and 180th [Divisions] in order from north to south, and the jap attack was stopped. Fighting continued on [March] 16th and 17th, by which time the japs had been driven back and the left of their line bent east and west. On the 18th of March, they had had enough and withdrew to the northeast. Chang Tse-chung was ordered to march his troops to Feihsien. [about 15 miles northwest of Linyi.]

The Chinese official history states that the five-day battle "broke the back of a [Japanese] brigade . . . killing more than half of its men . . . and our forces followed up with a pursuit which led to still greater achievements." Both claims bordered on the fictional, as so often happened in the heroics of Chinese nationalistic "histories." There was no pursuit of any kind. If there had been, with all three Chinese divisions participating, they might indeed have "broken the back" of a Japanese brigade. In beating off the enemy attack, the Chinese won the fight and inflicted severe casualties on the invaders. But they, too, suffered heavy casualties, and the 39th Division alone was in no condition to follow up the battle with a pursuit.

After spending a week refitting, on March 23 the Japanese again approached Linyi. Stilwell's account of the operation continues:

He [Chang Tse-chung of the 59th Corps] started off and had gotten well on his way [to Feihsien] when the japs returned to the attack. P'ang sent him a hurry call to get back, and he started at once. But the japs struck P'ang on March 24th, the day before he arrived. P'ang held on, and the next day when Chang arrived, he was in time to prevent the japs from getting around P'ang's left flank. The Chinese line ran roughly north and south with the 180th on the left, then the 38th, and then the 39th. After Chang formed line with P'ang, the japs continued their movements around the left flank, attacking from the north and northeast. The fight went on from March 24th·to March 28th, by which time the Chinese were in an east-west line at the southern limits of the city [Linyi]—the 39th outside on the east, the 38th and 180th outside on the west.

The Chinese fought stubbornly in front of Linyi, but their three half-strength and poorly equipped divisions could not withstand the constant assaults and artillery fire of the Japanese 5th Division. On March 25 and 26 enemy attacks against the Chinese left gradually forced the north–south line to rotate from the right, pivoting on the 39th Division, which held its ground, to an east–west position north of Linyi. On the twenty-seventh, Chinese began to give way all along the line, but they did not break. By March 28 they had been forced back to the southern edge of Linyi, and the Japanese attacks began to die down. Each side suffered heavy casualties, frequent hand-to-hand fighting taking a heavy toll of lives. As the guns fell silent on the night of March 28 and a blanket of darkness dropped over the smoking debris of the battlefield, the scarred earth between the original Chinese positions and Linyi was littered with dead and wounded, the sudden quiet broken only by pleading calls for water and aid.

Along the railway line the Japanese 10th Division, with a large number of tanks and armored vehicles attached, had been concentrating in the Tsouhsien area since early March. With two enemy divisions within 60 miles north of Hsuchow, Chiang Kai-shek ordered General T'ang En-po's 20th Army of five divisions from Kweiteh to the Hsuchow area. He also directed the 3rd Army Group of five divisions to move toward Yenchow on the railway east of Tsining "in a flank attack responding to operations" and General Sun Lien-chung's 2nd Army Group of four divisions to move from southern Shansi by rail to Hsuchow.

On March 14 the 10th Division took Chieh-ho just south of Tsouhsien; on the fifteenth it attacked the Chinese 122nd Division at Tenghsien, 30 miles north of Hsuchow. On the sixteenth, advance elements of the Chinese 85th Corps[5] reached the Lincheng area, 6 miles south of Tenghsien. Supported by planes, tanks, and heavy artillery, the Japanese captured Tenghsien on March 17 and broke into the Chinese positions at Lincheng on the eighteenth. General T'ang directed his 52nd Corps to deploy along the Grand Canal in the vicinity of Hanchuang and his 85th Corps at Yihsien on the railway—both towns about 15 miles north of Hsuchow.

On March 18 the Japanese 10th Division pressed on to occupy Hanchuang and to attack Yihsien. In the stubborn 24-hour battle through the town's streets and alleys, every officer and enlisted man of the Chinese 23rd Regiment, 4th Division, 85th Corps, was either killed or wounded. With the defense now wiped out, the Japanese stormed past Yihsien toward Taierhchuang.

Taierhchuang was a walled town of narrow streets and alleys covering an area about one mile long and one-half mile wide. Many of its one-story houses and shops had been built of local stone, rather than the usual mud bricks and plaster. The Grand Canal, about 50 yards wide and unfordable, ran past the town walls, as did a branch railway from Yihsien that connected with the Lunghai line to the south. Taierhchuang was surrounded by a flat plain dotted with low, rocky hills almost devoid of vegetation. Many of the houses on the wheat-growing farmlands and in the adjacent hamlets were also built of the plentiful local stone.

After blocking the Japanese 5th Division column at Linyi, the Chinese 5th War Area command decided to follow the German advisers' plan to draw the enemy from Yihsien toward Taierhchuang and attack with a double envelopment. General T'ang En-po's 20th Army, less the 110th Division, was then in position east of Yihsien and Tsaochang, about 12 miles north of Taierhchuang. General Sun Lien-chung's 2nd Army Group was moving toward the selected battle area. Its leading division, the 31st, commanded by General Ch'ih Feng-ch'eng, reached Taierhchuang on March 22. The division had a strength of about 9,000 men. General Ch'ih was ordered to carry out the initial phases of the plan, pending the arrival and deployment of the main body of the 2nd Army Group.

Leaving one brigade at Taierhchuang, General Ch'ih led the other to the vicinity of Yihsien on March 23. The Japanese reacted to this demonstration of force by dispatching a battalion reinforced by three tanks and four armored cars to drive off the Chinese. Since General Ch'ih refused to budge, the Japanese force was strengthened by a second battalion. At this, the Chinese took up positions on a nearby hillock where they waited until the Japanese had slipped around to attack from the rear. General Ch'ih then ordered one battalion to leave the hill positions and to remain concealed about one mile to the south. When the Japanese attacked what they thought was the Chinese rear, the detached battalion struck at the Japanese flank and rear. Caught by surprise, the Japanese withdrew to the northwest. By late afternoon, the strength of the Japanese force had been increased to a reinforced regiment of about 3,000 men; during the night it was further increased to about 5,000 men.

At dawn on March 24 the Japanese attacked the Chinese brigade's right flank, which deliberately fell back to let them pass. By 7:00 A.M., when the momentum of the assault had swept past the Chinese positions, General Ch'ih shifted the direction of his force to the east and attacked the enemy flank, but at 4:00 P.M. a new Japanese unit from Yihsien compelled him to fall back on Taierhchuang. Enemy attacks continued without letup until 8:00 P.M., when a Japanese unit broke into the town through the north gate. The 2nd Brigade of the Chinese 31st Division drove them out after a one-hour hand-to-hand fight.

On March 24, accompanied by deputy chief of staff Pai Ch'ung-hsi, Chiang Kai-shek arrived at Hsuchow—his first visit to any fighting front—to direct operations. Though formerly a sound tactician, Pai Ch'ung-hsi had sold himself on the theory of protracted defense to defeat the Japanese. He had even stated that China could afford to lose as many as 50,000,000 men in the process of wearing down the enemy—an attitude that nullified individual initiative and vetoed offensive action. However, both Chiang and Pai, by their presence 25 miles from Taierhchuang, could and later did claim credit for the action of the next two weeks.

During the night of the twenty-fourth General Ch'ih's troops kept up steady rifle and machine-gun fire to deprive the Japanese of sleep; by dawn the next day the east–west line occupied by his 31st Division ran just north of the walls of Taierhchuang. The Japanese attacked at 6:00 A.M., but within an hour were repulsed. For the rest of the day the Chinese positions were bombarded by artillery fire and aerial bombs.

After the Japanese morning attack had been stopped, General

Ch'ih reconnoitered toward Yihsien in an armored train. As he proceeded northward he passed a small column of Japanese marching to the rear. Since they were over 500 yards to his flank, he continued on to the next hamlet where he stopped the train and waited. When the weary enemy troops appeared, he opened fire and killed or wounded about 70 of them. Half of the remainder fled in panic to the northeast; the others rallied behind the stone walls of the village. After a brief exchange of fire, Ch'ih ordered the train to return to Taierhchuang.

That night, the twenty-fifth, about 3,000 troops of the Chinese 31st Division launched an attack against the Japanese. By 4:00 A.M. on the twenty-sixth the enemy lines had begun to crumble; before daylight the Japanese withdrew to the northeast. Late that afternoon the Chinese 27th Division[6] arrived. One of its brigades took up positions on the right of the Chinese line east of Taierhchuang; the other was placed in reserve south of the Grand Canal. Early on March 27 the Japanese attacked in full force, but the Chinese held their ground against one assault after another. At 1:00 P.M. a brigade of the Chinese 27th Division attacked the Japanese east flank; by 3:00 P.M. the end of the Japanese line had folded back on the center. The severe all-day fight ended abruptly, leaving several thousand casualties strewn over the bloody battlefield.

During the next few days of continual fighting, most of the Japanese 10th Division moved into the lines at Taierhchuang. Their daybreak attack on the twenth-eighth was repulsed by 7:00 A.M.; however, at 8:00 P.M. other Japanese elements managed to break into the town. They were driven out by 10:00 P.M. At dawn on the twenty-ninth the Japanese again attacked, were again repulsed, and were forced to resort to artillery and air bombardments. During the day, the Chinese 30th Division of Sun Lienchung's 2nd Army Group arrived and was assigned the left flank of the line west of Taierhchuang. Late that afternoon the first Chinese artillery units also arrived—two 150-millimeter and ten 75-millimeter guns. At 7:00 P.M. the Japanese succeeded in breaking into the town again. A house-to-house battle through the streets and alleys continued throughout the night.

On March 30 severe fighting inside the walls of Taierhchuang raged from daylight to dark, at which time the Chinese still held more than half the town. Japanese artillery and air superiority were useless in this congested melee; when either was employed, as many Japanese were killed as Chinese. Tearing each other apart in the savage street fighting, each side was compelled to rely on rifles, pistols, hand grenades, bayonets, and knives.

On March 31 General Sun Lien-chung arrived to take direct command of his 2nd Army Group; that same day the Japanese attacked again. The Chinese stood fast, but a midday counterattack by the Chinese was stopped dead in its tracks. Another Japanese assault at 4:00 A.M. on April 1 was supported by 11 tanks. Eight armored vehicles were either set afire or knocked out of action at point-blank range by Chinese 37-millimeter antitank guns.

Meanwhile, as Japanese attention was held by the struggle in and around Taierhchuang, the far more comprehensive German plan had been developing to the north of the intense battle area. On March 26 T'ang En-po's 20th Army launched a determined attack against Japanese forces in Yihsien and Tsaochang in an attempt to cut off their rear. His aggressive action paid off: over half the Japanese in the two towns were killed and the others driven off. Then T'ang abruptly shifted the main strength of his army to attack the enemy flank northeast of Taierhchuang. With this move, General Isogai's 10th Division suddenly found itself pinched between the Chinese 2nd Army Group and the 20th Army on the eastern half of the Taierhchuang defense line. By April 2 the main force of the Japanese 10th Division was threatened with complete encirclement and no means of resupply. At the same time, the Chinese 55th Corps of two divisions made a surprise crossing of a lake that formed part of the Grand Canal and cut the railway north of Lincheng.

At Linyi, 30 miles to the northeast, the Japanese 5th Division made a wide envelopment of the Chinese lines, captured Chuchen to the southwest, and dispatched a full brigade toward Taierhchuang to relieve the beleaguered 10th Division. On April 1 the Japanese brigade passed through Aichu and continued on its forced march to the southwest. General T'ang at once rushed a strong unit to block the direct road to Taierhchuang, then sent one division to force the Japanese brigade to the southeast toward Chahochen, a few miles east of Taierhchuang. This rapid move prevented the 5th Division troops from attacking the rear of the Chinese 20th Army and drove them into the same entrapped situation in which the 10th Division already found itself. The Chinese 52nd Corps of T'ang's 20th Army, the 75th Corps, and the 39th Division were now deployed east and northeast of Taierhchuang to block any possibility of a Japanese escape in that direction.

At this point the main strength of the Japanese 10th Division and one brigade of the 5th Division, plus attached troops, were more or less bottled up and sandwiched between seven Chinese divisions to the north of their positions and four to the south. The near-encirclement was commanded by two determined, highly resourceful Chinese generals, T'ang En-po (later described by the Japanese as one of Chiang Kai-shek's most capable and reliable generals) and Sun Lien-chung, who had wisely placed much confidence and responsibility in the hands of his 31st Division commander, 34-year-old General Ch'ih Feng-ch'eng.

On the night of April 3, in a desperate effort to force the Chinese defenders out of the town, the Japanese used tear gas in the east section of Taierhchuang, but without serious effect. They threw 30 tanks and 60 armored cars into the fight outside the walls, only achieving a temporary minor success in forcing the Chinese 27th Division back to the Grand Canal. The struggle on the fourth, fifth, and sixth was largely confined to the town and its immediate environs. By this time, both sides had almost reached exhaustion after 10 days of unceasing combat, and the Japanese were facing hunger and thirst as well. Neither Chinese nor Japanese any longer had the physical endurance to launch a large-scale decisive attack. On April 5, when the Japanese realized that two fresh Chinese divisions, the 21st and 110th, had moved in from the southwest and northwest, their will to fight broke completely.

But worn out as the Chinese were, when they saw that they held the Japanese in a vicelike grip and that their enemies were now facing a rapidly diminishing supply of ammunition, fuel for armored vehicles, and food and water, they were seized with wild enthusiasm. Men of the 20th Army and the 2nd Army Group rushed forward to the attack with renewed vigor. Japanese attempts at air drops failed; most of the packages fell behind

Chinese lines. The 2nd Army Group attacked from the south. Slowly the Japanese perimeter collapsed. The dead and wounded and their equipment lay sprawled over the battle-torn wheat fields. Gradually the roar of Japanese artillery was silenced for lack of ammunition. Without fuel, their tanks ground to a halt. Japanese infantry units were reduced to dependence on machine-gun and mortar fire, then only rifle and pistol fire, finally last-ditch bayonet charges to fight for their lives. Tasting victory at last, the Chinese showed no mercy as they mowed down the trapped enemy troops.

Early on the morning of April 7 nearly 2,000 exhausted, bearded, hollow-eyed Japanese dragged themselves through the breaches and over the rubble of their last defense post, the broken walls of Taierhchuang; before nightfall the ruined, burning town had been completely evacuated, except for the unburied dead. During that night the half-starved remnants of General Isogai's 10th Division and General Itagaki's 5th Division brigade fought their way through the narrow corridor in the Chinese encirclement and fled to the north and northeast. Before daylight, except for the occasional bark of a rifle or pistol administering a coup de grace to wounded Japanese, the battlefield that had been Taierhchuang lay silent under a black sky. For the first time since their attempted invasions of Korea under Hideyoshi had been disastrously repulsed in 1592–98, the Japanese had been forced to swallow the bitter pill of a major defeat at the hands of a despised opponent.

On April 8 the first gray light of dawn revealed a strange and eerie sight to the victorious Chinese armies—one they had never seen before. The grotesquely sprawled corpses of 16,000 Japanese soldiers lay where they had fallen in the churned-up wheat fields and among the collapsed stone walls of ruined farmhouses. Forty tanks, over 70 armored cars, and 100 trucks of various sizes dotted the flat, sandy earth, stalled where they had run out of fuel. Dozens of artillery pieces, their muzzles pointing every which way, lay scattered about. Thousands of machine guns and rifles, as if blown like chaff in a fitful wind, rested silently beside their silent owners.

Led by three bold, resourceful commanders, the scorned Chinese soldier had won a great victory over a superior enemy. But he had paid for it with the lives of over 15,000 of his own companions in arms and at least that many wounded. When General Ch'ih Feng-ch'eng mustered the remnants of his heroic 31st Division, only 2,000 of the original 9,000 stumbled wearily into line to answer the roll call.

But, like General Meade after his victory at Gettysburg, the Chinese failed to exploit their success and thus reap the full rewards that come with the decisive defeat of an enemy. They pursued the fleeing Japanese no farther than Yihsien, Tsaochang, Fushankou, and Hsiangcheng, less than 15 miles to the north and northeast of Taierhchuang. Had they pushed farther, they might have wiped out the Japanese division entirely.

The Battle for Hsuchow and the Loss of All East China North of the Yangtze River

After the battle of Taierhchuang, the National Military Council sat back in self-congratulatory euphoria to take credit for the victory. They used the short lull that followed the battle to "assess the overall situation": the Japanese were overextended and required large garrison forces as well as attack units, which would "take some time" to bring from Japan and Manchuria. Since the Japanese lacked the capability to move up the Yangtze River for an attack on Hankow, the assessment ran, a converging attack on Hsuchow could be expected in the near future. This last conclusion ignored the obvious fact that the capture of Hsuchow had been the Japanese objective since the middle of the previous December.

In addition, the members of the National Military Council decided that "having become greatly exhausted from prolonged fighting, the 5th War Area could not sustain much longer. As the situation was unfavorable, it was difficult to withdraw. The plains in eastern Honan and Anhwei lacked critical terrain for defense. In spring, as the Yellow River lacked water, there was no possibility of floods . . . [If] the enemy forces in north China and central China link up . . . the main strength of our forces would be defeated in detail." In other words, the groundwork was being laid for retreat before battle was joined.

Chiang now prepared for the withdrawal of a large intact army by shifting five corps, the 8th, 27th, 71st, 74th and 64th, consisting of ten "elite" divisions, to eastern Honan, Lanfeng and Kweiteh on the Lunghai Railway "to consolidate the rear of the 5th War Area." Committed to areas 50 to 75 miles west of Hsuchow, the five corps were placed well away from the expected scene of battle. In addition, General Lin Wei of the Board of Military Operations led a staff corps to Hsuchow to exercise supervision. However, his effect was limited by an express injunction from Chiang Kai-shek that the reinforcements of ten divisions were not to be committed to areas east of Hsuchow. Lin Wei was a staff man, not a combat leader, so even if he had been given a completely free hand, it is doubtful if Lin Wei could have turned the course of events.

Hsuchow, the strategic objective of the North China Front Army and the Central China Expeditionary Force, was an ancient trading center with a population of about 150,000 located on an offshoot of the Grand Canal. It had become vastly more important in modern times as a crossroads city at the junction of the north–south Tsinpu Railway and the east–west Lunghai Railway. As a transshipment point from both the Yellow and Yangtze river valleys to the north and south, it had direct connections with Lanchow, some 700 miles to the west, and with Haichow and the new port of Lienyunkang, 70 and 80 miles to the east. A bustling railway town, it boasted no distinction—despite its antiquity—save the most extensive cemeteries in China. The low gravelly hills and plains that encircled the city were covered with conical earthen grave markers for as far as the eye could see. The ancient stone roads running through this desolate waste were interspersed with countless stone *pailous* (arches erected as honorific memorials to distinguished citizens and virtuous widows). This sprawling semi-desert, unmarked by green fields or cultivated farms, was the last resting place for millions from bygone centuries. But the filthy streets of the city, which because of its location had been destroyed and rebuilt dozens of times, were full of life and activity, of dusty winds and hoarse, cracked voices. As a meetingplace of the north and south, Hsuchow was one of the few large cities in China where one might at the same time encounter a camel train from Peking and water buffalo from the Yangtze Valley. As in a seaport on main traffic routes—though 80 miles inland—its venereal disease rate, mostly syphilis, was among the highest in China. Missionary schools and hospitals had fought a long and losing battle against diseases that had been endemic for centuries.

Almost equally ancient, the slowly dying port of Haichow on the Shu River 70 miles to the east was even filthier. Here the only future was gradual disintegration because of the nearby port of Lienyunkang. Cramped within its stone walls, the population of Haichow was not only ridden with syphilis, but also—according to missionary doctors—was 65 percent infected with the eye disease trachoma. In startling contrast, Lienyunkang was a completely new city that had been built on high hills descending in rolling terraces to a magnificent harbor. The anchorage for ships was protected by 2-mile-long breakwaters and three towering islands a few miles offshore.

These two transportation centers, ancient and modern, and their railways were now the objectives of the Japanese army.

On April 15 the reequipped and reinforced Japanese 5th Division renewed the attack at Linyi with considerable vigor. A Chinese attempt to counterattack toward Chuchen, 25 miles to the northeast, was repulsed with heavy losses. The Chinese 92nd Corps of two divisions from southern Shansi was isolated by the Japanese before it was able to move into position to assist P'ang Ping-hsun's 39th Division. On the seventeenth the Chinese abandoned the town of Linyi. On the nineteenth, all resistance broke down completely; the 39th Division withdrew in considerable haste to Tancheng, 8 miles due south; the 38th and 180th divisions of the 59th Corps to the southwest beyond Matouchen on the west side of the I River about 12 miles from Linyi. On April 24, continuing to hammer at the retreating Chinese, the Japanese took Tancheng. At this point the 39th Division, having suffered heavy casualties during more than six weeks of almost daily combat, was withdrawn to the rear area. Chang Tse-chung then turned his 59th Corps to the southeast, recrossed the I River, and ran into the flank of the Japanese who were following up their success at Linyi. In the ensuing action at Taiwangchuang on April 26, General Chang's corps was roughly handled and forced to withdraw to the southwest. The Japanese continued a few miles farther to the south to a group of villages they occupied on April 27—Peilaokao, Fengchiayao, Peihsieh, Fangtsung-chuang, and Chiehchuang. On the same day General Fan Tsung-pu's 46th Corps of three divisions[7] arrived at the area of the villages from the south. General Fan's corps had come from Tungkuan at the great bend of the Yellow River about 250 miles to the west. His 28th and 92nd divisions closed in on the Japanese perimeter around the villages and attacked at once. That morning, General Chang Tse-chung's 59th Corps reversed its march to the southwest and attacked the enemy from the west.

The action that followed was described by Colonel Stilwell:

The japs attacked Fan [46th Corps] on April 28th and 29th without success. He and Chang [59th Corps] put on pressure and severe fighting took place at Peilaokao and Chiehchuang. The japs were cut off and were soon without food which their planes endeavored to deliver to them. But uncertainty as to their location resulted in most of the food being dropped behind Chinese lines. Sharp fighting continued up to May 5th, by which time the Chinese had taken Peilaokao and part of Chiehchuang. On this day a relief column of japs started south from Matouchen, but Fan had sent the 49th Division to block them off, and he had also sent some artillery to help. The 49th stopped the column, and on May 7th, the Chinese retook the remaining villages and liquidated the entire jap force there.

A footnote to Stilwell's account added: "Fan Tsung-pu is a rough-neck. Don't know what his losses have been. He's a good drinker." Chang Tse-chung was not only a burly roughneck, he was also a terrific fighter.

Meanwhile, the Chinese 60th Corps of three divisions had arrived in the Hsuchow-Taierhchuang area from Wuhan; the 69th Corps of two divisions from southern Hopei had reached a point east of Tancheng for an attack on the Japanese flank and rear at Linyi; and the 68th Corps of two divisions had moved from Hotseh just south of the Yellow River to Chinhsiang preparatory to an attack across the Grand Canal on the Tsinpu Railway north of Hsuchow. The attack fizzled out with no effect on the general situation. At the same time, General Shang Chen's 32nd Corps of two divisions and the 23rd Division were ordered to the Lanfeng-Hotseh area to prevent a possible Japanese attempt to cross the Yellow River in western Shantung.

After the victory at Taierhchuang, T'ang En-po's 20th Army of four divisions[8] moved north to establish defensive positions at Fushankou, about 15 miles east of the line of the Tsinpu Railway. On April 14 the Japanese attacked General T'ang's positions from the north and northwest. On the following three days the 20th Army stood its ground and fought off all Japanese assaults. But on the eighteenth enemy reinforcements from the Linyi area attacked the eastern end of the Chinese lines, thus threatening a complete envelopment and forcing T'ang to withdraw his four divisions to the southeast toward Peihsien, 8 miles east of Taierhchuang. The Japanese followed close behind the retreating Chinese column and reached the vicinity of Peihsien on April 20. At this point General T'ang turned to fight, and his troops stood fast. Colonel Stilwell's letter on the action that followed stated:

With the 4th, 25th and 2nd [divisions] in line from west to east, the fighting was confined to efforts by either side to capture this or that small village. The soil is very sandy, and the japs have not been able to use their tanks. The Chinese have refrained from digging trenches, and the jap aviation had great trouble in locating their positions. Besides the lack of definite targets, the jap artillery has no good observation—the hills all being in Chinese hands.

A typical example of this fighting was the jap attack on Lienfeng-shan, a village northwest of Peihsien. The garrison was one small battalion which was attacked by the japs as soon as it occupied the village on April 20th. On the 21st, two more battalions were sent in, but the Chinese strength even then was only 600 men. The japs were held off for four days, but approached gradually by rushes and by digging in as they advanced. On April 24th, [the Japanese] got a foothold inside the town. The garrison held on even after the japs attempted to get in from the east and south. Fighting continued until April 30th, when one hundred men of the Chinese garrison were all that was left. The jap attacks then stopped, with the Chinese still holding the western part of the village. Similar actions have been taking place all along T'ang's front. Villages change hands time and again, but neither side makes any material progress. Much of the fighting is hand to hand—with bayonets and grenades. Casualties on both sides have been very heavy.

One by one the villages were destroyed, the terrified peasants and farmers either killed or driven from their ancestral homes.

Meanwhile, General Yu Hsueh-chung's 51st Corps of two divisions was ordered from the Huai River front to the Taierhchuang area. Arriving on April 19, Yu's corps continued to the north and almost at once ran into the right flank of the Japanese column then following T'ang En-po's 20th Army toward Peihsien. A sharp fight took place, and General Yu's 113th and 114th divisions were pushed back for a distance of about one mile.

By May 8, after daily fighting by forward units and constant marches and countermarches by reserve, rear area, and "tying down" troops, the Chinese had established a 15-mile east–west defense line centered just north of Peihsien, 12 miles east of Taierhchuang. Nine Chinese corps consisting of 19 divisions (about 125,000 men) faced three Japanese divisions with a strength of about 50,000 men who were heavily supported by air, artillery, and armor. The more capable and aggressive Chinese commanders on the line—Yu Hsueh-chung, T'ang En-po, Chang Tse-chung, and Fan Tsung-pu—were now joined by General Liu Ju-ming, "that son of a bitch at Kalgan," who had escaped a justified execution by a political miracle, and General Lu Han of the 60th Corps, a highly efficient commander who six years later was to be closely associated with the American command in Yunnan province, and who with American planning and support was to overthrow the scoundrel warlord governor of the province, Lung Yun.

Having encountered greater Chinese resistance in the Hsu-chow-Taierhchuang area than had been anticipated, the Japanese North China Front Army's 2nd Corps of three divisions[9] on the Tsinpu Railway sector north of Hsuchow was reinforced by the 110th and 114th divisions. In addition, the 14th Division and the equivalent in separate brigades of two more divisions were sent to the Puyang-Yungcheng area on the Yellow River about 40 miles west of the railway. The 14th Division crossed the river on May 10 against little opposition from the Chinese 3rd Army Group; took Yungcheng on the south bank on the eleventh, Hotseh on the twelfth, and Chinghsiang on the fourteenth; and on the fifteenth cut the Lunghai Railway east of Lanfeng, 75 miles west of Hsuchow.

In the southern sector of the Tsinpu Railway, the Japanese Central China Expeditionary Force was reinforced to bring its 11th, 13th, 3rd, and Konoye divisions up to full strength and by several separate brigades. In early May the Chinese 26th Army Group of three divisions moved east from Hofei to attack the flank and rear of the Japanese in the railway corridor. The half-hearted attack—little more than a maneuver—was quickly turned into a disorderly retreat by vigorous enemy reaction, a retreat that continued for 20 miles west of the Chinese base at Hofei. At about the same time the Japanese 13th Division crossed the Huai River at two points in the vicinity of Pangpu and marched toward Suhsien, 30 miles north of the river. Coordinated with this thrust, the Japanese 9th Division and the Iseki Mechanized Brigade crossed the Huai 15 miles west of Pangpu, pushed north at once, and on May 9 captured Mengcheng. The Chinese 21st Army Group of five divisions gave up Mengcheng with no more than a token fight and withdrew for 20 miles to the west, then for no known reason continued in the same direction for another 15 miles—completely out of the combat zone. Since the 21st Army Group had failed miserably to carry out its mission to defend Mengcheng, the 77th Corps of three divisions was ordered from Hsuchow to Suhsien to block the northward advance of the enemy from the Huai River.

In coordination with the movements of the Japanese 13th and 9th divisions and the mechanized unit from the Pangpu area, one brigade of the 11th Division crossed the Yangtze in two columns: the first at Chinchiang, the southern terminus of the Grand Canal about 25 miles east of Nanking; the second at Nantung, 75 miles east of Nanking and 23 miles inland from the Yellow Sea. The first column brushed aside units of the Chinese 24th Army Group of five divisions to take Tienchang and Kaoyu, each about 25 miles north of the river, and pressed on against virtually no opposition toward Huaiyin, 60 miles north of the river. The second column simply marched north on the old road to Haichow through Tungtai and Yencheng toward Funing, over 85 miles north of the Yangtze. Units of the Chinese 24th Army Group put up no resistance whatsoever as they dissolved and scattered through the coastal countryside before the rapid Japanese advance.

The southern sector was collapsing, but not because of any lack of Chinese troops. In contrast to the vigorous actions of commanders in the Taierhchuang area, generals Hsu Yuan-chuan of the 26th Army Group at Hofei, Liao Lei of the 21st Army Group at Mengcheng, and Han Teh-chin at Kaoyu and Yencheng had refused to stand and face the Japanese. Their cowardly display of complete irresponsibility, typical of old-fashioned Chinese commanders, was best exemplified by the 24th Army Group whose five divisions of about 20,000 men broke and ran before the advance of one Japanese brigade of no more than 6,000 men that had been split into two columns. Because of their lack of dependability, or just plain fear of the Japanese, and their refusal to accept and to carry out orders, General Li Tsung-jen's 5th War Area was being pinched out of existence, and its remaining territory was too confined for maneuver of its 250,000 troops. Therefore the 3rd Army Group of five divisions and the 3rd Army of one division, already pushed into the zone of the 1st War Area, were transferred to that command. At the same time, in an effort to bolster a probable escape route, the 74th and 8th corps, each of two divisions, were concentrated at Kweiteh and Tangshan on the Lunghai Railway, 40 and 25 miles west of Hsuchow.

On the morning of May 12 the Japanese 9th Division and the mechanized brigade from Mengcheng stormed into Yungcheng, only 12 miles south of Tangshan on the railway. Then, after dispatching a security force to block any possible Chinese thrust toward Tangshan, this column turned east toward Hsiaohsien, 10 miles southwest of Hsuchow. On the same day the Japanese 11th and 3rd divisions, driving north on both sides of the railway line, were about to attack Suhsien and Chuhsikou, 20 and 15 miles south of Hsuchow.

Between May 11 and 15, in the area north of the Lunghai line, the Japanese 14th and 114th divisions were moving south from Puhsien and Yuncheng on the Yellow River through Hotseh and Chuyen toward Lanfeng on the railway and toward Chinghsiang. At the same time, the Japanese 16th Division swung to the southeast from the Tsinpu line to join the 10th, 5th, and 102nd divisions then facing the Chinese defense positions in the Pei-hsien-Taierhchuang area. On May 14 the 114th Division took both Chinghsiang and Yutai, the latter only 25 miles northwest of Hsuchow. As the Japanese noose grew steadily tighter, units of the Chinese 3rd and 21st army groups, the 74th Corps, and the 39th Division flailed helplessly against the western and southern perimeters of the relentless Japanese pressure. On May 14 the four Japanese divisions[10] facing the last reliable defenses at Taierhchuang and Peihsien opened a general attack against the Chinese lines. Battle-weary, hungry, and now frightened, exhausted Chinese troops began to give way under the steady pounding of air, artillery, and tank attacks. With the growing threats of encirclement and of being cut off from any possible escape, even good leaders like T'ang En-po, Chang Tse-chung, and Yu Hsueh-chung could no longer hold their men on the line.

As the last defenses began to crumble on May 15, "in order to avoid a decisive engagement against the enemy under unfavorable circumstances" the high command (Chiang Kai-shek) threw in the towel. He ordered the main forces of the 5th War Area "to begin the breakout to the southwest" to save themselves as best they could in an every-man-for-himself withdrawal. For many units whose commanders were now more terrified than their men, the breakout soon became a rout. The 24th Army Group (which if wiped out would have been no loss) was directed to remain where it was in northern Kiangsu "to conduct guerrilla operations," in other words to fend for itself and live off the already impoverished farmers and villagers of the countryside. The 69th Corps of two divisions and the Tsingtao marines were assigned the same mission in what was left of southern Shantung. A rear guard was left to hold the last perimeter around Hsuchow to cover the breakout of the outmaneuvered and outfought Chinese armies. On May 18, Peihsien and Taierhchuang, scenes of a great series of battles and symbols of great heroism, were abandoned. On the same day the Japanese closed in from the south and southwest to within 10 miles of Hsuchow. During the night of the nineteenth the last Chinese troops withdrew quietly and quickly from the great transportation center. In the end, after all the Hankow rhetoric about total victory, Chiang Kai-shek gave up without a fight.

When the Japanese entered the city on May 20, most of the population had fled, adding more tens of thousands to the slowly crawling river of humanity migrating toward the upper Yangtze Valley. Before the line had been cut at Lanfeng, the green-painted rolling stock of the Lunghai Railway had been moved to Sian and farther west. But trapped between its northern and southern terminals, much of the Tsinpu Railway's rolling stock had crowded into Hsuchow. Some had been shunted to the west, including the luxurious, dark-blue passenger cars of the Shanghai Express. As they gathered dust on a siding in distant Lanchow, camel trains from Khotan and Kashgar in Turkestan stalked past their locked doors. The first Russian truck caravans from Siberia and Hami, loaded with aviation fuel and munitions, raised clouds of gritty *loess* dust against their blank windows. What the Chinese could not move from Hsuchow they destroyed. During their last day in the city, exploding ammunition dumps set fire to parts of the deserted town. Barracks, government buildings, and railway installations blazed throughout that night. By morning the enormous marshaling yards were a tangled, smoking mass of burned-out steel skeletons of countless cars and locomotives, still hot as the Japanese poured into the ruined city to raise their flags in the triumph of a hollow victory. Although Chiang Kai-shek had now abandoned the people of all east and north China between the Mongolian-Manchurian borders and the Yellow and Yangtze rivers, his badly battered armies had not surrendered; and the Japanese had found no government officials with whom they could arrange for a cessation of hostilities and some form of new state they could dominate.

During the campaign to take Hsuchow, the Japanese had lost over 20,000 killed; the Chinese had lost probably three times that number in killed and in desertions, although the exact number of Chinese casualties in this or in any other campaign will never be known. No records of men wounded or killed were ever kept— except of senior officers. The five-month struggle had been characterized by the daring and ability of certain commanders; by the cowardice and ineptitude of others; by the floundering directions of the supreme commander, Chiang Kai-shek; and by the courage, self-sacrifice, and will to fight to the death of junior officers and enlisted men when given the inspiration to do so by a real leader.

As a footnote to the entire operation along the Tsinpu Railway between the Yellow and Yangtze rivers, the official Chinese history tidied up its record of the campaign with an astonishing bit of illogical military thinking and deduction: "Having been lured by our forces to eastern Honan, Kweiteh and Lanfeng, the enemy committed mistakes in dispositions, suffered from too wide a front, lacked depth, and made blind turning movements leaving his rear areas exposed. Accordingly, in late May, our 5th War Area withdrew its forces safely to western Anhwei and southern Honan." But despite any errors in judgment, the Japanese accomplished their objective and destroyed the effectiveness of a huge Chinese army.

The Loss of Amoy and Foochow

One of the oldest of the treaty ports created after the first Opium War 100 years earlier, Amoy was built on an island that formed part of a deeply indented bay. The foreign section near the Bund presented a conglomeration of architectural styles: Portuguese; Dutch; nineteenth-century British, French, and American. There was a white-pillared, red-brick Georgian mansion serving as the American consulate.

In the days of the clipper ships, Amoy had been a thriving and important port for the shipment of Fukien-grown tea. But it had long since been eclipsed—as had Foochow over 100 miles to the north—by the two commercial giants at the mouths of the Yangtze and Pearl rivers: Shanghai and Canton–Hongkong. By 1937 Amoy and Foochow had become sleepy relics of the past, still shipping some tea, featherweight Fukien lacquerware, porcelains, other local crafts, and dried fish. The harbors were always crowded with the slatted red sails of seagoing and fishing junks, but they seldom berthed a large modern steamship.

Though vessels of the Chinese Navy had participated to a minor degree in the Battle of Shanghai, most of them that had been unable to flee up river to Hankow and Chungking had been sunk by Japanese gunfire and bombs. At the time, other Chinese naval craft were stationed at ports south of the Yangtze River. At the outbreak of hostilities on July 7, 1937, the Chinese Navy was commanded by Admiral Yang, a tall, fiercely mustached individual who never seemed to go near a ship but who never missed a party. His "navy" consisted of twenty-nine small vessels of assorted types and vintage and twelve river patrol boats.

In early May of 1938 a small squadron of the Japanese 14th Fleet under the command of Admiral Ichiro Ouno appeared off Amoy. The naval force included one carrier and had four battalions (3,000 men) of marines aboard, of which three battalions were made up of Taiwanese. The Chinese defense force consisted of one provincial division, the 75th, some fortress troops, two batteries of antiquated coastal defense guns, and three warships of a type best described as a cross between a gunboat, a small frigate, and a very small destroyer. The total military manpower numbered less than 7,000 men.

On the morning of May 10, 11 Japanese ships and 18 planes bombarded two ancient stone forts and a small fishing village on the eastern coast of Amoy Island. When Japanese marines landed near Wutung, the crumbling northern fortress, the Chinese 75th Division pulled back about three miles. On the morning of the eleventh, enemy planes bombed and strafed the Chinese positions, the marines attacked, and the defense forces fell back to within a mile and a half of the city. On the same day three Japanese destroyers moved into the harbor and bombarded two old stone forts. That night, under cover of darkness, the entire Chinese defense force decamped from the city and the island, fleeing to the mainland in a confusion of junks, sampans, rafts, and anything that would float. After a brief fight at Kaoyu, across the bay from Amoy city, the defenders dissolved into the rugged hills of Fukien province to take up guerrilla warfare—possibly against their own people, since there were no Japanese beyond the island. By May 13 the show was over.

On May 23, Japanese naval ships bombarded several coastal villages in the vicinity of Foochow, over 100 miles to the north. On May 31 and June 1 enemy planes bombed and sank three Chinese gunboats in the Min River near the provincial capital and forced another to beach near the harbor entrance. During the next few days all Chinese army and navy installations were systematically bombed out of existence, though the city itself suffered but slight damage.

In the loss of the two ports, neither the poorly trained and equipped provincial troops nor the Chinese naval units had put up more than token resistance against the Japanese. This was probably just as well, for if they had fought they would have been slaughtered and the two cities at least partly destroyed.

7

Operations in Eastern and Northern Honan, February to June, 1938

MILITARY OPERATIONS IN THE CORRIDOR of the Pinghan Railway —beyond Chinese guerrilla activities—remained at a virtual standstill from mid-November, 1937, until early February, 1938. During this lull the Japanese attempted no action, merely holding their southern outposts: Anyang on the railway about 80 miles north of the Yellow River and Taming, some 40 miles to the northeast. Since the Japanese had withdrawn troops and support units from this sector to reinforce the Nanking and Tsinpu Railway fronts, the Chinese could have staged counteroffensives against the Anyang-Taming area at any time, but they failed to do so and thereby lost an opportunity to effect a partial relief of enemy pressure on the two active fronts. Instead of holding the Japanese at the points of their farthest southern advance, the Chinese 1st Army Group, under the command of Sung Che-Yuan, withdrew to south of Anyang, this so-called defense plan, in effect, offering their enemy free passage west of the Wei River and the Pinghan Railway line. After T'ang En-po's 20th Army of five divisions and Chang Tse-chung's 59th Corps of three divisions had been shifted to the Tsinpu Railway front, the main strength of the 1st War Area on the Pinghan Railway was moved to the south bank of the Yellow River, leaving the entire area to the north in jeopardy.

By February, 1938, the Japanese North China Front Army, commanded by General Terauchi, had been deployed from the

Anyang-Taming area to northern Hopei. This force consisted of the 14th Division, commanded by General Doihara, the evil genius of the Kwantung Army, parts of the 108th and 11th divisions, and supporting air, artillery, and armored units. Its total strength was about 45,000 men.

General Cheng Chien, commander of the 1st War Area, had under his command three army groups containing a total of 46 divisions, 2 cavalry divisions, 1 separate infantry brigade, 3 cavalry brigades, and 6 supporting artillery regiments, with a total strength of approximately 290,000 men.

Of the senior commanders in the 1st War Area, General Hsueh Yueh, commanding the Eastern Honan Army of six divisions and later known as the Tiger of Hunan, was probably the most outstanding. Independent and tough to the point of downright rudeness, he was not always trusted by the generalissimo. When he decided to be, Hsueh Yueh was a great fighter.

On February 7 a column of the Japanese 14th Division crossed the Wei River at Taming, brushed aside spotty Chinese resistance, and took the undefended town of Nanloh, 11 miles to the south. On the same day a second Japanese column, supported by planes, tanks, and artillery, attacked the lightly held Chinese positions at Pao Lien Temple, a few miles south of Anyang. When the Japanese executed a double envelopment, the Chinese garrison at Anyang withdrew hastily, but in good order, to previously prepared positions at Chihsien and Taokou, 25 miles to the south. There they joined newly reinforced units of the 53rd Corps of two divisions and the New 9th Division. Sung Che-yuan, "hoping to achieve sustained resistance," then deployed his 1st Army Group in depth—a depth between 35 and 40 miles to Hsinhsiang—again subscribing to the Chinese penchant for risking but a small part of the total force and thereby permitting the enemy to pick off units one by one.

The Japanese column from Taming continued its southward thrust parallel to and some 30 miles east of the strung-out Wei River defenses, taking, against no resistance of any kind, Puyang, Changyuan, Fengchiu, and, on February 16, Hsinhsiang. By this 130-mile envelopment, the Japanese were now striking at the rear of a poorly planned Chinese defense line. On the fifteenth, General Sung pulled his army back to prepared defenses just north of

Hsinhsiang; then, in the face of attack from three sides, he broke out to the west toward Huchia, about 11 miles away. The breakout became a six-day rout, the army marching as far each day (an average of 12 miles) as its exhausted, demoralized, and now half-starved men could stagger. General Sung's two corps, closely pursued by the Japanese 14th Division, continued their westward flight to the vicinity of Hsiahsien and Chiangtienchen, where they finally came to a halt on March 3—safe at last after one of the most ignominious performances in the entire eight months of hostilities.

Having no one to fight, the Japanese 14th Division returned to the area of the Pinghan Railway, its troop commanders congratulating themselves on the small expenditure of ammunition required to rout a Chinese army group of over 45,000 men. The operation had turned out not to be a pursuit, but a huge game of tag in which the Japanese had never been able to catch up with their intended victims. Sung's 1st Army Group had been in no condition for combat operations of any kind. During its headlong flight thousands of men had thrown down their weapons; other thousands had shed their uniforms and melted into the countryside to disappear as farmers or to organize into small marauding bands to live off of the helpless peasants and villagers. After its rout, the 1st Army Group was finally sent south of the Yellow River for "replenishment." From then until the capture of Hsuchow on May 20, Chinese operations in the 1st War Area were linked with and in support of Li Tsung-jen's forces in the corridor of the Tsinpu Railway. A considerable transfer of troop units, both Japanese and Chinese, took place from the Pinghan Railway corridor to the east. The 139th Division from Shang Chen's 20th Army Group, Liu Ju-ming's 68th Corps of two divisions, and Sung Che-yuan's 69th and 77th Corps of five divisions were sent to the 5th War Area south of the Yellow River. All but the 139th Division acquitted themselves poorly. After the Battle of Taierhchuang, the Japanese 14th Division moved from the Pinghan Railway sector to concentrate at Puhsien and Puyang, 10 and 20 miles west of the Yellow River at the point where its course turned to the northeast, preparatory to effecting crossings at these points. The 20th Army Group's 23rd Division was ordered to Yuncheng opposite Puhsien to block the expected enemy crossing. The Chinese 39th Corps of two divisions was concentrated along the Lunghai Railway between Chengchow and Kaifeng to prevent a Japanese crossing in that general area.

In early May, Hsueh Yueh's Eastern Honan Army of three corps (strengthened by two more) was ordered by Chiang Kai-shek to take positions along the Lunghai Railway. The mission was characteristically vague and subject to individual interpretation: "to stop the enemy and cover the Lunghai Railway so as to facilitate the operations of the 5th War Area."

On May 12 the Japanese 9th Division, moving rapidly north from the Huai River, took Yuncheng and turned northeast toward Hsiaohsien, less than 20 miles from Hsuchow. The enemy column then headed for Tangshan on the Lunghai Railway, where it was delayed by the Chinese 74th Corps. At this time the reinforced Japanese units north of the Lunghai line were closing in on Hsuchow, and the Chinese defense of the railway center had begun to fall apart. By May 20 Hsuchow was captured, and most of Li Tsung-jen's troops escaped to the southwest.

On May 14 the Japanese 14th Division crossed the Yellow River at Puhsien and captured Hotse. Caught by surprise and enveloped on their left, the Chinese suffered heavy casualties. Those who could break out fled in complete disorder to Tung-ming, 20 miles west of Hotse, and to Kaocheng, 30 miles to the southwest. With his command in shambles, General Li Pi-fan, the 23rd Division commander, committed suicide. On May 16 a Japanese column from Hotse bypassed the few units of the Chinese 23rd Division still holed up near the river, and after a forced march of 45 miles, cut the Lunghai Railway at Yifeng, east of Lanfeng. On the eighteenth the main body of the Japanese 14th Division reached the area of the Lunghai Railway.

At this time Chiang Kai-shek flew to Chengchow, 70 miles west of Lanfeng, in order to lend his tactical wisdom to the rapidly deteriorating situation. He had barely deplaned at the airfield when his grating voice began to bark out orders. General Hsueh Kweiteh, two days' march to the east of Yifeng, and to leave Yueh was ordered to attack the Japanese 14th Division from sufficient troops at Kweiteh and Tangshan "to delay the westward movement" of the Japanese 111th and 114th Divisions. The shattered 23rd Division, then in no condition for any kind of action, was directed to make a flank attack against the enemy in the east—another vague assignment subject to almost any interpretation. Though his plan to strike at the Japanese 14th Division from both east and west might well have blunted its rapid advance, the generalissimo's orders ignored coordination and timing between the units involved.

When attacked by the Chinese at Neihuang, near Lanfeng, and at Yifeng, the 14th Division crossed the railway line at night, moved to the southwest, and slipped out of the trap. Eight Chinese divisions plunged after the Japanese in hot pursuit. On May 2 General Doihara reversed the direction of his 14th Division and circled around Hsueh Yueh's forward elements. Then moving rapidly to the northwest, he captured a part of Lowang, only 10 miles east of Kaifeng, and Chuhsingchi and Sanyichai, both north of the railway line. Although Doihara's marches and countermarches were baffling, Hsueh Yueh determined to attack from the south and east. The Chinese 39th Corps of two divisions was ordered to block any Japanese attempt to escape the threatened encirclement, but its attack never got off the ground, its units simply firing their weapons in place. After two days of fighting the Japanese had not budged from their positions. Meanwhile, another Japanese force crossed the Yellow River at Kuantai, northwest of the combat area, and took Lanfeng. Having run rings around the slower moving—and slower thinking—Chinese, Doihara now dug in, encircled the Lanfeng-Lowang-Kuantai area with his troops, and fought off Chinese attacks while he waited for reinforcements.

On May 27 the Chinese 71st and 64th corps, each of two divisions, again attacked from the east and south, broke through the enemy positions, and recaptured Lanfeng and Lowang, which cleared the Japanese block of the Lunghai line. Rolling stock that had been held east of Lanfeng was rushed through to Kaifeng, Chengchow, and farther west. Fighting between the railway and the river continued for the next two days, with small towns and villages exchanging hands repeatedly. The constant attacks and counterattacks achieved little result except the usual destruction of villages and the dislocation of surviving peasants.

Meanwhile, on May 21 in the corridor between the Tsinpu Railway and the Grand Canal, the Japanese 11th and 114th divisions began a rapid southward thrust from Tsining in two columns. Troops of the Chinese 3rd Army Group were generally driven like stampeding cattle before the enemy advance; however, the 74th Corps did put up some resistance at Fenghsien and at Tangshan on the Lunghai line. The reported bitter fighting over the 65 and 75 miles of the two southward routes "lasted until May 24th when our [Chinese] forces withdrew to the west" with all speed. Whatever resistance took place must have been in the nature of a fast, running fight. The Japanese pursued the retreating Chinese along the railway line toward Kweiteh, a part of the enemy forces diverting to Yucheng and then turning south. Hsueh Yueh's 8th Corps "conducted sustained resistance at Yucheng and Kweiteh," sustaining a stalwart defense for all of two days, from May 26 to 28. Then, from the official Chinese history: "As the forces of the 5th War Area broke out safely, our forces abandoned Kweiteh and withdrew to the west and southwest." On the same day, Liu Ju-ming's 68th Corps broke out of Hsiaohsien, 30 miles southwest of Hsuchow, and continued until it reached Pochow, about 45 miles farther, on May 30. There a brief stand was made, and "having repelled the enemy pursuit forces, the corps [the 68th] received orders to withdraw to Huaiyang, 50 miles farther to the southwest." In this case, repelling the enemy pursuit forces really meant that the Japanese did not wish to stray too far from the Tsinpu Railway line. Having driven Liu Ju-ming and his rabble a good 60 miles to the west, the Japanese returned to the main scene of activity.

On May 31, "in order to avoid a decisive battle against the enemy on the eastern Honan plains," Chiang Kai-shek ordered most of the troops of the 1st War Area to withdraw west of the Pinghan Railway, again conceding the fight without having committed even one-half of the troops available for resistance in that area. However, he directed General Shang Chen "to conduct sustained resistance in the area of Kaifeng, Chungmu [20 miles to the west], and Weishih [30 miles to the southwest]." But the driving force of the Japanese, with a strength of nearly 60,000 men, proved too great for General Shang's command of less than 40,000. Although the Chinese fought off Japanese assaults for six days, they were finally compelled to pull out of Kaifeng, which the Japanese entered on June 6.

And another of China's ancient walled cities fell to her enemies. Though never an imperial capital, Kaifeng had been an important fortress since the Shang dynasty (1766–1122 B.C.). Built on the approximate site of the walled town of Chengchou, Kaifeng's environs had yielded a great wealth of pottery from Neolithic times as well as from the Shang and Chou dynasties, magnificent bronzes, inscribed bones, and other artifacts from ancient foundations and deep burial sites. Kaifeng and the more important cities of Loyang and Sian to the west had played an integral part in the history of the Yellow River valley from which most of China's culture emanated. Under the Manchu dynasty, Kaifeng was designated by imperial decree as one of two cities permitted to receive Jewish immigrants from Russia in the seventeenth and eighteenth centuries. Over several generations these east European Jews, many originally with blond hair, gradually assimilated with the local Chinese. A few of their descendants still bear the blond heritage with oriental features.

By June 8 Japanese troops had driven General Shang Chen 10 miles beyond Chungmu and out of Weishih, about 10 miles west of the Chialu River. Japanese cavalry had pushed as far as Hsincheng on the Pinghan Railway, 30 miles west of the Chialu.

At this stage of affairs, Chiang Kai-shek began to panic. He visualized an imminent Japanese occupation of the entire area between the Yellow and the Yangtze rivers. His stronghold of Wuhan (Hankow) was in danger. If he lost Hankow, he might lose the dwindling support of the Chinese people—perhaps even that of his armies. His position as titular leader of China could be overthrown. Uppermost in his mind was the maintenance of himself in power. Desperate with fear that the Japanese armies were about to descend upon him, he ordered Shang Chen to blow up the dikes of the Yellow River at Huayuankou, east of Chengchow, in order to block off the three rampaging enemy columns. Time and again he telephoned frantically to insist that his orders be carried out at once. But having been assigned the mission, General Shang delayed irrevocable action—hoping the order would be rescinded—until he was able to move all of his 32nd and 39th corps troops to safety.

The original dikes, reputedly over 4,000 years old, had been planned and constructed by a legendary ruler of China known to posterity as the diligent Yu. However successful at the time, Yu's engineering genius had failed to control the floods of later times. Over the centuries, instead of dredging the river bottom—a project for which the Chinese possessed neither equipment nor knowledge—the dikes had been built higher and higher. During each annual flood stage, heavy deposits of silt had raised the muddy bottom, thus requiring higher dikes, until the river itself was often as much as 20 to 30 feet higher than the surrounding countryside. Chiang Kai-shek was well aware that destruction of any section of the massive dikes would loose a gigantic flood onto the flat plains of Honan and beyond into Anhwei.

When Shang Chen finally ordered the explosive charges set off, the silt-filled waters tore through the breach and over the farmlands toward the southeast. Before the rampaging waters settled into the course of the Chialu River, thence to the Huai, and finally into the Yangtze near Chinchiang, 11 large towns and over 4,000 villages were flooded; the crops and farmlands in much of Honan, Anhwei, and Kiangsu provinces were destroyed and ruined through loss of topsoil; and well over 2 million people were left without homes or means to survive. Thousands of small boats and cargo junks rode the muddy waters until wrecked or grounded on distant islands of soggy land. On the old lower course of the river, now carrying little more than a trickle, hundreds of craft were stranded with their tall masts pointing at crazy angles. The vast destructive flood built up a hatred of Chiang Kai-shek and his government in the hearts of millions of his disillusioned people.

But the Japanese advance was stopped. Finding themselves about to be trapped in the flood, troops of the three enemy divisions hastily retreated to the east. Not all of them escaped; those who did not were quickly annihilated by Shang Chen's troops.

A mere sideshow in comparison to the great struggles in the Shanghai-Nanking and Taierhchuang-Hsuchow battles, the east and north Honan operations clearly pointed up the lack of dependability of most commanders in the 1st War Area. Shang Chen and Hsueh Yueh had stood out as men willing to fight and able to get the most out of their troops under difficult conditions.

But with rare exceptions the other commanders had shown themselves to be looking over their shoulders for escape routes even before they had been engaged in combat. In most situations they had been outmaneuvered by the Japanese, and through their timid, blundering actions they had sacrificed thousands of their men for nothing.

8

The Hankow (Wuhan) Campaign, June 10 to November 12, 1938

THE SOGGY FARMLANDS of the Honan plains did not long delay the next Japanese move. Before mid-June, troops of the 2nd and 11th corps, using the Tsinpu Railway, shifted to the south of the main flooded areas and began to advance westward, while Japanese forces from the Nanking area began to move up the Yangtze River. Chiang Kai-shek and his National Military Council were forced to the unhappy conclusion that Japanese capabilities and intentions not only threatened the temporary capital, Hankow, but also endangered the large cities of Changsha and Nanchang, as well as the entire lake region south of the Yangtze.

At this time the Japanese high command was assembling troop units to be employed in the most far-reaching operation they had yet mounted in China—one that was planned to knock out all further organized military resistance, destroy Chiang Kai-shek, and finally force a settlement of the increasingly expensive venture to subjugate China. As organized in early July, the Central China Expeditionary Force under the command of General Shunroku Hata consisted of two corps, a separate army, and three air brigades. The 11th Corps, commanded by General Okamura, was made up of five divisions[1] and the Taiwan Infantry Brigade with a total strength of about 125,000 men, including supporting artillery and armored units. The 2nd Corps, now commanded by Prince Naruhito, consisted of four divisions,[2] which with supporting units numbered over 100,000 men. The separate army command, units of which could be attached to the two corps as needed, consisted of five divisions[3] plus the three air brigades; it numbered about 130,000 men. The air brigades were equipped with about 200 tactical aircraft, both fighters and bombers. In addition, General Hata could count on considerable support from ships and aircraft, since during the summer high-water season vessels of up to 10,000 tons could navigate the Yangtze River up to Hankow. The Japanese army and air strength for the projected campaign was close to 380,000 men.

The Chinese defending forces consisted of a huge conglomeration of troops from two war areas: the 9th, reconstituted and greatly augmented from the Wuhan Garrison Command, along the Yangtze River and south of it; and the 5th, which was north of the river. The 9th War Area, commanded by the able and forceful General Ch'en Ch'eng, consisted of the 1st Army Corps, 2nd Army Corps, the Wuhan (Hankow), Garrison and various attached units and support troops: all in all nearly 450,000 men in 58 divisions and 1 separate brigade. The 5th War Area, commanded by General Pai Ch'ung-hsi with Li Tsung-jen as titular commander and deputy, consisted of 49 divisions organized into two army corps, four army groups, three armies, and three independent corps—a total of about 340,000 troops.

The total of all Chinese troops available to meet the Japanese threat, including various regional and fortress troops, was close to 800,000. Though greatly outclassed by enemy superiority in training, equipment, and artillery, air, and naval support, the Chinese had the advantages of interior lines of operation, natural defensive barriers of mountains and numerous large lakes in summer flood stage, and a still more or less friendly population.

The National Military Council, parroting Chiang Kai-shek's deductions and decisions, issued an estimate of the situation ("the enemy's attempt to attack Hankow became more obvious"), followed by the usual operational guiding principles: "A powerful force will support Matang fortress [150 miles downriver from Hankow], compel the enemy to deploy east of Poyang Lake [40 to 80 miles south of Matang], and prevent the enemy from moving up the Yangtze River to Kiukiang [100 miles downriver from Hankow]. The main force will concentrate in the vicinity of Hankow and take advantage of the natural barriers of

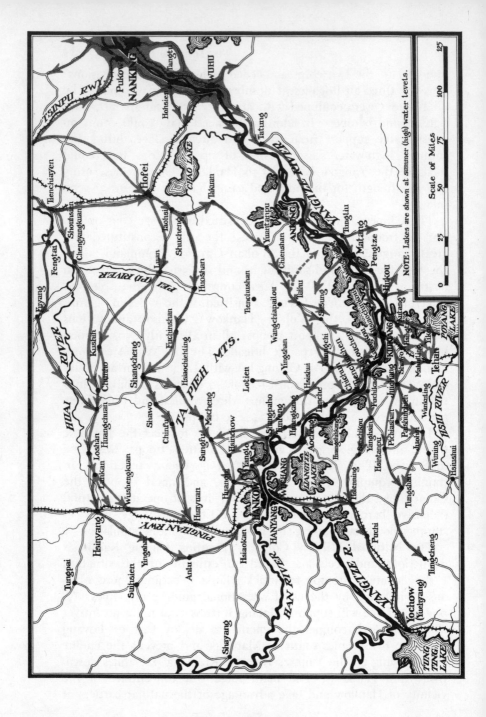

The Hankow Campaign

Poyang Lake and the Ta Pieh Mountains [a 100-mile range about 60 miles northeast of Hankow]."

The 1st War Area command in the Pinghan Railway corridor was assigned a minor role: guerrilla operations in northeast Honan and western Shantung, the defense of the Yellow River, occupation of prepared positions from which to "assume the offensive at the opportune time," and the dispatch of six of its divisions to other battle areas.

The 5th War Area command, originally in the corridor of the Tsinpu Railway, of which not much was left under Chinese control, was assigned a far more important role. It was ordered to concentrate its 3rd Army Corps (nine divisions) under the command of General Sun Lien-chung in the vicinity of Shangcheng, about 100 miles northeast of Hankow and halfway between the Pinghan and Tsinpu railways, in order to attack any Japanese forces attempting to move toward Hankow in that area. The 26th Army Group (three divisions) was directed to concentrate in the area from Luan and Huoshan on the Pi River to Shucheng and Tiencheng, 175 miles northeast of Hankow, in order to block any western move of the Japanese from the Hofei–Chao Lake area. The 27th Army Group (three Szechwan divisions) was ordered to defend the Anking area, 180 miles downriver from Hankow, and to attack the flanks of any Japanese forces moving west along the Yangtze River—a contradictory order: if Anking were defended, the Japanese could not move along the Yangtze. The 24th Army Group (four divisions) was directed to defend north Kiangsu province, the railway lines and roads of which had been lost a month before. This force was also ordered to conduct guerrilla operations against the enemy-held southern sector of the Tsinpu Railway—a completely meaningless directive.

The 3rd War Area, originally Kiangsu and Chekiang provinces, but now pushed into the mountains of southern Chekiang and Anhwei south of the Yangtze, was ordered to organize river defense between Tungliu and Matang, 25 and 40 miles upriver from Anking, and to be ready to assist in the defense of Anking. It was also directed to construct defense works along the branch railways and principal roads in the area where the borders of Anhwei, Chekiang, and Kiangsi met.

The 9th War Area, under General Ch'en Ch'eng, was directed to concentrate its main strength on a defense arc 60 to 75 miles north, east, and southeast of Hankow. A force of undesignated size was ordered to the Susung area, 25 miles east of Kuangchi, "to delay and wear out the enemy." General Hsueh Yueh's 1st Army Corps was ordered to conduct a vigorous defense of Matang, 150 miles downriver from Hankow. The 25th Corps of two divisions[4] was located along the Kiukiang-Nanchang railway line. The 18th Corps of three divisions[5] was located in the area of Hukou, just south of the Yangtze and 15 miles east of Kiukiang. The 66th Corps of two divisions[6] was directed to be in readiness along the Nanchang-Chuchow rail line just south of Poyang Lake, presumably to block any Japanese attempt to outflank the river defenses by encircling the lake. The 94th Corps of two divisions[7], the 2nd Corps of two divisions plus attached "fortress" troops[8], and the 75th Corps of two divisions plus attached "fortress" troops[9] were directed to "assume the defense of Wuhan." The 30th Army Group of two corps containing four divisions[10], already concentrated south of the river, was shifted from Chang Fa-kuei's 2nd Army Corps command to come directly under the National Military Council.

General T'ang En-po, in command of the Honan-Hupei border region north of Hankow, was directed to concentrate his 31st Army Group[11] against "the flanks of the enemy moving south along the Pinghan Railway and assisting in the operations" at Hankow. He was also directed to dispatch "a powerful force" to assist the 1st War Area in the Yellow River region "should the enemy advance from south of the Lunghai Railway to the west or southwest." The 68th Corps of two divisions[12] under the innocuous and cowardly Liu Ju-ming and the 95th Division were ordered to "occupy positions" in the Piyang reserve area under the command of the 5th War Area.

The air force, recently augmented by the purchase of 100 light bombers and fighters from the Soviet Union, was concentrated at the Hankow and Nanchang airfields—both vulnerable targets for attack. Planes were ordered to bomb enemy ships on the Yangtze "day and night"—though neither the Chinese nor the Japanese were equipped to fly missions at night—and to attack Japanese airfields at Nanking, Wuhu, and Anking. The navy—all

35,000 surviving tons of it—was directed to support fortifications along the river and to harass Japanese shipping.

In most details the so-called operational guiding principles were as vague as to missions and objectives as was the label under which they masqueraded as military orders. They were full of unrealistic pomposities directing "powerful forces" to march here, there, and everywhere about the countryside; directing the "tying down, delaying and wearing out" of an opponent who had no intention of acceding to any of the three; directing forces to "occupy positions and defense works" that were 100 miles and more from the nearest enemy soldier; directing "guerrilla operations" that seldom materialized; directing "attacks on the flanks" of an enemy who had long since learned that flank attacks could be turned against the slow-moving Chinese by outflanking them and putting them to rout. The whole tone of the directive was one of delay, step-by-step withdrawal, and defense in depth that presaged retreat and eventual acceptance of defeat. Like most antiquated Chinese military thinking, the operational guiding principles for the defense of Hankow were the product of a sort of dream world of correct words and resounding phrases. Not once in the long-winded document was a commander ordered to stand in place, face the enemy, and fight. By instinct, a few leaders would fight anyway. Most would welcome the escape clauses and turn tail.

This time Chiang Kai-shek's military chessboard was the largest over which he had ever shifted his pawns. He had issued the orders, but with few exceptions could not be certain that his generals would carry them out. He could depend on men like Ch'en Ch'eng, Hsueh Yueh, Shang Chen, T'ang En-po, Sun Lien-chung, Chang Tse-chung, and Hu Tsung-nan. But of 22 other commanders of army or higher rank and over 40 corps commanders, he was not sure whether they would accept the orders at all and had long since been forced to put no faith in their preparations for future actions. But having contributed his military wisdom, which as usual deprived combat commanders of all individual initiative, Chiang Kai-shek rested from his mighty labors to await the next Japanese move. He did not have long to wait.

Wuhan, the great prize of the Yangtze Valley, was actually three cities at the junction of the Han and Yangtze rivers: Hankow, Hanyang, and Wuchang, with a combined population of about 1.5 million. Because Hankow with nearly 1.2 million people was the largest and most important of the three, foreigners usually referred to the complex of cities as Hankow, though the Chinese called them Wuhan. Hanyang, with a population of 100,000, was the center of a number of steel and iron mills and related factories. On a high bluff on the south side of the Yangtze, Wuchang had a population of about 200,000. It was the temporary seat of the executive branch of the government—Chiang Kai-shek—and the location of the national military headquarters. About 550 miles upriver from the mouth of the Yangtze, in flood season Hankow was the head of navigation for ocean ships of 10,000 tons or less. Roughly halfway between Ichang, 250 miles upriver at the start of the great Yangtze gorges, and Nanking, Wuhan had become the financial, commercial, and manufacturing center of the rich Yangtze Valley. Because of its central location and importance, American-educated Chinese had labeled it the Chicago of China. Others, with the steel mills of Hanyang in mind, called it the Pittsburgh of China. In any real comparison, it was neither. Its workers had long made the city a center of unrest and dissension. The 1911 revolution against the Manchu dynasty had broken out in Hankow, and the extreme left wing of the Chinese government had set up a regime of its own in Hankow until it and its Russian advisers had been driven out by Chiang Kai-shek and the conservative elements of the Kuomintang in 1927.

Consulates of the more imperial-minded nations, including Japan, were located in the busy city. Though the Japanese and others had had military detachments in Hankow to guard their nationals, concessions, and commercial interests, all foreign troops (except a small force of French Annamites) and all Japanese civilians had been evacuated shortly after the outbreak of hostilities in July, 1937.

Hankow was also the center of the great lake region of the Yangtze Valley. For ages, numerous shallow lakes, both north and south of the river, had acted as catch basins for summer floods and had thus saved the richly silted farmlands of the valley from destructive ravages such as repeatedly occurred along the lower reaches of the Yellow River. The two largest, Tung Ting Lake and Poyang Lake, each had dry-season areas of about 2,000 square miles. Located south of the Yangtze, the two lakes not only dictated road and communications routes on the high ground between them but also gave prosperity to a number of large cities clustered near their shores.

At Hankow the rise and fall of the river between floods and dry seasons varied so rapidly that although the city boasted a Bund or quayside esplanade, ships, sailing junks, and men-of-war all tied up at large floating pontoons lashed by heavy hemp and bamboo cables to shoreline stanchions. Access from the Bund to the pontoons and river craft was by boardwalks whose slopes varied from steep to horizontal depending on the level of the river. There was no bridge connecting Hankow with Wuchang; construction of such a span was deemed at that time to be impossible. All cross-river traffic was by rickety ferryboats and uncertain, wallowing sampans. The smaller stream separating Hanyang and Hankow was bridged at several points.

From a distance Hanyang was a forest of spindly smokestacks belching dark clouds into the sky. At closer range it was dismal, dirty, and blackened by soot. Wuchang was drab, its military buildings and barracks fittingly gray, its large presidential residence gloomy and dark but offering a wide view of the busy waterfront across the river. In contrast, Hankow near the Bund —however crowded with the flotsam of war—showed the Edwardian pomp that characterized most foreign construction in the major cities of China. The British consulate faced the Bund from the midst of tree-shaded lawns and gardens. Typically, the nearby American consulate was housed in an upper floor of the Asiatic Petroleum Building, with apartments for the consul general on a floor below. The large, seedy-looking Grand Hotel de Hankow, which provided rooms and French cuisine for visitors, was now so jammed with guests that it seemed more like a crowded tenement. From late morning to early morning its bar-lounge was filled with newsmen, military officers, diplomatic officials, foreign businessmen, and Chinese prostitutes with such names as Autumn Moon and Lotus Blossom. The town's few restaurants were equally crowded, particularly one operated by an attractive half-Austrian, half-Chinese woman who served remarkably good gimlets and Wiener Schnitzel.

In mid-March of 1938, after about six weeks in Peking, I was ordered to Hankow as assistant military attaché to observe and report on the situation in central China. In the same War Department orders, Colonel Stilwell was ordered to Lanchow in far northwest Kansu province to report on Russian activities and shipments through there, and Captain Roberts was sent to the French Indochina border area of south China.

By this time travel in China away from the ports had become difficult. Of necessity my route to Hankow from Peking was by rail to Tientsin, to Mukden, and south to Dairen where I boarded a Japanese ship, the *Nagasaki Maru*, which first stopped at Chefoo on the north coast of Shantung before dropping me off at Shanghai. From there I took a British Butterfield and Swire coastal ship that put in at Amoy (then still in Chinese hands) and finally at Hongkong.

Outwardly undisturbed by the war, Hongkong epitomized the nineteenth-century power of the British Empire at its unchallenged height. The Peak, rising abruptly above the narrow shelf on which most of the city was crowded, and the adjacent wooded islands and waterways made it one of the most magnificent harbors in the world. Dozens of commercial and naval ships had dropped anchor in the busy roadstead, smaller vessels nudged the Bund and docks of Hongkong and Kowloon, and ferries darted back and forth across the bay like waterbugs on a pond. The tall masts of countless junks clustered like a forest of barren trees or, with lateen sails hoisted, glided majestically on their missions. Everywhere stern-oared sampans scuttled in and out of the rippling shadows cast by large ships. A mass of dingy, multistoried Victorian buildings out of which rose the white tower of the Hongkong and Shanghai Bank stood hard by the water's edge, then climbed part way up the precipitous slope of the Peak and gradually thinned out into the homes and gardens of the rich and the important. On starlit nights the lights on the waterfront seemed to sweep upward, as if to join the stars.

After waiting two days for a reservation, I boarded a trimotor plane that lumbered off with creaks, groans, and rattles. The airfield was so hemmed in on three sides by high ridges that takeoff gave one the feeling of flying straight up out of a hole in the ground. John Gunther was also a passenger; he was on his way to gather material for his *Inside Asia*. Two days after our arrival at Hankow, his insides suffered a disruption and he was forced to spend most of the next few weeks in a hospital.

Unable to find a place of my own in Hankow, I finally wound up sharing a room and bath at the YMCA hostel with Walter Bosshard, the Swiss photographer. The place was bursting at its seams with guests, but it was clean and the meals were reasonably good. I told Bosshard my problem. Stilwell had instructed me to contact both the Chinese Communist representatives in Hankow and the German military mission and to find out what they were doing. But how was I to meet Chou En-lai and General von Falkenhausen? Or at least the officers on their staffs? Fortunately Bosshard knew the German general and a number of his officers. He was sure he could arrange meetings, which he did within a few days.

Baron Alexander von Falkenhausen (later *gauleiter* of The Netherlands) was a tall, thin, rather frosty-eyed member of the Junker class. He had been sent to China by Hitler, after the recall of General Hans von Seeckt, to head the mission of about 70 German officers whose purpose was to advise and assist in the training of the Chinese army. At our first meeting, Falkenhausen bemoaned the fact that most of Chiang Kai-shek's generals ignored his and his staff's highly professional planning and tactical advice; they favored their own brand of military chess inherited from the bow-and-arrow days of ancient dynasties. This I could well understand after what I had observed in other parts of China. In the ensuing months, both the old gentleman with thick pince-nez trembling on the bridge of his patrician nose and the various members of his staff were of great assistance to me in my job of gathering and reporting military information.

The original German mission under General von Seeckt had come to China in 1928. A competent and dedicated group of officers, they had planned and supervised the training of 30 selected Chinese divisions, which had become Chiang Kai-shek's most dependable troops. The Germans had laid out the defense system north of the Lunghai Railway and had strongly advised against precipitating the disastrous Shanghai-Nanking campaign.

Getting in touch with Chou En-lai was a tougher nut to crack, since I felt it essential that I meet him under auspices acceptable to him. So Bosshard arranged for me to meet Agnes Smedley at a luncheon in the YMCA dining room. Though not a member of any Communist party, she had spent months in the cave city of Yenan and worshiped Chu Teh and his sturdy 8th Route Army. She was now a correspondent for the *Manchester Guardian*— when she took time off from her aggressive assaults on the foreign community for money and hospital supplies to alleviate the neglect with which the Chinese treated their sick and wounded soldiers. She was without much conventional charm or femininity; her face was squarish, as was her figure. Her blonde hair, streaked in shades of sun-scorched yellow, was cut in an indifferent bob; she wore clothes for the sole purpose of covering her body, with no thought of fashion. Though a relative of the Marine Corps general Smedley Butler, she had little use for most military officers, except of course her beloved Chinese Reds. In her eyes the military were all politically naive, an opinion she promptly stated in an abrupt and somewhat harsh voice. But after this initial phase of putting me in my place, she settled down and we got along pleasantly enough. During coffee I invited her to have Wiener Schnitzel the next evening at the Austrian-Chinese restaurant. Though her eyes widened momentarily with surprise, she accepted. That evening, after the third gimlet, Agnes set her glass down with a thump and said flatly:

"What's this all about, Captain Dorn? I know damned well I'm not the type that *your* type asks out on a date."

"I want you to introduce me to Chou En-lai and to ask him to be frank with me."

"Well, at least you're honest about it. That's to your credit . . . aside from all these drinks. I like honesty. Even though I think I'm being taken in, I'll see what I can do. I've got an appointment with Chou tomorrow morning."

We finally shook hands across the table, and I began a long friendship with this intense, unhappy woman. A radical with a great soft heart, she refused to submit to any form of discipline and distrusted all political leaders.

She introduced me to Chou En-lai the following afternoon. After more than an hour's talk, I found myself deeply impressed with the man. That was the first of many meetings during the seven months I remained in Hankow. I learned to respect his intelligence, his toughness, his pragmatism, and his frankness in discussing the political-military situation. His thick eyebrows shaded large, luminous eyes that could sparkle with humor and blaze with intensity. Though he always dressed in the simplest gray, uniform-type apparel, his manner and charm gave him an air of vibrant distinction.

Before long it seemed that half of China had descended on Hankow to be there for the kill. While we waited for the inevitable—by day each doing his own job—the town's nightspots were like New Year's Eve. Japanese air raids added to the tenseness temporarily forgotten in each night's rollicking. Every man knew that it was only a question of time until Japanese soldiers marched through the city, once again victors in the long series of struggles. In all minds were nagging thoughts of Nanking, Paoting, and Shanghai, of the Japanese burning and pillaging, raping and murdering. Men drank more than usual; women's voices became more strident, parties more frequent.

When news of the victory at Taierhchuang was announced in April, the city went wild. The excitement produced an outburst of impromptu parades, exploding firecrackers, rifle fire, whistles, sirens, and blaring bugles. But the uncontrolled elation ended a little over a month later with the gloomy news of the fall of Hsuchow. Everyone realized that the tri-cities would be the next big prize for the Japanese.

As the weeks went by, an increasing number of Japanese air raids acted as constant reminders of the city's approaching doom. Usually about midday, wailing sirens gave the first insistent warnings. Like a vast pulse beat, the drone of distant engines gradually filled the air. Then came the menacing glint of Japanese bombers and their fighter escorts approaching the city in perfect formation, followed by the angry bark of antiaircraft batteries and the rapid bursts of white smoke balls in the blue sky as countless shells exploded harmlessly in the direction of the now plainly visible planes. The defending fighter planes of Russian "volunteer" fliers darted like angry wasps in and out of the unbroken

Japanese formations, trying to zero in on the bombers. Chinese aircraft zoomed upward, too, boring into the steadily advancing enemy squadrons as antiaircraft shells burst indiscriminately among friends and foes, but seldom hitting either. And the bedlam of death and destruction: the deep groan of a fighter diving for a kill; the victim exploding in a great flash, its wings and tail section falling to the earth like oversized leaves; another, its engine afire and out of control, trailing a comet tail of black smoke as it streaked downward in a long, slanting dive, finally to blow up in a shattering burst of flame and billowing smoke; now and then two planes colliding in midair with a great splash of fire and blackish clouds. Within minutes, strings of bombs cut through the air like shrieking knives to fall on Hanyang's mills and arsenal, on Wuchang's headquarters and barracks buildings, on Hankow's outlying suburbs. The deafening roar of multiple explosions and the breathtaking concussions were followed by vast mushrooms of heavy smoke ballooning upward over the red glare of crackling fires. Then, having delivered their packages of annihilation, the still-intact but battered Japanese formations wheeled in a wide graceful arc to return to their bases, trailed and harried by both Russian and Chinese fighters bent on wreaking vengeance.

Usually the Chinese defenders lost as many planes as the Japanese. The antiaircraft fire was completely ineffective but spectacular to watch; it also reassured the cringing populace. On one raid in which 130 planes participated, 29 were destroyed. Unfortunately, most of the Chinese pilots were as inept as their Italian instructors, all of whom had departed China in a hurry just after the outbreak of hostilities. The comparatively few Chinese who had had American or Russian training had learned their craft well. Captain Claire Chennault, retired from the U.S. Army Air Corps because of deafness, along with a few American instructors on contract to the Chinese government, had succeeded in injecting competence and responsibility, whereas swashbuckling glamor had formerly been the Chinese conception of a pilot's life. But the American group did not have enough personnel, potential students, or planes to turn the tide against Japanese air superiority.

The Russian fliers and their aircraft—four fighter and two bomber squadrons—had been sent to China by Stalin ostensibly to help the Chinese. Actually it was to give the fliers training under combat conditions and to inflict as much harm as possible on the Japanese air force. Housed apart from the contamination of Chinese political ideas, the stolid, humorless Russians com plained constantly about the food prepared by their Chinese cooks. Their wants—borsch, black bread, potatoes, chunks of beef, and heavily sweetened tea, all virtually unheard of in Chinese cooking—did not harmonize with what was available—wonton or shark's-fin soup, steamed bread, rice, chicken or pork, and jasmine-flavored tea. By 1939, in addition to the squadrons sent for training and combat purposes, Stalin had extended three loans to China totaling $250 million, had delivered 400 aircraft, and had trucked in large amounts of aviation fuel, bombs, and munitions. He ignored Mao Tse-tung's Communists as being too weak and unruly. Ever the cold-blooded pragmatist, Stalin was on the side with the most combat divisions.

In May, since all reports indicated an ominous quiet on the Yellow River, I decided to go up the Pinghan Railway to Chengchow to find out what was going on. My request to make the trip was disapproved by the Chinese G-2 office, so I departed quietly the next morning without permission. I soon found out what was going on: nothing, except for intermittent air raids on the railway station and marshaling yards at Chengchow and casual strafing attacks on the rest of the city. Japanese troops were entrenched along the north bank of the river about 10 miles from the city; Chinese troops along the south bank. The opposing ground commanders had informally agreed to maintain the status quo for the time being and had arranged to exchange food and other amenities. I returned to Hankow.

After the fall of Kaifeng on June 6, the Chinese information office announced to the press and attachés that over 200 Japanese prisoners were being transported by rail from Chengchow to Hankow, a trip of about 250 miles. Eager for pictures and stories, the press corps readied their cameras, sharpened their pencils, and waited for the arrival of the enemy soldiers. Since no explanation for the delay came from the information office, they belabored me to find out from Chinese intelligence why the prisoners had not arrived.

"The trains are very crowded," was the embarrassed reply to

my query. "They are also very slow during wartime." Finally, after repeated demands, the intelligence office informed me: "There are no longer *any* Japanese prisoners."

"What happened? Where are they?"

"They all died on the way."

"Died! How could they?"

"The train was attacked by very angry townspeople at every station. The guards could not hold them off."

"The guards had guns. The people had nothing but their bare hands."

"That is correct, captain. But you can not expect Chinese guards to open fire on their own people to protect the hated Japanese soldiers."

"So the prisoners were torn to pieces by the mobs?"

"That is so, captain. Very sad, but that is so."

The flooded Honan plains did not delay the next Japanese move in the southern corridor of the Tsinpu Railway. The four divisions of the Japanese 2nd Corps[13] seized Fengtai, Shouhsien, and Chengyangkuan, west of the Tsinpu line and about 100 miles north of the Yangtze River. In rapid thrusts the Japanese took Hofei, 50 miles farther south on a branch line from Pangpu to Wuhu. The 6th Division, detached from the 11th Corps of five divisions and the Taiwanese Brigade,[14] immediately moved 35 miles south of Hofei to Takuan. Encountering almost no resistance, the 3rd Division occupied Taohsi, 25 miles southwest of Hofei, and established a wide perimeter that enabled the Japanese 2nd Corps to concentrate in the area west of Lake Chao.

At this point, without yet having made a stand of any kind, the Chinese 26th Army Group of three divisions, the 21st Army Group of five divisions, the 77th Corps of two divisions and the 51st Corps of two divisions made a precipitate withdrawal of 30 miles to defensive positions just west of the north–south Pei River—a move that vacated an area 30 miles wide and 100 miles long. The defense line was anchored at Fuyang, Luan, Huoshan, and Tienchushan.

Meanwhile, Japanese naval vessels covered the vanguard of enemy troops moving up both banks of the Yangtze from Wuhu toward Tatung and Anking. Tatung, about 90 miles upriver from Nanking, fell to the Japanese without a fight. On the evening of the twelfth, after an all-day battle, the Chinese pulled out of Anking under cover of darkness, retreating toward Chienshan, 30 miles to the west on the main road paralleling the river. Under constant attacks, the Chinese reached Chienshan on June 15, where they held off the assaulting Japanese until the eighteenth, then fell back to Taihu, 18 miles southwest of Chienshan. While this action was under way, the Japanese 6th Division captured Takuan on June 11. The Chinese defenders fell back to Yuantanpu, 25 miles to the southwest and only 6 miles from Chienshan. On June 26 the Chinese 26th Army of three divisions attacked the flank and rear of the enemy near Taihu, and the 31st Corps of three divisions with the 20th Corps of two divisions struck them head on. This coordinated attack by eight Chinese divisions was too much for the Japanese to handle. On June 29, after three days of severe fighting and heavy casualties, the Japanese were compelled to retreat northeast to Chienshan and southwest toward Wangchiang near the Yangtze River. As usual, the Chinese failed to follow up on their success at Taihu. Instead, the 26th Army Group fell back to its former defensive positions west and northwest of Chienshan and extending from Wangchiapailou to Tienchushan, while the 31st Corps remained in the vicinity of Taihu. Neither unit did anything for over a month after the Japanese withdrawal on June 29.

On June 20 a Japanese naval force of one light cruiser, four destroyers, and a number of armed patrol boats escorting army troops marching upriver had progressed about 30 miles from Anking to within 10 miles of the Matang fortress. (The Chinese use of the term fortress is misleading: in their parlance a fortress was any permanent or semipermanent defensive position in which either mobile or fixed artillery pieces or mortars were emplaced. At points on the seacoast and along the Yangtze a few crumbling old stone forts, in the north a number of ancient castles, and throughout China many hastily constructed redoubts on commanding heights passed as forts or fortresses.) Matang was the strongest defensive position on the Yangtze. A heavy boom of woven bamboo cables had been stretched across the river about 5 miles west. On June 24 Japanese naval vessels and bombers bombarded Matang, while army units attacked the outer defenses.

The Chinese 53rd and 167th divisions were engaged in a seesaw battle with the Japanese until noon on the twenty-sixth, when the enemy broke through the Chinese positions and entered the town. A Chinese counterattack achieved a brief success, but the end results were a large number of casualties on both sides, the complete rout of the defenders, and the loss of Matang on June 27. The fortress commander had been killed; the commander of the 167th Division was executed because he had managed to survive the defeat of his troops. Chiang Kai-shek had decreed that Matang be held at all costs; therefore its loss called for a scapegoat on whom the generalissimo could wreak his vengeance.

On June 29 Japanese destroyers and gunboats rammed through the Matang boom and proceeded to Pengtze, 10 miles upriver. On July 3, units of the Japanese 101st and 116th divisions, continuing the advance up both banks of the river, swept all Chinese resistance before them. At the same time, a Japanese naval force approached Hukou, another fortress on the south side of the river about 18 miles west of Pengtze. A regiment of marines landed near Hukou and attacked its outer defenses. The entire Japanese 101st Division arrived to join battle with the Chinese 26th Division. Though the Chinese put up a determined resistance and engaged in hand-to-hand street fighting through the town, by July 5 the Japanese had cleared all Chinese from Hukou and its defenses. On the sixth the Chinese 18th Corps of two divisions[15] belatedly arrived to reinforce the already defeated 26th Division. The corps attacked the Japanese—now defending Hukou—but it was too late. By July 8 the fight was over; the Japanese 101st Division was in undisputed control of Hukou. Having failed to press its attack, the Chinese 18th Corps was standing by, waiting for the next enemy move. In one month the Japanese had advanced over 100 miles from their initial positions east of Tatung.

With the preliminary thrusts and counterthrusts out of the way, each side girded itself for the main event—the impending pincer movements from the north, northeast, east, and southeast toward Hankow. General Ch'en Ch'eng and his 9th War Area command were assigned the principal mission of its defense. His massive force of 58 divisions now had for its operational sector Kiangsi province west of Poyang Lake, Hunan, Hupei south of the Yangtze, the Wuhan area and Tienchiachen on the Hupei-Kiangsi border just north of the river. General Li Tsung-jen's 5th War Area command, consisting of 23 corps of 49 divisions, was assigned Honan, Anhwei, and everything in Hupei north of Ch'en Ch'eng's sector as its defense zone.

By mid-July the Japanese Central Expeditionary Army under General Hata, consisting of 13 divisions, 1 separate brigade, and 3 air regiments, plus naval support from ships moving up the Yangtze, had made its principal dispositions in preparation for the offensive. The 2nd Corps of 4 divisions had completed its concentration in the area from Hofei to the southwest. The 11th Corps of 5 divisions and 1 separate brigade was assigned the area south of and along the Yangtze River; the separate army of 4 divisions was assigned the Nanking-Shanghai-Hangchow area, the Yangtze River valley as far upriver as Matang, and the area between the Yangtze and the Huai rivers.

General Hsueh Yueh had failed in his special mission of compelling the Japanese to deploy east of Poyang Lake; having seized the initiative in early June, the Japanese had maintained their full mobility of action. Hsueh Yueh was now ordered to hold Kiukiang, 100 miles downriver from Hankow, and the area west of Poyang.

Kiukiang and Hukou, 18 miles apart, commanded the outlet of Poyang Lake into the Yangtze. Of far more importance, Kiukiang, once the location of a British concession, was the northern terminus of the railway to Nanchang, which connected with Changsha to the west and with Hangchow to the east. The busy river port was thus the freight transfer point on the Yangtze for much of the produce from the rich lake region. A few miles south of Kiukiang a pine-covered spur of the Kiu Ling and Mu How mountain ridges terminated not far from the river. The area was high enough to be cool in summer, and a pleasant resort community had been established at Kuling by foreign missionaries. In time, foreign businessmen and Chinese government officials enlarged the original village until it became the most popular summer place on the Yangtze River. At the outbreak of hostilities in July, 1937, Chiang Kai-shek and Madame Chiang had settled down in Kuling for the season—or so they thought.

General Hsueh Yueh concentrated the bulk of his 9th Army

Group of fourteen divisions west of the lake and its wide outlet to the Yangtze, with the 8th and 29th corps, each of two divisions, in Kiukiang itself. General Chang Fa-kuei was ordered to defend the area along the river west of Hsueh Yueh's sector with his 2nd Army Corps of twenty-one divisions. North of the river, the 21st, 26th, and 27th army groups of 10 divisions took up defensive positions in the area of Susung-Taihu and the eastern flank of the Ta Pieh Mountains. The 4th Army Corps' 68th, 84th, and 86th corps, plus the 2nd, 7th, 26th, and 55th corps, a total of 14 divisions, were directed to hold the road that paralleled the river 15 to 20 miles north of its banks from Huangmei, 15 miles west of Susung, to Hankow. The 2nd Army Group of 4 divisions and the 31st, 59th, and 71st corps of 8 divisions were ordered to defend the area east of the Pinghan Railway and north of the Ta Pieh Mountains.

Before daylight on July 23, units of the Japanese 101st Division from Hukou landed from river craft and established a strong foothold just north of Kutang on the stream flowing from Poyang Lake and 8 miles south of the Yangtze. The landing was covered by naval gunfire and bombing and strafing attacks. Even with eight divisions in the immediate area, it apparently did not occur to Chinese commanders to try to prevent the enemy troops from coming ashore. While the landing was in progress, the Chinese did nothing; by the time the landing had been completed, a series of uncoordinated, piecemeal Chinese attacks came too late to dislodge the Japanese. Kutang was occupied on July 24. On the same day, Japanese troops stormed ashore at Kiukiang and at a nearby inlet called Lake Machang. Though the landing had been preceded by naval gunfire and air attacks, relatively slight damage had been inflicted on the town. Fighting along the river and near the lake continued until June 26, when the eight Chinese defending divisions, numbering between 45,000 and 50,000 men, broke out and abandoned Kiukiang to no more than 10,000 men of the two attacking Japanese divisions. The Chinese forces retreated to prepared positions south of Shaho and 16 miles below the Yangtze. As had happened so many times before, the knowledge that prepared positions existed to the rear obviously weakened the will of the Chinese commanders and their troops to stand up and fight. So Kiukiang, the most important river port between Hankow and Wuhu, fell into the grasp of the Japanese after less than two days of defense.

On July 25th, Japanese naval vessels and aircraft turned their full attention on Hsiaochihkou opposite Kiukiang on the north bank of the Yangtze. At the same time, the 6th Division smashed through the Chinese positions at Taihu, nearly 40 miles north of the river, knocking aside resistance by the 7th, 31st, 68th and 84th Corps. Then, after a contested march of about 25 miles, the Japanese launched an attack against the twelve divisions of the Chinese 21st, 26th, and 27th Army Groups and the 2nd Corps at Susung and Huangmei. The five divisions of the Chinese 31st and 68th Corps put up a good running fight against determined enemy attacks, but the other sixteen Chinese divisions in the area fell back slowly after each new assault. In the end, all of the Chinese units withdrew to the line that had been established in early June and had since been strengthened. By August 5 the Japanese 6th Division had secured the entire Taihu-Huangmei-Susung area.

Although Kiukiang had suffered but slight damage from enemy air attacks and Chinese demolitions, in the weeks after its capture it became the victim of a new outburst of Japanese rage—the scene of ruthless murder, rape, vandalism, and looting. Its ceramics and tile factories were deliberately wrecked, the shards of their output scattered through the debris-cluttered streets. Houses and shops were torn apart, their doors, walls, and rafters ripped out for firewood. Suburban districts and nearby villages suspected of harboring guerrillas or anti-Japanese elements were burned. A number of men, proportionate to the magnitude of the community's supposed offense, were seized and shot, their women raped and murdered. Water craft, so vital to a river and lakeside populace, were confiscated, destroyed, or set adrift on the Yangtze.

In June, a change of heart, or perhaps an intuitive whim, caused Hitler to recall the German military mission from China. Though the Führer had signed the Anti-Comintern Pact with Japan in November, 1936, he had maintained a posture of neutrality toward the Sino-Japanese conflict and had continued to sell arms and equipment to the Chinese government. Since before the outbreak of hostilities, he had considered Chiang Kai-shek completely anti-Communist in attitude and action. But Japanese protests over the presence in Hankow of General von Falkenhausen and his staff had finally convinced the German dictator that he should order his officers to leave China.

For 10 years the mission had provided the only professional military touch to the Chinese army. Dedicated to their own strict army traditions, von Seeckt and later von Falkenhausen had been appalled at the organization, training, and equipment of Chinese troops. Though their advice often went unheeded, they had worked hard to build up Chiang's military posture. The generalissimo's actual control had extended over only a relatively small portion of the entire army. When dealing with provincial commanders, with forces still commanded by the old warlord generals and the Kwangtung-Kwangsi clique, and with Communist troops, Chiang and his National Military Council had been compelled to negotiate, rather than command, to dangle the carrot of new equipment and cash stipends before unwilling generals.

Both of the German chiefs of mission had urged Chiang to merge under-strength divisions to make full-strength outfits, to abolish units that had proven themselves to be useless, to cut down on top-heavy staffs and headquarters troops, to weed out inept and venal commanders, and to appoint one dependable man as commander-in-chief with absolute authority in the field. But Chiang, the politician, had never held sufficient power to institute such revolutionary innovations. Having failed to convince the generalissimo to undertake a complete restructuring of his armies, the Germans had won him over to the advisability of placing 30 German instructors on the staff of the Whampoa Military Academy and of concentrating training and reequipment on an elite corps of 30 divisions. The latter project had progressed well until July, 1937; but in his disastrous effort to bring on foreign intervention at Shanghai, Chiang had thrown his best troops into the hopeless battle and had lost most of them.

When it had become apparent that Japan intended to take over China, von Falkenhausen had advised a war of maneuver, mobility, and aggressive hit-and-run tactics. He had urged seizing the initiative and shifting to offensive action on a large scale. But Chiang and his generals had cowered behind their stationary defenses, only to be mowed down by superior firepower or forced by Japanese maneuvers to retreat. Their military philosophy had remained unchanged for centuries: given time, China could outlast and absorb any external enemy. This had worked during the bow-and-arrow days, so why not now? After all, staggering losses in military manpower and even more staggering losses among the civilian population could always be sustained by China's vast numbers.

When von Falkenhausen received the recall order, he and his staff seriously considered whether or not they would obey. After days of soul-searching and delay, the majority bowed to the tenets of their own military background and departed for Germany. However, a few elected to remain in China in order to continue advising a man and his generals lacking the good sense and humility of spirit to accept advice from anyone. (A few officers of the German military mission were still in Chungking in 1942–43, persona non grata in their homeland, still striving to help the Chinese army.)

On July 11, 1938, nearly 1,000 miles north of the steamy Yangtze Valley, the Japanese Kwantung Army of Manchuria became embroiled with Soviet Russia's Far Eastern Army at Changkufeng close to the junction of the Korean, Manchurian and Siberian borders. Since the Japanese occupation of Manchuria in 1931–32, there had been hundreds of clashes between border patrols. Although each side had suffered a fairly large number of casualties, most of the individual skirmishes amounted to little more than irritating pinpricks. But in 1937, when Stalin began to purge his Far Eastern Army and thus weaken its officer corps, the ever aggressive Kwantung Army saw an opportunity to test the strength of its old enemy. In June of 1937 the Japanese had made several well-organized, battalion-strength, probing attacks along the border. In the face of swift and determined Russian reaction, Japanese troops returned to their own side of the bleak, imaginary line in each case.

In May, 1938, Stalin resumed his insane purge of the Far Eastern Army with a vengeance. By July 1, the toll of purged officers was so large—over fifty percent of the commanders and staffs—that the Japanese concluded that Russian combat effectiveness must have been seriously weakened. The temptation to act was too great for them to resist.

On July 11th, the Kwantung Army command ordered one division to attack and seize the heights of Changkufeng dominating the adjacent border areas. Though clearly in Russian territory, the steep hill mass had been unoccupied by troops of any nationality until shortly before the attack. To their surprise, the Japanese butted up against a well dug-in force of Soviet troops determined not to yield an inch of ground. The defenders were quickly reinforced with additional infantry and artillery units. The Russian air force sent Japanese planes scuttling back to their bases, then bombed and strafed the exposed enemy positions. The battle continued intermittently for one month. Every Japanese attack failed. On August 10 the clash ended with a Japanese withdrawal from assault positions to Korean and Manchurian territory.

Somewhat dazedly the Japanese finally awakened to the humiliating truth that they had been rudely set back on their heels. In view of their overextension in China, they were in no condition to risk further embroilment with Soviet Russia. The terms for a cease-fire were agreed upon within two weeks.

By late August, troop concentrations and preliminary thrusts indicated the Japanese battle plan for the pincer movement to take Hankow. Three divisions of the 11th Corps[16] were poised in the area south of the Yangtze River just west of Kiukiang ready to strike out in three columns. The Chinese National Military Council correctly assessed the situation as to probable Japanese routes and objectives. They could hardly have done otherwise. With their heavy equipment, artillery, and tanks, the Japanese were confined to main roads and, because of supporting naval units, to dependence on the Yangtze River. But when the entire Chinese government, trailed by the foreign ambassadors and their staffs, evacuated Hankow and Wuchang in early September, the bulk of the armies lost much of their will to fight. With the abandonment of the tri-cities for the safety of Chungking, 550 miles farther upriver, army, corps, and division commanders realized that Wuhan would be taken and that their commander-in-chief was deserting his troops in order to preserve the core of his regime and personal power in the craggy, inaccessible city at the confluence of the Kialing and Yangtze rivers. To many soldiers—with a few notable exceptions, such as Hsueh Yueh—the battle was already lost; it would be no more than a series of delaying actions, withdrawals, and breakouts to save their own skins.

In addition, the will to put up stiff resistance in the defense of Hankow had been dangerously sapped by an epidemic of malaria throughout most of the Chinese units in the humid Yangtze Valley. Never plentiful, the supply of quinine had run out completely, and replenishment from the Netherlands Indies had been cut off by the Japanese blockade of Chinese ports. The outbreak was particularly virulent among northern troops unaccustomed to the hot, humid river and lake regions. Entire units were laid low; tens of thousands of men were reduced to dragging weakly from one position to another. However, the general debilitation among Chinese troops was more than offset by an epidemic of violent intestinal disorders among the Japanese. This condition had developed from carelessness or ignorance in maintaining pure water supply and had been aggravated by poisoned and contaminated village wells. The Chinese custom was to drink only boiled water before it had had time to cool, either brewed into tea or drunk alone to quench thirst; the Japanese troops paid dearly for breaking this most important health rule of the Far East. At one time during the summer the greater part of an entire division was incapacitated. The lull in the campaign from early July to mid-August was necessary for both sides.

In January, 1938, months before departing for Chungking, Chiang Kai-shek had summoned the governor of Szechwan, General Liu Hsiang, to Hankow to discuss the proposed movement of the entire national government to Chungking in his province. Liu had plainly indicated his disinclination to play host to a flood of national and senior military figures. He had inherited his practically autonomous domain from an uncle and considered it a family fief. While in Hankow, he had truculently expressed his unwillingness to grant permission for what he saw as an invasion of his rights and authority. His whole manner had been that of a foreign potentate reluctant to grant asylum to a defeated ally. To correct this potentially embarrassing situation, Liu Hsiang was invited as the honored guest to an elaborate banquet. That night, after the festive dinner, he was seized with agonizing stomach cramps. By daylight he was dead. It was officially announced that Liu Hsiang, the highly esteemed governor of Szechwan, had died of a sickness in the stomach. A lavish state funeral was held, and Liu's remains were shipped to his family burial ground at Chengtu, the capital of Szechwan. Chiang Kai-shek immediately appointed General Chang Ch'un, whose loyalty he felt he could depend upon, to the suddenly vacant position of governor of the province.

The offensive against Hankow began on August 20 with the five divisions of the Japanese 11th Corps operating as three well-coordinated offensive forces. The 101st and 106th divisions, after moving south on the Kiukiang-Nanchang Railway, made a forced landing at Hsingtze on the northern outlet of Poyang Lake. They immediately attacked the Chinese 9th Army Group of 14 divisions, then entrenched in an arc extending from east of Juichang, 8 miles south of the Yangtze, to south of Shaho and along the railway line to Nanchang. At the same time the Japanese 27th Division attacked the defense positions at Juichang. The capture of Juichang on August 24 could have opened the roads leading to the west for the Japanese 106th, 9th, and 27th divisions; but the stubborn resistance of the Chinese 1st Army Corps and the attached 20 divisions of the 2nd Army Corps[17] against repeated enemy assaults stopped the Japanese dead in their tracks. Finally, with massive air, tank, and artillery support—and heavy casualties on both sides—the Japanese broke through the Chinese positions just north of Mahuiling, about 20 miles south of Kiukiang. By September 21 the Japanese 101st Division had battled its way to a point just north of Tehan, on the railway 35 miles south of Kiukiang, where it was again stopped. On October 1, after repeated attacks and counterattacks for 10 days, the Japanese succeeded in seizing Yikou, a few miles east of the railway on the northwest shore of Poyang Lake. Their 27th Division then attempted to push west from Juichang, but it was stopped near Pichiashan by the 5 divisions of the Chinese 12th and 52nd corps before it had been able to advance 10 miles. Meanwhile, the Japanese 101st and 106th divisions turned west and southwest to attack the 12 divisions of the Chinese 9th, 26th, and 30th army groups in the area of Paishuichieh and Wanchialing, 30 miles southwest of Kiukiang. On October 6, determined assaults with heavy air and artillery support managed to ram through the Chinese positions at Paishuichieh, but got no farther. Instead, the Japanese divisions were badly mauled in the constant attacks and hand-to-hand bayonet charges. By October 10 the toll of Japanese casualties was so high (over 10,000 men) that the 4 infantry regiments of the 106th Division had been rendered temporarily incapable of further offensive action and the 101st Division was compelled to break off the battle. For a change, the Japanese were forced to assume a defensive stance. Had it not been for the chronic Chinese reluctance to go on the offensive and the heavy casualties they had sustained at Wanchialing, Hsueh Yueh could have enveloped the weakened east flank of the Japanese, pushed rapidly to the northeast, and placed a large force in the enemy rear. Had he done so at once, it is possible that he could have disrupted the entire time schedule of the Japanese 11th Corps. But he allowed the opportunity to pass.

In General Chang Fa-kuei's 2nd Army Corps combat sector— west of Hsueh Yueh's zone of operations both north and south of the Yangtze—action began with the Japanese attack on Juichang on August 22. With the fall of that important road junction two days later, 6 Chinese corps containing 13 divisions[18] faced the Japanese 9th and 27th divisions to block the opening of the two roads leading to the west. For nearly seven weeks the Japanese battled against stubborn Chinese resistance in bitterly contested delaying actions; by October 10 they had been unable to gain more than 15 miles of ground. In the constant ebb and flow of the battle, the countryside was devastated. In late August, Japanese marines and the Taiwanese Brigade landed at Kangkou, a small river town northeast of Juichang, and proceeded upstream toward Matouchen on the south bank and toward Wushihchieh on the opposite shore. In the meantime, on August 28 and 29, the Chinese 7th, 31st, and 20th corps of 7 divisions carried out a surprise attack against Huangmei, the Japanese 6th Division's base 20 miles north of the river. Though the Chinese inflicted heavy casualties on the enemy, they did not follow up their initial advantage and take the town. On the morning of August 30 the Japanese counterattacked and drove the Chinese back to their former positions. The Japanese 6th Division then began to move west and south from Huangmei. By September 9 it had broken through the main Chinese defense lines and had taken Kuangchi, 12 miles northeast of the river fortress of Tienchiachen. The south-driving column rolled back the Chinese line toward the river and on September 10 linked up with the marines and the Taiwanese Brigade near Wushihchieh. Though strongly resisted, this enemy move divided the Chinese forces north of the Yangtze, cutting off the 9 divisions of the 7th, 31st, 68th, and 84th corps. Of these 4 corps, the 7th withdrew to Yingshan, 30 miles to the west in an area that had been designated as a base for future guerrilla operations; the 84th, after a 20-mile forced march, managed to rejoin the main Chinese defense forces. Meanwhile, on the south bank, 7 Chinese corps[19] containing 15 divisions held their ground at Matouchen against air, naval, and ground assaults for nearly two weeks of bloody fighting. Finally Matouchen fell to the Japanese on September 12, but it was not until October 3 that the Taiwanese Brigade with the support of naval units succeeded in forcing a landing at Fuchikao on the south bank opposite Tienchiachen. As an indication of the stiff Chinese resistance, it took the Japanese three weeks to advance 15 miles upriver from Matouchen, though their troops were heavily supported by naval gunfire and constant air attacks. Wushihchieh on the north bank was not captured until September 16.

With the capture of Kuangchi northeast of Tienchiachen and of Wushihchieh to the southeast, the Japanese 6th Division moved rapidly toward the fortress of Tienchiachen from the north, northeast, and southeast. At this time, naval units and the Taiwanese Brigade were in position to attack from the river. The nine divisions of the Chinese 26th, 48th, 84th, and 86th corps attacked the Japanese on their north flank. But the 6th Division fended off all Chinese assaults and pressed on to attack the fortifications of Tienchiachen. The Chinese 2nd Corps of two divisions[20] was trapped within the perimeter of the defensive positions. The Japanese began the attack on the Chinese outer defense lines on September 19, but they made no progress in the face of heavy artillery, mortar, and machine-gun fire from the defending troops who well knew there was now no escape for them. Attempting to ram through the heavily seeded mine-fields in the river, the Japanese lost a number of gunboats and smaller river craft; not, however, "scores of enemy ships and motor boats" as claimed in the official Chinese account. Other Japanese craft were put out of action or damaged. Four Chinese gunboats were sunk by enemy aircraft. After a bitterly contested 10-day fight and several thousand battle casualties, the Tienchiachen fortress was captured on September 29. All Chinese troops who had not been able to escape were executed forthwith. When they entered the town, the Japanese found that they had won no prize. The once-prosperous river port was a battered ruin of burning buildings, demolished structures, and blackened debris. Most of the fortifications had been blasted into crumbling ruins during the battle; what little had remained intact had been blown up in accordance with the Chinese policy of leaving nothing for the enemy but scorched earth. The riverside pontoons had been drenched with oil, set afire, and cast adrift to float into Japanese vessels. And the Chinese 26th, 48th, 84th, and 86th corps began a slow withdrawal from Chichun, north of Tienchiachen, toward Hsishui and Shangpaho to the northwest.

Prior to the beginning of its wide, end-run envelopment north of the Ta Pieh Mountains, the Japanese 2nd Corps had concentrated its 3rd and 10th divisions at Luan on the Pei River, its 13th and 16th divisions in the vicinity of Huoshan, 20 miles to the south. For the defense of this sector the Chinese 5th War Area command had deployed in depth the forces at its disposal—strung out for 140 miles. The 77th Corps of 2 divisions was opposite Luan on the west side of the Pei River; the 51st Corps of 2 divisions was in Huoshan. Their missions were to block Japanese attempts to cross the river and move to the west by the two main roads. The 71st Corps of 3 divisions was deployed at Fuchinshan, 30 miles northwest of Huoshan, and at Kushih, 50 miles northwest of Luan. Presumably the 2 corps at the Pei River, with a maximum strength of less than 25,000, were expected to carry out the impossible task of stopping Japanese forces numbering 80,000 men backed up by 6 battalions of attached artillery in addition to their organic artillery units, tanks, and air squadrons. The 2nd

Army Group of 4 divisions was deployed at Shangcheng, 60 miles northwest of Huoshan, and at Macheng, 40 miles south of Shangcheng. The 59th Corps of 2 divisions was in defensive positions at Huangchuan, 85 miles northwest of Luan; and the 1st Corps of 2 divisions was deployed at Hsinyang, 50 miles farther to the west. One of the 31st Corps' 3 divisions was placed 12 miles east of Shangcheng, expecting to fight a decisive battle in the area. The remaining troops in this sector of the 5th War Area were held in reserve—meaning to be preserved for later political-military bargaining purposes. This characteristic of drawn-out deployment in depth not only predicated the expectation of defeat, but inexcusably set up 18 divisions to be picked off one by one. Had Chiang Kai-shek ordered the concentration of these 100,000 troops for a determined fight at the Pei River crossings, it is quite possible that they could have delayed the Japanese offensive or even have stopped it before it was able to gain momentum.

On August 27 the Japanese 2nd Corps began its offensive by attacking at Luan and Huoshan. Two days later the Japanese crossed the Pei River against little Chinese resistance and pushed on to the west. Having swept the Chinese 51st Corps before them, the north Japanese column, the 3rd and 10th divisions, reached the defensive positions at Kushih on September 3. But at Kushih, the 51st Corps joined one division of the 71st Corps behind prepared positions and held off enemy attacks for three days. On September 6 the Chinese abandoned Kushih and fell back 15 miles to a defense line just east of Chunho. The Japanese south column, the 13th and 16th divisions, met stronger resistance on the road to Shangcheng and was held up until September 11 at Fuchinshan, about 20 miles northwest of Huoshan. After driving the Chinese out of Fuchinshan, the Japanese pressed on toward Shangcheng, 30 miles to the northwest. For the next five days, nine Chinese divisions from the 2nd Army Group, the 31st, 71st, and 77th corps, fought a series of delaying actions as they gradually fell back on Shangcheng. Finally, in the words of the official Chinese history, "the enemy's absolute superiority changed our original plans to fight a decisive battle east of Shangcheng. On September 16th, our forces abandoned Shangcheng and fell back to . . . Shawo [12 miles to the south] . . .

and the passes in the Ta Pieh Shan. Enemy failure shattered his design to move along the Shangcheng-Macheng highway." In more honest terms, the enemy failure had resulted in the defeat and withdrawal of the Chinese, not to mention Japanese advances of about 70 miles along both roads leading to the northwest. The Chinese were routed because of their stubborn adherence to tactics of so-called deployment in depth and because of their refusal to attack. Chinese claims that up to September 16 over 15,000 Japanese troops had been killed were manifestly absurd. With the usual ratio of killed to wounded, this claim, if correct, would have meant that the Japanese 2nd Corps had lost nearly half of its strength in battle casualties.

Meanwhile, the Japanese north column attacked the Chinese positions at Chunho, broke through the lines, and captured the town on September 12. Troops of the Chinese 51st and 71st corps withdrew in disorder for about 18 miles to new defense positions east of Huangchuan. There the three divisions of the 59th Corps put up a determined fight, but again "superior fire power, air support and indiscriminate gas attacks" brought on the eventual defeat of the Chinese defenders. (The accusation that the Japanese used gas in this sector has not been substantiated.) Huangchuan was taken on September 19. In precipitate flight, Chinese forces paused briefly at Loshan, 25 miles to the west, where they put up token resistance; Loshan was abandoned on September 21. The Chinese fell back to Lankan, 10 miles farther west. At this point the Chinese 1st Corps of two divisions counterattacked and forced the Japanese to pull back to Loshan, but on September 28 the Japanese 3rd Division, supported by artillery and air units, counterattacked. The engagement lasted for two days. By the thirtieth the Chinese fell back to the vicinity of Hsinyang to prepared positions parallel to and about 5 miles east of the Pinghan Railway for sustained resistance. The resistance did not sustain itself very long. A Japanese column from the 3rd Division at Lankan drove through the south end of the defense lines, cut the railway 10 miles south of Hsinyang, and continued toward Wushengkuan, 8 miles farther south. On October 12 the Chinese abandoned Hsinyang without a fight and retreated to the west, southwest, and south.

By October 10–12 the five Japanese columns advancing toward

Hankow from south of the Yangtze River, along the river, from just north of the river, from the northeast, and from the north had reached points 60 to 75 miles from their goal. The noose in the great pincer movement was steadily tightening.

As the hot summer days gave way to October, the people of doomed Hankow seemed to be seized with a strange mix of emotions: terror and the hysterical urge to flee before the arrival of the Japanese; numb resignation among the old and those too exhausted by previous flights to leave the city; driving determination for haste among the hundreds helping to evacuate half-starved, bewildered orphan children who had been brought from ruined villages to Hankow; deep dread among the thousands of bloody, filthy, wounded soldiers struggling to keep ahead of the enemy, begging for a bowl of rice, a clean bandage, a ride on a truck, a place to rest—even as their hollowed, feverish eyes showed they knew their pleas would not be heard. Bands of looters slipped through the streets at night, snatching food and valuables; they were shot on sight by the police. The foreign community, growing ever smaller, wound itself into a sort of nightly dance of death in bars, restaurants, and emptying hotels. Chinese government officials decamped at night, leaving no word of their destinations. Streams of refugees numbering hundreds of thousands left the city by cart and wheelbarrow, on foot, on overloaded trucks and jammed trains, by boat and junk, each trying desperately to cling to as many of his possessions as he could carry. Men and women in the struggling columns fought for food. Shots frequently rang out, and another body was kicked into a roadside ditch or thrown into a stagnant canal. Going about their now meaningless business, the consulates strove to maintain a calm air of efficiency for the Chinese to see, and to prop up their own sagging spirits, as if the world about them was not collapsing into a complete breakdown of all order and control.

As stragglers and deserters slunk through the city seeking their own means of solitary escape, fires in the Chinese city sent quavering spirals of black smoke into the hot, blue sky. Some shed their uniforms for any rags they might find or steal. All had cast aside their weapons and so had to fight for food with their bare hands.

During the summer, before the exodus from Hankow began, I had tried with little success to visit the fighting fronts. A train going north on the Pinghan Railway, onto which I had fought my way through crowds of uneasy troops, stopped less than 100 miles from Hankow to disgorge its load of soldiers at a small station. I had hoped that it would also disgorge me to make my way toward the front as best I could, either on foot or by military truck; but the military police had had other ideas and had firmly escorted me back to the empty coach. Within minutes the train had begun to back down the tracks. A few hours later it had rolled into the Hankow station where I bid a none too polite goodbye to my guards. They, having been fortunate enough to reach the city, had undoubtedly slipped off among the deserters to a temporary surcease from war.

Later I had better luck on a hot, dirty train trip to Nanchang to visit General Hsueh Yueh's headquarters, from where I hoped to go north to his fighting front. At least I reached Nanchang and was received by General Hsueh and his English-speaking aide, General Ho; but that was as far as I got. During most of the interview, General Hsueh was either stone-faced or scowling. Every time he glanced toward me his cropped hair fairly bristled. To all my questions regarding troop movements and operations plans the answers were that such information was either a military secret or *pu shih ni-ti shih* ("none of your business"). When I requested permission to go to the forward area near Tehan, I was told flatly that I could go back to Hankow and nowhere else —in effect, get the hell out of the 1st Army Corps' zone of operations.

My bruised ego was mollified at the American Methodist mission and school. The fatherly old gentleman who directed its operations invited me at once to be his guest for as long as I remained in Nanchang. That evening after dinner he became almost oratorical as he enlarged on the significance of Chiang Kai-shek's conversion to Christianity. Though I pointed out that many of Chiang's actions and those of his secret police could hardly be described as exemplifying Christian principles, the kindly old missionary was not in the least convinced. He stated that the generalissimo had enormous responsibilities in the present difficult times; that he was often compelled to direct actions he would rather avoid; that he could not be held liable for the sins of all of his subordinates. Besides, he read the Bible with Madame Chiang every day, proving that he was a sincere and devout Christian. I dropped the subject.

On another trip from Hankow, I went to see General Chang Fa-kwei at Changsha. Arriving on a steaming hot evening in the bedlam of the railway station, I pushed through a mass of jostling, sweaty people to a rickety four-story inn at which I planned to stay the night. Built around the well of a central court, all of the rooms opened onto balconies on which noisy groups of people chattered and from which the refuse of meals and chamber pots rained in an intermittent waterfall of filth. The place was stifling; it reeked of garlic and uncleared sewage. Its only lights were sputtering candles and smoking kerosene lamps. Its thin walls vibrated with the constant shouts and yells of guests, and it was the worst kind of a firetrap. The distraught manager told me with apologies that I should not stay in his hostelry. It would be dangerous during the night. Some of the men at the inn would stop at nothing to steal my money. It would be much better if I went to the Standard-Vacuum Company compound for the night. I did, and found a haven of cleanliness and quiet, disturbed only by the echoes of sounds from the city. All of the American wives and employees, except one, had been evacuated. The assistant manager, the sole remaining American, was a hospitable young man delighted at the opportunity to talk to one of his own kind. To fill in the dull days and nights of his stewardship he had taken up soap sculpture, an entirely new craft to me. Scattered about his quarters were a dozen examples of his work, one of green soap nearly 16 inches in height. To make that, his masterpiece, he had laboriously pressed cake after cake of wet soap to form a large block out of which he had carved an unusual nude figure with outstretched arms, Paul Robeson singing "Old Man River."

The next morning I called at Chang Fa-kuei's headquarters and got no farther than the outer gate. The sentries called the officer of the guard, who shook his head in mock dismay over all the trouble I had gone to in order to see the general. He was out of town. All of his staff were out of town. His aides were out of town. So sorry. I wandered off to the famous "Yale in China" university and hospital. The outpatient clinic was mobbed with wailing children, keening mothers, and silent old men and women hoping patiently that the white doctors could cure their ills and open sores with a foreign magic their own herb specialists did not have. The American and Chinese doctors were making a valiant effort.

The next day another visit to the 2nd Army Corps headquarters brought forth a captain who stopped me at the outer gate. This time, General Chang Fa-kuei and his entire staff were at the front; it was not known when they might return. My proposal to visit the general in the forward areas met with hard-eyed disapproval and the information that a train would be leaving for Hankow within the hour; and to ensure my safety in the streets, a guard of soldiers would escort me to the station. I was so escorted.

In early September Colonel Stilwell had radioed to Hankow to ask if I would accept a one-year extension to my four-year tour of duty in China, due to terminate in October, if it could be arranged. According to what we used to call the "Manchu Law," American officers of the combat arms were not allowed at that time to remain away from troop duty for more than four years. I agreed to the extension, and somehow Stilwell managed to have me transferred to the Chemical Warfare Service in order to circumvent the traditional policy of the Manchu Law. But some horrified chairwarmer in the adjutant general's office in Washington discovered this dastardly trick, and promptly had me transferred back to the Field Artillery with orders to return to the states at the proper time.

So I was to return to Peking, pack up my belongings, and beat the deadline of the Manchu Law. But how? I could not leave Hankow by air. The Japanese had recently shot down three civilian planes on the way to Canton, and all other planes had been grounded. Two important bridges on the railway to Canton had been bombed out. No one could say when they might be rebuilt and service restored. But I reserved space on the first train leaving Hankow for Canton.

John Davies threw a farewell party at his apartment, but the specter of what we all knew was about to happen haunted the dinner, and we were only partially successful in our efforts to act carefree and cheerful. Agnes Smedley read a poem she had composed, then informed us that before the Japanese entered Hankow she would slip out of town to join Chinese guerrilla forces.

After several days, word came that the first train for Canton would depart the following morning. The temporary bridges, I learned, might not hold up under the weight of a crowded train, but they had to be tried out some time. With mixed feelings I crossed the river on the ferry, drove to the Wuchang station, and pushed into the milling crowd. It seemed impossible for anyone to squeeze through that tight-packed mob to the waiting train, but with the aid of the resourceful half-Chinese son of L.C. Arlington, the author of *In Search of Old Peking*, I finally managed to shove, gouge, and ram my way to the compartment assigned to us.

The antique wooden coach must have been one of the first built after the invention of the steam engine. Its two upper and two lower berths (boards with thin mattresses and paper-thin cotton blankets) had already been locked in position for sleeping. Two other occupants of the compartment had arrived before us and of course had preempted both lower berths. One was the fattest Chinese I had ever seen. The other was a very attractive young woman who forthwith presented her business card, a seven-inch-long affair with her name printed in large black characters. Arlington whispered to me in English that she was a high-class prostitute and that all expensive professionals used huge cards like hers. Then with a brisk manner he assumed command of the compartment. First he talked the fat man into moving to an upper berth: it would be grossly discourteous of a Chinese, Arlington argued, not to offer an important foreigner the best they could provide. The fat man looked dubious, but in the interests of international relations, he managed to swing his enormous bulk into the berth above the one now assigned to me. I would have felt better—and safer—had all that bulk not been overhead, but Arlington refused to consider altering his arrangements. The prostitute, he decided, should retain possession of her lower berth. About that time the train grunted and lunged its clanking way out of the station.

The dining car served two meals a day: tea, rice, and *congee* (a gruel of rice cooked for hours in an excess of water) for breakfast; a variety of Hunanese food with fiery peppers and sauces in the late afternoon. The latter could be washed down with tea, *pai ga-erh* (a potent liquor distilled from sorghum), or great quantities of *huang chiu* (yellow wine served hot). Meals were cheerful and noisy social gatherings. Before the trip of two and a half days and 600 miles was over, the occupants of our compartment, with an additional skinny little Chinese who fastened onto us like a leech, had become friendly and companionable—even the fat man. The prostitute, on a brief rest from business, was not only fun but also entertained us by reading the most wonderful fortunes with cards and in the lines of our palms.

Moving at a bare crawl, the train negotiated the first wobbly bridge without mishap. A hundred miles farther on it tackled the second with a little more speed and confidence as the timbers shook and groaned under its weight. Then, within 100 miles of Canton, it stopped in the midst of farmlands in the open countryside. With much shouting and blowing of whistles, the passengers were ordered to detrain in a hurry and to take cover in a large patch of woods a few hundred yards from the tracks. Soldiers with Luger pistols and bayoneted rifles herded us into groups crouching under the doubtful protection of the trees. With his pistol at the ready, a particularly mean-looking, slant-eyed corporal stood behind me to make sure I did not raise my eyes skyward, since it was well known to the Chinese that blue eyes reflected light and therefore could flash signals to enemy fliers.

About nine o'clock on the third morning, the train chugged to a stop in the Canton station. The whole area was a shambles from repeated Japanese bombings—twisted rails, burned-out sheds, yawning craters, and the scattered debris of the last raid. In the best tradition of Chinese bureaucracy, a barrier at which all incoming passengers were required to present their identity papers stood at the guarded exit. Just as my new friends and I debarked with our assorted luggage, warning sirens wailed to announce the approach of a wave of bombers. As in the past, the planes would probably head straight for the station and yards and be overhead before the hundreds of passengers could possibly edge through the barrier. I knew that my diplomatic passport would get me through quickly, but what about my companions? I couldn't leave them stranded. Something had to be done fast. A sudden inspiration saved the day for them. I shouted to the prostitute: "You're my mistress. They'll understand and accept that." To Arlington: "You're my Chinese secretary." To the fat man: "You're my Number One house man." And to the skinny one: "You're my coolie. Grab my bags. Now, all of you! Run like hell and hit that goddam barrier with a rush!"

Displaying the passport with my haughtiest air, I identified myself and my staff to the guards. They ushered us through the barrier and out of the station with all the smiling deference due such an obviously rich and important foreigner, particularly after the sergeant had palmed a $20 bill. On the street, we all breathed a quick sigh of relief and leaped to grab the few rickshas whose operators were still brave enough—or poor enough—to be awaiting fares. Then with our luggage piled about us in the vehicles, the prostitute suddenly called a halt before we started off. She announced that since I had helped them out of danger, they would now all escort me to the safety of my hotel in Shameen, the sacrosanct island in the river that had been a foreign concession for nearly 100 years.

The ricksha men took off at a dead gallop, dashed across the guarded bridge, and pulled up at the entrance of the very British Victoria Hotel. A bearded Sikh doorman in elegant uniform and high turban was duly impressed with my entourage, dirty and travel-stained as we were. I bid a genuinely fond farewell to my friends and urged them to get out of the center of the city as quickly as possible.

After a bath and a change, I phoned Frank Roberts, who had left word at the desk that he was in Canton. We met for lunch at the staid British club, set as usual in a tree-shaded garden. The rear windows of the dining room faced the Chinese Bund across the narrow river—tall, battered buildings, some blackened by fires, others pockmarked by 50-caliber bullets from strafing attacks. Their blown-out windows seemed to stare in blank hopelessness at the neat safety of Shameen.

The next morning, Roberts and I boarded a British steamer for the 80-mile trip down the estuary of the Pearl River to Hongkong. From the first-class deck we watched lush green hills and peaceful fishing villages gradually merge into bustling water traffic as the ship approached the proud crown colony. We went straight to the clean, cool comfort of the Hongkong Hotel where Roberts's wife Peggy was waiting to welcome us. After months in the wreckage of the Yangtze Valley and the hot, slow train trip to Canton, the meticulous service and quiet of the hotel was a blessed relief. Two days later I boarded the Canadian Pacific liner *Empress of Japan* bound for Shanghai. There I transferred to a smaller Butterfield and Swire ship enroute to Tientsin.

By the middle of October, Chinese resistance in the operations zone of the 9th War Area south of the Yangtze had begun to crumble. Exhausted and no longer able to withstand the pounding of Japanese ground and air attacks, General Hsueh Yueh's 9th, 30th and 26th Army Groups of twenty-six divisions were nonetheless still clinging to their positions just north of Wankuling and Tehan, both cities about 30 miles south of the river and less than 20 miles apart. But when a strong enemy column executed a rapid move around the west flank of the 1st defense line and seized Juohsi, the 30th and 26th Army Groups abandoned Wankuling at once and fell back to the south bank of the Hsiu River, flowing from west to east into Poyang Lake about 10 miles south of the now collapsed defense line. Renewed attacks by the Japanese 101st Division finally won Tehan on October 28th. By October 31 the entire 1st Army Corps had withdrawn to the south bank of the Hsiu, where military operations remained at a standstill until the following spring. In Chang Fa-kuei's 2nd Army Corps zone of defense, the Japanese 27th Division steadily, but slowly, forced back the five divisions of the 3rd Army Group and 52nd Corps toward Pichiashan, 15 miles west of Juichang. On October 18, after a two-day battle, the Japanese forces captured Pichiashan, then pushed on to Hsintanpu, 16 miles to the west. They took Yanghsin on the eighteenth. By the nineteenth the Japanese 106th Division had turned to the northwest and was attacking southwest of Huangshihkang, only 45 miles from Wuchang. But the fight had gone out of the Chinese; after a heavy bombardment, they retreated and left wide open the route to Wuchang along the south bank of the Yangtze. Skirting the east and north shores of Liangtze

Lake, the Japanese 106th Division rushed through undefended Aocheng and reached the outskirts of Wuchang on October 25.

In other operations in this sector, the Japanese 27th Division captured Tungshan on November 6 after a halfhearted show of Chinese resistance, then pushed on to Tungcheng, 40 miles to the southwest, which fell on November 11. The Japanese 9th Division pressed forward to take Hsienning on the Hankow-Canton railway line, 50 miles south of Wuchang, in late October. Then, driving down the railway, they captured Puchi in early November. Finally, on November 12, the 9th Division took the important city of Yochow (Yuehyang) on the railway at the northern exit of Tungting Lake. The Chinese 2nd Army Corps fell back 22 miles to the south bank of the Hsinchiang River, which flowed into Tungting Lake, and established a line of defensive strongpoints that ran in an easterly direction and linked up with the 1st Army Corps on the Hsiu River. Beyond patrolling and relatively minor probing attacks, the western half of these 9th War Area positions remained inactive until the fall of 1939.

After the loss of Tienchiachen in early October, the combined force of 11 divisions from the 11th Army Group[21] and the 26th, 86th, and 2nd corps fell back to establish a new defense line running through Hsishu and Lanche, north of the Yangtze and about 15 miles northwest of the fortress. In mid-October the Japanese 6th Division launched a heavy attack against the center of the line, at the same time sending a column around the Chinese south flank toward Huangkang on the river some 15 miles to the rear of the defensive positions. Alarmed, as usual, at this threat to their line of retreat, Chinese resistance collapsed completely. The Japanese took Hsishu on October 19 and immediately went into pursuit of the routed Chinese divisions fleeing toward Shangpaho, 30 miles to the northwest. Meanwhile, the enemy flanking column took Huangkang, turned inland, and attacked the Chinese 55th Corps of 2 divisions at Tunfeng, 10 miles to the north. At this point, Chinese commanders were ready to panic, which they did at the first sign of an enemy attack. The Japanese simply marched into both Shangpaho and Tunfeng. With the goal now so near, the two Japanese columns plunged on in frantic haste to take Sungfu and Hsinchow, the latter less than 20 miles northeast of Hankow, and turned to the southwest. On October 24 they seized Huangpi, 10 miles north of the city. By this time all Chinese resistance had dissolved into a helter-skelter scramble for escape to the west. Within a week the bulk of the defeated Chinese troops managed to straggle into a defensive line about 20 miles west of the Pinghan Railway, but the 7 divisions of the 21st Army Group and the 7th Corps remained in the hilly country south of the Ta Pieh Mountains to conduct guerrilla operations, meaning to hole up and live off the countryside.

North of the Ta Pieh Mountains in the operations zone of the Japanese 2nd Corps, its 16th and 13th divisions, after taking Shangcheng on September 16, were relatively inactive until mid-October. Then they attacked positions held by the seven divisions of the Chinese 2nd Army Group and 71st Corps about 12 miles to the south. A counterattack by the 71st Corps forced the Japanese to pull back temporarily. But the enemy 13th Division reacted with a vengeance, smashed through the Chinese lines, forced a passage through the rugged Ta Pieh Mountains at Hsiao-chiehling, and captured Macheng, 30 miles south of the battle area. The Japanese 16th Division pursued the fleeing 2nd Army Group and 71st Corps through Chinfu, in the mountains 15 miles south of the Chinese positions. It then headed toward Huayuan, 40 miles north of Hankow on the Pinghan Railway. The Chinese 2nd Army Group and 71st Corps panicked when they discovered that the Japanese 3rd and 10th divisions were moving south along the railway line toward Wushengkuan, 50 miles west of Chinfu. In their precipitate and disorderly flight of 85 miles they lost much of their equipment and hundreds of men by desertions. The rout finally stopped 30 miles west of the Pinghan line, where with a river between them and the enemy they crawled into defensive positions—a safe haven at last, since they were passed by and ignored until the following April. Huayuan was occupied by the Japanese without opposition on October 22. They immediately pushed south along the railway line and on October 24 linked up with the 6th Division at Huangpi, just north of Hankow.

Farther north, the Japanese 3rd and 10th divisions, having seized Hsinyang on the Pinghan line on October 12, attacked the Chinese 31st Corps of three divisions and the 13th Division, which were deployed at Wushengkuan to block any farther southward movement of the enemy. The block was removed by the first Japanese assault, and Wushengkuan was captured without a fight on October 15. The defending Chinese troops had had enough. They fled to Suihsien, 40 miles directly to the west—instead of withdrawing to the south along the railway—and occupied the southern end of another defense line already being prepared by the 1st Corps after its rout from Hsinyang. According to the official Chinese history, the 1st Corps had "moved to the mountainous area northwest of Hsinyang . . . to seek exterior lines so as to ensure freedom of movement." The corps found the exterior lines—exterior to the whole battle area—but the freedom of movement was neither sought nor employed. Though the six Chinese divisions on the line could have attacked the Japanese flank and rear at any time and could have cut the railway behind their forward elements, they remained inactive during the next six months, except, of course, to forage through the countryside. In mid-October, when the Japanese 3rd Division moved south to attack Yingshan, 30 miles below Hsinyang, the Chinese command decided that the withdrawal route of the main force of the 5th War Area was threatened. Once again, the chronic trauma concerning an enemy on the flank and rear filled the minds of Chinese commanders with a frantic urge to withdraw with the greatest possible speed. Having well over 100,000 troops within 50 miles of Yingshan, it apparently did not occur to General Li Tsung-jen and his senior commanders to concentrate all available forces and to strike hard at the two columns of advancing Japanese numbering at most no more than 30,000 men. After meeting but slight resistance at Yingshan, the Japanese pressed on unopposed to Anlu, 20 miles farther south. Then the Japanese 3rd Division turned to the southeast through Hsiaokan and on October 25 entered the northwest outskirts of Hankow.

General Lo Cho-ying's Wuhan Defense Garrison of seven divisions plus the 26th Corps of two more divisions had already folded in a frenzied race to escape the Japanese trap by river craft, cart and trucks. But despite its haste to make a getaway, most of the 26th Corps found itself caught in the lake area around Hankow by the rampaging, wildly exultant troops of the Japanese 6th and 16th divisions.

After four and a half months the great Japanese pincer movement was finally succeeding. On October 25, enemy columns were about to pour into Hankow from the northwest, north, northeast, and east. They had already entered Wuchang from the south, and a sizable fleet of naval units and transports was steaming upriver to disembark troops on the waterfront Bund. The Chinese apologists who authored the official history of the war wrapped up the disastrous campaign in a neat face-saving package of words for the record: "On October 25th, our forces, having abandoned Wuhan, withdrew to the line from the Hsiu River to the Hsinchiang River, Shayang [on the Han River 75 miles west of Hankow] and Suihsien. Coupled with [absurdly high claims of Japanese casualties—over 200,000 out of a maximum of 380,000 engaged—and of huge losses in ships, gunboats, and aircraft] the advance evacuation of the people and matériel of Wuhan, the objective of a war of attrition was realized." When viewed in a more realistic light and coupled with the loss of over 1,000,000 officers and men, probably twice that many civilians, staggering amounts of arms and equipment, all of China's seaports (Canton fell on October 21), most of the railway lines, most of the major cities, north China, Shantung, the Yangtze valley, and all territory adjacent to the occupied lines of transportation and communication, the Chinese claim of realization of the objectives of a war of attrition was in fact a catastrophic disaster for its hundreds of millions of people.

The entry of Japanese troops into Hankow, so long dreaded in view of Nanking's ghastly fate, was almost anticlimactic. The Chinese threat to make scorched earth of Wuhan was frustrated by property owners who quietly removed most of the explosives and charges. However, the Japanese concession, a vacant and unloved symbol of the invaders, suffered some damage. The Hanyang arsenal was destroyed, as were a number of military installations in Wuchang. On the morning of October 26, as early sunlight brushed the surface of the river, the people of Hankow waited, silent and fearful. A few foreign gunboats, emblems of American, British, and French concern in the past, remained tied to their riverside pontoons. At the French concession, over which its European overlords had not relinquished authority, a flimsy barricade had been erected—an almost silly reminder of former Gallic military might. A barbed-wire fence, a sandbagged emplacement for a lone machine gun, a tired old armored car, and a frightened group of civilians, sailors, and Indo-Chinese guards trying to look their bravest and most defiant awaited the arrival of waves of occupying Japanese troops and tanks. They were not long in coming.

The rising-sun flag of Japan, proudly flying from the short mast of a speeding patrol boat, suddenly flashed its red and white on the river. It was followed by six destroyers and a flotilla of gunboats, all ready for instant action, with guns leveled on the city. They dropped anchor in an ominous line, silent and now motionless but for grinding anchor chains and slight ripples in the water around them. The silent wait continued: grim Japanese eyes glaring at the Bund, fear-widened Chinese eyes peeping from behind shuttered windows at the ships. Then a transport nosed around a bend in the river. It was followed by another, then another, and finally by what appeared to be a whole fleet. Each ship dropped anchor beside the protecting guns of the destroyers. Troops, armed for combat, clambered down the gangways into landing craft, chugged across the water, and landed at the Bund. During the day, tens of thousands climbed out of their flat-bottomed boats, stretched their cramped legs, scowled at the prize they had won, and poured like a brown flood through the city. Meanwhile, Japanese units from Huangpi and Yanglo, led by officers on tall, skinny horses, marched through the streets of Hanyang and the Chinese sections of Hankow.

Japanese flags were raised triumphantly; banzais were shouted with rifles upheld at arm's length. When found, Chinese stragglers and wounded who had been unable or too weak to escape were shot in the head. If they were near the waterfront, their bodies were kicked into the river; if they were too far off in the city, they were left lying in bloody heaps where they had fallen. But there were no disorders, no looting, no burning, no murders of civilians, no raping or brutalizing of terrified women. General Hata had issued stern orders on the conduct of his victorious army.

In the afternoon a band was put ashore to play the short-legged, grim-faced Japanese commander to his billet. The tuneless, tinny blare of horns and bugles echoed through the streets, each bandsman striving his independent utmost in an ear-splitting rendition of what was meant to be a martial air. Then the army's complement of patriotic prostitutes landed.

By nightfall, Hankow and the adjacent cities of Wuchang and Hanyang were completely in the hands of the Japanese army. The few remaining foreigners and hundreds of thousands of Chinese breathed a vast sigh of relief, for it was clear that Hankow would be spared the devastation that had been visited upon Nanking.

But the Japanese found no Chinese officials with whom they might arrange some kind of settlement of this costly military venture from which they could not extricate themselves. Their feet were mired in the endless morass of Asia's core. They were being sucked ever deeper into the quicksands of its unlimited space.

9

The Fall of Canton and Political Actions

The Fall of Canton
OCTOBER 12–21, 1938

AFTER THE EASY CAPTURE of Amoy on May 12, 1938, and the subsequent seizures of Foochow and Swatow, Canton was the last
remaining seaport through which China could import war materials. Although the railway station and yards and the center of the
city had been bombed repeatedly, the Japanese high command
had hesitated for months about occupying the teeming capital of
Kwangtung province. The risk was great that the British in Hongkong and the leased territory of Kowloon—only 85 miles by
water and 100 by rail from Canton—might react strongly if their
great bastion of power and commerce were threatened. If Japanese actions caused the British to rouse themselves from their
preoccupation with Hitler's Germany, the United States would
probably feel moved to do more than just dust off the Open
Door policy and issue statements on international law and obliga-
tions. It could not be overlooked that the combined British and
American navies were still nearly three times as powerful as
that of Japan. Heavily fortified Hongkong and the British Navy
just east of the mouth of the Pearl River estuary more or less
blocked the direct water approach to Canton. The presence of
Portuguese authority at Macao, 40 miles across the estuary from
Hongkong, was not considered worthy of attention.

Canton had had a long history of involvement with European poweis. It had been the site of the first British, Dutch, and French factories for trade with the outer world, the original bone of contention in both the first and second opium wars of the 1840s, and for decades the most important treaty port on the coast of China. Known by the Chinese as the birthplace of revolutions, it had long been a hotbed of turmoil and unrest. Its cantankerous, argumentative populace had been a magnet attracting the thoughts of the rebellious, bringing them to a boil, then spewing out dissension throughout China.

Situated on the delta of the twisting branches of the Pearl River, the city of 1.5 million people sprawled in raucous confusion through countless dank alleys and a few streets and filthy canals. Trade had brought great wealth to its more astute merchants and bankers, abysmal poverty to its masses. Disease-ridden and malodorous, Canton was an unlovely place of unusually tall houses and slums of such squalor they could be compared only to those of Calcutta. Its waterways, inlets, and canals were slowly flowing channels of sewage-laden slime upon which a sizable portion of the population dwelt in a variety of boats and junks. Tens of thousands of these water people had never set foot on dry land, living out their desperately impoverished existence on the waters in a daily struggle to survive.

Canton completely lacked the serene nineteenth-century overtones that characterized its imperial neighbor Hongkong. Having been planted on hundreds of flat, muddy islands, it was devoid of the awe-inspiring majesty of the British city built on the steep slopes of its dominating Peak. But it could boast of one island of calm order in the midst of all its cacophony—Shameen, the foreign concession that housed the symbols of western imperialism. Though Japanese aircraft had dive-bombed and strafed the city directly across the narrow channel from Shameen, they had never so much as cracked a window in the British-operated enclave—a measure of Japanese respect for the still-unchallenged might of the British Empire.

For months the Japanese 14th Fleet had prowled up and down the China coast from Shanghai to the south imposing the blockade of all ports north of Canton. Like hungry dogs waiting for a prize bone, its ships had patrolled off Hongkong, impatiently eyeing China's last major access to the sea. Plans for taking the city had been drawn up, refined, and rehashed down to the most minute detail. Japanese troops and transports had been allocated for the operation, but after the fall of Swatow, they had waited through five months of inaction. General Mikio and his 21st Corps of three divisions, the 11th, 18th and 104th, had been assigned responsibility for ground operations. About 100 aircraft would support the assault on Canton and the 14th Fleet would back up the landings. With corps troops and supporting units General Mikio commanded about 70,000 men; however, it had been decided that no more than one-fourth of this force would be required in the initial phase of the operation.

On the other side, General Yu Han-mou, commander of the 12th Chinese Army Group, and the man responsible for the defense of Canton, had made no plans for resisting an enemy attack. He had placed all of his bets on the British presence in Hongkong to protect him from Japanese offensive operations. An old-fashioned type, Yu had won his senior rank by adherence to the military principle of loyal inaction—never doing anything wrong, and never doing anything right either. An avid pursuer of personal wealth through use of his position, he was inept as a commander and negligent in his duties. Scattered throughout the Canton area in convenient billets having little relationship to defensive positions, his poorly trained, ill-equipped 12th Army Group consisted of three corps, the 62nd, 63rd, and 65th, of seven understrength divisions, two separate brigades and the Humen fortress command. Its total strength was less than 55,000 men. The Humen fortress, a complex of prepared positions constructed around an old stone fort armed with a number of artillery pieces up to six-inch caliber, was located on the eastern shore of the Pearl River estuary about 30 miles below Canton. In the hinterland of Kwangtung and Kwangsi provinces, several hundred thousand miscellaneous troops, militia regiments, and peace-preservation units on garrison and police duties could be made available to reinforce Yu's 12th Army Group. But from his safe post at Chungking, Chiang Kai-shek had decided, like Yu, that the British would act as a shield for his southern port.

Finally, an event in Europe was interpreted by the Japanese as the sign for which they had been impatiently waiting. On September 29, 1938, Neville Chamberlain and Edouard Daladier, buying time at Czechoslovakia's expense, signed the Munich agreement with Italy and Hitler's government, accepting the German occupation of Sudetenland. The British capitulation emboldened Japanese Imperial Headquarters to give the go-ahead for the attack on Canton. If their ally, Germany, could overawe London—and, therefore, Hongkong—why could not Japan?

On the morning of October 12, the Japanese landed at Bias Bay. The Chinese commander at Bias Bay put up no defense whatever against the Japanese landing. On the appearance of enemy warships and transports, he and his entire force fled in panic to the Tung River, between 50 and 60 miles to the north, leaving the land route to Canton wide open. During the landing operations, one small Japanese vessel struck a mine and sank. There were virtually no other Japanese casualties.

After taking Tamsui, 10 miles inland the enemy continued to advance in three columns. The Japanese column marched 80 miles from Tamsui to Huiyang on October 15, to Polo on the Tung River on the sixteenth, and reached Tsengcheng on the eighteenth. The right column's advance of 105 miles breezed through Pingshan on the fourteenth, Hengli on the fifteenth, then Pingling and Paitan, reaching Tsunghua on October 19. The third column of two regiments moved northwest to Changshuitou on the Canton-Kowloon Railway, which it occupied on October 15, then to Shihlung on the Tung River on October 17. From Changshuitou, one regimental combat team marched 45 miles south against no opposition to occupy Paoan at the mouth of the Pearl River estuary, 25 miles northwest of Hongkong, on October 18th. Finding no Chinese troops, this column turned north and marched unopposed to Humen "fortress", which it attacked from the land side, or rear, on October 22nd.

At this time, the four Japanese columns at Tsunghua, northeast of Canton; at Tsengcheng and at Shihlung, east of the city; and at Humen to the southeast; were all within 30 to 40 miles of their goal. In the words of the Chinese account: "As our water and land transportation were destroyed, it was most difficult for troops to mass." Water transportation had indeed been destroyed, or knocked out of action. Seven gunboats and four PT boats of the River Defense Command had been sunk by Japanese aircraft; nine other assorted craft had slipped through the network of waterways attempting to hide until they, too, had all been sunk. Thus the un-heroic Yu Han-mou decided to abandon the Canton area. He and his undependable 12th Army Group—though they had not once stood up to fight the invaders—withdrew in the greatest haste to a defense line running through Chingyuan and Hengshih, 40 miles north of Canton; Liangkou, 50 miles to the northeast; and Hsinfeng, 90 miles to the northeast. The "defense" of Canton thus ended in one of the most ignominious examples of sheer cowardice, or downright treachery, since July 7, 1937. However, following the usual pattern, a force of two brigades was left in the rugged hills between Changshuitou, Tamsui and Paoan "to conduct guerrilla operations, tie down the enemy and sabotage his lines of communications." Disinclined to conduct either guerrilla or sabotage operations and soon deducing that the enemy was equally disinclined "to be tied down," this force gradually dissolved into the neighboring farms and villages.

The Japanese paraded into the city of Canton on October 21. Two days later, after an air and naval bombardment that lasted all of 40 minutes, Humen fortress was abandoned by its remaining Chinese defenders. The Japanese established a defense perimeter around Canton, then moved 25 miles up the Pearl River to its junction with the Peh River at Samshui on the twenty-fifth. Another column occupied Namhoi, 10 miles southeast of Canton, on the same day. Since there had been no British military reaction to his activities, General Mikio showed his contempt for the Union Jack by sending his troop transports up the wide estuary and river past Hongkong to debark his troops directly on the Bund at Canton.

During the next month, in order to concentrate the occupying forces, now numbering over two divisions, Japanese garrisons on the Tung River at Polo, Huiyang, and Hengli, about 70 miles east of Canton, were reduced to outpost size, as were the garrisons at Tsunghua and Paitan, 35 and 40 miles northeast of the city. When word of these Japanese readjustments reached Yu Han-mou at his headquarters 30 miles north of Tsunghua, he moved belatedly, and slowly, into action. His troops marched cautiously toward Tsunghua and Paitan. On their approach, the Japanese outposts pulled back to 'l'sengcheng. Thus, on November 24, Tsunghua and Paitan were recovered by the Chinese. Similarly, as the Japanese relinquished their occupation of the Tung River towns, 30 to 50 miles east of Tsengcheng, and abandoned their 100-mile line of communications from Bias Bay, the Chinese recovered Pingling, Polo, Huiyang, and Hengli.

The fall of Hankow and Canton ended the major phase of military operations of the Sino-Japanese conflict. During the next three years, 12 offensives and counteroffensives, some of major proportions, and countless guerrilla operations kept China in turmoil and its people in agony. Millions died of privation or were killed as a direct result of battle. In their war of attrition— in a sense, a non-war—the Chinese had by December, 1938, lost to the invader most of the requisites that could have made their country independent. And in their war of aggression, the Japanese, though they held those requisites by deploying an occupying army of over 1 million men, found that their hands were empty. They had accomplished their military objectives but had not succeeded in achieving their political ends. They had not conquered the Chinese people, the majority of whom were rural, living in small towns and villages and on farms.

The Japanese armies had been unable to extend their control for more than a few miles on either side of the main lines of communication. Except in the Peking-Tientsin area, much of Shantung province, and the Shanghai-Nanking area, Japanese occupation was confined to urban centers and the railways or main roads connecting them. A map of the invaders' domination would show long, snakelike arms traversing China north of the Yangtze River, with numerous islands of unoccupied and more or less undisturbed territory. Though large forces of nationalist and provincial troops had been left behind to conduct guerrilla operations from these islands, most of these troops were gradually being forced into banditry at night and farming by day in order to keep alive. Beyond minor forays against Japanese communications lines and supply areas, their activities were ineffective, though a constant source of irritation to enemy commanders. In general, the people of the unoccupied areas continued their district, county, and village systems of government. Since they had never known the benefits of modern life, their existence was little changed from the past. Abandoned by the distant government to which they had tendered the formality of a sort of allegiance, they had been left to their own devices. Thus stranded, they soon began to grasp at any straw of paternal authority and deliverance from their isolation. The straw came in the form of Communist cadres from the northwest, preaching a land owned by and worked for the benefit of the people. Most of the landlords fled; their lands and houses were seized and distributed among the downtrodden. Millions of peasants accepted this unexpected largess, and if they did not always understand the teaching that went with it, they were more than willing to be converted to the unfamiliar doctrine that allowed them to keep the fruits of their labors. Hundreds of thousands of troops and local militia defected to the cause of the men from the northwest. For the first time in their military service they found that they were treated as men to be respected; that hard work, attendance at primitive schools, and loyalty to the new masters brought decent food and decent uniforms. More important, they found a purpose and a pride they had never known before. And so, under the noses of the Japanese conquerors, the seeds of a new revolution were planted.

Japanese Naval and Air Strength
EARLY 1938

Although American, British, and Japanese naval strengths had been limited by treaty at the Washington Conference of 1921–22 to a respective tonnage ratio of 5:5:3, none of the signatories had given much more than lip service to their pledges. The Japanese military expansionists, by far the greatest violators, had never conceded that the liberals who had agreed to the treaty represented the will of the emperor. In their eyes the placement of Japan in a weaker naval category than the United States and Great Britain had been a national affront that they refused to accept. Since they had defeated and destroyed most of the Russian fleet at Tsushima in 1905, they had been unwilling to accede to any inferior naval position. Regardless of mere treaties or agreements, if their ideal of a Japan supreme over all other nations was to be achieved, a navy inferior to none was a necessity. The question of the morality involved in side-stepping an international covenant to which Japan had agreed on paper had never entered their inflexible, determined minds.

In 1938 the Japanese navy's combat ships included 10 modern or fairly modern battleships, 5 aircraft carriers, 26 cruisers, 79 destroyers, and 41 submarines. Overage vessels still suitable for combat included the antique *Izuma* of Shanghai fame, 13 cruisers, 26 destroyers, and 16 submarines. At the time, 2 aircraft carriers, 2 cruisers, 6 destroyers, and 3 submarines were in various stages of construction. The total tonnage of all combatant ships was less than 900,000.

An expansion program—in violation of the 1922 treaty—was then under way. It was designed to add 3 battleships, 5 aircraft carriers, 7 cruisers, 43 destroyers, and 8 submarines to the fleet. During the next two years, this schedule of construction was expanded to add 3 more battleships, 4 pocket battleships of about 15,000 tons each, and 8 more submarines. Three of the 5 planned carriers and 11 of the planned destroyers were commissioned before the end of 1941, as were all 16 of the projected submarines and many auxiliary, noncombat vessels of all types. Older cruisers were modernized with heavier armor and guns. All carriers were brought up to date with modern equipment.

The naval expansion program was designed to give Japan a battle fleet of 17 battleships, 4 pocket battleships, 12 aircraft carriers, 48 cruisers, 154 destroyers, 76 submarines, and the necessary auxiliary vessels, provided, of course, that all old ships were still seaworthy and combat-ready when new construction was completed.

In 1938, estimates of Japanese air strength varied widely, since the actual number of aircraft was carefully guarded. A reasonable guess was that Japan then had available about 4,000 aircraft of all categories except heavy bombers. The construction of new airplanes had been accelerated on the advice of German technicians using modified German designs. At the time, Japan was capable of producing about 2,000 military aircraft annually in her own factories, provided the construction of commercial aircraft was virtually eliminated. In order to speed up production, cut costs, and simplify pilot training, the Japanese eliminated certain features that were considered essential by other nations, such as two-way radios in fighter and light bomber aircraft, except in lead or command planes.

In late 1938 and during the succeeding three years, the naval and air strength of Japan made her a formidable adversary to any nation, and an overwhelming one to a country like China with its dearth of military technology.

League of Nations Actions
OCTOBER, 1937, TO JANUARY, 1939

On October 6, 1937, three months after the incident at the Marco Polo Bridge, the assembly of the League of Nations adopted a resolution concerning Japan's military aggression in China. The document declared that Japan was in "contravention of . . . the Pact of Paris of April 27, 1928," then lumbered on with the adoption of its Far Eastern Advisory Committee's report and expressed moral support for China and little else. Having accomplished this great work, the assembly then voted for adjournment.

On the same day, United States Secretary of State Cordell Hull stated that "the Government of the United States has been forced to the conclusion that the action of Japan in China is . . . contrary to the provisions . . . of the Kellogg-Briand Pact of August 27, 1928," whose 23 signatory nations had renounced "aggressive" war. Like most international statements of principle, the Kellogg-Briand Pact lacked teeth to enforce its provisions. This American statement and the League's slap on the wrist in no way restrained the Japanese armies then aggressively battling at Shanghai, Shihkiachuang, Teh Hsien, and Taiyuan.

A conference of the powers at Brussels on November 15, 1937, failed to effect mediation. In this case, the powers consisted of an assortment of governments whose policies toward China and aggressive war ranged from star-gazing to cynicism. They included Portugal, Latvia, Bolivia, and Ecuador as well as Great Britain, France, the Soviet Union, and the United States. The Japanese government remained unimpressed by their deliberations.

On February 2, 1938, the council of the League of Nations was moved to adopt another resolution regarding the situation in the Far East. The general tone of this document was "more in sorrow than in anger." It was laced with such expressions as "notes with regret," "deplores," "recalls," is confident," etc. The council noted with regret that hostilities in China continue and have been intensified since the last meeting of the Council"—a situation that had been noted with less pomposity by every newspaper in the world, not to mention hundreds of millions of the Chinese people. Continuing, it deplored, "this deterioration in the situation." After recalling in detail the resolution and recommendations of October 6, 1937, the document asked for "the most serious attention of the Members of the League to the terms of the above mentioned resolution," then stated that the Council "is confident that those States represented on the Council for whom the situation is of special interest, will lose no opportunity in examining, in consultation with similarly interested powers, the feasibility of any further steps which may contribute to a just settlement of the conflict in the Far East." Having again delivered itself of meaningless sympathy, the council adjourned. And again Japan, whose militarists had every intention to continue aggression in China, ignored the League council. And China, who so desperately needed concrete forms of assistance, was left by itself to face the unremitting pressure of its enemy.

On May 14, 1938, the League council delivered another resolution: "Having heard the statement of the representative of China on the situation in the Far East," the council "earnestly urged Members of the League to do their utmost to give effect to the recommendations contained in previous resolutions of the Assembly and Council in this matter, and to take into serious and sympathetic consideration requests they may receive from the Chinese Government in conformity with the said resolutions; expresses its sympathy with China in her heroic struggle for the maintenance of her independence and territorial integrity . . . and in the suffering . . . inflicted on her people." Another section followed, recalling "that the use of toxic gases is a method of war condemned by international law," and requesting "the Governments of States who may be in a position to do so to communicate to the League any information that may be obtained on the subject."

One indication of the extent of American sympathy for China was the beginning of unrestricted sale of scrap metal to Japan, all of which was converted into war materials of one kind or another. British sympathy was exemplified by a business-as-usual policy throughout the Far East. Reference to the use of toxic gases was the result of Chinese accusations that gas had been employed by the Japanese against their troops. Since the Japanese had been able to obtain their objectives with conventional ground and air weapons, it had seldom been necessary, or desirable, to use gas.

On September 19, 1938, the League council tried a new tack. At the request of the Chinese government, it extended an invitation to the Japanese government to negotiate a settlement of the conflict in China. In its formal communication, the council stated that under the provisions of Article 17 of the League covenant Japan would have the same rights in dealing with the dispute as would a member state, namely China.

On September 22, 1938, the Japanese government thumbed its nose at the council in a flat refusal to accept the invitation. "The Imperial Government is firmly convinced that means such as those laid down in the Covenant cannot provide a just and adequate solution of the present conflict . . . and its attitude . . . has been clearly stated on many occasions . . . therefore . . . the Imperial Government regrets its inability to accept the Council's invitation." Though couched in formal diplomatic language, the Japanese reply was clearly a request to the League of Nations to mind its own business and keep its hands off the Sino-Japanese conflict.

But on October 3, 1938, when it learned that the League council had adopted a report that member states might "individually apply Article 16 [sanctions] of the Covenant to Japan by virtue of Paragraph 3, Article 17," the Japanese Foreign Office struck back. In a public statement it declared: "By thus invoking Paragraph 3, Article 17, the League of Nations recognizes the existence of a state of war between Japan and China, which is inconsistent with . . . the profession, in order to protect the interests of Member States in China, that no state of war existed."

The Japanese government then threatened to adopt countermeasures "against any country resorting to measures of sanction against Japan." With a pious "for the sake of world peace," the statement went on to point out Japan's cooperation with the League in social and technical fields, only to be confronted by "a greatly deplorable attitude . . . and of slandering at every turn the actions of Japan in China." The threat of sanctions against Japan had "made clear [to the Japanese] the irreconcilability between the positions of Japan and the League, as a result of which Japan cannot . . . maintain the policy of cooperation she has hitherto pursued with the League." The Japanese statement then complained that the League council had been "misled by intrigues of certain foreign powers," and ended with a warning that any member state having in mind sanctions against Japan had better "give full consideration to possible consequences." Thus, before any misguided members of the League of Nations might take action, Japan threw down the gauntlet by its defiant stand.

On January 20, 1939, apparently unaware that its resolutions accomplished nothing but an increase in the Japanese government's irritability and determination to pursue its own course, the League council issued another futile resolution. After rehashing all of the previous council and assembly resolutions and recommendations, reminding readers that the Chinese had rejected Japan's claim to establish a new order in the Far East, and "taking note . . . that a number of States have been taking individual action" to aid China, the resolution's final paragraph ended with a hedged invitation to members of the League to participate in "effective measures, especially measures of aid to China."

The League of Nations, scorned by Japan's high-riding militarists, was totally ineffective in trying to stop the aggression in China. Its ponderous deliberations and effluent resolutions were no match for Japan's bombs and bullets, just as they had been no match for Italy's troops and tanks in Ethiopia in 1936. And so the agony and the struggle went on.

Japanese Puppet Regimes in China
DECEMBER, 1937, TO NOVEMBER, 1938

In accordance with Japanese military reasoning, the Chinese government either should have 'sued for peace or should have asked for a settlement of the conflict after the fall of Hankow and Canton. Having been pushed to Chungking in the far reaches of Szechwan province, Chiang Kai-shek's near-bankrupt regime should have welcomed any opportunity to preserve the remnants of its authority and to accept the benefits of cooperation with Japan. But it did not, any more than it had on previous Japanese attempts to reach some kind of terms or to set up regional governments.

The first "national" puppet regime established under Japanese military auspices was the Provisional Government of the Chinese Republic at Peking. Inaugurated on December 14, 1937, it was the instrument of Japan's Kwantung Army of Manchuria to stake out its claim to control of north China before the Japanese armies in central China could gobble up the entire prize. The Peking provisional government was organized with a façade of authority —administrative, deliberative, and judicial committees to which selected Chinese were appointed. Theoretically the committees and their numerous subcommittees and departments had certain governing powers, but behind the front of Chinese officials were hordes of Japanese advisers who took their orders from the military command in north China. Japanese intelligence officers, or spies, were assigned to each department to ensure no deviation from the will and desires of the Kwantung Army.

The Chinese who fronted the complicated double structure of the provisional government were carefully chosen elderly gentlemen, fond of airing their pet thrushes on warm spring days, most of whom could boast of few achievements beyond a lifelong study of the classics, perfection in calligraphy, and endless discussions with other bewhiskered old scholars on interpretations of poetic couplets. A few who had been partly educated in Japan had acquired a more practical outlook regarding the machinery of government. But the minds of the majority seldom descended from the clouds of the ancient precepts and political teachings of

Confucius and Mencius. This state of mind suited the Japanese overlords perfectly, since their primary objective was to destroy all thoughts of democracy and Communism among their Chinese subjects. The dignified old mandarins, whose tired eyes were barely able to distinguish between a Japanese and a Chinese soldier, accepted the dictates of their new masters, implanted their seals on whatever documents were put before them, and turned happily back to their own world of abstruse philosophy, singing birds, and ancient poetry.

A month before, in November, 1937, the Kwantung Army had made another power grab by unifying the Chinese provincial governments of north Shansi, south Chahar, and "Inner Mongolia" under the name of Mengkiang. Although this regional, rather than national, fiction had been called the Federation of the Autonomous Governments of Mongolian Provinces, it included only one of the three; not having been conquered, Ninghsia and Kansu were not under its jurisdiction. A closely advised Federal Council of Mongolians and Chinese was established with its capital at Kalgan in Chahar. A Mongolian prince, Teh Wang (Prince Teh), was set up as chairman. A plump, syphilitic hedonist who wore a long queue that left greasy pendulum strokes down the back of his dirty brocade robes, Teh Wang claimed descent from Kublai Khan, as did most Mongolian princelings, whose lineages were usually vague. Teh had a large following among the semiautonomous clans, but because of his predilection for the pleasures of the flesh, he was easily manipulated.

After the Japanese peace overtures of January 2, 1938, were transmitted by Doctor Oscar Trautmann, the German ambassador, and failed to produce a "sincere" reply from the Chinese government, Premier Konoye declared that the Japanese government would cease all further dealings with Chiang Kai-shek's regime. He also stated that he looked forward to the establishment of a new Chinese regime and harmonious coordination. The Japanese did not long delay the pursuit of the harmonious coordination they professed to seek.

On March 28, 1938, the Reformed Government of the Chinese Republic was inaugurated among the ashes and blackened ruins of Nanking. Though this creation of the Japanese Central China Army assumed national pretensions, its actual area of jurisdiction was confined to the occupied territory between the Yellow and the Yangtze rivers. The structure of the hastily organized reformed government was similar to that of the rival provisional government at Peking—three boards with subordinate departments infested with Japanese advisers. Its Chinese front men were, like those at Peking, conservative and old-fashioned in their views, but younger and less steeped in the classic tradition. Many were simply out-of-work dissidents anxious to climb on any bandwagon that might place them in positions of some power. Since the reformed government was intended to be no more than a stopgap until a permanent form of national government could be organized, both the northern and central cliques of the Japanese army in China were soon involved in its operation. Both factions agreed on General Wu Pei-fu, a former Peking warlord living in enforced retirement, as the figurehead to lead the Chinese people into the harmonious reconciliation with Japan. Unlike most other warlords of lowly origin, Wu Pei-fu had the slender features and bearing of a man born into an aristocratic family of Manchu blood. He had passed in the old classical examinations, spoke the court language of Peking, and genuinely hoped to restore order and a strong nationalist government to China. He had had a loyal army of his own; because his troops had always been paid their full salaries, they had spared the countryside the ravages and desolation the Chinese people had learned to expect from their own soldiery. A capable military commander for his time, Wu had been no politician and had lost out to more unscrupulous types in the general scramble for power in the 1920s; however, he had won a measure of esteem and respect throughout China. To the Japanese he represented conservative prestige. But General Wu surprised his Japanese sponsors by refusing to take office as long as their troops remained in China. Wu Pei-fu died the next year.

The Japanese second choice to head their Nanking government was Wang Ching-wei, vice-president of the Kuomintang and president of the Chinese government's executive Yuan from 1932 to 1935 (roughly the equivalent of premier). Wang was a man consumed with vanity and personal ambition; the spoiled darling of the leftists, he was without principles. His political life had been one of frustration aggravated by envious resentment of

Chiang. Kai-shek, who had usurped the power he thought should have been his. In the heady Canton days of the early 1920s, he had allied himself with Eugene Ch'en, a half-Negro radical, and Sun Fo, the fat, ineffectual, left-thinking son of Doctor Sun Yat-sen. Wang had helped to set up several left-wing separatist regimes in Canton and, once, a right-wing government with T.V. Soong, the brother of the future Madame Chiang Kai-shek. When real trouble or danger loomed, Wang had always managed to slip out of Canton to the safety of Hongkong or Shanghai, where he nursed his bitterness over failures until the next opportune moment. After Sun Yat-sen's death, Wang had claimed to be his spiritual successor and therefore head of the party and the government. He had partly succeeded in his pretensions as leader of the left wing of the Kuomintang and as acting head of one of Canton's many so-called national governments. But he had no control of the army, then commanded by his chief rival for supreme power, Chiang Kai-shek. Chiang also had had an eye fixed on a position for himself far above that of commanding general of the southern army. When Wang made a political move to seize power, Chiang had struck rapidly. Claiming that he had discovered a plot to kidnap him and ship him off to Vladivostok, Chiang Kai-shek, on March 26, 1926, had arrested dozens of left-wingers and Communist sympathizers in Wang's Kuomintang. Scared out of his unheroic wits by the sudden wreckage of his following, Wang found that he was suffering from a serious health condition. He deserted his few remaining supporters and hurriedly sailed for Europe. But in 1927 he had slipped back into China and had surfaced as the head of the Soviet-supported government at Hankow. But again Chiang Kai-shek thwarted his ambitions by destroying his effort to establish a Communist-oriented national government.

Aware of Wang Ching-wei's past, the Japanese military were confident that he would not be difficult to overawe and control. In April, 1938, Chiang Kai-shek authorized and backed secret attempts to come to a settlement with the Japanese based on the sovereignty, administrative independence, and economic equality of China. Emissaries from both sides met at Hongkong and Shanghai. It was probably during the early stages of these devious proceedings that the Japanese approached Wang Ching-wei, Chiang's chief representative at the negotiations, with their offer of the presidency of the reformed government at Nanking. For months Wang attempted to bargain with the Japanese for more power before officially accepting their offer. But his mind had been made up from the beginning, his verbal minuet with the invaders nothing but a face-saving performance to justify his traitorous intentions. His principal demands (funds from the foreign-operated customs service, taxes and salt revenues, the opening of the lower Yangtze to commercial navigation, and an increase in police powers) were met with bland, vaguely worded Japanese promises. Meanwhile, Wang issued a bellicose statement on "endless courage, patience and endurance so that our war of resistance may be won." By late August, still negotiating in Nanking, Wang's relationship with the Japanese had become so involved that he lived in constant fear of assassination by his countrymen. By that time he had become a creature and virtually a prisoner of the Japanese military.

In an effort to reconcile the rival factions in the Japanese army in China—the northern Kwantung clique and the southern Yangtze Valley clique—the United Council of China was created on September 22, 1938. Members of the council were appointed from the two rival governments at Peking and Nanking. Since each faction was out for its own prestige and financial gain, meetings accomplished nothing but to provide a forum for airing grievances and voicing recriminations to each other. (The united council was dissolved on March 30, 1940.)

On November 3, 1938, after the fall of Canton and Hankow, the Japanese government issued a statement explaining its benevolent purpose in the conflict with China: "the establishment of a new order which will insure permanent stability in East Asia. The new order has . . . a tripartite relationship of mutual aid and coordination between Japan, Manchukuo and China in political, economic [and] cultural fields, . . . joint defense against communism, [the creation of] a new culture and . . . economic cohesion throughout East Asia." It went on to declare: "What Japan desires of China is that that country will share in . . . this new order . . ."

On December 19, 1938, Japan's aims were enlarged upon by Foreign Minister Hachiro Arita in a speech to the Japanese Diet.

His pious exposition was intended to make Japan's high-minded goals clear to the world and, of course, to the recalcitrant Chinese. "It is . . . of benefit to the Chinese themselves . . . to lift China from its present semi-colonial state to the position of a modern state. . . . The new order . . . a relationship of mutual aid and coordination between Japan, Manchukuo and China, signifies the creation of solidarity between these three countries . . . enabling each nation to maintain its independence and develop its individuality." Though Arita stressed the economic, rather than political, aspect of the new order, he ominously stated that a certain degree of coordination would be necessary since the principle of equal commercial opportunity "must be applied under restrictions demanded by the requirements of national defense . . . and security." In other words, Japan's benevolence did not go so far as to free China to pursue its own policies for the benefit of its people.

Meanwhile, the slippery Wang Ching-wei was playing a double game with the Japanese in Nanking and the Chinese in Chungking. In his role as Chiang Kai-shek's chief negotiator for a settlement of the conflict, for which Germany volunteered her good offices as mediator, Wang had failed. In all probability he had never really tried to reach an agreement with the Japanese. But in his role as a candidate for the title of president of the Reformed Government of the Chinese Republic, his discussions with the enemy were beginning to pay off. By December he was ready to accept Japanese suzerainty over his country. He interpreted his decision to collaborate with the Japanese as a pragmatic acceptance of a situation that would not change: the Chinese cause was lost; Chiang Kai-shek could not resist much longer. The Japanese had assured him that they had no intention to destroy China as a nation, that it would benefit China in the long run (and hopefully Wang Ching-wei) to accept Japanese plans for cooperation in their new order. In his manifesto, Wang did not mention that at last he would be president of the reformed China, that he would have supreme power, and that he had bested his old rival, Chiang Kai-shek. His public declaration calling for the support of his fellow Chinese raised outraged cries of indignation among the intended victims of his calculated perfidy.

On December 22, 1938, Premier Konoye issued a new series of demands regarding the Chinese folly of anti-Japanism. Since Wang Ching-wei was now in the pocket of the Japanese military, Konoye bared his fangs in a threat to achieve the complete extermination of Chiang Kai-shek's Kuomintang government. He demanded that China recognize the puppet state of Manchukuo, conclude a treaty with Japan to wipe out Communism, agree to the presence of Japanese troops at specified points throughout China, designate Mengkiang (Inner Mongolia) as a special anti-Communist area, and extend to Japan facilities for the development of China's natural resources.

On December 26, Chiang Kai-shek repudiated Konoye's demands. He had no other choice. The breakdown of his own overtures for peace and the defection of Wang Ching-wei were the last straws breaking any attempt to reach a settlement with the Japanese. Chiang's statement pulled no punches in accusing Japan of absurd utterances, of attempts to hoodwink the world; it described the rebirth of China envisaged in the plans of the new order for East Asia as meaning the destruction and enslavement of China with Japan the sole beneficiary. Chiang then declared that Japan was "dominated by a horde of militants who knew no law and order . . . but conquest. If they are allowed to continue to hold sway, the fate of Japan is doomed." He concluded his long statement with a firm reiteration that China intended to resist to the end regardless of any sacrifice.

Meanwhile, Wang Ching-wei had organized the semblance of a party—the orthodox Kuomintang—composed of other defectors willing to support him. This rubber-stamp group dutifully elected Wang to the presidency of the puppet Reorganized National Government of China. The formal inauguration took place in Nanking on March 30, 1938, billed as the return of the national government of China under the benign principles of the deified Sun Yat-sen. The next day, Chiang Kai-shek's government at Chungking issued futile orders for the arrest of 77 of Wang's ignominious henchmen. Wang Ching-wei had achieved his burning ambition to supremacy, even though his position had no more substance than a paper kite. His reorganized government played out the charade that it was the true executive authority of a China now cleansed of evil and restored to its capital.

On November 30, 1938, Japan extended formal recognition to and concluded a treaty with Wang's regime. The wording of the secret treaty designated the puppet organization as the National Government of the Republic of China. For administrative purposes it carved China into four general areas—the northeast, Mongolia, north China, and central China. It included provisions for joint defense against Communist activities, for economic development, for special facilities for Japan, and for Japan to station troops indefinitely in north China and Mongolia. The withdrawal of troops from other parts of China and the questions of taxation and restoration of requisitioned property were left up to Japanese discretion. On the same day a joint declaration by Japan, Manchukuo, and China guaranteed respect for each other's territory and mutual cooperation; thus Japan achieved Chinese recognition of sorts of its other puppet, Manchukuo.

The Chinese government at Chungking immediately denounced Wang's regime as an "illegal organization whose acts . . . are null and void in respect of all Chinese citizens and all foreign countries." The statement branded Wang Ching-wei as an "arch-traitor" and declared the treaty to be "totally devoid of legality and [with] no binding force whatsoever."

The Wang Ching-wei government was not recognized by any other state until July 1, 1941. Under pressure and complaints from Japan, Germany and Italy extended recognition on that date. Shortly after, Rumania, Denmark, and Spain followed suit.

10

The Battles for Nanchang, Mid-February to May 9, 1939

AFTER THE FALL OF HANKOW in the autumn of 1938, Chiang Kai-shek gathered together the dejected faithful for a series of military conferences at Nanyueh and Wuking. The ostensible purpose of the meetings was to solicit advice from the senior generals on what to do next; their actual purpose was to give the generalissimo a receptive forum before which he could air his views. He announced that it was time to shift from the defensive to the offensive and emphasized the future importance of political maneuvers, propaganda, and guerrilla warfare—all areas of failure in the past. Then in his clipped voice he called for persistence, loyalty, harmony, and other national virtues, such as accepting the shame and disgrace of defeat. His verbal divertissement ended with an upbeat note: a vow to take revenge.

Of necessity, the new offensive war required a new order of battle. Commands were fitted like pieces in a jigsaw puzzle into areas and sectors not occupied or isolated by the Japanese. General Wei Li-huang, known as 100-victory Wei for his successes against the Chinese Reds in southern Anhwei and northern Kiangsi provinces, would command the 1st War Area in what was left of Honan and northern Anhwei. Well padded and of dignified appearance, General Wei was a man of integrity who had occasionally been forced into doubtful decisions by the involved politics of the Chinese army. In true feudal fashion he had been assigned by Chiang Kai-shek the revenues from four rich *hsien* in Hunan as a reward for his services against the Reds.

General Wei's command consisted of the 2nd Army Group of the 30th, 42nd, and 68th corps, and the 3rd Army Group of the 12th Corps, the 76th Corps, and the 40th Corps, the latter commanded by the jovial P'ang Ping-hsun. The entire force included 12 divisions, 1 infantry brigade, 1 cavalry division, and 1 cavalry brigade with a total strength of about 90,000 men.

The slippery old warlord General Yen Hsi-shan commanded the 2nd War Area in what was left of Shansi province and the southern part of Shensi. His troops consisted of the 14th Army Group of three corps,[1] still commanded by Wei Li-huang from a distance of over 200 miles in his own war area; the 4th Army Group of three corps;[2] the 5th Army Group of three corps;[3] the 7th Army Group of four corps,[4] commanded by Fu Tso-yi; the 8th Route Army, a virtually independent force commanded by General Chu Teh; the 9th Corps; and 3 separate divisions. The command included 32 divisions, 14 infantry brigades. 5 cavalry divisions, and 3 cavalry brigades with a strength of about 280,000 troops of mixed quality as to training and equipment.

The 3rd War Area, in Fukien province (less the occupied coastal ports) and in what was left of Kiangsu, southern Anhwei, and Chekiang, was commanded by General Ku Chu-tung, a political hack and a rear-area commander who never went closer than 50 miles to any front. His command consisted of the 25th Army Group of one corps and one division;[5] 10th Army Group of two corps;[6] 32nd Army Group of two corps and one division;[7] 23rd Army Group of two corps;[8] and the 4th Corps. General Ku's forces included 22 divisions and 2 infantry brigades with an approximate strength of 155,000 men.

The 4th War Area was commanded by Old Ironsides, Chang Fa-kuei, whose sturdy clang of iron was rapidly changing to the tinkle of silver in his pockets, and whose former toughness was already diminished. His war area was located in the southern provinces of Kwangtung and Kwangsi (less Canton) simply because he had marched off to that region with all of the troops he could gather. His command consisted of the 9th Army Group,[9] the 16th Army Group,[10] and the 12th Army Group.[11] The 12th Army Group was commanded by General Yu Han-mou, the "defender" of Canton, whose lack of loyalty to the nationalist government was exceeded only by that of Old

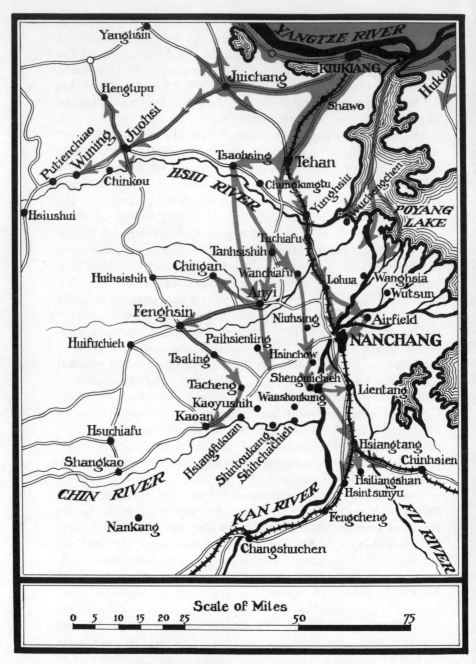

The Japanese Offensive to Take Nanchang

Ironsides himself. This undependable force included 18 divisions and 2 infantry brigades with a strength of about 130,000 men.

The 5th War Area, commanded by General Li Tsung-jen, was confined to southern Anhwei straddling the Yangtze, Hupei north of the river, and southeastern Honan. Li's command consisted of the 33rd Army Group,[12] commanded by the redoubtable "roughneck" Chang Tse-chung of Hsuchow fame; the 11th Army Group;[13] the 22nd Army Group;[14] the 29th Army Group;[15] and a guerrilla army of two corps.[16] It included 26 divisions, 1 cavalry division, 1 cavalry brigade, and a miscellaneous rabble of local militia and peace-preservation units, with a strength of approximately 180,000 men.

The 8th War Area, in Kansu, Ninghsia, Tsinghai, and western Suiyuam, was commanded by General Chu Shao-liang, who was assigned a mixed bag of Mongolian and Chinese units with inflated rank and command designations far beyond those warranted by the number of their troops. This command consisted of the 17th Army Group,[17] all Mongol; three corps,[18] one Mongolian and two Chinese; one Mongolian cavalry corps;[19] two Chinese cavalry corps;[20] and one Chinese division. As an example of the inflated character of the units, the three cavalry corps contained only 4 brigades instead of the normal 12 brigades. In overall strength, the 8th War Area included 6 infantry divisions, 9 infantry brigades, 4 cavalry brigades, and miscellaneous peace-preservation units, with a strength of about 75,000 men. (The Peace Preservation Corps, with units all over China, consisted of partly trained, poorly armed local groups, usually of regimental size. Because of their local character and lack of conventional training, the peace-preservation units were best suited to guerrilla activities.)

The 9th War Area, in northern Kiangsi, Hupei south of the Yangtze, and Hunan province, had as its titular commander General Ch'en Ch'eng. The acting commander, and de facto commander, was General Hsueh Yueh. The 9th War Area command consisted of the 19th Army Group[21] under the pudgy, bespectacled, and indecisive Lo Cho-ying; the 31st Army Group[22] commanded by the forceful T'ang En-po; the 74th Separate Corps; a guerrilla army of two corps;[23] the 1st Army Group[24] commanded by Lung Yun; the 27th Army Group;[25] the 30th Army

Group;[26] and the 20th Army Group[27] commanded by General Shang Chen. Lung Yun, the ex-bandit, ex-warlord governor of Yunnan who had grown vastly rich through a monopoly of the opium traffic in his province, as well as through prostitution, blackmail, and a monopoly of all building materials and construction in the Kunming area, never got within 600 miles of the war-area headquarters at Changsha. General Shang Chen was a loyal officer whose family's aristocratic background of officialdom under two imperial dynasties made him suspect to Chiang Kai-shek and others of similar low origin. The entire command included 52 divisions and miscellaneous special units with an approximate strength of 355,000 men.

The 10th War Area, sandwiched between Yen Hsi-shan's 2nd War Area and the Red stronghold in northern Shensi in order to block any possible expansion by the Chinese Communists, consisted of the 34th Army Group[28] and the 16th Corps. It included nine divisions, one infantry brigade, one cavalry division, and one cavalry brigade, with a total strength of less than 65,000 men.

The Shantung-Kiangsu War Area, straddling the border of those two provinces, was commanded by General Yu Hsueh-chung who had valiantly tried to thwart Han Fu-chu's machinations in Shantung. His command consisted of three regular corps,[29] a corps of guerrilla troops, and miscellaneous detachments that included seven divisions, with a strength of about 50,000 men.

The isolated Hopei-Chahar War Area, commanded by General Lu Chung-lin, consisted of three corps[30] and various units of the Hopei militia. It included five infantry divisions, one cavalry division, the equivalent of one division of militia, and guerrilla units. Its total armed strength was about 35,000.

This tabulation of the new command structure does not include scattered units of provincial troops, independent guerrilla organizations, numerous peace-preservation corps elements, local militia, and various semimilitary and semi-independent organizations throughout free China. The combined strength of these detached units was probably in the neighborhood of 400,000 men. In addition, numerous nontactical hangers-on and paramilitary attachments, which accompanied all regular combat units in the field, probably numbered as many as 250,000 throughout the Chinese army. Thus China could count as "troops" a total of approximately 2,100,000 men, about half of whom could be classed as combat-effective (meaning that they carried a weapon of some kind).

At this time the Japanese had 11 divisions, 4 infantry brigades, and 1 cavalry division in north China; 10 divisions and 1 cavalry brigade in central China; 2 divisions in south China; and numerous garrison, supply, support, and civil-government troop organizations throughout China; along with 270 army planes and about 250 navy planes in support of ground troops. This was an overall strength of about 1,000,000 men, of which, however, no more than 550,000 were combat troops.

During the four-month lull after the capture of Hankow, the Japanese high command in China realized fully that the chief stumbling block to their plans for controlling the Yangtze River and the adjacent lake region was General Hsueh Yueh and his 9th War Area command in northwest Kiangsi and Hupei. Therefore the general staff worked out detailed plans for offensives aimed at the capture of Nanchang, south of Poyang Lake, and Changsha, south of Tung Ting Lake, both of which were in Hsueh Yueh's command sector.

Meanwhile, the Japanese navy, which in this land war had played a minor role compared to that of the army, surveyed the coastal scene for further conquest and glory. After the seizure of Canton, the maintenance of the sea blockade and the transportation of troops from Japan had become frustrating for a service that yearned to flex its armor-plated muscles. Having temporarily run out of worlds to conquer, the eyes of the Japanese navy focused on the large island of Hainan off the south coast of China.

Hainan, the home of the primitive Hakka tribes, lay within the French sphere of influence that had been guaranteed by the Franco-Japanese entente of 1907. The Japanese Foreign Office brushed that detail aside with a statement that "conditions in China have undergone a complete change" since 1907 and that Hainan "has become a very important base for Chinese military operations," which, of course, it never had. A previous agreement in 1897 between France and China regarding the island was dismissed as not binding upon Japan. Also, because of the situation in Europe in 1939, France was in no condition to take action to thwart Japan's intentions vis-à-vis the island.

In mid-January, 1939, General Mikio's 21st Corps, which had taken Canton in October, was directed to provide the landing and occupying troops for the seizure of Hainan. On February 10, 1939, under cover of naval gunfire and air support, the somewhat overworked Taiwanese Brigade stormed ashore on nearly empty beaches near Haikou on the north coast of the island. There was no Chinese resistance of any kind. Peace-preservation defense units fled in panic to the mountainous interior at the first appearance of the Japanese task force. The landing troops moved inland at once and occupied the capital, Kiungshan, then proceeded to fan out over the north half of the island. A few days later the Japanese navy appeared off Yulin, a port of the south coast. Troops were landed without opposition, and in the best tradition of the Japanese navy the conquest of Hainan was complete.

The first Japanese objective in the plan to destroy Hsueh Yueh and his 9th War Area command was the capture of Nanchang. The 11th Corps, commanded by General Neiji Okamura, was assigned responsibility for carrying out this mission. The corps consisted of the 6th, 101st and 106th Divisions, the 120th Cavalry Regiment, 22nd Artillery Regiment, one battalion of marines and one brigade of the 116th Division—about 75,000 troops. Since Japanese plans envisaged the use of Poyang Lake and its outlet to the Yangtze River, about 30 gunboats and a large number of smaller armed craft were attached to General Okamura's command. The Japanese 3rd, 13th, and 16th divisions were directed to block any possible reaction by the Chinese 5th War Area command north of the Yangtze.

Facing the enemy along the Hsiu River, 40 to 70 miles north and northwest of Nanchang, were the troops of Hsueh Yueh's command. Available in the Nanchang sector were the 19th Army Group of four corps,[31] the 5th Reserve Division, three peace preservation regiments of the Poyang Lake garrison and two guerrilla regiments with the equivalent strength of twelve divisions under General Lo Cho-ying; the 74th Corps of three divisions; the Hunan-Kiangsi-Hupei Guerrilla Army of two corps;[32] 128th Division and four additional regiments of guerrilla troops, totaling the equivalent of six divisions; the 1st Army Group of three corps[33] which included six divisions; and the 30th Army Group of two corps[34] composed of three divisions and one infantry brigade. In early April, the 32nd Army Group of two corps[35] and one separate division, totaling five divisions, was shifted from the 3rd War Area and attached to General Hsueh's command.

General Hsueh Yueh's thirty-five divisions and one brigade in the Nanchang sector, including the guerrilla forces, had a strength of about 230,000 men. The twenty-four divisions of the 31st, 27th, 30th and 20th Army Groups—all in Hsueh Yueh's 9th War Area command—were not employed in the Nanchang operations. They were deployed to oppose an expected Japanese thrust toward Changsha, 170 miles west of Nanchang.

In mid-February, 1939, the front in the 9th War Area extended from a point on the east shore of Tung Ting Lake, about 25 miles south of Yochow, in an easterly direction toward Juohsi on the Hsiu River, then along the south bank of the river to its outlet into Poyang Lake. The line crossed the Kiukiang-Nanchang rail line about 15 miles south of Tehan and 35 miles north of Nanchang. In preparation for the planned offensive, the Japanese 6th Division concentrated in the Juohsi area, the 106th Division in the Tsaohsing area about halfway between Juohsi and the north–south railway, and the 101st Division on the railway line south of Tehan. One brigade of the Japanese 116th Division, one battalion of marines, and a flotilla of small naval craft assembled around Hukou where Poyang Lake flows into the Yangtze.

At this point, with the Japanese 11th Corps poised and waiting, the Chinese National Military Council woke up to the fact that in the words of the official history, an "enemy attempt to attack Nanchang . . . gradually became apparent," but that "it would be some time after March 15th when the enemy would begin the attack." The orders that spewed forth from distant Chungking were an enlightening example of Chiang Kai-shek's military myopia, his inability to keep his fingers off the smallest detail, and his propensity to meddle to the confusion of the main issue.

The highlights of Chiang Kai-shek's instructions were:

(1) Deploy only necessary forces in Wuning [15 miles southwest of Juoshi] and maintain powerful forces on the Nanchang front. Keep the 32nd Corps and the 20th Army Group in the vicinity of Nanchang under the command of the 19th Army Group.

(2) The employment of the 1st Army Group should be based on the operational plans of the Generalissimo's headquarters in Kweilin [400 miles southwest of Nanchang]. It must not be employed hastily.

(3) The 3rd War Area should constantly watch the situation. . . .

(4) Water outlets in Poyang Lake and rivers . . . should be blockaded and guarded.

(5) The highway from Wuning to Hsiushui [35 miles to the southwest] . . . should be completely destroyed.

The 9th War Area will deploy the 19th Army Group . . . to garrison Nanchang. The 19th Army Group will deploy the 32nd, 79th, 49th and 70th Corps [12 of its 14 divisions] to garrison Wuchengchen and . . . to the west on the south bank of the Hsiu River . . . The 30th Army Group [of two corps[36]] with the 78th Corps attached will . . . garrison . . . Wuning. The 31st Army Group [of five corps[37]] will . . . garrison southern Hupei and northern Hunan. The 1st Army Group [of three corps[38]] and the 74th Corps will be retained in Liling and Luyang [in] the vicinity of Changsha as mobile forces.

Chiang's detailed and often contradictory orders removed all possibility of initiative from General Hsueh Yueh. Chiang Kai-shek reduced his field commanders to the status of mere aides-de-camp with the sole task of transmitting his orders. The result was that extremely few dared to make decisions of any kind without detailed instructions from Chiang, usually too late to counter rapid enemy moves.

On March 17, one Japanese brigade and a battalion of marines from Hukou arrived by boat to attack Wuchengchen at the junction of the Hsiu River and Poyang Lake. At the same time, one brigade of the Japanese 101st Division attacked Tuchiafu, on the railway 30 miles north of Nanchang. The Chinese 14th and 5th reserve divisions at Wuchengchen and along the west shore of the lake held their ground, as did the 142nd Division at Tuchiafu. Repeated enemy assaults failed, and on March 23 the three Chinese divisions still held their positions.

At dusk on March 18 the Japanese 101st Division, less one

brigade, and the 106th Division deployed along the north bank of the Hsiu River at Tsaohsing and Changkungu, 15 miles west of the railway line. After a heavy artillery preparation that cleared the south bank, the Japanese crossed the river on March 20 and came up against two divisions from the Chinese 79th and 49th corps. The other three divisions of these corps had been "deployed in depth" and took no part in the engagement that followed; in the ensuing three-day fight, during which the two Chinese divisions gave ground slowly, the other two divisions of the 79th Corps were unable to cross a small flooded river and, when called upon, did not join the battle. The Japanese compelled the Chinese to withdraw through Chingan and Tanhsi for a distance of 20 to 25 miles to a line running just north of Fenghsin, Anyi, and Wanchiafu, about 25 miles northwest of Nanchang. On March 23, enemy armored units rammed through the center of the Chinese line and stormed into Anyi. The next day they took Wanchiafu and Fenghsin. The Chinese fell back to a new line anchored at Niuhsing, less than 12 miles northwest of Nanchang, and at Tacheng, 25 miles to the west.

Meanwhile, on March 20 the Japanese 6th Division launched an attack from Juohsi against the 8th and 73rd corps of four divisions from the Hunan-Hupei-Kiangsi Border Guerrilla Command some 10 miles northeast of Wuning, forcing the Chinese to pull back for over 10 miles. On the twenty-first, the bulk of the Japanese 6th Division forced its way across the Hsiu River east of Chinkou and attacked the 78th Corps of the 30th Army Group in a week-long series of indecisive engagements. During these attacks and counterattacks the 8th Corps was ordered to make a thrust in four columns from Henglupu, 12 miles northwest of Juohsi, toward Japanese rear areas at Juichang and Tehan on the Kiukiang-Nanchang railway line. These halfhearted attempts petered out before they got well off the ground. The guerrilla divisions of the 8th and 73rd corps were then relieved by the 72nd Corps of two regular divisions. While the relief was still in progress, the 8th and 73rd corps pulled out without warning and headed rapidly toward the mountainous area to the west and safety. Taking advantage of the situation, the Japanese attacked the 72nd Corps before it had had a chance to complete the relief, at the same time striking hard at the flank of the 78th

Corps, also from the 30th Army Group. The two Chinese corps retreated in disorder. The 72nd abandoned Wuning on March 29 and continued abandoning its defense sector until it reached Putienchiao on the Hsiu River 25 miles southwest of Juohsi. Caving in under constant Japanese pressure, the 78th Corps retreated for 25 miles to the south before it stopped to rest.

While the inept performance at the western end of the defense sector was in progress, the 1st Army Group of six divisions and the 74th Corps of three divisions were ordered to move by forced marches to the area of Huifuchieh-Kaoan-Hsiangfukuan in preparation for an attack on the flank of the Japanese 106th Division. The forced marches were made with slow, dragging feet. By March 27 only the advance elements of the 74th Corps had reached Hsiangfukuan, 35 miles west of Nanchang. On the same day, advance guards of the 1st Army Group managed to reach the vicinity of Huifuchieh, about 20 miles to the northwest. The 74th Corps' contact with a flank detachment of the Japanese 106th Division was brief—so brief that the Chinese immediately withdrew to "positions to confront the enemy southwest of Kaoan," nearly 20 miles from their contact at Hsiangfukuan. The commanding general of the 1st Army Group did not wait to contact the enemy, but at once pulled back his six divisions for a distance of about 20 miles. The 70th Corps of two divisions, then about 12 miles west of Chingan, was ordered to attack the enemy flank east of Chingan to enable the three divisions of the 79th Corps, now trapped east of the rapidly advancing Japanese columns, to break out toward the Tacheng area. With Nanchang about to fall, the gallant 70th Corps beat a hasty retreat to Hsuchiafu, 40 miles to the south. Most of the 79th Corps made it to safety without the assistance of other Chinese units.

In a move that under the best conditions could have accomplished little, the Chinese 102nd Division from the 3rd War Area command blundered onto the scene "to defend the highway from Nanchang to Fenghsin," which had already been lost. When the division commander reached a point 15 miles southeast of Fenghsin and suddenly realized that he had stepped into a rapidly deteriorating situation, he turned tail and beat a hasty retreat to Fengcheng on the Kan River nearly 40 miles to the southeast and a good 30 miles south of Nanchang. On March 24, with the 32nd Corps of three divisions and the 5th Reserve Division outflanked and about to be cut off at Tuchiafu and Wuchengchen, General Lo Cho-ying ordered these units to withdraw to Nanchang at once—distances of 30 and 40 miles from their precarious locations. On March 26 the Japanese 106th and 101st divisions broke through the now demoralized Chinese on the Tacheng-Niuhsing defense line. There was no stopping them. The 106th Division pushed on for another 10 miles to Hsinchow, and the 101st pushed 20 miles to Shengmichieh, both on the Kan River, which flowed through Nanchang only 10 miles away. Followed closely in its frantic withdrawal from Tuchiafu by brigades of the enemy 101st and 116th divisions, the Chinese 32nd Corps was not only compelled to fight constant rearguard actions but also had to fend off the Japanese column on its right flank. In a desperate effort to reach Nanchang, part of the Chinese corps succeeded in breaking through and across the route of the two Japanese divisions. But blocked by Japanese forward elements, two of the corps' divisions, the 139th and 141st, gave up and did not pause in their flight until they reached Changshu-chen, nearly 50 miles south of Nanchang. On March 26 the bulk of the 32nd Corps' third division, the 142nd, finally managed to reach Nanchang—just in time to face the full force of two assaulting Japanese divisions.

On the morning of March 27 the Japanese launched a full-scale attack against the city from the north, west, and south. The trapped Chinese troops, now compelled to fight for survival rather than defend the town, fell back through the narrow streets and alleys in a day-long house-to-house struggle. By nightfall the remnants of the Chinese 142nd Division had managed to break out of the burning city, fleeing to Chinhsien, 33 miles to the southeast. The Japanese 11th Corps had captured Nanchang in an operation that took but 11 days. During the final assault and street fighting, large areas of the city were either badly damaged or burned.

Several hundred thousand more terrified refugees straggled in a bewildered stream of uprooted humanity to the south and southwest.

The Chinese 27th and 30th army groups withdrew along the

Hsiu River toward Hsiushui. The routed 19th Army Group, less the 32nd Corps, and the 74th Corps fell back to the area of Hsuchiafu-Shangkao-Nankang, some 60 miles southwest of fallen Nanchang.

Having gained their objective with the capture of Nanchang, the Japanese 11th Corps released the brigade of the 116th Division to rejoin its parent unit in the area east of Hukou and along the Yangtze River. The 6th Division was shifted to Yochow, north of Changsha on the Hankow-Canton railway line. This left only the 101st and 106th divisions with their cavalry and artillery attachments to hold the Nanchang area encompassed by Wuning, nearly 70 miles northwest of the city; Fenghsin and Tsaling, about 55 miles to the west; and Hsiangtang, 20 miles to the south. The 101st Division garrisoned Nanchang and its vicinity; the 106th, the area to the west and northwest for a distance of 60 to 70 miles.

On April 16, 1939, Chiang Kai-shek directed the 9th War Area command to cut the Kiukiang-Nanchang rail line and to recapture Nanchang. The counteroffensive was scheduled to open on April 24 under the command of General Lo Cho-ying, who had just lost this area. Employing the 32nd Army Group, the 5th Reserve Division, and his own 19th Army Group, General Lo's plan was typical of him. His orders bristled with such expressions as "to attack," "to advance toward," "to maintain a state of readiness," "to maintain surveillance," and "for the defense of." But no unit of the command was ordered to seize or gain an objective on a fixed timetable of successive missions.

On April 21, elements of the Chinese 49th and 74th corps crossed the Chin River and engaged Japanese outposts at Tacheng; at Wanshoukung, 12 miles north of the river; and at Shengmichieh, 10 miles farther north. The 74th Corps also attacked Kaoan in force, which was quickly abandoned by the Japanese. By April 26 the Chinese had reoccupied Hsiangfukuan and Tacheng north of the river, Shihtoukang on the river, and Shengmichieh at the junction of the Chin and Kan rivers 10 miles south of Nanchang, and had entered the outskirts of Niuhsing, only 5 miles northwest of the city. Caught by surprise at the unexpected speed of the Chinese thrusts, the overconfident Japanese 101st Division drew in its outposts to Wanshoukung and prepared to stand fast. The Japanese 106th Division followed suit and took up a defensive stance in the hilly Chingan area, 20 miles northeast of Fenghsin. Fairly large probing attacks by the Japanese failed to drive the Chinese out of Kaoan and Tacheng, but the 101st Division held Wanshoukung and forced the Chinese column to pull back from the Niuhsing area.

On the same day, April 21, the Chinese 184th and New 10th divisions of the 1st Army Group attacked enemy outposts west of Fenghsin. By the twenty-fourth, they had forced the Japanese to fall back into the town itself. The New 11th Division continued to "maintain surveillance over the enemy at Chingan" from a distance of about 15 miles—meaning that it did nothing but sit on its hands. Meanwhile, a large unit of the Chinese 182nd Division moved toward its objective, Tanhsishih, 40 miles east of its original starting point. It did not get much farther. After 10 days of intermittent fighting and maneuvering, troops of the Japanese 106th Division still held their positions along an arc with a radius of 20 miles from Chingan that extended from Paihsienling through Tsaling and Fenghsin to a point about 5 miles east of Huihsishih and 15 miles north of Fenghsin. The Japanese had pulled in their outpost positions, but the Chinese had merely nibbled around the edges.

While the Chinese 30th Corps attacked the Japanese force at Wuning, one regiment from the 78th Corps made an unopposed 45-mile march south of the Hsiu River to Changkungtu, 10 miles west of the railway. After reaching its objective on May 4, this unit contacted guerrilla forces north of the river on both sides of the railway line.

On April 23 the Chinese 10th Reserve Division and 16th Division of the 32nd Army Group attacked Japanese defensive positions at Hsintsunyu and Hsiliangshan between the Fu and Kan rivers about 20 miles south of Nanchang. At the same time the Chinese 5th Reserve Division and 79th Division, from their assembly areas 20 miles east of Nanchang, crossed the Fu River at two points. The 5th Reserve Division reoccupied undefended Wutsun, 5 miles west of the river, and pressed on to attack Japanese positions south of Wanghsia, only 6 miles east of the

Nanchang airfield. After crossing the Fu River, the 79th Division headed directly toward Nanchang and attacked Japanese positions some 14 miles east of the city. To its surprise, the Japanese 101st Division now found itself under heavy pressure by units of the 32nd Army Group from the east and south and by the 9th Reserve Division and 105th Division of the 49th Corps from the southwest and west. At all points of attack the Japanese put up stiff resistance, but the Chinese "human sea" tactic flooding in from so many directions at the same time proved too much for them. On April 25, Chinese assaults engulfed Shihchachieh, 25 miles southwest of Nanchang, and Hsintsunyu and Hsiliangshan to the south of the city. To the north, the Chinese 5th Reserve Division and 79th Division stormed through their first objectives, then pressed on toward Nanchang and the airfield, 7 miles to the northwest. On the twenty-sixth, the Chinese took Hsiangtang, 15 miles south of the city, rammed through Shawochang, and attacked the Japanese at Lientang, 8 miles south of Nanchang. From the west, a unit of the Chinese 105th Division slipped through Japanese positions at Niuhsing, infiltrated the defenses of Nanchang, and managed to enter the western outskirts of the city.

Up to this point the Chinese counteroffensive had met with unusual success. Then, on April 27, the Japanese air force bombed Chinese positions heavily, forcing the attacking troops to halt their advance. Taking advantage of the slowdown on April 28, the Japanese 101st Division counterattacked to the east, south, and west; but Chinese reaction was prompt and vigorous. On April 30, General Chen An-pao, commander of the 29th Corps, led his 26th Division across the Fu River near Hsiangtang to assault Japanese defenses at Lientang. The recapture of Lientang and the enemy withdrawal back to Nanchang spurred other Chinese units into an enthusiastic renewal of the offensive around the city. The nearly encircled Japanese were gradually forced into a steadily tightening perimeter by Chinese troops grown reckless with the taste of victory. Casualties were heavy during the ensuing five-day battle. By May 5 the Chinese 5th Reserve Division had recaptured the airfield and pushed on toward Nanchang. Other Chinese units stormed into the railway station at the edge of town. For three days Chinese and Japanese fought from house to house. The city's battered buildings became heaps of rubble when the Japanese opened up with heavy artillery barrages and air attacks. Reinforcements from the Japanese 116th Division made possible a series of enemy counterthrusts within the city's confines. But the savage toe-to-toe fighting continued until May 8, when General Chen An-pao was killed and General Liu Yu-ching, commander of the 26th Division, was severely wounded. When this news of the loss of the two generals spread among Chinese troops, all offensive spirit suddenly seemed to vanish into thin air. The nearly victorious attackers stopped in their tracks, slunk back from street barricades, and began to slip off toward the rear. On May 9, in the words of the Chinese history: "our forces received orders to stop the attack, and the entire front returned to what it had been." The counteroffensive had blown sky high.

What caused the Chinese suddenly to withdraw when victory was within their grasp? Why had not the forceful Hsueh Yueh stepped in to save the battle? He was sulking, perhaps, because the generalissimo had designated one of his subordinates to command the operation; as overall commander, he had lost face. But why should he not now move in to pick up the pieces? During the counteroffensive, Chinese troops had fought with great gallantry. They had almost won the battle. Then, having lost two heroic leaders, they had withdrawn. Why the general collapse? Perhaps it was not the nature of defense-minded senior commanders to visualize sustaining an offensive. Perhaps they feared the Japanese counterattack and reprisals that would surely have followed their success. So the Chinese armies fell back to the defensive posture in which they felt more comfortable. The official history of the campaign sought solace in the thought that "the blow and tying down we dealt against the enemy contributed greatly to the over-all situation."

11

Operations in North Hupei West of the Pinghan Railway, April 25 to May 20, 1939

IN EARLY APRIL, 1939, during the lull between the fall of Nan-chang and the abortive Chinese counteroffensive to recapture it, Chiang Kai-shek cast his eyes toward the southern end of the Pinghan Railway as a likely arena in which "to harass and tie down the enemy." The region for this latest game of military chess lay south of the Huai River in northern Hupei province. Its principal points of reference were Hsinyang, on the railway about 90 miles north of Hankow, and Anlu, about 60 miles north-west of Hankow. The Chinese labeled the ensuing operations the Battle of Sui-Tsao after the towns of Suihsien and Tsaoyan. For the opening move, Chiang Kai-shek shifted T'ang En-po's 31st Army Group from the 9th War Area in northern Hunan to Tsaoyang to reinforce Li Tsung-jen's 5th War Area command.

By late April, when Chinese troop deployments indicated a threat to the Japanese position in the area north of Hankow, General Neiji Okamura, commander of the 11th Corps, reacted by dispatching three divisions and one cavalry brigade to the vicinity of Hsinyang and to the area southwest of Anlu. This task force, operating under 11th Corps command, consisted of the 3rd, 13th and 16th Divisions and the 4th Cavalry Brigade. The 16th Division concentrated in the Chunghsiang-Yangtzechen-Tungchiaochen area east of the Hsiang River about 30 miles west of Anlu; the 13th Division west of the Piao River about 10 miles north of Anlu; the 3rd Division in the Yingshan area, 5 to 15 miles west of the Pinghan Railway and about 10 miles north of

Anlu; and the 4th Cavalry Brigade astride the Hankow-Ichang Road some 40 miles south of Anlu. The enemy force assigned responsibility for the area had a total strength of about 70,000 men.

For its "spring offensive" the 5th War Area command had reorganized its major units into a Right Flank Army, a Left Flank Army, a River Defense Force, and four army groups directly responsible to the war-area command. The Right Flank Army, commanded by the forceful "roughneck," General Chang Tse-chung, consisted of the 33rd Army Group of three corps composed of seven divisions and two cavalry brigades; the 29th Army Group of two corps containing four divisions; and one separate division—a force of twelve divisions and two cavalry brigades with a strength of about 90,000 men. General Chang retained direct command of the 33rd Army Group and of his highly dependable 59th Corps. The Left Flank Army, commanded by the rather colorless General Li Pin-hsien, consisted of the 11th Army Group of two corps composed of five divisions and one separate division—a total of six divisions with a strength of approximately 40,000 men. The River Defense Force consisted of one corps of two divisions; two separate divisions; and one peace preservation regiment—four divisions with a strength of less than 28,000 men. The 31st Army Group, commanded by the capable and forceful General T'ang En-po, consisted of two corps of six divisions with a strength of about 40,000 men. The 21st Army Group consisted of two corps of four divisions with a strength of 30,000 men. The 2nd Army Group, commanded by General Sun Lien-chung, consisted of two corps of four divisions with a strength of approximately 30,000 men. The 22nd Army Group consisted of two corps of two divisions with a strength of 20,000 men. Thus, Li Tsung-jen had a total available strength of over 280,000 men with which to conduct the planned operations.

On April 25th, the Generalissimo ordered General Ku Chu-tung, commander of the 3rd War Area, "to step up the offensive along the Yangtze River and tie down the enemy." He also directed General Hsueh Yueh of the 9th War Area "to continue the attack on Nanchang, reinforce Tungshan, exploit success and attack Yuehyang [Yochow]."

According to the Chinese history: "In late April, the 5th War

Area ceased its attack and redeployed its forces." Actually, there had been no Chinese attack any place in the zone of the 5th War Area, though there had been much huffing and puffing about the spring offensive that had not yet got off the ground. But there was a considerable shifting around of various units. The River Defense Force moved into the area between Ichang on the Yangtze and the Piao River south and southwest of Anlu. The Right Flank Army was deployed along the Hsiang River north of Chunghsiang, 35 miles west of Anlu. The Left Flank Army took up positions in the Lishan-Taerhwan area, 20 to 30 miles northwest of Anlu. The 31st Army Group's 13th Corps of three divisions deployed in the Tangliangtien-Tienhokou area, about 30 miles north of Anlu. The 85th Corps of three divisions, also from the 31st Army Group, was deployed nearly 20 miles to the rear of the 13th Corps in the Wushanchen-Lutouchen area. The 22nd Army Group was sprawled for over 25 miles from Tsaoyang, 43 miles northwest of Anlu, through Maotsefan to Changkangtien, 23 miles northwest of Anlu, "for mobile employment." The 21st Army Group was directed to conduct guerrilla operations east of the Pinghan Railway in the general area where the borders of Honan, Hupei and Anhwei provinces meet. The 68th Corps of two divisions—attached from the 1st War Area— was directed "to maintain surveillance over the enemy at Hsinyang."

The plan for the spring offensive was typically defensive in character. The Chinese would occupy positions in depth in the rugged Tahung and Tungpo mountainous areas flanking the narrow Piao River valley between Tsaoyang and Suihsien. From these strongholds they were directed "to wear out the enemy . . . awaiting the enemy to go deep into the Sui-Tsao Basin, and shift to the offensive before destroying him." The entire concept of the 5th War Area command was based on attrition rather than action.

But the Japanese 11th Corps reacted to Chinese troop deployments by striking first. On April 30 its 3rd Division attacked the three divisions of the Chinese 84th Corps[1] at Haochiatien and Hsuchiatien, 5 and 12 miles west of the railway and about 15 miles north of Anlu. On May 1, after piddling resistance, the 84th Corps withdrew for about 15 miles to the vicinity of Lishan and Taerhwan. North of Lishan, the Japanese attack was stalled by General T'ang En-po's 13th Corps[2] on May 2. After a four-day fight, the attack against the 84th Corps at Taerhwan met with more success. Again claiming that the Japanese had used poison gas, the 84th Corps abandoned Taerhwan and the nearby village of Kaocheng. The corps "fell back to positions on the west bank of the Piao River"—and left a large hole in the Chinese defense line. On May 5 the Japanese 3rd Division attacked the 13th Corps at Tienhokou. Fighting continued for 24 hours, and the attack was again stalled.

Provided with excellent intelligence and having no intention of being drawn into the trap of the narrow Piao Valley, the Japanese main thrust came from the south. On May 1 the 13th and 16th divisions and the 4th Cavalry Brigade attacked the Chinese 37th and 180th divisions in the area between Chunghsiang and Chingshihchiao, 8 miles to the northeast. Hurling the weight of the attack at the boundary between the two divisions, the Japanese quickly forced a wedge toward Tenglo, 10 miles north of their jumping-off line. Though the Chinese 77th Corps and 55th Division crossed the Hsiang River and attacked the flank of the advancing Japanese, the 34th and 56th divisions,[3] only 10 miles east of the battle area, did nothing. On May 5, after a four-day seesaw struggle, Japanese troops rammed their way through the Chinese positions to Liushuikou—a push of 5 miles—where they were temporarily stopped by the Chinese 38th Division. During the next two days, Japanese assaults and superior artillery fire forced the Chinese back for 20 miles to Tsaoyang, which was captured on May 7.

The Japanese had now encircled the planned Piao Valley trap. With the loss of Tsaoyang, Chinese resistance collapsed completely, their defense lines simply falling apart. On May 10 the Japanese marched almost unopposed into Huyangchen, 10 miles north of Tsaoyang, and their cavalry took Hsinyeh, 18 miles farther to the northwest. On May 12 the cavalry captured Tangho, nearly 20 miles east of Hsinyeh, and Nanyang, 12 miles farther north. Also on the twelfth, a Japanese column from Hsinyang seized Tungpo, 20 miles west of the railway. The Chinese forces east of Tsaoyang now found themselves in a pocket nearly 20 miles wide and over 35 miles long—virtually caught in their own trap. With the exception of the 39th Corps' two divisions and the 13th Corps' three divisions, the entire Chinese force rushed pell-mell to escape before the 20-mile gap at the north end of the trap was closed. The two corps that were left behind took up positions in the mountains on each side of the Piao River valley, presumably still waiting hopefully for the Japanese to enter their trap, which they never did.

The 33rd Army Group was ordered to attack Japanese rear areas south of Liushuikou, but the commander, Chang Tse-chung, suddenly seemed to have lost his taste for battle. If any hostilities ever did take place in this area, they were of a very minor nature indeed. The 2nd Army Group was directed to launch a counteroffensive from Hsihsinchi and Paoanchai, north and northeast of Nanyang, to recapture Nanyang and Tangho. But the Japanese had accomplished their purpose of breaking up any Chinese spring offensive and protecting the Pinghan Railway north of Hankow. They had no desire to garrison the rugged territory that lay 40 to 50 miles west of the railway line. In any case, they did not have sufficient strength to do so. So they now withdrew their forces through Tungpo to the area just west of Hsinyang. As the Japanese pulled back, the Chinese reoccupied Hsinyeh, Nanyang, Tangho, Tsaoyang, and Tungho and hailed this action as a great victory. It was not; in fact, the reoccupation of the various towns and villages was accomplished without firing a shot.

In the words of the Chinese official history: "By May 20th, the original front lines were restored." The 25-day spring offensive, with all its brave plans, amounted to a complete cipher for the Chinese, except for several thousand dead and wounded, burned villages, ruined crops, and fleeing refugees.

The Nomonhan Incident

MAY 11 TO SEPTEMBER 15, 1939

Far from the Yangtze Valley and the Sino-Japanese conflict, other violent events filled the world with shock and fear during the summer of 1939. One, which directly affected the war in China and presaged events in Manchuria 6 years later, was the so-called Nomonhan incident. Continuing from May until September, it was to be the most important military clash between Soviet Russia and Japan until the latter's collapse in 1945. In July an accelerating series of world-shaking actions brought war to Europe, and eventually to the entire world. Within the next 10 years, the vast continuing struggle was destined to destroy both the Japanese Empire and Chiang Kai-shek's government in China.

Since 1935, the borders between Manchuria and Outer Mongolia had been the cause of constant friction and dispute. From 1935 to 1937 hundreds of armed clashes had occurred between the bellicose Kwantung Army of Japan and the Soviet Union's Far Eastern Army. The 50-year-old enmity between the two protagonists had not been allayed by the German-Japanese (and the later Italian-Japanese) Anti-Comintern Pact of November, 1936, nor by the Sino-Russian nonaggression pact of August, 1937.

Dissension between Japan and Russia, constantly stirred by the Kwantung Army, had been further exacerbated by Stalin's devious plans in the Far East. Since the signing of the nonaggression pact with China he had not only rotated Russian air squadrons to bolster China's fight against Japan and to provide combat training for his aviators, but had by 1938 provided Chiang Kai-shek with about 400 planes, fuel, and munitions on a fairly large scale. In addition, Moscow had made two loans to China in 1938, each of $50 million, and a third loan in 1939 of $150 million. Caring not a whit for China's predicament, Stalin's purpose in supporting the nationalist government was designed to strike at and contain his old enemy Japan. Pragmatically, he had calculated that Chiang Kai-shek, commanding the most divisions and the most power in China, was far more capable of hurting Japan in the long run than were the comparatively weak Chinese Communists, to whom he gave no aid of any kind.

By 1939, unable to settle the prolonged and worsening situation they had created in China, the Japanese military and their Foreign Office had begun to fear that Russia, Great Britain, the United States, and China might combine to bring about the downfall of the empire. Later events were to prove that this fear was not entirely unfounded.

At the time, 30 Russian divisions, most of which were a part of the Soviet Far Eastern Army, and an estimated 2,300 tanks and 1,700 planes were stationed throughout the vast area of Siberia.

(After the German attack on Russia in the summer of 1941, about one-half of the ground forces and about 1,000 planes were transferred to the Russian western front. Later the number of troops in Siberia was gradually increased to an estimated strength of 800,000 men with approximately 1,000 planes and 1,000 tanks.) In the summer of 1939, the Far Eastern Army and its supporting troops numbered over 600,000 men. At the time of the July, 1937, outbreak of hostilities with China, the Japanese Kwantung Army in Manchuria had only six divisions, plus supporting and line-of-communication troops, scattered throughout their occupied territory—a force of about 250,000 men. By May, 1939, Japanese strength in Manchuria had been increased to nine divisions, which with supporting troops, numbered around 400,000 men.

Still smarting from its defeat at Changkufeng in July and August, 1938, the Kwantung Army selected Nomonhan as the most likely spot for a test of the fighting quality of the recently purged Soviet Far Eastern Army. There were dozens of other border areas where the boundary between Manchukuo and Outer Mongolia were in dispute, but Nomonhan, 1,600 miles north of Chungking, was near enough to the old Chinese Eastern Railway to ease the difficult logistics problems of supporting an operation on the border. Also, Japanese intelligence had indicated that the Russian garrison at this point was not large. The staff of the Kwantung Army saw a quick victory over the hated Soviets, one that would enable them to settle the troublesome border questions on their terms. To ensure success, the Japanese assembled a full division, the 23rd, with supporting troops and aircraft for the planned vest-pocket war.

As might be expected, the Japanese and Russian versions of the incident vary considerably. According to the official Japanese records, the clash started on May 11, 1939, when a force of Outer Mongolian troops crossed the Khalka River and attacked a lightly manned observation post of Manchurian troops. Although the Mongolian force succeeded in overrunning the post, it was quickly replaced by Russian troops of the Far Eastern Army. The Russian story claimed, of course, that Japanese units had overrun a Russian border post.

By May 14 the bulk of the waiting Japanese 23rd Division and the 2nd Air Group had moved up to test Soviet reaction. On May 18 the Japanese attacked without warning. Caught by surprise, the weaker Russian units were forced by the vigor and superior strength of the assaults to pull back from their outposts and forward positions. During the next few weeks the Japanese continued the pressure until they had not only seized all of the disputed ground, but had also entered territory recognized by both sides as being in Mongolia. Then, having pushed their opponents around more or less at will, they dug in for a long stay. Additional troops of the Kwantung Army's 6th Corps reinforced the 23rd Division to almost twice its original strength. Meanwhile, the Russians increased their forces at the front with one mechanized division, two Mongolian cavalry divisions, and supporting air units. On June 18 the Soviets attacked, but without decisive results. Intermittent probing attacks by each side continued throughout July, but the Russians made no serious attempts to recover all of the lost ground.

However, the Japanese Kwantung Army had not reckoned on General Georgi K. Zhukov, commander of the Far Eastern Army. He had made no secret of the reinforcements he had sent to his forward units, but well to the rear he had also been assembling the equivalent of nearly 4 infantry divisions, 2 additional cavalry divisions, about 350 tanks, 340 armored cars, 15 battalions of supporting artillery, and an estimated 300 combat aircraft. By early August he was ready to move.

On August 20 he struck with the full power at his disposal. Stunned by massive infantry, artillery, tank, and air attacks, augmented by freewheeling cavalry squadrons operating all over the place, the Japanese fell back, rushed in reinforcements, and fought savagely to hold their positions. Within five days the largest armored battles in history were being fought over the flinty, treeless battlefield. The border dispute had erupted into full-scale combat involving over 150,000 troops. In the end the Japanese were overwhelmingly defeated and forced to retire from the disputed territory. They admitted officially that they had suffered 18,000 casualties and had lost over 100 planes. To its bitter chagrin and complete loss of face, the Kwantung Army had learned the hard way not to tamper with aroused Russians, particularly those commanded by General Zhukov. On September 15 a cease-fire agreement was signed by the antagonists, but the boundaries were not clearly defined for another two years.

The Japanese attempted to censor all news of their defeat, but

18,000 casualties are not easy to hide. Moscow took pains to inform the world—particularly China—of their victory. The news heartened the Chinese; it proved again that the Japanese could be defeated, but unfortunately, they were compelled to admit, not by Chinese armies.

But that summer of 1939 the heady news from Europe and America seemed a guiding star to China's future: virtually all the European powers were suddenly at war; Japan, allied to Germany and Italy, could be drawn into the conflict; possibly even the United States. At last there seemed hope for China.

On July 26 the United States abrogated its trade treaties with Japan. Although this action hurt the island empire in many categories of essential commodities, it built up more resentment than it did harm to Japan. It did not stop the enormous shipments of scrap metal from the United States that were earmarked for conversion into munitions.

On August 23 Stalin and Hitler signed a nonaggression pact. This threw the foreign ministries of both China and Japan into complete confusion. It made Japan's Anti-Comintern Pact with Germany utterly meaningless. In Chinese eyes, that was fine; but what about their own nonaggression pact with Russia?

On September 1 Germany invaded Poland. At every encounter its huge army of 1.7 million men and its blitzkrieg tactics overwhelmed the poorly equipped Polish army of less than 600,000. Alarmed at the speed of the German advance from East Prussia, Silesia, and Czechoslovakia, and fearing that its slice of the Polish pie might be gobbled up by Hitler's legions, Russia invaded Poland from the east on September 17. After heroic but futile defense, the nearly destroyed Polish capital, Warsaw, surrendered on September 27, only to suffer the massacre of a large part of its population. On September 29 the Hitler and Stalin governments divided prostrate Poland between them, with the Germans getting the lion's share.

To the Japanese militarists, that was how things should have gone in China, if the stubborn Chinese had only had enough sense to appreciate the benefits to be gained from the new order in Asia. To the Chinese, that was what could have happened to them had they not resisted Japanese aggression.

12

The First Battle of Changsha, April 13 to October 8, 1939

Just as Nanchang had been an irritant in Japanese eyes, so in early August was Changsha, 170 miles west of Nanchang and 85 miles south of occupied Yochow. Aside from its strategic location in the lake region south of the Yangtze River, Changsha, with a population of over 500,000, was the largest city in Hunan, capital of the province, and center of the rich agricultural area south and east of Tung Ting Lake. A prize so near could not be ignored by the invaders; the Imperial General Staff promulgated detailed plans for its seizure.

General Okamura, commander of the 11th Corps, was assigned the 6th, 106th, 33rd, 3rd (split into two brigade task forces) and 101st Divisions, one brigade of the 13th Division (the Nara column), supporting artillery and air units, and over one hundred small gunboats and armed water craft for the planned operation against Changsha. Not including sailors and marines manning the river and lake flotilla, his offensive force numbered about 120,000 men—a strength deemed adequate to overwhelm any armies the Chinese might field for the defense of the city.

In early September, when Okamura's troops had already been disposed preparatory to the attack, the Imperial General Staff again adjusted the command structure of the armies in China, the purpose being to achieve one overall coordinated command. On September 12, Headquarters China Expeditionary Force was activated at Nanking with General Nishio in command. He was assigned control of all operations, civil affairs, and military govern-

ment not only in central China but also over the North China
Front Army. The new unified Japanese command consisted of six
corps and all attached units from Mongolia to Canton. It had a
strength of over 1 million men; however, because of strung-out
garrison functions in the huge areas of occupied China, no more
than a relatively small percentage of this number could be
brought to bear on any specific operation.

The Chinese 9th War Area, General Ch'en Ch'eng commanding, with responsibility for the defense of Hunan and northwest
Kiangsi provinces, consisted of six army groups, seven separate
corps and one separate division. The 19th Army Group, consisting of the 32nd and 49th Corps of four divisions, was commanded by General Lo Cho-ying, the non-hero of Nanchang.
Considerably reduced from its former size, the Army Group now
had a strength of close to 32,000 men. The 1st Army Group,
whose commander, Lung Yun, still preferred the safety of his
broken-down palace at Kunming to the risk of facing a court
martial and a firing squad, consisted of the 58th and 60th Corps
of four divisions plus the 2nd Advance Column of peace preservation troops. Also reduced in size, it had a strength of about 34,000
men. The 30th Army Group consisted of the 78th and 72nd
Corps of four divisions, the Hunan-Hupei Border Area Advance
Force made up of the 8th Corps of two divisions, the 3rd
Advance Column of three peace preservation regiments, the 1st
Advance Column and one Hupei peace preservation regiment.
This rather mixed bag of troops had an approximate strength of
55,000 men. The 15th Army Group consisted of the 52nd, 37th
and 79th Corps of eight divisions with a strength of about 54,000
men. The 20th Army Group, commanded by the faithful but
unappreciated General Shang Chen, consisted of the 53rd, 54th
and 87th Corps of seven divisions with a strength of about
50,000 men. The 27th Army Group consisted of but one corps,
the 20th, of two divisions. It had a strength of about 18,000 men.
Seven separate corps, the 73rd, 4th, 70th, New 6th, 74th, 5th and
99th, were comprised of seventeen divisions. These units and the
11th Division, directly under the command of Headquarters 9th
War Area, had a total strength of close to 115,000 men. Thus,
General Ch'en Ch'eng had under his command a total of forty-
seven divisions and six peace preservation regiments with an

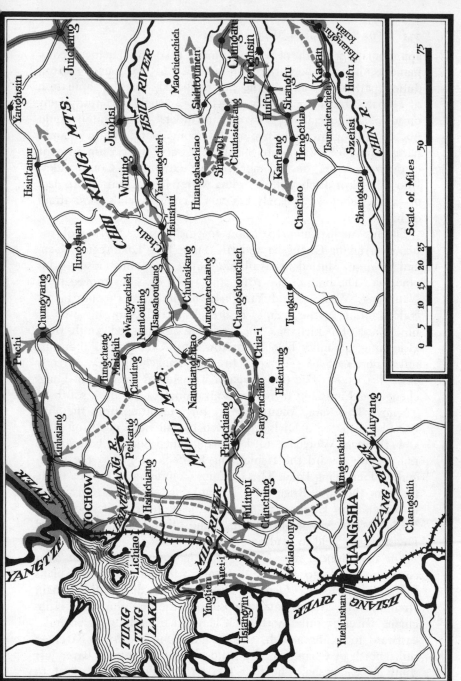

The First Battle of Changsha (Broken lines show Japanese withdrawal.)

approximate strength of 365,000 men. Like the Japanese commanders, he also bore the responsibility for extensive garrison duties, particularly among the hot-tempered, volatile population of Hunan. Unlike the enemy, however, he could not always rely on all of his generals to carry out his orders. He definitely could not depend on an aggressive spirit among many of his subordinates. Though he was aware that he must accept a certain amount of incompetence, he did not forgive cowardice. Commanders who shirked or disobeyed his orders were relieved, court-martialed, or—a few—shot. Fortunately Ch'en Ch'eng's generals were afraid of him.

During August, in preparation for the implementation of the plans for taking Changsha and the Tung Ting Lake region, General Okamura shifted his available units to positions closer to his objective. The bulk of the 101st and 106th divisions moved from Nanchang, Wuning, and Yunghsiu, 75 miles to the north, for concentration in the vicinity of Fenghsin and Chingan, over 50 miles west of Nanchang. The 33rd Division moved south from Hsienning, 45 miles below Hankow, and Chungyang, about 60 miles northeast of Yochow, to the Tungcheng area directly east of Yochow. The 6th Division was shifted west from Tungcheng and Linhsiang to its concentration area 10 miles south of Yochow. The Nara Column, a task force made up from the 26th Brigade of the 13th Division, moved by rail from north of Hankow through Wuchang to Linhsiang, then marched about 10 miles south toward the Hsinchiang River flowing into the north end of Tung Ting Lake. The Uemura Column, a task force made up from the 29th Brigade of the 3rd Division, was transported by water from Hankow to concentrate about 15 miles south of Yochow. The Muragami Column, the other brigade of the 3rd Division, was held in readiness north of Yochow.

On the Chinese side, Chiang Kai-shek directed the 9th War Area command "to crush the enemy with pre-determined plans for mobile defense." General Ch'en Ch'eng disposed his main strength in a series of parallel positions: the first along the Hsinchiang River 75 miles north of Changsha extending for 60 miles eastward to Wangyachieh, the second along the Milo River 45 miles north of Changsha, the third along the Liuyang River just south of Changsha. The first two streams flowed from east to west into Tung Ting Lake; the third from east to west into the north flowing Hsiang River on which Changsha was located. The fourteen corps of thirty-five divisions on the northern Hunan (Changsha) front were directed to "bank positions" in the Mufu Mountains between the Hsinchiang and Milo Rivers, and to take up "multi-layered positions in Changsha to resist and wear out the enemy." The 4th and 52nd Corps, totaling six divisions, along the Liuyang River between Changsha and Liuyang town, were directed to "await the opportunity to conduct flanking attacks and destroy the enemy." At this time, there were no enemy flanks within 90 miles.

On the eastern flank of the command in northern Kiangsi, the 19th, 1st, and 30th army groups, with the strength of sixteen divisions, were deployed along a 60-mile line extending from Hsiangfukuan on the Chin River 150 miles east of Changsha, northwest to Huifu, west to Shihloumen, and north of Yankangchieh on the Hsiu River about 140 miles northeast of Changsha. The 183rd and New 14th divisions were directed to march east through Maochienchieh toward Tehan on the Kiukiang-Nanchang Railway to disrupt Japanese rear areas.

The Japanese offensive to capture Changsha fell into three more or less separate—though coordinated—operations from the north and northeast. The first operation took place in northern Kiangsi. On September 13 the Japanese 106th Division, pushing west from Chingan and Fenghsin on the eastern front, attacked the 184th Division at Huifu on the Chin River section of the Chinese defense line. On the fifteenth the Japanese 101st Division attacked the 58th Corps[1] and the 32nd Corps[2] in the vicinity of Hsiangfukuan, 14 miles south of Fenghsin. The Chinese held their ground for two days, but on September 17 the enemy broke through the defense positions near Huifu, turned south, and reached the vicinity of Tsunchienchieh, a penetration of nearly 15 miles. With its flank and rear now threatened, the Chinese 58th Corps and 32nd Corps withdrew from Kaoan on September 18 to Huifu, a second village with the same name as the one mentioned previously, on the Chin River south of Kaoan. Thus the southern end of the defense line was abandoned. However, the Chinese 49th Corps[3] held its positions on the south bank of the river from Kaoan to the east. At this time the hard-pressed 184th Division of the 60th Corps broke out and retreated 10 miles to the west. The 51st Division of the 74th Corps then rushed up from the south to block any farther Japanese advance at Tsunchienchieh. Meanwhile, the 15th Division moved south from the Hsiu River to Chiuhsientang to reinforce the center of the crumbling Chinese line, and the 183rd Division moved to Shangfu, 10 miles west of the Japanese breakthrough at Huifu.

Early on September 21 the Japanese 106th Division and a task force from the 101st Division captured Shangfu, then made a forced march of 15 miles to the northwest, apparently headed for Hsiushui on the Hsiu River. The Chinese at once took advantage of the now weakened Japanese rear and recaptured Kaoan on the twenty-second and Hsiangfukuan, 8 miles to the northeast, on the following day. The Chinese 49th Corps was ordered to anchor the eastern end of the Chin River line, and the 32nd Corps shifted some 60 miles west to Tungku in order to block a column of the Japanese 101st Division that was expected to push through Shangfu and Chaochiao, 25 miles beyond. The Chinese 51st Division moved from the south toward Chaochiao to reinforce the New 13th Division of the 78th Corps. The bulk of the corps, the 57th and 58th divisions, deployed rapidly in the Szehsi-Shangkao area north of the Chin River, with the 58th Corps about 15 miles to the west. The result of these marches and countermarches was a confused, fluid situation with each side thrusting toward the flank and rear of the other very much like two dogs chasing each other's tails.

At dawn on September 22 the Chinese 183rd Division reached Shangfu and immediately occupied defensive positions. At noon, elements of the Japanese 106th Division attacked; in the early afternoon, they smashed through the lines and forced the Chinese to pull back for 14 miles to Kanfang. On the twenty-third the 15th and 184th divisions arrived to reinforce the 183rd Division. Also reinforced, the Japanese column attacked: after two days of severe fighting, they took Kanfang and continued their westward drive. The Chinese 15th and 183rd divisions pulled back to the northwest; the 184th Division counterattacked from the south. On September 26 the Chinese 57th Division of the 74th Corps attacked the rear of the advancing Japanese column at Hengchiao and Shangfu, 7 miles apart. On the twenty-seventh the Chinese recaptured Shangfu and defeated a relief column of one battalion that had been sent back from Kanfang to salvage the situation. The 184th Division renewed its attack on Kanfang at once. Meanwhile, the Chinese New 15th Division, marching south from the Hsiu River, ran head-on into advance units of the Japanese 106th Division marching toward Hsiushui, and intense fighting broke out. On September 28 the New 10th Division of the Chinese 58th Corps occupied positions at Chaochiao to block the enemy's westward advance. On October 1 the Chinese 57th Division recaptured Hengchiao, nearly 20 miles to the Japanese rear, and the Chinese 184th Division took Kanfang by assault. Although the Japanese column could have been in bad trouble, cut-off completely from its rear areas, it attacked the Chinese defenses at Chaochiao and took them on October 2. Farther westward advance was blocked by waiting Chinese units. Unable to fall back to the west, the Japanese column turned northeast with the object of joining the main force of the 106th Division. The Chinese 32nd and 60th corps jabbed repeatedly at the flanks and rear of the retreating column, hounding it over the entire 20 miles to Shawoli.

At Huangshachiao the Japanese 106th Division was having considerable difficulty fending off constant attacks by the Chinese New 14th and New 15th divisions of the 72nd Corps and by the two divisions of the 78th Corps.[4] On the morning of October 3 the Japanese began to retreat toward Shawoli, 8 miles to the east, intending to join the retreating column from Chaochiao: the combined enemy forces might be able to pull their chestnuts out of the fires being fed by the enthusiasm of Chinese troops smelling victory. On October 5 the Chinese 51st Division attacked Chiuhsientang from the south in order to cut off the Japanese avenue of retreat. On the seventh the combined enemy columns fell back toward Chiuhsientang and Shihmenlou, 5 miles to the north. In a joint attack of wild violence, the Chinese 51st and 57th divisions recaptured Chiuhsientang on October 8, then kept right on the tail of the now disorderly column of Japanese as they beat a retreat to the northeast. On the ninth the Chinese 32nd Corps took Shihmenlou and continued to harass the enemy as he struggled toward Chingan, 18 miles farther to the east. In the four-day battle the Japanese had their noses badly bloodied and suffered severe casualties. Finally, on October 14, the routed enemy troops reached the safety of Wuning and Chingan, stumbling into the same positions from which they had started a month before. Their offensive in northern Kiangsi had been a complete failure.

The Chinese armies glowed with the exhilaration of victory over their hated enemies, but unfortunately they rested on their hard-won laurels and did not follow up the great advantage they had gained.

The second operation in the Changsha offensive was in northeastern Hunan and southern Hupei. In early September the Chinese 3rd and 197th divisions from the 8th Corps of the Hupei-Hunan Border Area Advance Force attacked the enemy north of the Chiukung Mountains near Yanghsin and northeast of Tungshan. Sparsely occupied by the Japanese, this rugged area was about 160 miles northeast of Changsha. At the same time, the Chinese 20th Corps[5] attacked elements of the Japanese 33rd Division in the Hsienning-Chungyang area close to the Hankow-Canton railway line about 140 miles north-northeast of Changsha. The Chinese 79th Corps[6] was deployed in positions from Wangyachien to Maishih, Chiuling, and Huanganshih on a 35-mile-long east west line starting at Peikang on the Hsinchiang River. On September 19, in expectation of enemy offensive action from the Chungyang area, 25 miles north of the line's right flank, the 20th Corps was ordered to march south and to anchor the east end of the line at Nanlouling and Taoshukang.

On September 22 the Japanese 33rd Division attacked the positions of the 140th Division at Wangyachien and Maishih. By nightfall the next day the Japanese had penetrated the line both to the east and to the west of Wangyachien. On the twenty-fourth they continued to drive toward the south. At this time the Chinese 20th Corps was arriving at Nanlouling and Taoshukang. In a vigorous counterattack the Chinese 140th Division struck hard at the west flank of the advancing enemy troops; although the Japanese suffered heavy casualties, the 140th Division was not able to stop their southward push. On September 26 the Japanese took both Nanlouling and Taoshukang. Leaving garrisons in the two towns, the main body of the Japanese 33rd Division continued its drive to the south.

On September 28, advance elements of the Japanese 33rd Division reached Chuhsichang and Lungmenchang, 16 miles south of the east end of the Chinese defense line. On the same day, the Nara Column, a brigade of the Japanese 13th Division that had previously been engaged in operations nearly 50 miles to the west, marched eastward along the Milo River and captured Pingchiang, 35 miles southwest of Lungmenchang. On September 29 the Chinese 79th Corps, the Hupei-Hunan Border Area Advance Force, and the 27th Army Group, the equivalent of eight divisions now placed under the command of the 27th Army Group, were ordered to destroy the enemy, still moving south from Lungmenchang, in the area of Chia-i. To accomplish this objective, the 20th Corps was ordered to attack the Japanese at Changshouchieh, 12 miles south of Lungmenchang. The 79th Corps was directed to block the enemy advance at Hsienlung, 13 miles farther to the southwest. If successful, the Japanese 33rd Division would be boxed in between those two towns. Meanwhile, the 3rd Division of the Chinese 8th Corps attacked enemy rear elements at Nanlouling and Taoshukang, 30 miles to the north at the eastern flank of the original Chinese defense line. On September 30, advance elements of the Japanese 33rd Division passed through Changshouchieh, and the 13th Division brigade was approaching Sanyenchiao, 13 miles east of Pingchiang. Less than 20 miles apart now, the two Japanese units were exerting great pressure to effect a junction. On October 1 the Chinese 79th Corps attacked at Hsienlung. After a fierce fight and heavy casualties on both sides, the Japanese 33rd Division was forced to pull back. On October 2, both Hsienlung and Chia-i were recaptured by the Chinese.

On October 3, a part of the Japanese 13th Division brigade succeeded in breaking through the Chinese block at Sanyenchiao to link up with the 33rd Division, then just north of Chia-i. The bulk of the brigade, under constant attacks against its flanks and rear guard by the Chinese 79th Corps, pulled back in disorder to Pingchiang. From there, in an effort to join the 33rd Division, it headed for Nanchiangchiao, 23 miles to the northeast. Meanwhile, the remainder of the brigade fought its way toward

Changshouchieh. The Chinese 98th and 82nd divisions of the 79th Corps kept close on the heels of the Japanese, now in a virtual rout toward Pingchiang to the west and toward Changshouchieh to the northeast. The latter force was under continuous attack on both flanks by the Chinese 20th Corps. In near panic because of the hornets' nest they had pulled down about their heads, the Japanese fled at night toward Nanchiangchiao and Lungmenchang. The enemy effort to divert troops from the close defense of Changsha had been frustrated by Chinese determination and, above all, by leadership. The routes over which the running battles had stormed were strewn with Japanese dead and wounded, discarded arms and equipment. Generals Amagasu of the 33rd Division and Nara of the 13th Division brigade had bitten off more than they could chew and had failed completely.

Still not ready to accept defeat, on the night of October 3 the Japanese 33rd Division sent a column from Chuhsichang to assist the 106th Division. The relief force took Chalu, 15 miles to the east, before daylight. Its advance elements managed to reach a point about 4 miles west of Hsiushui. But the Chinese 72nd and 78th Corps[7] had already deployed southeast of Hsiushui for a counterattack on the 106th Division in that area. On October 4 the Chinese New 16th Division was rushed to Hsiushui for its defense; on the fifth the other three divisions of the two Chinese corps lined up along the south bank of the Hsiu River prepared to strike.

Meanwhile, on October 3 the Chinese 3rd Division[8] and 140th Division[9] had begun to attack the east and west flanks of the Japanese forces at Nanlouling and Taoshukang, a few miles south of the original defense line's right flank. On the sixth the 3rd Division was ordered to move through Chalu (Chachin) and the 20th Corps of two divisions[10] to the northeast in order to assist the 30th Army Group in its projected counterattack on Hsiushui. On the same day the 98th Division[11] reoccupied and cleared the area around Pingchiang. On October 7 the Chinese recaptured Nanchiangchiao. Now completely cut off from the Japanese 33rd Division and the bulk of its own 13th Division brigade, the remnants of enemy troops from Nanchiangchiao fled to the north and northwest toward Linhsiang on the railway 18 miles east of Yochow. In a similar situation and about to be annihilated by attacking Chinese, the Japanese in the vicinity of Nanlouling scrambled out of their predicament in a near rout to Tungcheng, 10 miles to the northwest.

Faced with Chinese attacks from the west, southwest, south, and east by the eight divisions of the 72nd, 78th, 8th, and 20th corps and already badly battered, the Japanese 33rd Division had had more than enough. On October 8 it beat an unbecomingly hasty retreat from Hsiushui for 8 miles along the Hsiu River, then turned north to push through the rugged Chiukung Mountains. But, exhilarated with success, the Chinese were not yet through with them. On the ninth the Chinese 3rd Division reoccupied Hsiushui. On the same day, from prepared ambush positions in the lower ridges of the mountains, the 197th Division[12] descended like howling dervishes on the retreating Japanese column. Unable to use their full strength and artillery in the narrow, twisting pass, the Japanese were mowed down by the hundreds; but the depleted 33rd Division finally managed to cross the mountainous area. By October 14 a chastened General Amagasu had led his bedraggled and weary troops into Tungshan, 45 miles north of Hsiushui, and Yanghsin, 55 miles northeast of the scene of his humiliation. He, too, had learned that given leadership and a taste of victory, Chinese troops could and would fight with great determination and ferocity.

The third phase of the Changsha offensive occurred north of Changsha. Nearly 50 miles to the west along the Hankow-Canton railway line as it skirted the eastern shore of Tung Ting Lake and the Hsiang River, the Chinese 52nd Corps of three divisions,[13] with the 60th Division of the 15th Army Group attached, had initially deployed along the western half of the northern defense line following the south bank of the Hsinchiang River. It was charged with maintaining liaison with the 79th Corps[14] on its eastern flank. The Chinese 70th Corps,[15] with the 95th Division attached, had deployed along the eastern shore of Tung Ting Lake from the mouth of the Milo River to Hsiangyin, about 5 miles south of the outlet of the Hsiang River. The 73rd Corps, less the 15th Division, had been designated as the general reserve. After moving from Hsiushui through Pingchiang, it concentrated near the railway line about 15 miles east of the Hsiang

River and 30 miles north of Changsha. The 20th Army Group's 53rd Corps[16] and 54th Corps[17] and the 11th Division concentrated along the west bank of the Hsiang River from Hsiangyin to Changsha. The 4th Corps[18] concentrated north and northeast of Changsha.

On September 18 the Japanese 6th and 3rd divisions, less one brigade, opened the offensive by attacking Chinese outposts along the north bank of the Hsinchiang River, 70 miles north of Changsha. Within the next three days, all Chinese troops were driven to the south bank. During the night of September 22 a large flotilla of Japanese gunboats, commandeered junks, and miscellaneous water craft with one brigade of the 3rd Division aboard anchored in Tung Ting Lake just south of the mouth of the Hsinchiang River. At dawn on the twenty-third, troops of the brigade landed near Lichiao, south of the river mouth. At the same time the Japanese 6th Division, supported by air attacks and artillery barrages, forced a crossing of the river between the north–south railway line and the town of Hsinchiang. Shallow water made it possible for the enemy to ford the stream. Twenty-five miles to the south, the Muragami Column, made up of Japanese marines and the second brigade of the 3rd Division, made a second landing from the lake between the mouths of the Milo and Hsinchiang rivers about 48 miles north of Changsha. At the Hsinchiang River defense line a bloody battle with some hand-to-hand fighting lasted all morning, but by noon, the Chinese 2nd Division's section of the line in the area of the railway had broken. The division was forced to withdraw from its positions west of Hsinchiang town. The 180th Brigade of the Chinese 60th Division[19] was rushed forward to plug the gap. Meanwhile, at the mouth of the Milo River, Chinese mortar and artillery fire from the 95th Division[20] succeeded in putting about 20 Japanese landing craft out of action before they reached the shore of the lake. However, the majority of Japanese marines and 3rd Division troops had already completed the landing in the vicinity of Yingtien before 5:00 A.M. Just east of the shoreline, the 95th Division and troops of the Chinese 70th Corps[21] put up a stubborn resistance; by 4:00 P.M. the muddy flats were littered with the casualties of both sides, and heavy enemy air attacks compelled the Chinese to pull back.

During the early hours of darkness on September 23 the Japanese took four villages along the south bank of the Hsinchiang River in the vicinity of Hsinchiang town. South of the Milo River they were firmly entrenched around Yingtien. On the twenty-fourth the Chinese 15th Army Group ordered its 52nd Corps to reinforce the hard-pressed 95th Division. But that night it, too, was forced to pull back for three miles. The Chinese 60th Division, near Hsinchiang town, was ordered to withdraw to positions south of the Milo River in the vicinity of Kuei-i on the railway line.

On September 24, as it withdrew south from the Hsinchiang River, the 52nd Corps of three divisions launched a series of counterattacks against the Japanese. Constant fighting and heavy casualties slowed down the enemy advance, but before the day was over, unremitting Japanese pressure forced a break in the sector of the Chinese lines held by the 25th Division.[22] At the same time the Chinese 95th Division near the mouth of the Milo River was compelled to withdraw from its positions. Badly mauled by five days of continuous fighting, the 95th was relieved by the 19th Division of the 70th Corps. That night the 52nd Corps and the 60th Division were ordered to pull back farther from positions south of the Milo River to a line extending from the railway bridge at Kuei-i for about 5 miles to the east. The 70th Corps[23] was directed to remain at its defense positions west of the bridge. On September 25, violent assaults by the Japanese 3rd Division broke through the line held by the 19th Division and again forced the Chinese to pull back. The timely arrival of reinforcements from the 95th Division and a determined Chinese flank attack halted the enemy breakthrough, and the new defense positions held fast.

On the morning of September 26, against strong Chinese resistance, the Japanese 6th Division forced a crossing of the Milo River near Kuei-i, where the river was deep, the assault being carried out with the use of boats and rafts. Casualties were heavy; fighting near the river degenerated into a confused series of combats between small units, even between individuals. By early afternoon the Chinese began to withdraw.

Meanwhile, General Ch'en Ch'eng had decided "to lure the enemy into the vicinity of Changsha for a decisive battle." To implement his plan, he ordered the 52nd Corps, less the 195th Division and the attached 60th Division, to drop back as rapidly as possible for 15 to 20 miles from the Milo River area. Two regiments of the 195th Division were left just south of the river as a rear guard to delay the Japanese advance. By 7:00 P.M. on the twenty-sixth the main force of the Chinese corps had reached its ambush positions running from north to south on the west side of the railway line. The 70th Corps of 2 divisions, with the 95th Division attached, received similar orders, including the designation of a delaying rear guard of 2 regiments. By 7:00 P.M. on the twenty-sixth the bulk of this corps had reached its north-south positions east of the railway line. The 73rd Corps, less the 15th Division and with the 195th Division attached, took up positions at Chiaotouyi, 15 miles north of Changsha, and at Fulinpu, 25 miles north of Changsha. Its mission was to attack the flanks of the advancing Japanese column. The 59th Division of the 4th Corps was moved to Changsha and the area southeast of the city. The other 2 divisions of the 4th Corps[24] were deployed in the vicinity of Changshih, 18 miles southeast of Changsha. Their mission was to strike to the north or to the northwest, depending on which road the main Japanese thrust might follow. The 11th Division was shifted to Yuehlushan, across the Hsiang River from Changsha. The 87th Corps[25] was directed to remain in its positions west of the Hsiang River about 35 miles northwest of Changsha. Its mission was to cross the river and to attack the west flank of the advancing Japanese. By the night of September 26, 13 Chinese divisions had occupied positions in what amounted to a gigantic ambush that extended for some 35 miles. Ch'en Ch'eng's trap was ready to be sprung.

On September 27, as Chinese resistance seemed to wither before advance enemy elements, the overconfident commanders of the Japanese 3rd and 6th divisions ordered their troops to press on to the south without delay. With only the annoyance of the Chinese rear guards to interrupt their almost uneventful march toward Changsha, leading Japanese components reached Chinching, Fulinpu, and Chiaotouyi, 15 to 25 miles north and northeast of Changsha, on the morning of September 30. One advance patrol managed to get as far as Yunganshih, 16 miles due east of Changsha and 20 miles south of Chinching.

That night the Chinese struck from every direction. Caught by surprise, the Japanese suddenly had to face over 60,000 screaming Chinese on their front, rear, and both flanks. At the same time Chinese forces some 60 and 120 miles to the east attacked the Japanese 33rd, 101st, and 106th divisions, and Chinese attacks in the 5th War Area threatened enemy supply and ammunition installations north of the Yangtze. General Okamura's 11th Corps found itself in a very serious situation. Or, as the Chinese history politely understates: "the enemy found the situation most difficult to cope with." By the evening of October 1 the Japanese 3rd and 6th divisions had pulled back their advance elements. The main bodies of the two divisions then began to fight their way out of the trap in an effort to escape by the same routes over which they had so confidently strutted but a few days before. Chinese on their flanks and rear gave no peace to the disconcerted Japanese in their disorderly retreat. On October 3, General Ch'en Ch'eng's enthusiastic troops continued the hounding pursuit by three roads leading to the north. During the retreat the Japanese suffered several thousand casualties and lost great quantities of arms and equipment. By October 8 they had scrambled across the Hsinchiang River to their old positions south of Yochow, and the original Chinese positions along the south bank of the river had been restored.

General Okamura's 11th Corps had been badly defeated, and at a great cost in dead and wounded, Changsha had been saved. General Ch'en Ch'eng had demonstrated superb planning and forceful generalship in a widely dispersed and complicated operation. Mobility and offensive tactics—in contrast to defensive tactics from fixed entrenched positions—had routed the Japanese, though it had taken three and one-half times the number of Chinese to do so. Though Japanese operational plans had been bold, the commanders charged with carrying them out had not been able to respond to unexpected, fluid situations. Ch'en Ch'eng had used his great asset of manpower to offset superior equipment and arms. Unfortunately he was not permitted by Chiang Kai-shek to follow up his victory by launching an offensive to retake the upper Yangtze Valley, even though he had five Japanese divisions on the run and badly depleted in strength. The Chinese soldier had shown that given real leadership he could hold his own in battle.

13

The Campaign in Southern Kwangsi, Mid-November, 1939, to Mid-November, 1940

THE FALL OF HANKOW AND CANTON in late 1938, expected by the Imperial General Staff in Tokyo to wring from Chiang Kai-shek's government a settlement of the conflict in China, had accomplished little more than to extend farther the already over-extended Japanese lines of communication. By all logic—Japanese logic—the Chinese had been defeated in war and therefore should have sued for peace; but they still refused to discuss the generous terms offered by their Japanese benefactors. The Tokyo staff was nonplussed: its armies had taken Nanchang, but they had only thrashed about in northern Hupei; and worse, the invincible machine of His Imperial Majesty had been defeated at Changsha by an inferior Chinese rabble they had had full confidence they could destroy. Something had to be done to end the costly embroilment on the continent. For want of a better solution, the Japanese lashed out again, this time in south China. The objective would be Nanning, the capital of Kwangsi province. The ostensible purpose was to cut the road connecting Hanoi in French Indo-China with Nanning, Kweilin, and Changsha and thus eliminate one more avenue for military supplies to the Chungking government. It mattered little that almost no war munitions were being imported over this route. It was a road on the maps and therefore should be cut. Besides, the Japanese had an air base for combined army and navy operations on the island of Hainan, 100 miles from the coast of Kwangsi.

General Kinichi Imamura was assigned command of the 21st Corps and given a somewhat vague mission to carry out the impending operations in Kwangsi. When it reached its planned strength in January, 1940, the corps would consist of the 5th and Konoye divisions, one brigade of the 18th Division, and the Taiwan Composite Brigade. In early November, the Japanese 4th Fleet, which included the aircraft carrier *Kaga*, was ordered to cover and support the concentration of the 21st Corps in the vicinity of Haikou, the northern port on Hainan island. The fleet was to support the coastal landing operations, its marine contingents to take part in the assault. Not including the naval-personnel of the 4th Fleet, General Imamura would have a ground strength of about 65,000 men. About 100 aircraft, both land- and carrier-based, were made available to support the 21st Corps. In early November these planes bombed and strafed the cities and larger towns of the province to soften up and terrorize the civilian population.

Aware of the Japanese preparations, the generalissimo's headquarters at Kweilin, 225 miles northeast of Nanning, issued orders for the defense of Kwangsi. The 16th Army Group's 46th Corps of three divisions[1] was assigned the mission of defending the coastline from Fangcheng to Chinhsien, Hopu, and Lienchang—a shoreline distance of well over 100 miles, impossible for 18,000 troops to cover. The other corps of the 16th Army Group, the 31st of three divisions,[2] was directed to defend "key localities on the banks of the Hsi River" that emptied into the Gulf of Tonkin at Hopu. "Positions were prepared in advance . . . in the hope of offering gradual resistance and wearing out the enemy before fighting a decisive battle by the Yung River," 70 miles inland. In other words, General Pai Ch'ung-hsi, the "director" of the Kweilin headquarters, was prepared to give up a large area of the province before the battle was joined. From the beginning of the conflict with Japan, General Pai, though an able theoretical tactician, had been the leading exponent of fighting a long war of attrition, of "wearing out the enemy," of sacrificing land and the Chinese people, rather than facing the aggressors and battling it out.

Pai Ch'ung-hsi's command consisted of 5 army groups, 3 separate divisions, attached medium artillery units, and about 100 air-

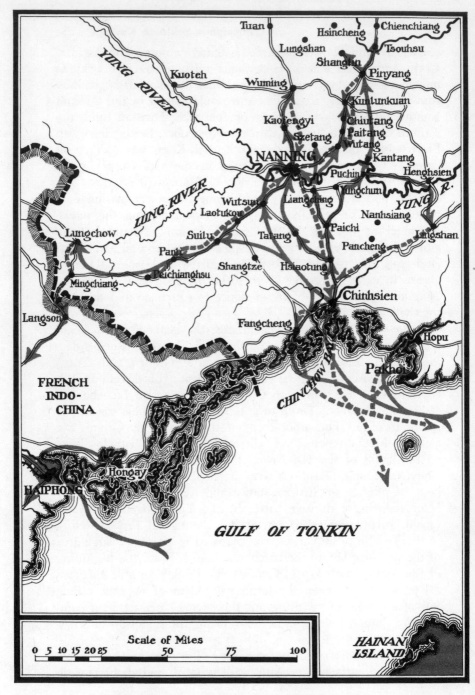

The Campaign in Southern Kwangsi (Broken
lines show Japanese withdrawal.)

craft of the 2nd Route Air Force. Three of the army groups and the air units had been sent from Hunan, Kwantung, and Szechwan to build up strength to combat the expected Japanese offensive. The command consisted of the 16th Army Group comprised of the 31st and 46th corps of 6 divisions; the 26th Army Group of 4 separate regiments; the 35th Army Group composed of the 64th Corps of 2 divisions; the 37th Army Group of the 66th Corps containing 2 divisions; the 38th Army Group comprised of the 2nd, 5th, 9th, 99th, and 36th corps containing 13 divisions; the 43rd, New 33rd, and Kwangsi Pacification Headquarters divisions, plus attached artillery and air units. The total strength of the 26 divisions, 4 regiments, and attached artillery was about 190,000 men. The 5th Corps, which included the only motorized division in the Chinese Army, the 200th, was commanded by General Tu Yu-ming, or Tu Li-ming, a vacillating and often sulky individual more interested in enriching himself than in risking the depletion of his troops and equipment by standing firmly against the enemy. (Later, during the disastrous first Burma campaign of early 1942 and during the training of the Chinese Expeditionary Force in Yunnan in 1943–44, General Tu was to be closely associated with the American ground effort to assist China. At the Chinese Communist takeover in 1949, Tu Li-ming was captured and imprisoned by the Reds. He was chained hand and foot to the stone walls of his cell, where he died, still chained, three years later. In the Burma campaign of 1942, General Tai An-lan, commander of the 200th Division, proved to be a bold, tenacious fighter in the defense of Toungoo and during the withdrawal through Mandalay to Hsipaw, where he was killed in action.)

On November 15 the Japanese 5th Division and the Taiwan Brigade, under an almost unnecessary cover of air support and naval gunfire, landed on the coast of Chinchow Bay near Pakhoi. Meeting little resistance, the enemy quickly seized Chinhsien, the terminus of the road from Nanning, Pakhoi, and Hopu. The Chinese New 19th Division and most of the 46th Corps hastily fell back to Shangtze, on the road to Nanning and 45 miles north of Chinhsien. The rest of the 16th Army Group with the strength of about one corps of three divisions pulled back to the Nan-hsiang-Pancheng area, 60 miles northeast of Chinhsien. The Japan-

ese 5th Division pressed closely on the heels of the retreating
Chinese along the Chinhsien-Nanning road; the Taiwan Brigade
was on the Hsiaotung-Paichi road running due north toward the
Yung River nearly 100 miles above Chinhsien. The disorderly
rout of the six Chinese divisions and four regiments[3] did not
slow down until they had all crossed the Yung River. The original
two Japanese columns, now split into four columns, reached the
river on November 21. On the twenty-second the Chinese 135th,
170th, and 200th divisions "raced" to the vicinity of Laotukou,
28 miles west of Nanning, to Nanning, and to Szetang, 20 miles
northeast of Nanning, as "reinforcements." But when a Japanese
column crossed the Yung River at Liangching, 20 miles east of
Nanning, the near presence of the enemy prompted further withdrawals by these three Chinese divisions. On the same day,
November 23, the Japanese captured Szetang. With enemy
troops now on their left flank, a part of the Chinese forces in
and around Nanning panicked on the twenty-fourth and fled
from the city in great disorder. Forced to stop for breath at
Kaofengyi, 20 miles to the north, they dug in and took up a
defensive stance. The bulk of the Chinese rushed to the northeast, skirted Japanese-occupied Szetang, and finally stopped to
take up "in-depth positions" at Paitang and Kunlunkuan, 52 and
64 miles northeast of Nanning.

The Japanese columns, having now advanced between 75 and
100 miles from the landing beaches in nine days, experienced considerable difficulty in keeping up with the retreating Chinese.
When rested sufficiently, the Japanese attacked the defenses at
Kaofengyi on the twenty-eighth. The next day they rammed
through the Chinese positions and pushed on to Wuming, 20
miles farther north. The eastern Japanese column seized Wutang,
14 miles east of Szetang, and continued their drive to the northeast. They captured Paitang on December 1 and Kunlunkuan on
the fourth. Up to this time the enemy advance had encountered
only token resistance. General Imamura had accomplished his
mission of isolating Nanning with surprising ease. He ordered
his troops to take up defensive positions in place at Wuming and
Kunlunkuan. Unless otherwise directed, they had gone far
enough.

The Chinese having staged an ignominious performance, General Pai Ch'ung-hsi reorganized and redeployed in preparation for a counteroffensive:

(1) The 16th Army Group, now called the West Route Force, was divided into two columns. The 1st Column[4] was directed to "attack the enemy at Kaofengyi, operate in Szetang and Wutang, assist the North Route Force in . . . destroying the enemy at Kunlunkuan and . . . attack northwest of Nanning." The 2nd Column[5] was directed to assemble about 35 miles southwest of Nanning from which area it would attack Tatang, 30 miles south of Nanning, Wutsun, 20 miles southwest of the capital, and Nanning itself.

(2) The 38th Army Group was designated the North Route Force. Its 5th Corps of three divisions, the hesitant General Tu Li-ming commanding, was directed to move from Pinyang and to attack the Japanese at Kunlunkuan, 42 miles to the south. Its second mission was to support the East and West Route Forces in the attack on Nanning. The 99th Division of the 99th Corps was ordered to attack the enemy south of Kunlunkuan and to coordinate with the 5th Corps in destroying Japanese forces in that area. Its second mission was to move to the hilly country below Wutang, 30 miles south of Kunlunkuan, from which location it was to attack the enemy at Liangching, 23 miles east of Nanning, and nearby villages on the Yung River in order to block routes to the north.

(3) The 26th Army Group was designated the East Route Force. Its 46th Corps of two divisions,[6] acting as the 3rd Column, was directed to assemble at Lingshan, 50 miles east of the Nanning-Chinhsien Road. Using mobile, guerrilla type tactics from that area, it would deny the main road to the enemy and block northward movements of reinforcements. The 66th Corps[7] of two divisions was ordered to "operate toward . . . Kantang [35 miles northeast of Nanning] and later to cross the [Yung] river" at Yungchun, 10 miles south of Kantang, in order to disrupt all enemy activity on the Nanning-Yungchun Road paralleling the south bank of the river.

(4) The 99th Corps, now made up from the 92nd and 118th Divisions, was directed to concentrate in the vicinity of Pinyang as the general reserve.

General Pai Ch'ung-hsi's rather complicated plans and orders called for the utilization of but fifteen out of the twenty-six divisions available to him.

On December 18 the Chinese counteroffensive began. On the same day the North Route Force reoccupied Kunlunkuan and a village a few miles to the south. On the nineteenth the West Route Force recaptured Kaofengyi. On the twentieth the Japanese counterattacked and drove the Chinese out of both places. But the Chinese New 22nd and 92nd divisions had blocked the road against the movement of enemy reinforcements and supplies between Wutang and Paitang, 20 miles south of Kunlunkuan. In order to hold Kunlunkuan against Chinese attacks, the Japanese were forced to airlift troops, rations, and ammunition to the battle area. From high ground northeast of the town, the Chinese 159th Division was able to pour in mortar and artillery fire on the beleaguered Japanese in the valley below, and Chinese planes bombed and strafed their positions. The fight lasted from December 25 to 31, when the Chinese New 2nd and 159th divisions stormed the crippled enemy force and routed the remnants in a house-to-house cleanup. In addition to killing several thousand men of the Japanese 5th Division, the Chinese also killed General Nakamura, commander of the 12th Brigade. While the fight at Kunlunkuan was in progress, the Chinese first column attacked Kaofengyi, but failed to recapture it. The Chinese 46th Corps (the third column) kept up a series of unremitting attacks to block the Nanning-Chinhsien road.

Just prior to the December 18 counterattacks, a column of the Japanese 5th Division moved from Suilu, 40 miles southwest of Nanning, to Lungchow, 35 miles farther west and only 25 miles from the border of French Indo-China. On the approach of enemy troops on December 21, Chinese militia units, after the barest show of resistance, withdrew from Lungchow. When the Japanese column attempted to return over the same route, it was intercepted by the Chinese second column[8] near Wutsun and was badly mauled by superior numbers; the Japanese survivors of the encounter beat a hasty retreat toward Nanning. On January 4, 1940, the Chinese recovered Chiutang, 5 miles south of Kunlunkuan. Again defeated by superior numbers, the Japanese fell back to Paitang where they dug in to defend the high ground in that area.

At this time the Chinese forces "underwent replenishment preparatory to a continuation of the attack." During the quiet replenishment period of three weeks, the Japanese succeeded in reinforcing their battered 5th Division, nearly one-third of which had been casualties. They also rushed in the Konoye Division and one brigade of the 18th Division. General Imamura was relieved as commander of the 21st Corps and replaced by General Seichi Kuno.

On January 25 the Japanese 18th Division brigade and a part of the 5th Division moved north on the main road to attack the Chinese positions at Wuming, 40 miles north of Nanning. At the same time the Konoye Division marched east on the Nanning-Yungchun road; turned north; captured Kantang, 10 miles north of Yungchun, on January 30; and continued toward Pinyang, over 80 miles northeast of Nanning. Chinese forces retreated before the weight of the fresh enemy division, fell back within the defense perimeter of Pinyang, and were cut off.

On February 2 an air-supported Japanese assault took Pinyang and vicinity. Contrary to the usual procedure when threatened on the flanks or rear, the Chinese 2nd and 36th corps of four divisions at Kunlunkuan, south of Pinyang, did not withdraw. On February 3, having pushed 25 miles north from Pinyang, the Japanese took Tsouhsu and forced the Chinese New 33rd Division to withdraw toward Chienchang. On the fourth a Japanese column occupied undefended Shanglin, 20 miles west of Pinyang. Meanwhile, the Chinese 64th Corps of two divisions, after a 50-mile march from Kueihsien, attacked Pinyang from the east. Although the ensuing three-day fight was inconclusive, it pinned down the enemy defenders and enabled the Chinese 46th Corps to reoccupy Kantang on the third and Yungchun on February 4. Over 30 miles southwest of Pinyang, the Chinese 66th and 99th corps of four divisions fought off Japanese attacks and held their positions for six days. Finally, on February 8, the enemy succeeded in taking Wuming, and the Chinese withdrew to the north.

With Kunlunkuan firmly in Chinese hands, the Konoye Division at Pinyang was cut off from resupplies of any kind. Out on a limb, the Japanese withdrew from Pinyang toward Kunlunkuan on February 9. On the eleventh the Japanese 18th Division brigade and elements of the 5th Division began to pull back from Wuming toward Nanning. The Chinese poured into the vacuum created by the withdrawal and on February 18 reoccupied Kaofengyi, 20 miles farther south.

The bulk of the Chinese troops north of the Yung River were withdrawn to Tuan, Hsincheng, and Lungshan, over 60 miles north of Nanning, for another period of "replenishment preparatory to resuming the offensive." Holding forces were left to maintain surveillance over the enemy on the two main routes leading north and northeast from Nanning. This replenishment period lasted for nearly a month. Meanwhile, the Japanese 18th Division brigade was ordered back to Canton. The Japanese 21st Corps, now consisting of the 5th and Konoye divisions and the Taiwan Brigade, continued to hold Nanning, Chinhsien, and Fangcheng and the roads connecting them. The Chinese deployed strong forces to the east and west of the Nanning-Chinhsien road and north of the Yung River. As a move preliminary "to resuming the offensive," the Chinese East Route Force (the third column) of four divisions plus three separate regiments[9] moved west from Lingshan, some 70 miles southeast of Nanning.

On March 12 the Chinese 46th Corps seized a section of the Nanning-Chinhsien road, thus cutting off Japanese forces to the north. At the same time, Chinese north of the Yung River attacked the outer defenses of Nanning. On March 14, one Japanese regiment with attached artillery and cavalry units moved north from Chinhsien to force the opening of the road. Simultaneously, a 5,000-man column of the Japanese 5th Division moved east from the Nanning-Liangching area to Puchin on the Yung River at the end of the eastern road leading north from Chinhsien. One regiment continued to move along the river and captured Yungchun on March 15. It then proceeded toward Lingshan where it ran head-on into the Chinese 64th Corps of two divisions on the sixteenth. After a day-long engagement the Chinese withdrew to the northeast. The Japanese occupied Lingshan on March 17. There, on March 20, in the rugged hills, the

64th Corps turned to make a stand. But the enemy had no desire to push into that difficult area, so the sudden courage of the Chinese corps meant very little at the time. On March 21 the Chinese 93rd Division of the 9th Corps crossed the Yung River near Henghsien and moved rapidly, to the southwest, thus cutting the road between Yungchun and Lingshan. The Japanese pulled back to Lingshan at once. They were followed closely by the Chinese 156th Division of the 64th Corps. On March 24 the 156th Division attacked Lingshan from the northeast, the 46th Corps of two divisions attacking from the south. On the twenty-fifth the enemy was forced to retreat westward from Lingshan. By constant attacks on the north flank of the retreating column, the Chinese 93rd Division forced it to turn to the southwest and south. Hounded by four Chinese divisions on their flanks and rear, the Japanese eventually reached the Nanning-Chinhsien road.

Frustrated by the hit-and-run tactics and unexpected mobility of Chinese attacks, the Japanese 21st Corps was more than ready to sit back, suspend operations, and consolidate its positions at Nanning and the road leading to the coast. It had suffered fairly heavy casualties and was as badly in need of replenishment as were the Chinese. This time the replenishment period—with no more than minor probes and patrol actions—lasted for two and one-half months.

On June 17 a Japanese regimental column—having been sufficiently replenished—moved to the southwest on the road leading from Nanning to Hanoi in French Indo-China. On the night of the eighteenth the column took Suilu, 45 miles from Nanning. The Chinese 135th Division withdrew for about 20 miles along the road to Panli. On June 23 the Japanese overran Panli. The Chinese withdrew toward Mingchiang, 50 miles west of Suilu and only 10 miles from the Indo-China border. With the capture of Peichianghsu, about halfway between Panli and Mingchiang, on June 24, the Japanese controlled the road and river crossings in the border area. On June 26 the Chinese 135th Division withdrew from Mingchiang—again with almost no resistance—and fled to the high, rugged mountains just east of the border "to continue the resistance" that had not yet started. On June 29, about 3,000 Japanese troops started to move north toward Lungchin (Lungchow), 20 miles from Mingchiang. The mountain town was senselessly bombed by enemy aircraft. There was some fighting along the road, but the Chinese 131st Division, sent to assist the 135th, did not await the outcome. After hearing the sounds of a firefight, the division commander quickly decided that it was not his duty to assist the 135th Division or the 188th, then north of the Lung River barrier. He withdrew his unit in great haste to the north bank of the river "to stop the enemy" from a good safe distance. When both the 131st and 188th divisions moved still farther north "to stop the enemy," a task force was left in Lungchin "to prevent the enemy from crossing the river." This preventive measure failed in short order. On the evening of July 2 the Japanese crossed the river on rafts, landed against no opposition whatsoever, and occupied Lungchin. The performance of the Chinese 31st Corps' three divisions, about 18,000 men before wholesale desertions into the mountains reduced their strength, had been nothing short of cowardly.

Another two-month replenishment period followed the ignominious conduct of the Chinese 31st Corps. In September, during the long pause in activity, the Japanese 5th Division was ordered to French Indo-China. The Konoye Division and the Taiwan Brigade were now the only large Japanese units in Kwangsi province. During the latter half of September, Chinese troops repeatedly cut the Japanese line of communications between Lungchin and Nanning. Although the line was restored after each break, the constant fighting in this area took a heavy toll of both Japanese and Chinese. On October 13, elements of the Chinese 188th Division of the 31st Corps crossed the Lung River east of Lungchin; its main strength then assaulted the town from the southeast. At dawn, the Chinese broke through the west gate; street fighting within the town walls continued until 9:00 A.M., when, according to the Chinese history, "the enemy poured in reinforcements to launch counterattacks." Actually there were no Japanese reinforcements within 20 miles, but now fighting for their lives, the 2,000 remaining Japanese troops overwhelmed more than 10,000 Chinese with the ferocity of their counterattacks. The Chinese withdrew to a safe distance outside the city walls. That night, October 14, they pulled 2 miles farther back. With the two divisions of the 46th Corps, the 31st Corps had now surrounded Lungchin; and since the road back to Nanning was blocked, there was but one possible exit for the besieged Japanese—the road to Mingchiang (Pingchiang).

On October 26, after having failed in a number of sorties to break through the circle of Chinese troops, the Japanese broke out through the river gate, crossed the Lung on the same rafts they had used in arriving, and fought their way south on the road to Mingchiang and Indo-China, 10 miles beyond. After the enemy cleared Lungchin, the commander of the 31st Corps ordered his troops "to storm" the empty town; it was "recovered" on October 18.

The 16th Army Group[10] was then ordered to secure the entire Lungchin-Mingchiang-Nanning area—meaning to massacre all Japanese wounded and stragglers, a task of which even that hopeless unit was capable. The 35th Army Group's 64th Corps[11] was directed to move south on the Nanning-Wuming and the Nanning-Pinyang roads, to attack the enemy wherever he might be encountered, and to recapture Nanning. The two divisions of the 66th Corps[12] crossed the Yung River near Yungchin, marched to the southwest, cut the Nanning-Chinhsien road, and linked up with the 16th Army Group to keep the road blocked. The 64th Corps, "fighting courageously" against small Japanese outposts, reoccupied Kaofengyi and the lightly held villages on the Nanning-Pinyang road. On October 29 it pressed on toward Nanning from the north and northeast. Meanwhile, a column of the 155th Division crossed the Yung River to attack Japanese forces on the south bank; but finding none there, it recrossed the river on the same day to rejoin the rest of the 64th Corps. The Japanese on the north bank of the Yung had already fallen back toward Nanning and were then engaged in keeping the road to Chinhsien on the coast open as their only lifeline. On October 30 the Japanese 21st Corps evacuated Nanning; its 23,000 remaining troops were on the march toward Chinhsien, over 100 miles to the south. Like jackals, the Chinese trailed and harassed the enemy column along the entire route; but like jackals keeping at a safe distance, they failed to inflict any serious harm on the Japanese. When they reached the Chinhsien-Fangcheng area, the Japanese embarked on waiting transports to sail back to Hainan and Canton. The last transport departed from the roaring flames of Chinhsien on November 17, 1940, leaving behind a string of burned-out towns and villages and a ravaged countryside.

Why had the Japanese, who seldom relinquished a conquest, abandoned their year-long operation in southern Kwangsi? Mainly because their move into Indo-China had effectively cut the supply lines from Saigon to Kwangsi and Yunnan. The maintenance of a garrison at Nanning and along the road to the coast was no longer necessary. The difficulties and expense in supplying a permanent occupation of the province were not worth the effort involved.

At the outset of the campaign, the Japanese command had correctly gauged the inferior quality of the Chinese forces in Kwangsi and had had quick initial success; but it had failed to reckon on the resiliency of the Chinese. Nor had the Japanese the capability of pouring in a force strong enough to destroy Pai Ch'ung-hsi's armies. Had they thought it a military advantage to hold Nanning and the line of communications to Chinhsien with the available troops, they would have fought it out and never have withdrawn. But having tackled what turned out to be a bad bargain, the Japanese high command had cut its losses and had got its troops out of Kwangsi.

Highlighted by some bold, courageous moves, Chinese operations in general had been pitifully ineffectual and at times almost farcical—had it not been for the dead, the uncared-for wounded, and the peasants driven from their homes and farms. In the year-long operation there had been four replenishment periods totaling seven months of inaction. Had Pai Ch'ung-hsi been able to instill in his commanders and troops a will to fight, and had he made a determined stand with even half of his 190,000 troops on the beaches from Fangcheng to Chinhsien, Hopu, and Pakhoi, the Japanese would probably have recognized the futility of the operation at once and gone no farther than their beachheads. Instead, he dallied and the people of the province suffered, their towns and villages in ruins, their crops destroyed, and their hearts as full of hatred for their own armies as for the Japanese.

In late February during one of the frequent replenishment periods of the then three-months-old Kwangsi campaign, Chiang Kai-shek called a military conference at Liuchow, about halfway between Nanning and Kweichow and over 80 miles from the nearest combat. As former secretary general of the aviation commission—appointed by the generalissimo in May, 1936, and compelled by pressure from senior generals to resign in April, 1938— Madame Chiang accompanied her husband to the meeting. Although she had derived great satisfaction from her military position, her enthusiasm was not matched by generals who detested her constant intrigues and interference in matters they considered to be solely masculine. In addition to reviewing the military situation as he saw it, the generalissimo offered his tactical views for the guidance of his senior commanders. The assembled generals were first told that they should "deepen their self criticism and alertness" and analyze the enemy's "tactical merits and weaknesses."

In order to counteract the enemy's "four tactical merits," the generals were enjoined to base their military actions on the following principles.

(1) Speed. "Attack the enemy . . . [and] appear where you are not expected." Then, "exhibit the coyness of a maiden; afterward emulate the rapidity of a running hare."

(2) Hardness. "Defend a position at all costs."

(3) Sharpness. "Conical break-in and bold advance"—the first part of which is not to be found in any known lexicon of military terms, the second not in the nature of many Chinese commanders.

(4) Secrecy. "Keep the enemy guessing."

The generalissimo also proposed solutions for the enemy's four tactical weaknesses.

(1) Minority. "Capable of only small unit harassing tactics"— ignoring the fact that small units of Japanese troops then in China numbered about 1 million men who had managed to harass the Chinese armies with considerable success in division and corps organizations.

(2) Shortness. "Capable of only short-time combat"—a conclusion that disregarded the months-long Japanese campaigns against Shanghai, Nanking, Hsuchow, and Hankow.

(3) Shallowness. "Capable of only shallow distance attacks"—but in fact the Japanese advances had covered thousands of miles from the Manchurian-Mongolian border to the Yangtze Valley and beyond.

(4) Emptiness. "Lack of reserve forces and emptiness in rear areas."

Having disposed of the enemy's strengths and weaknesses, the generalissimo expounded on tactics and countermeasures for exploiting the enemy's weaknesses and "breaking" his merits. "Balance speed with steadfastness; hardness with fortitude; sharpness with ambush; secrecy with discipline; and [be] willing to sacrifice."

Quite satisfied with the guidance he had just dispensed, Chiang Kai-shek dismissed his generals and flew back to the safety of Chungking. But the war ground on, and Chiang's words could not inspire the hapless Chinese armies.

The collapse and surrender of France and the establishment of the powerless Vichy government under Marshal Pétain in 1940 opened the greedy eyes of the Japanese Imperial General Staff to visions of further aggrandizement in French Indo-China. Occupation of the northern province of Tonkin would block the trickle of military supplies moving into China by road and railway, but with France helpless to resist, Japan could now initiate the master plan to take over all of southeast Asia and the rich islands to the east—the Philippines—and to the south—the Netherlands Indies.

The four kingdoms of Indo-China (Tonkin, Annam, Laos, and Cambodia) and the delta dependency of Cochin China had been tributary to the emperors of China since the thirteenth century. While in the service of the Mongol emperor Kublai Khan as a minister of state, the intrepid Venetian explorer Marco Polo had accompanied a Chinese army to Tonkin around 1300 as a sort of political commissar. The first French acquisition in the area had been made in 1867. In 1885, during the heyday of imperialistic land grabs, France had wrested all of Tonkin and Annam from under the Manchu wings and not long after had acquired the other three provinces by force and negotiation.

Wisely, the French governors had subsidized and had permitted the still-reigning royal families to maintain their shabby courts at Lauang Prabang in Laos, in a small replica of Peking's Forbidden City at Hue in Annam (somewhere along the line the king of Annam had metamorphosed himself into an emperor), and in a fanciful palace near the Silver Pagoda at Phnom Penh in Cambodia. The French government had even undertaken the stupendous task of clearing the jungle and reconstructing the ancient and imposing capital of the Khmers (Cambodians) at Angkor Wat. In Tonkin and Cochin China, it had built the cities of Hanoi in the rice-growing delta of the Red River and Saigon just north of the lush and steamy delta of the Mekong River. Engineers had built railways along the coast linking Hanoi, Haiphong, and Saigon and, in 1895, a line from Hanoi to Kunming in China's Yunnan province. The latter had established Yunnan as a French sphere of interest—the principal French interests in that province being its tin and tungsten mines, opium, and markets for manufactured goods. Kunming, at an elevation of nearly 6,000 feet and with a population of about 500,000, soon blossomed with a stone Catholic cathedral, a spade-bearded French bishop, a haphazard French Club, a French convent, French schools, a French bank, and French business agencies—the hallmarks of a long stay.

In Indo-China, Hanoi, with a population of 300,000, had been transformed into a prosperous French provincial city, complete with a beautiful park and lake, a fine museum of history and art, a renaissance Hotel de Ville, and a tree-shaded *place* surrounded by the governor's residence, hotels, and street cafés. Haiphong, with a population of about 200,000, was its bustling port. The noisy docks were, before 1940, crowded with ships, and the entire harbor area was covered with a film of black dust from the coal mines of nearby Hongai. Saigon, with its 1.5 million people, was actually two cities in one—the sprawling French capital and southern seaport containing an imposing palace, government buildings, hotels, business structures, and busy docks; and Cholon, the huge Chinese rabbit warren of twisting alleys across the river.

The practical French had taken Indo-China for every piaster they could wring from its people. By oriental standards the country was a prosperous land with great rubber plantations, hardwood forests, and a large annual surplus of rice for export. Its unhappy history had been characterized by incredible violence and bloodshed. Under the French-imposed peace its people had learned to smile and dance and murder each other with an almost charming gaiety, until the shadow of a Frenchman fell across their paths. The French were hated by both their Catholic converts and by the Buddhist majority. To the Japanese, this rich province of the helpless Vichy government would be the first steppingstone on their southward march to Thailand, the Philippines, the Netherlands Indies, Burma—perhaps even to India and Australia.

On July 2, 1940, the Japanese government formally presented its proposal to occupy French Indo-China to the Japanese emperor for his approval. Prior to the conference, there had been a sharp dichotomy between the ministers who advocated "going south" and those who favored "going north" in an attack on the Soviet Union. The latter argued that since Russia had been vigorously attacked by Hitler's legions, this would be an ideal time to strike at the old enemy in Siberia. Eventually, the "go south" faction prevailed. When the ministers filed into the conference room at the imperial palace, they were agreed on one plan to be offered to the emperor for his divine approval. Based on long-standing tradition at imperial conferences, the emperor's role was to sit looking as imperial as he could, to listen, and to say nothing. His formal approval would be indicated by silence; his seal would be affixed to the document in question after the meeting had adjourned.

The ministers sat rigidly at attention on each side of two long tables while they awaited the arrival of the divine presence. When the emperor entered the council chamber, they leaped to their feet at attention. No one spoke. Wearing an army uniform, in which he looked quite unmilitary, His Imperial Majesty seated himself in a thronelike chair on a raised dais. Weak-chinned and owl-eyed behind round spectacles, he focused his myopic gaze on the wall at the far end of the room, probably wishing he could get back to his marine studies. The ministers sat rigidly, hands on knees, staring woodenly at each other across the tables. The feet of the shorter men barely touched the floor.

Prince Konoye, the premier, rose, bowed to the emperor, and read the crucial paper in a low, respectful voice—Outline of National Policies in view of Present Developments. The proposed plan called for the occupation of French Indo-China by military force if pressure on the Vichy government failed to produce the desired approval, even at the risk of war with the United States and Great Britain. Finished reading, Konoye bowed and sat down. It was then Minister of War Sugiyama's turn to rise, bow, and state that he agreed, after which he resumed hands-on-knees position of respect. The chief of the navy general staff, Admiral Nagano, next went through the procedure adding that he felt it necessary to go south regardless of all risks. The president of the privy council, Toshimichi Hara, demurred by posing several slightly embarrassing questions. Foreign Minister Matsuoka observed that diplomatic measures would probably fail. In the end, General Sugiyama talked down the barely suggested opposition of the liberals and called for a vote. The Indo-China policy was unanimously approved. To do otherwise would have been unseemly in the presence of the emperor. His silence having signified approval, His Imperial Majesty left the room. A new phase of Japanese aggression had been initiated.

The 1938 occupation of Hainan and the Paracel Islands and the May 30, 1939, annexation of the Spratley Islands halfway between the Philippines and Indo-China had already pointed the way toward Haiphong; but an air of legality and diplomatic niceties were now in order. Although France had categorically denied that any gasoline, trucks, or other military supplies had been shipped by road or rail from Indo-China to Yunnan, and had offered to accept Japanese inspectors to verify the facts in the matter, nonetheless a Japanese naval squadron was sent to Haiphong in late June. Shortly thereafter, a small army of Japanese inspectors arrived at Hanoi, Haiphong, and Kwangchowan. On July 23, under German pressure, the Vichy government accepted a Japanese demand to establish a military base and to be granted the use of airfields in Tonkin as a prerequisite of conducting the inspections. On further German insistence, the Vichy government was compelled to "negotiate" additional concessions through its powerless colonial governor and its ambassador in Tokyo. This tragic farce ended with an agreement with Japan on September 22, 1940, to permit the entry of Japanese troops into the northern province of Indo-China. Defeated and prostrate, France had no other choice. The ink had hardly dried on the signatures to the agreement when Japanese armed forces began to pour into Tonkin through Haiphong and later from Kwangsi province in China.

Meanwhile, the Japanese government demanded—with an actual threat of war—that Britain close the Burma Road running from the port of Rangoon to Lashio and Kunming and seal the border between Kowloon (Hongkong) and China. Her back to the wall after Dunkirk, the British government requested American assurance of joint action should a refusal to comply bring on hostilities. But the United States, low on munitions that had gone to England and suffering from the penury of an ever-reluctant Congress, was in poor shape to promise military assistance even to its closest ally. To pacify the Japanese militarists, Prime Minister Winston Churchill announced that the Hongkong border would be sealed and that the Burma Road would be closed for three months. China's last land link, its umbilical cord to the outer world, was cut on that day. However, the Burma Road was quietly reopened on October 18, 1940, at the expiration of the three-month period.

With newly whetted appetites for more worlds to conquer, on August 1, 1940, the military-controlled Japanese government issued a statement that envisaged far wider horizons than those of the past. Overnight the new order in East Asia expanded into the new order in Greater East Asia. Imperialistic plans for aggression now knew no boundaries: "Japan's national policy lies in the firm establishment of world peace . . . and in the construction . . . of a new order in Greater East Asia resting upon the solidarity of Japan, Manchukuo and China." The extent and nature of this pious, all-men-are-brothers declaration were not defined. But Japan's intent was clear—to seize every undefended territory she could.

A heady vision of the postwar world had begun to crystallize in the minds of uniformed men of power determined to raise the Japanese Empire to the heights of glory to which it should be elevated. They pictured a world divided into four great spheres, with that of Japan the loftiest of all. The emperor would rule over all of east and southeast Asia, the Pacific islands, India, Australia, and eastern Siberia. The Soviet Union, pushed back from its possessions bordering the Pacific, could reign undisturbed over European Russia and the bleak wastes of Siberia from the Urals to Lake Baikal. Germany would control Europe and the Mediterranean. For a time, the two American continents would be left to their own devices—a situation that would be solved eventually by the two dominating powers on the eastern Atlantic and the western Pacific. And Japan would have overcome for all time her two great concerns—the need for oil and the need for raw materials.

14

The Chinese Winter Counteroffensives, November 26, 1939, to Late March, 1940

PRIOR TO THE WINTER of 1939–40, Chiang Kai-shek and the National Military Council misinterpreted Japanese reluctance to be drawn deeper into the interior of China as a lack of military capability. Having successfully wrecked the enemy offensive against Changsha in September, there was some slight justification for Chinese optimism, but not for their reasoning. The static Japanese military posture at the time was due to overextended lines of communication, a refusal to admit that military victories and occupation of territory could not accomplish the political goal, and conviction that slow starvation must eventually bring Chiang Kai-shek's government to its knees. Although it would be difficult for the Japanese high command to concentrate sufficient troops to mount a major offensive, it was not impossible.

By the latter part of 1939 the Japanese had increased their combat forces in China to 25 divisions plus 20 separate brigades, which raised their overall strength to about 1.2 million men. The North China Front Army, under the operational control of the China Expeditionary Army, consisted of the 1st Corps of three divisions and four brigades in Shansi; the 12th Corps of two divisions and three brigades in Shantung and north Kiangsu; the Mongolian Garrison Corps of one division, one infantry brigade and one cavalry brigade in Chahar and Suiyuan; and three divisions, four infantry brigades and one cavalry brigade in Hopei and north Honan—a force of nine divisions, twelve infantry brigades and two cavalry brigades. Under the direct command of the

China Expeditionary Army were the 11th Corps of eight divisions and two brigades in the general area around Hankow; the 13th Corps of four divisions and four brigades in the lower Yangtze area; and the 21st Corps of four divisions and two brigades in south China—a force of sixteen divisions and eight separate brigades which were supported by the 3rd Air Group of six air regiments and six air squadrons. The Japanese armies in China were capable of striking out in almost any direction they chose. At the time, the reality was not so much Japanese weakness, but whether a major effort would be worthwhile.

The rotation of many Japanese divisions back to Japan and their replacement by home-trained units without battle experience—a normal procedure in the Japanese army—had convinced the generalissimo that enemy combat effectiveness had deteriorated and that "its total fire power and mobility were inferior." Therefore, he would "seek the initiative, conduct multiple-front attacks . . . tie the enemy down" and thereby demonstrate to the Western world that China was carrying on a valiant defense in which no sacrifice would be too costly in order to save the country from aggression. Hence, the so-called winter offensives. In October, 1939, the National Military Council issued orders to each war-area command prescribing its part in the planned offensives. All war areas were directed to initiate their roles in the program "by the end of November and early December respectively." Had they all done so with vigor and the maximum strength at their disposal, the Japanese army in China would have been in extreme difficulty.

The 1st War Area—Honan and northern Anhwei—began its attacks on December 1, 1939. Its 3rd Army Group was ordered to use the 81st Division and some 40,000 guerrillas to cut the Lunghai Railway near Kaifeng "and lure the enemy" (to what was not specified). The 2nd Cavalry Corps was ordered to block enemy reinforcements from Hsuchow at Kweiteh, 40 miles east of Kaifeng. The 36th Army Group was to launch an attack on Poai and Hsinhsiang north of Chengchow on the Yellow River, the New 5th Corps to attack north and south of Anyang on the Pinghan Railway and the 9th Corps to attack in the Poai area.

The 3rd Army Group guerrillas cut the Lunghai Railway at

three points east of Kaifeng, while its 81st Division attacked Lanfeng and Kaifeng. Troops entered Kaifeng on December 16 and, before they were forced to withdraw, burned a number of Japanese installations in and around the city, as well as large areas of the city itself. The 2nd Cavalry Corps assaulted the east gate of Kweiteh, temporarily occupied the nearby small airstrip, burned 600 barrels of aviation fuel, and blocked enemy reinforcements from the east. On December 6 the New 5th Corps partly destroyed four railway bridges north and south of Anyang, all of which were repaired by the Japanese within a few days. On December 13 the 47th Corps raided two railway stations. The 9th Corps cut the Pinghan Railway 20 miles north of the Yellow River and attacked Hsincheng, 35 miles north of Chengchow. On January 1, 1940, elements of the 4th Division, 9th Corps, broke into the town "and spent a day mopping up enemy troops." Several hundred small-arms weapons were captured. Though the Japanese suffered some casualties in these activities, the number claimed by the Chinese was greatly exaggerated. Then the troops of the 1st War Area fell back to their original defensive positions and the great winter offensive ended for them.

The 2nd War Area—Shansi and southern Shensi—started the winter offensive by deploying its 40th and 27th corps "to maintain surveillance over the enemy" near Changtze, about 90 miles north of the Yellow River. Its 14th, 5th, and 4th army groups moved toward the Anyi area, 60 miles northeast of Tungkuan at the big bend of the Yellow River. The 61st and 34th corps moved from western Shansi to cut the rail line from Taiyuan to Chuwu and Houma, about 90 miles northeast of Tungkuan. Other units of the command made feints that accomplished nothing.

On December 3, aware of the Chinese troop movements, the Japanese attacked the 14th, 5th, and 4th army groups near Anyi. A seesaw fight continued for nine days, with the inferior Japanese force compelled to pull back. By December 20 the Chinese had managed to inflict fairly heavy casualties on the Japanese and had cleared a 70-mile section of the railway. The three remaining enemy strongpoints in the area were completely surrounded. In late December, about 2,000 Japanese launched a counterattack in the Anyi area, but without much success. In early January, 1940, the Chinese 98th Corps and 7th Division counterattacked, also without conclusive results, although the Chinese had at least seven times as many troops as the Japanese. The Chinese record described this prolonged engagement with: "A confrontation resulted." It was a standoff. The Chinese 4th and 5th army groups then joined the 14th Army Group in another attack in the same general area of the railway, but on December 15 a force of about 5,000 Japanese, supported by air and artillery, counterattacked. On December 18, after a three-day battle during which both sides suffered considerable casualties, the contending forces called it quits and pulled back to their original positions. The Chinese announced that "by mid-January, 1940, the enemy was completely routed." He was not. Each side had had enough, and neither had the strength or the will to best the other.

Meanwhile, about 80 miles to the north, on December 13 and 14, the Chinese 27th Corps succeeded in taking Japanese outposts on the outskirts of Changtze and Tunliu. On January 1, 1940, the enemy reacted sharply with a counterattack by between 4,000 and 5,000 troops. The Chinese 46th and 8th reserve divisions held their ground until January 3, at which time they in turn launched a counterattack. The Chinese history has an interesting comment on this engagement: "As the enemy was sandwiched, suffered heavy losses and fled, our forces followed in pursuit and pressed near the outskirts of Changtze"—where they had been all the time. The Japanese had merely pulled back a few hundred yards from their forward positions, a move that imaginative Chinese propagandists magnified into a flight. While this was going on, the Chinese 40th Corps attacked Japanese outposts a few miles south of Changtze. On January 5 it recaptured three outlying villages. By January 24 the Chinese had recovered three more villages on the road leading south and on the twenty-eighth were still engaged with the Japanese east of Changtze, which the latter still held.

At this point, the 2nd War Area's offensive came to a halt with the triumphant announcement of nearly 14,000 casualties inflicted on the Japanese—although about one-third of that number appears correct. Then, as troops crawled into their winter quarters, the remaining spirit of military cooperation disappeared as Nationalist generals accused their Communist counter-parts in the 8th Route Army of "instigating rebellions, seizing food from the people and forbidding them to sell food to government forces. As a result, supply difficulties greatly affected operations." The charges were ridiculous and self-serving: no Nationalist troops had ever been known to *buy* food when on campaign—"requisitioning" was the accepted practice by all Chinese armies; and, however unwanted they might be, the Communist troops of the 8th Route Army were just as much a part of the 2nd War Area command as any Nationalist unit.

But the damage was done, and the friction created by these charges eventually heated to open hostility in the Hungchaio Incident in October, 1940. A more immediate result, however, was that the brouhaha afforded an excellent opportunity for the warlord General Yen Hsi-shan to take his troops out of the combat area and back to the relative safety of his home province.

The first move of the 3rd War Area—Anhwei south of the Yangtze, northeastern Kiangsi, and areas to the east—to join the winter offensive was an outpouring of blustering orders to its Left, Central, and Right Flank Forces directing them to accomplish the impossible. In the record, this all sounded very belligerent. The 32nd Army Group was ordered to "step up the attack against . . . Nanchang and harass Nanchang." For over six months there had been no attack against Nanchang to step up. The 23rd Army Group of 12 divisions from the 50th, 21st, 86th, and 25th corps and the 18th Corps of 2 divisions were designated as the Yangtze River Front Army to consist of three flank forces. This aggregation of 14 divisions was directed to operate along the south bank of the Yangtze from Wuhu, 60 miles above Nanking, to the Kiukiang–Poyang Lake area. Among other objectives, the Right Flank Force was ordered "when necessary . . . to capture Tatung [on the river] . . . at once" and to send a "powerful force . . . to Wuhu to harass and tie down the enemy." The Central Flank Force was ordered to attack Tatung and later the area around Kweichih, across the river from Anking, as well as "to cover artillery shelling and mine laying." The Left Flank Force was directed to "organize two columns built around one infantry regiment," which were to approach the riverbanks, attack enemy ships, and lay mines. Two divisions with attached artillery and engineer troops were to act as the reserve in the vicinity of Taiping, about 55 miles back from the river.

On December 16 the three flank forces began their moves toward the Yangtze. By the eighteenth the 144th Division had reoccupied two undefended villages, the 10th Reserve Division three villages and part of a fourth, the 16th Division two villages, the 190th Division three hamlets, and the 147th Division three villages, one of which was on the riverbank. No fighting was involved because there were no Japanese anywhere near to fight. However, as the Chinese units of the Central Flank Force approached the river, notably the 10th Reserve and 16th divisions, they ran into both enemy outposts and fire from naval gunboats. Before they were able to extricate themselves from the situation into which they had stumbled, the Japanese inflicted heavy casualties in their ranks. Since the two divisions were floundering around helplessly in an effort to escape further punishment, they were relieved by the 40th and 67th divisions on December 20. Two days under enemy fire had been all they could take.

On December 23 the Japanese 15th Division landed troops at several points along the river. They moved immediately to attack the Chinese where they had dug in at the first sounds of gunfire. On December 28 the Right Flank Army was directed to hold its existing positions, while its main force undertook "to infiltrate into the river banks near Tikang, Wuhu and Tatung" with five columns of regimental and battalion size, to which were attached artillery, engineer, and mine-laying detachments. The Central and Left Flank Forces were given similar instructions to attack Japanese shipping with artillery and drifting mines.

In the Kan River area west of Poyang Lake, Chinese plainclothes detachments slipped into Nanchang to sabotage enemy installations during the nights of December 12 and 18. The effect of their efforts was minor. On December 21, elements of the 32nd Army Group attacked the outskirts of Nanchang. They achieved little more than to rouse the Japanese garrison.

On December 13, in the area of Hangchow, the Chinese 192nd and 62nd divisions of the 10th Army Group reoccupied two villages and a small part of the outlying suburbs of the city.

During the night they set fire to enemy installations and warehouses, as well as Chinese shops and houses. Apparently the Japanese garrison commander was not unduly alarmed, for after establishing a perimeter of outposts, he dispatched only one regiment of his 22nd Division to disrupt the sporadic Chinese activities south of Hangchow. At dawn on January 22, 1940, the enemy regiment crossed the Chientang River, which flows into Hangchow Bay, and landed north of Hsiaoshan. After a brief exchange of fire, the Chinese "2nd resistance and defense column" ceased to resist and defend, and melted away before the Japanese advance. By noon on the same day the Japanese entered Hsiaoshan and were marching toward Shaohsing, about 25 miles to the east. On January 25 the Japanese column encountered the 6th, 8th, 2nd, and 5th resistance and defense columns at various points along the road. On January 27, thousands of Chinese militia attacked from every direction, convincing the Japanese regimental commander that a return to Hsiaoshan would be advisable.

Thus ended the winter offensive operations in the 3rd War Area. Nine river transports of varying sizes had been damaged, but water traffic on the Yangtze had not been interrupted. Not reticent in its claims, the 3rd War Area command reported that its troops had killed over 10,000 Japanese. It is, however, doubtful if they killed as many as 1,000 men, since at no time had they come to grips in a determined fight.

In the 4th War Area—Kwangsi and Kwangtung provinces—winter operations were centered in two separate locations, Nanning (see Chapter 13) and Canton. On December 8 the Japanese 104th Division advanced north from Canton in three columns. Its mission was to create a diversion to forestall the dispatch of Chinese reinforcements to southern Kwangsi. Since the purpose of this move was to pin down troops of the 4th War Area, the Japanese made no effort either to move with speed or to bring about a major engagement. But on December 17, when the Chinese 158th Division attacked the enemy's left column about 30 miles northwest of Canton and checked its progress, the Japanese rushed in reinforcements and counterattacked. After two days of fighting, the positions remained unchanged. On

December 20, additional elements of the Japanese 18th, 104th, 38th, and Konoye divisions joined the three columns. The left column of 104th Division troops, proceeding north along the Canton-Hankow railway line, attacked Pachiangkou, nearly 50 miles northwest of Canton, and captured it on December 24. On the twenty-sixth the Japanese crossed the North River; on the twenty-seventh, the Lien River; on December 31 they reached the vicinity of Yingteh, 30 miles north of Pachiangkou. The enemy's center column, the 1st Brigade of the Konoye Division and elements of the 38th Division, kept pace with the left column until it captured and moved north of Liangkou on December 25. There, at Lutien, it was attacked by the Chinese 64th Corps and its advance checked. The enemy's right column, troops of the 18th Division, moved north from Tsengcheng, 30 miles northeast of Canton, on December 20; on the twenty-third it took Lungmen, 25 miles to the north. On the twenty-fifth a part of the column held off a Chinese attack southwest of Hsinfeng, while the main body pressed on to capture Wongyuan, 40 miles to the north, on December 30.

With the arrival of the 54th Corps on the scene, the Chinese launched a series of coordinated counterattacks in nine separate areas: the 35th Army Group at Pachiangkou, Liangkou, Lutien, and Tsengcheng; the 64th Corps at Wongyuan; the 54th and 2nd provisional corps at Yingteh; and a mixed force at Lungmen. The overwhelming numbers of attacking Chinese proved too much for the Japanese. After a sharp engagement on January 1, 1940, the Chinese 54th Corps recovered Wongyuan on the second, Kantu on the fourth, and Chingtang on the fifth. On January 3 the 2nd Provisional Corps attacked Yingteh, capturing it on the fifth. The enemy fell back to Chingyuan, 45 miles north of Canton. An attack by troops of the Chinese 64th and 2nd provisional corps succeeded in forcing the enemy to evacuate Chingyuan on January 10 and to retire toward Canton. On January 11 the Chinese recovered Tsunghua; on the twelfth the 14th Division recaptured Pachiangkou, and on the sixteenth, Yinchanao, about 10 miles to the south.

Then, having demonstrated that they could force the Japanese to pull back in the face of vigorous attacks and superior numbers, the Chinese 35th and 12th army groups failed to follow up on their advantage. When they reached their old defensive positions about 50 miles north of Canton—Chingyuan, Chishih, Hengshih, and Liangkou—they quit, settling themselves as comfortably as they could for another hoped-for spell of inactivity. Instead of pressing on to attack Canton, General Chang Fa-kuei satisfied himself with exaggerated reports on the number of Japanese his armies had killed. The now-rusted Old Ironsides chilled at the thought of undertaking that major offensive action.

In the 5th War Area—western Anhwei, northern Hupei, and southern Honan—General Li Tsung-jen issued orders for participation in the winter offensive, but with the exception of orders to recapture Hsinyang, the directive prescribed no definite objectives and only limited operations, which could not be expected to achieve results of any importance.

On December 12 the 32nd, 49th, and 128th divisions of the River North Army moved up to the west bank of the Han River. The 6th, 13th, and 41st divisions crossed at two points and pushed on toward the Yunglung River, roughly parallel to and about 40 miles east of the Han. During the night of the fifteenth the 55th and 4th reserve divisions crossed the Han north of Sha-yang, about 100 miles upriver from Hankow. By December 16 the five Chinese divisions had recovered seven minor enemy outposts between the two rivers, but had encountered strong Japanese resistance near Szekang, west of Yunglung. On the seventeenth, about 2,000 infantry and artillery troops of the Japanese 116th Regiment, 13th Division, with 15 tanks, held off repeated dawn-to-dusk Chinese assaults at Szekang and nearby Hsientao. Just before darkness the Chinese took both places. On December 18 a truck column of 2,000 Japanese reinforcements was intercepted and outflanked by the Chinese. In the ensuing engagement, over 600 Japanese infantry and cavalry troops were isolated from the main column; though some managed to extricate themselves, more than half were cut to pieces. On December 22 the Japanese counterattacked, drove the Chinese back from their positions with heavy losses, and cleared a vital link on the road from the east. At the same time, additional Japanese infantry and tank reinforcements attacked the left flank of the Chinese lines with considerable success. Unable or unwilling to stand in place and fight it out, and having suffered fairly heavy casualties, the Chinese again pulled back. On December 23 the Chinese 55th and 13th divisions were ordered to cover the withdrawal of the 6th, 41st, and 4th reserve divisions to the west bank of the Han River. By the thirty-first all Chinese troops had crossed and had crawled back into their original positions west of the river. For the River Front Army the winter offensive had ended with no results other than the loss of a few thousand men and further devastation of the farms and villages in the area.

On December 12 the 74th Division of the Chinese Right Flank Army crossed the Han River and attacked a Japanese force south of Chunghsiang. On the same day the Chinese 77th and 59th corps and the 29th Army Group swarmed across the river, reoccupied two undefended villages north of Chunghsiang, and attacked small enemy outposts at four others; on the thirteenth they recaptured these and two additional villages. On the eighteenth they came up against two infantry battalions of the Japanese 13th Division who held their ground against repeated piecemeal attacks. But on the nineteenth a coordinated Chinese assault was launched causing sufficiently heavy casualties to compel the Japanese to retreat southward on December 21. On the twenty-second the Chinese again attacked at Chunghsiang and three neighboring villages, but without success. On December 26, Japanese strength in the Chunghsiang area was reinforced by one regiment and 20 tanks. The next day the Japanese attacked Chinese positions and on the twenty-eighth took Changshoutien, 20 miles north of Chunghsiang. Here the Chinese 84th Corps held its lines while the 74th Division and 59th Corps launched a flank attack from the south against the enemy positions. By December 31 the two sides were facing each other along a line running for several miles through Changshoutien. With only minor sorties during the next four days, they continued to confront each other. On January 5, 1940, a Japanese attack forced the 29th Army Group to withdraw from its positions on favorable high ground, but a counterattack with the aid of the 55th Division regained the lost ground before nightfall. Between January 9 and 13 the Japanese force at Huangyang, about the center of the lines, was increased to three regiments. Before the Japanese had a chance to attack, the Chinese made a night assault on

January 14 and succeeded in regaining high ground at the south end of the line; but by January 17 the Chinese 13th Division had been forced back from the north flank of the line to the banks of the Han River, where it fought for three days to avoid being pushed into the water. Fighting in the sector of the Right Flank Army continued until January 20, then subsided, since the Japanese had prevented the Chinese from carrying out their mission. The official Chinese history wrote of this phase of the operations with a terse: "A state of confrontation resulted"—in other words, nothing.

On December 12 the Left Flank Army, though busily "maintaining surveillance" on Suihsien, 50 miles northeast of Chunghsiang, found time to attack a few enemy outposts west of its point of interest. Another force cut the road leading east from Suihsien; in doing so, it came up against troops of the Japanese 3rd Division, who did not indicate a disposition to move from their roadblock. On the fifteenth the left flank of the Chinese 22nd Army Group fell back about 10 miles after a vigorous enemy attack, but on the 18th, the Chinese bounced back and recaptured two of the villages they had just lost. Since neither side sought a decision in this sector, no further action occurred until December 28, when the Chinese reoccupied an undefended village and "beat off enemy reinforcements" at four points of attack. After that heroic performance, this exercise in standing still culminated in an inactive standoff for the remainder of the winter offensive period.

The Southern Honan Army opened its phase of the winter offensive on December 12. On the thirteenth the Chinese 92nd Corps moved into three villages west of the Pinghan Railway and marched to the southeast. But on the fifteenth the Japanese intercepted the march and recaptured one of the villages they had lost two days earlier. At the same time the Chinese 30th and 68th corps advanced to the railway line and cut enemy communications north and south of Hsinyang, "reaping many [unspecified] gains" in the process. A small Japanese column, moving north to intercept the Chinese, was stopped before it accomplished its purpose. On the night of December 22, two Chinese regiments acting as advance guards pressed toward Hsinyang. On the twenty-sixth the Chinese 27th Division joined the two regiments in an attack on Hsinyang, but they failed to take the town. On January 5, 1940, two Japanese battalions, reinforced with artillery, attacked the 68th Corps and forced it to pull back. To salvage a potential debacle, the Chinese 30th Corps attacked enemy troops then moving through the gap in the line created by the withdrawal of the 68th Corps. The fight continued all day on January 8, with neither side able to best the other, but on the ninth the commitment of the Chinese 85th Corps saved the situation. The Japanese force was compelled to withdraw.

Meanwhile, the Northern Hupei Army on the right flank of the Southern Honan Army moved into the picture. On December 28 its 92nd Corps of four divisions was ordered to strike to the southeast and reach the area of Kuangshui, 15 miles south of Wushengkuan, by January 1, 1940, which it did. Beginning on January 5, the 92nd Corps attacked the Japanese in six villages west of the Pinghan Railway. This enabled the Chinese 23rd Division to press forward to the area between Wushengkuan and Kuangshui. On January 7 the Chinese 4th Division recaptured Huashan, west of the railway line. On the seventeenth the Chinese 4th, 21st, and 142nd divisions were heavily engaged with enemy forces near Huashan and three neighboring villages. By the twenty-second the battleground had expanded over a large area west of the railway, but after days of seesaw fighting in and around nine villages, each side broke contact. And the winter offensive ended for the Northern Hupei Army.

From the east of the railway line, the East Hupei guerrillas had been making ineffectual stabs at troops of the Japanese 39th Division since mid-December. Though they had accomplished nothing of any importance, the Chinese history credited them with "reaping considerable gains" of an unspecified nature.

In mid-December, the 6th War Area—southern Hupei and western Hunan—made its sole contribution to the winter offensive by dispatching its 116th Division of the 53rd Corps to assist the 4th Corps of the 9th War Area in an abortive attack on Linyueh, north of Yochow. This was followed by a raid on a small railway station between Linyueh and Yochow, during which a number of cars were burned. Then, quoting the Chinese history: "as the enemy was divided into several columns to make an enveloping

. . . attack, our forces broke out and massed in the vicinity of Kaochin," a good 20 miles to the west, from which safe vantage point they rested for the remainder of the winter.

The role of the 8th War Area in the winter offensive—Kansu, Ninghsia, Tsinghai, and Suiyuan in the far northwest—was "to tie down the enemy and to respond to operations of the main effort," which was about all that the National Military Council felt it could expect of its conglomerate troops. Its 35th Corps, with two brigades attached, was ordered to attack Paotou on the railway; the 6th Cavalry Corps was to sabotage the line between Kueisui, 90 miles east of Paotou, and Salachi, about 50 miles east of Paotou, and prevent Japanese reinforcements from moving to the west.

The first Chinese move, in mid-December, was the reoccupation of lightly defended Anpei, 45 miles west of Paotou, by the 81st and 35th corps. Moving east, the two corps reached the outskirts of Paotou during the night of the nineteenth and entered the city at dawn on the twentieth. During the street fighting that followed, the Chinese 101st Division captured a Japanese strongpoint at Chientzekou, about halfway between Anpei and Paotou, then marched to the east. Meanwhile, the Chinese New 6th Brigade wiped out enemy remnants between the two towns. At the same time, Chinese guerrillas destroyed part of a column of Japanese reinforcements on the road between Paotou and Kuyang, about 40 miles to the north. The Chinese 32nd and 101st divisions moved in on this action and wiped out enemy troops trying to escape from Kuyang to the east. By noon on December 22 the Chinese had squeezed the Japanese defenders of Paotou into the southwestern corner of the town and were pressing in for the kill. At this time about 2,000 Japanese infantry, artillery, and tank reinforcements were approaching Paotou by truck to relieve the beleaguered troops inside the walls. The column was attacked by the Chinese a few miles east of the town and stopped dead in its tracks after having suffered heavy casualties. Hit-and-run tactics of Chinese cavalry and guerrilla troops on the Japanese flanks and rear and determined infantry frontal assaults had been too much for the column. However, on the night of December 24 additional Japanese reinforcements arrived. Overawed by artillery, tank, and air attacks, the Chinese pulled back and "changed dispositions to confront the enemy."

By late January, 1940, with the buildup of strength in the Paotou area, the Japanese commander felt it safe to strike out to the west beyond the end of the railway. On February 3 the enemy took Wuyuan, 90 miles west of Paotou; on the fourth, Linho, 50 miles farther to the west. The Chinese "withdrew to the outskirts [of both towns] awaiting the time to stage a counter attack."

On March 16, leaving the New 4th Division to keep the Japanese occupied at Linho, the Chinese 35th Corps, Suiyuan guerrilla force, and Wu-lin (Wuyuan-Linho) Garrison Brigade slipped around Linho and made a forced march to the east along the gully of a dry river bed. On the night of the twentieth the Chinese burst into Wuyuan, fighting the surprised Japanese through the streets and alleys until 4:00 P.M. on the twenty-first. By that time the last enemy troops had either been driven off or shot off the ancient city walls. On March 22 the exultant Chinese drove the enemy out of another nearby village. The Japanese rushed reinforcements to Tatsaichu, about 6 miles north of Wuyuan, and immediately attacked the Chinese 101st Division in that area. The fight there lasted for three days, with neither side gaining or losing ground. But on March 25, when the enemy force was further increased and provided with air and artillery support, the Chinese lines began to crumble. On the twenty-sixth the Japanese recaptured Wuyuan. Though the Chinese fell back, they continued the attack from four directions. By March 30 the Japanese commander decided that he had accomplished his punitive mission to inflict heavy casualties on troublesome Chinese forces; he ordered his troops to withdraw to the east. That night and during the next day the Japanese evacuated Wuyuan and began the eastward march toward Anpei and Paotou. On the morning of April 1 the Chinese reentered the smoking, battered ruins of the town. On April 3 the Chinese 11th provisional and 3rd cavalry divisions, having followed closely on the enemy's heels, recovered two towns between Wuyuan and Anpei.

At this point, 8th War Area participation in the winter offensive came to a dead halt. Poorly equipped Chinese troops had again demonstrated conclusively that surprise, boldness, and mobility could severely hurt better armed Japanese. No one in

Chungking had expected them to do any more than "tie down" their opponents. They had tied the Japanese in knots. But General Chu Shao-liang, the commander, had no stomach to follow up his advantage.

On December 12 the 9th War Area command—northwest Kiangsi, Hupei south of the Yangtze, and Hunan—threw elements of the 19th, 1st, 30th, 27th, and 15th army groups into the winter offensive. The 19th Army Group's 58th Corps and 184th Division of the 60th Corps attacked the Japanese 34th Division at Wanshoukung and Shihtoukang, 18 and 30 miles southwest of Nanchang; at Tacheng and Hsiangfukuan, 38 and 50 miles to the southwest; and at several other points. The Chinese quickly cut Japanese lines of communications and reoccupied six villages near Fenghsin south and west of Nanchang. During the night of the thirteenth they burned several storage depots north of Fenghsin, and the 139th Division of the 32nd Corps attacked Chingan, 22 miles to the southwest. On the night of December 21 the Chinese stormed into Chingan and set fire to Japanese installations as well as Chinese property in the vicinity. The 141st and 139th divisions infiltrated a number of fairly large units behind enemy positions, and wrecked rail and telegraph lines around Anyi, 25 miles northwest of Nanchang; Tehan on the railway 43 miles north; Juohsi, 30 miles west of Tehan; and between Lohua and Niuhsing within 7 miles of Nanchang.

At the same time, the Chinese 78th Corps of the 30th Army Group attacked the 213th Regiment of the Japanese 33rd Division at Wuning, 48 miles west of Tehan, and forced it to pull back. The Chinese 72nd and 8th corps attacked the enemy's 40th Division in the vicinity of Hsintanpu, nearly 60 miles west of the Kiukiang-Nanchang railway; Tungshan, 28 miles to the northwest; Yanghsin, 18 miles to the northeast; and Painichiao, 15 miles southwest of Tungshan. All communications were disrupted in the general area. The 72nd Corps recaptured Hsintanpu, and the 8th Corps took two other small towns. On December 14, two regiments from the Japanese 33rd and 40th divisions counterattacked the freewheeling 72nd and 8th corps. By the nineteenth the Japanese had been compelled to withdraw from the battle area. The Chinese resumed their destructive activities in the Tungshan-Hsintanpu area. By January 10, 1940, elements of the Chinese 72nd Corps, 3rd Division, and 3rd Advance Column had wreaked havoc with all telegraph, road, and rail communications in Japanese rear areas.

Meanwhile, the Chinese 1st Advance Column, consisting of the 27th Army Group, cut the Canton-Hankow railway at three places between Yochow and Wuchang (Hankow), one of which was just south of Puchi, about 50 miles below Wuchang. On December 12th the 20th Corps of the 27th Army Group reoccupied Chungyang, 15 miles southeast of Puchi, and proceeded to wreck all communications and means of travel in that area. The corps also turned back Japanese reinforcements attempting to reach Chungyang. Beginning on December 16 the Chinese 73rd Corps attacked the enemy on their front and managed to "tie them down" in that vicinity for nearly a month. On December 13 the 3rd and 19th divisions of the Chinese 70th Corps moved to attack a Japanese force southwest of Chungyang. They cleared the enemy out of a number of villages, then turned toward Puchi where they intercepted Japanese reinforcements again attempting to move south along the line of the railway. Bridges had been destroyed and sections of tracks had already been torn up.

In mid-December a column of the 79th Corps' 82nd Division of the 15th Army Group made a quick stab at the Canton-Hankow railway line about 25 miles north of Yochow, routed guards from the Japanese 6th Division, and cut the line. The bulk of the 82nd Division, with the 98th and 140th divisions and two additional attached regiments, attacked the enemy garrisons at Tashaping and Tungcheng, 40 miles east of Yochow, and completely surrounded the latter town. The Chinese then turned west, recaptured two small towns, and pressed on to the outskirts of Yochow. At the same time, the Chinese 4th Corps, moving up from the southeast, and the 116th Division of the 6th War Area, coming from the southwest, attacked Linyueh (Linhsiang) on the railway about 30 miles northeast of Yochow. About to be cut off, troops of the Japanese 6th Division counterattacked at six points around Linhsiang, but as the Chinese drove them out of one village after another, the enemy was compelled to retreat toward Yochow.

As in other war areas, operations in the 9th War Area ground to a halt in mid-January. Thousands of troops on both sides had been killed or wounded—probably as many as 50,000. The most powerful command in China had accomplished little more than a series of sharp pinpricks and burnings. Chinese dependence on sabotage and commando-type raids, no matter on how large a scale, had "tied down" the Japanese, but there had been no determined effort to turn small successes into a major drive to destroy the enemy.

In the Hopei-Chahar War Area, the 69th Corps, New 6th Division, and guerrilla forces attacked the enemy's "key localities south of Shihkiachuang" along the Pinghan Railway, and between Tsangchow and Tehchow, south of the Yellow River, along the Tsinpu Railway, all of which meant exactly nothing to the winter offensive.

The Shantung-Kiangsu War Area duplicated the operations of the Hopei-Chahar command. The only differences in their activities were the designations of troop units involved and the location of their "employment"—in this case, the southern sector of the Tsinpu Railway. There, the 51st, 57th and 89th Corps "sabotaged" the line in the vicinity of Taian, Tenghsien and Chuhsien. However, at no time was Japanese traffic on the railway disrupted for more than a few hours by Chinese acts of sabotage.

The Chinese records claim that between November 26, 1939, and late March, 1940, "some 77,386 enemy troops were killed, over 400 enemy troops and 2,743 rifles captured." The absurdity of such gross exaggeration is evident when the killed-to-wounded ratio of 1:2.5—after the first five months of conflict—is considered. If the Chinese figures were correct, the Japanese had suffered over 270,000 casualties in both killed and wounded—about 23 percent of all their troops in China, which would have compelled them to withdraw from the interior to enclaves in the Hopei-Shantung, Canton, Shanghai-Nanking, and coastal-port areas. A more reasonable estimate of Japanese casualties—killed and wounded—is not more than 50,000. Chinese military casualties probably totaled over 150,000, civilian casualties considerably more. As for the claimed 400 Japanese prisoners, they should be added to the number killed in combat, because as was customary, they were all murdered.

The Chungking government also declared: "The Chinese Communists took advantage of this opportunity to attack our guerrilla forces, garble [sic] up local militia units and enlarge their territories causing heavy losses to our winter offensive." This meant that the Chinese Communists had moved into the vacuum created by the withdrawal of nationalist troop units and that local militia, like the local populace, accepted Red leadership since they had no other.

Actually, Chinese Communist troops had withdrawn to safe bases in the rugged Wutai Mountains of the Shansi-Hopei border areas and into the precipitous Chungtiao Mountains north of the Yellow River in southern Shansi. The Japanese had soon found to their cost that it was not only impossible to dislodge them, but even to find them. From their wild mountain fastnesses the Communists had struck in every direction in a constant series of raids that completely disrupted enemy lines of communication. They had driven off Japanese railway guards and torn up miles of track on the Tatung-Taiyuan and on the Shihkiachuang-Taiyuan railways. They had destroyed bridges throughout the two provinces, had cut out great sections of telegraph and telephone lines, and had burned enemy supply depots and barracks. In their postwar "monographs" dealing with the conflict, the Japanese somewhat grudgingly conceded that the Chinese Communists "displayed great skill in guerrilla operations" and in employing to the fullest extent the elements of surprise and speed.

The reality of the entire winter offensive was simply that it was grist for the propaganda mills of Chiang Kai-shek's government: China was fighting desperately for her life with her back to the wall; China's armies were defending their homeland, battling the enemy to the last man in every province; China had been impoverished by Japanese aggression and needed billions of dollars to carry on her struggle for existence; the Chinese people had rallied around the standard of Chiang Kai-shek, fighting the enemy with bamboo clubs and farm tools. Actually, the Chinese people were fleeing by the millions as much to escape Chiang's troops as the Japanese invaders.

It was a secondary matter to Chiang Kai-shek and his corrupt bureaucracy that close to 400,000 of his troops and people had died or had been maimed during his winter offensive, that millions of refugees had been uprooted from their homes and farms, in order to achieve a propaganda victory and to persuade the U.S. government to intervene against the Japanese.

15

Operations in Hupei, April, 1940, to March, 1941

IN CHIANG'S BECLOUDED THINKING, the "real" enemy was still Mao Tse-tung and his Red Army in the north and the "real" issue was a confrontation with the Chinese Communists after his American sympathizers had handed China back to him. Chiang Kai-shek's military tactics never could have defeated the Japanese, nor any other aggressive foe willing to fight for its objectives. True, had he concentrated sufficient troops against the enemy in a determined offensive, the sheer weight of their numbers might have forced the Japanese to withdraw from most of the Chinese hinterland. But the capability for that action and most of the equipment he had been squirreling away were reserved to destroy the Chinese Communists.

Justification for his callous disregard for the Chinese masses came from the self-delusion that the military "successes" of his guerrilla forces in the so-called winter offensives had been real. Therefore the 1940–41 guerrilla activities that followed were born of a misguided conviction, or wishful thinking, that the Japanese armies could be "tied down," "worn down," and eventually "knocked down" by harassment in occupied and adjacent areas of the country.

The Japanese wished to maintain a military status quo while they established their puppet government and expanded its influence over China. In order to preserve the security of their conquests and the safety of their troops, they had no choice but to react with punitive mopping-up operations against Chinese guerrillas and other forces in threatened areas. Chinese military activities in Hupei were countered by Japanese offensives and brutality in Shansi, Hopei, Kiangsi, and Hunan.

To meet the annoyance and the time-consuming challenges of Chinese guerrilla raids in Hupei, General Katsuichiro Enbu, now commander of the Japanese 11th Corps, assembled a sizable force. But he failed to realize that conventional armies, no matter how large or how powerful, cannot defeat tenacious guerrilla-type forces by matching numerical strength and superior arms against hit-and-run tactics. He could compel the Chinese to fall back as his corps advanced, but he could not compel them to remain "withdrawn" except from the larger towns and main lines of communication.

In mid-May, 1940, General Enbu concentrated his 11th Corps at key localities from the area of Hsinyang on the Pinghan Railway 100 miles north of Hankow to the vicinity of Chunghsiang near the Han River about 90 miles to the southwest. At the time, the corps consisted of the 3rd, 4th (all of which did not arrive from Manchuria until June 1), 13th, and 30th divisions; the 6th and 40th divisions, each less one brigade; and the 20th and 185th separate brigades—a force equivalent to six divisions containing about 130,000 men. By late October the 11th Corps had been reinforced by the 39th Division and the 15th and 17th divisions, each less one brigade, with a total strength of 40,000 men. Before the conclusion of the three antiguerrilla campaigns, the 11th Corps had a strength of approximately 170,000 men.

General Li Tsung-jen, in whose 5th War Area the three operations took place, had under his command six army groups[1] consisting of 13 corps of 31 divisions, 1 cavalry division, and 2 separate brigades; 5 separate corps[2] with 10 divisions and 1 cavalry division; the River Defense Force of 2 corps[3] and 1 separate division for a total of 7 divisions; and the Eastern Hupei Guerrilla Force consisting of 2 corps of 2 infantry and 5 guerrilla divisions. The 5th War Area command included a total of 50 regular infantry divisions, 5 guerrilla divisions, 2 cavalry divisions, and 2 separate brigades, with a strength of nearly 380,000 men, more than twice as many troops as were ever at the disposal of the Japanese 11th Corps.

The Battle of Tsaoyang-Ichang
MID-APRIL TO JUNE 10, 1940

In late April a column of the Japanese 3rd Division from Hsinyang drove the Chinese garrison out of Mingkang, 23 miles to the north. On May 1 the same enemy troops took Shihtzuchiao, on the railway 7 miles farther north; from that point the division marched to the west with the apparent intention of striking from the northeast against Tsaoyang, 65 miles west of Hsinyang. At the same time the Japanese 13th Division began to move in two columns from Chunghsiang toward Tsaoyang, 60 miles north of their base. Meanwhile, the Japanese 39th Division at Suihsien, about halfway between Hsinyang and Chunghsiang, attacked troops of the Chinese 11th Army Group in a feint to draw the Chinese into a long, drawn-out fight some 35 miles southeast of Tsaoyang and thus assist the pincer movement of the 3rd and 13th divisions.

General Li Tsung-jen reacted to the first Japanese moves by directing the River Defense Force of seven divisions to defend the general area of Ichang, the important river port on the Yangtze about 110 miles upriver from Hankow. The 33rd Army Group of seven divisions and one cavalry division was ordered to block the northward move of the Japanese 13th Division from Chunghsiang. In the center, the Chinese 45th Corps of two divisions from the 22nd Army Group and the 84th Corps of two divisions from the 11th Army Group were ordered to stop any move of the enemy 39th Division to the west and north of Suihsien. The 30th and 60th corps of five and one-half divisions from the 2nd Army Group were ordered to take up positions east of Tungpo, 25 miles northwest of Hsinyang. The 41st Corps of two divisions from the 22nd Army Group was directed to act as the war area reserve in the vicinity of Hsiangtung at the junction of the Han and Pai rivers. The 29th Army Group of four and one-half divisions was "held in readiness" in the Tahungshan area between Japanese-held Suihsien and Chunghsiang. The 31st Army Group "awaited the opportunity to strike the invading enemy" west of the Han River. Other troop units of the 5th War Area command were not mentioned in the initial orders, presumably because it was planned to hold them back from participation in the impending operations.

Having taken Mingkang and Shihtzuchiao against light Chinese resistance, the Japanese 3rd Division turned west toward Piyang on May 1. On the same day the 40th Division brigade took Hsiaolintien, 18 miles northwest of its base at Hsinyang, then turned west toward Tungpo. On May 5 the two Japanese columns captured Piyang and Tungpo, and continued their westward drive. After assaulting and capturing Tangho, about 55 miles west of the railway, on May 7, the 3rd Division turned southwest to advance on Tsaoyang, while the 40th Division troops pressed on from Tungpo. Although General T'ang En-po's 31st Army Group, with the 68th, 92nd, and 30th corps attached (a total of 13 divisions), nibbled at "the flanks and tail end of the enemy," their halfhearted attacks failed to slow down the Japanese progress toward Tsaoyang. T'ang En-po, who had been one of the most aggressive and resourceful of Chinese commanders, had either lost his will to fight or had received secret orders to preserve his army group intact.

From the Japanese southern flank at Chunghsiang, the 13th Division moved out rapidly. On May 3 it took Changshoutien and Tienchichi, 15 and 20 miles north of its base. On May 6 the Japanese occupied Fengyao, 22 miles northwest of Chunghsiang. On the seventh they brushed aside feeble Chinese resistance at Wangchiatien and attacked General Chang Tse-chung's 33rd Army Group just west of Teinchichi and Huanglungtan. In that fight General Chang personally led a counterattack that failed. The Japanese broke through the Chinese positions and drove on past Changchiachi to Shuangkou, 65 miles north of their jumping-off positions and only 15 miles west of Tsaoyang. On May 8, enemy cavalry troops galloped into Hsinyeh, some 10 miles farther north.

Meanwhile, the Chinese 29th Army Group, which had been holding itself "in readiness" at Tahungshan, discovered that it was more than ready to make a getaway from what had now become a very dangerous location. After a precipitate 45-mile withdrawal to the vicinity of Wangchiatien, its bewildered commander, General Wang Tsan-hsu, suddenly found his troops embroiled with rear elements of the Japanese 13th Division.

Realizing that he was trapped behind the enemy advance, he attacked to break through the Japanese column in order to escape to the west—which he did.

In the Japanese center at Suihsien, the 39th Division and 6th Division brigade delayed making any move until May 4, when they pounced on the Chinese 11th Army Group. On the fifth the Japanese overran Kaocheng and Anchu, about 15 miles north and west of Suihsien. The Chinese wilted under the vigorous attacks of the two enemy columns and fell back in disorder for 10 miles to a defense line of sorts extending from Huantan to Tanghsien. On the Chinese right flank of this sector, the 33rd Army Group "encountered reverses in its operations"—got the hell kicked out of it—and was about to break into a rout when one division of the 11th Army Group prevented its line from collapsing completely. Then, leaving the 178th Division to delay the enemy at Tanghsien as best it could, the 11th and 33rd army groups of 10 infantry and 1 cavalry divisions threw in the towel. Without further resistance, they retreated toward Tsaoyang. They had been outmaneuvered and outflanked by an inferior force. When the 33rd Army Group's 74th Division reached the Chang-chiachi-Shuangkou area, it found the escape route from Tsaoyang to the west blocked by elements of the Japanese 13th Division.

North and northwest of Tsaoyang, General T'ang En-po aroused himself sufficiently to launch his 31st Army Group into vigorous attacks against the enemy at Tangho and Hsinyeh, which he recaptured on May 8 and 9. His action came too late. The 11th and 33rd army groups were then in a mad scramble to escape encirclement. On the seventh the Japanese took Suiyangtien and Wuchiatien, each less than 10 miles from Tsaoyang. On the same day, "in order to break out," the panicked Chinese forces hastily abandoned Tsaoyang. Even the redoubtable Chang Tse-chung could not hold back the rout to the west banks of the Han and Pai rivers. During the exodus from the town the 178th Division acted as rear guard, suffering very heavy casualties, including its division commander. On May 8 the Japanese marched triumphantly into Tsaoyang from the north, east, southeast, and west.

On May 10 the Japanese completed the occupation of the Hsiangtung plain, the area east of Hsiangtung at the junction of the Han and Pai rivers and south of Tsaoyang; but by this time the Chinese had begun to recover from the effects of their defeat and were ready to strike back. General T'ang En-po's 31st Army Group, General Sun Lien-chung's 2nd Army Group, and the 92nd Corps of the 11th Army Group (a total of 11 divisions) suddenly moved south against the right flank of the Japanese 3rd Division and 40th Division brigade. The 39th and 75th corps moved east from the Hsiangtung-Shuangkou area at the same time. The 29th Army Group and Chang Tse-chung's 33rd Army Group, with a total of 12 divisions, pushed north from Yicheng area to strike at the left flank of the Japanese 13th Division. Overnight, some 75,000 enemy troops spread thinly throughout the area between the Pinghan Railway and the Han River found victory turned against them by over 250,000 aroused Chinese—in particular, two enraged generals, Chang Tse-chung and T'ang En-po. Meanwhile the 94th Corps of 3 divisions was tearing up Japanese rear areas at Yingshan, Yunmeng, Chengshan, and Tsaoshih, only 8 to 20 miles west of the Pinghan line and within 20 miles of Suihsien and Hsinyang. At the same time, the East Hupei Guerrilla Force swung 5 divisions into action and seized three towns on the railway between Hsinyang and Hankow. In surprise attacks the 68th Corps[4] and 92nd Corps[5] (four and one-half divisions) recaptured Piyang, Tungpo, and Mingkang, within 25 miles of Hsinyang. Possession of the latter two towns was a serious threat to the rear and north flank of the Japanese 3rd Division and 40th Division brigade.

General Enbu's 11th Corps was in trouble. On May 11 it began an eastward withdrawal from the Tsaoyang area. Chinese infantry and cavalry troops clawed at the Japanese flanks and rear with constant attacks. Not satisfied with this measure of vengeance for his recent humiliation, General Chang Tse-chung rammed his 33rd Army Group of seven infantry and two cavalry divisions into the south flank of the Japanese 13th and 39th divisions in a furious attempt to block their route to the east and to pin them between his and the other Chinese armies in hot pursuit. On May 16, T'ang En-po's 31st Army reoccupied Tsaoyang, immediately veered eastward, and drove the remaining enemy troops toward the embattled 33rd Army Group. On the same day, Chang Tse-chung assumed personal command of his Guard Battalion and 74th Division in a wild charge into the thick of enemy troops attempting to retreat over the few clogged and intercepted roads. At noon, as he roared orders to the vanguard of his army and wrathfully slashed the air with his sword, he was cut down by a burst of Japanese machine-gun fire. The gallant "roughneck" died at the forefront of his men. With his death the Chinese counterattacks evaporated. Pressure on the enemy stopped dead; smoking guns fell silent. That afternoon, sensing an unexpected opportunity, the Japanese mustered all their strength to launch a vigorous counterattack. On May 17 an enemy spearhead bulldozed its way through the now listless Chinese ranks and again captured Tsaoyang. The Chinese forces fell back to Hsinyeh and Hsiangtung on the west banks of the Pai and Han rivers "awaiting the opportunity to launch the counter offensive"—an opportunity that was not to come for over four years.

In the latter part of May the Japanese 4th Division from Manchuria and the 18th Separate Brigade completed their concentration in the Shayang area, 35 miles south of Chunghsiang. On the night of May 31, columns of the Japanese 3rd and 39th divisions crossed the Han River near Yicheng and Ouchiamiao, 30 and 35 miles southwest of Tsaoyang. On June 1 the 3rd Division took Hsiangtung from the still-inert Chinese forces. The full division then marched to the southwest and on June 3 captured Nanchang, about 20 miles below Hsiangtung. On the same day the 39th Division took Yicheng. The two Japanese divisions then moved to the south in parallel columns about 15 miles apart toward Ichang on the Yangtze, about 75 miles from Nanchang and Yicheng.

The ancient city of Ichang, with a population of close to 100,000, was the largest and most important river port between Hankow and Chungking. A prosperous commercial and transshipment point just below the start of the great Yangtze gorge, Ichang and the valley to the east were best known as the original home of the tangerine and Mandarin orange, the ancestors of the modern orange.

After the entire Japanese 3rd Division had pulled out of Hsiangtung on its way toward Ichang, the Chinese 41st Corps[6] moved into the town "after attacking the enemy fiercely" where there was no enemy to attack. On June 4 the Chinese 77th Corps of three divisions[7] reoccupied Nanchang after the Japanese had passed through that place on their southward march. Official Chinese reports of another "fierce attack" consisted of no more than a few rear-guard skirmishes. The Japanese had had no intention of holding Nanchang, and had only taken it in the first place because it was on the best road to Ichang. Some 70 miles to the south, the Japanese 13th Division and 6th Division brigade crossed the Han River at Shayang and Chiukou and moved west on the Hankow-Ichang road. To block the advance of the enemy's south column, the Chinese River Defense Force of seven divisions took up defensive positions astride the road a few miles west of the river. But on June 6 the enemy broke through the Chinese lines after a brief fight and took Shihlipu and Shihhuichiao, both about 7 miles west of the river. On the same day the Japanese 39th Division, moving south from Yicheng, took Chingmen with little effort, then turned southwest toward Tangyang to link up with the 3rd Division. Although the Chinese River Defense Force claimed to have "fought hard against the enemy along the line from Chingmen to Chiangling," they had already been outflanked by the Japanese 3rd and 39th divisions, the left flank of their defense line having been rolled back for a stretch of nearly 30 miles. To the north the Chinese 2nd Army Group reoccupied Yicheng after it had been vacated by the Japanese and continued to follow—"to pursue"—the enemy to the south. On the 7th, Chiangling, the southern anchor of the Chinese positions, was captured by the Japanese 13th Division following a brief firefight. The Chinese fell back to a new "defense line" about 20 miles to the west that extended for 40 miles from Tungshih on the Yangtze through Tangyang to Yuanan.

On the morning of June 9 the three Japanese divisions attacked all along the line. By that afternoon the right (south) end of the line had collapsed under assaults by the enemy's 13th Division. That night the Chinese again fell back across the Tsu River to positions that formed an arc extending from within 5 miles of Ichang through Kulaopu and Shuanlienshih to Tangyang. When the enemy took Kulaopu and Tangyang by assault on the tenth, the Chinese abandoned the remains of their crumbling defense line and crowded into the immediate vicinity of Ichang. The Japanese continued unnecessary pressure for three days—unnecessary because there was no heart in the Chinese defense of the city.

Then, "having suffered prohibitive losses, [the Chinese] took the initiative to abandon Ichang."

At this time the Chinese 2nd and 31st army groups, trailing the Japanese 3rd and 39th divisions from the north, reached the vicinity of Tangyang and Chingmen, 30 and 50 miles northeast of Ichang. Their "pursuit" had been conducted at a much more leisurely pace than the "flight" of the two enemy divisions. On June 16 the two Chinese army groups with the 77th and 18th corps counterattacked the Japanese in the Ichang area. On June 17 the 18th Corps succeeded in entering Ichang, but it was forced out of the city within a few hours. The 2nd Army Group and 77th Corps[8] concentrated their attacks in the Tangyang area, the 31st Army Group in the vicinity of Chingmen. Meanwhile, the Chinese 5th and 32nd divisions crossed the Yangtze to attack the Japanese at Shayang and Shihlipu, but they failed to come within miles of their objectives. On June 18 the Chinese called off their counterattacks and fell behind new defensive positions to "maintain surveillance over the enemy." The Japanese had not only given Li Tsung-jen's 5th War Area troops a sound drubbing and taken the prize of Ichang, but had also laid waste a large area of western Hupei province. Both sides had suffered heavy casualties during the operations—about 20,000 Japanese and probably as many as 50,000 Chinese—and had lost large quantities of weapons and equipment. The greatest loss to the Chinese was the death of General Chang Tse-chung.

Operations in Central Hupei
NOVEMBER 23 TO EARLY DECEMBER, 1940

For five months after the fall of Ichang, the Chinese 5th War Area command engaged in no more than intermittent guerrilla activities against the Japanese in central Hupei between the Han River and the Pinghan Railway. By what amounted to a gentlemen's agreement, neither side had undertaken any major operations along a general line from Hsinyang on the Pinghan Railway through Suihsien, Chunghsiang, Chingmen, and Tangyang to Ichang on the Yangtze River. The Japanese had withdrawn from Tsaoyang when they no longer had any need to occupy that area.

The Chinese had indulged their penchant for needling with guerrilla activities, but they had never constituted a threat to enemy tenure in Ichang, Hankow, or the territory between. Nevertheless, they were a constant annoyance that General Enbu of the Japanese 11th Corps decided to end.

To carry out his purpose, Enbu deployed five task forces, which he assembled in the vicinities of Tangyang (the Kayashima Force), Chingmen (the Muragami Force), Chunghsiang (the Hirabayashi Force), Chuchiafu between Chingmen and Chunghsiang (the Kitana Force), and Suihsien (the Hanjima Force). Each task force had the approximate strength of one division. The Kayashima Force was composed of the 18th Composite Brigade and one brigade of the 40th Division; the Muragami Force had the entire 39th Division with attachments; the Hirabayashi Force had two brigades from the 17th and 15th divisions; the Kitana Force had one brigade of the 4th Division and the Kususe Armored Force; the Hanjima Force consisted of the 3rd Division. The armored unit was equivalent in strength to one regiment.

Chinese intelligence, more often based on intuition than on rational deduction from available facts, concluded that Japanese dispositions "indicated the enemy attempt to encircle our forces on both banks of the Hsiang [Han] River," presumably to destroy them. On the contrary, the Japanese intention was to chastise rather than to annihilate.

Having convinced itself that the enemy was about to launch a major offensive, the 5th War Area command's preparations to meet the threat were of a surprisingly minor nature, involving but 6 corps of 14 divisions out of the 22 corps of 57 divisions at its disposal. The 30th and 77th corps of the River West Army, the 44th and 67th corps of the Right Army Group, which was in the center, and the 41st and 45th corps of the Central Army, on the left, were directed "to adopt the tactics of checking a rampant enemy by employing the main force to intercept the enemy's outer flanks at the opportune time." If any corps commander managed to decipher that, he must have been possessed of an unusually clairvoyant nature indeed. But since many had risen from lowly peasant origins and could barely read and write, and since others would follow their usual pattern of obeying orders at their own pleasure, the effect of these written instructions was probably insignificant one way or another. The 59th Corps was directed "to push to the Hsiangtung area ready to respond to the operations [on] both banks of the Hsiang [Han] River," a position over 50 miles from the nearest Japanese unit, the Kitana Force. There were no orders for the other 15 corps of the 5th War Area command.

On November 25, about 1,000 troops from the Japanese 18th Composite Brigade at Tangyang, west of the Han River, easily broke through the defense positions of the Chinese 77th Corps and pressed on for another 20 miles to Hangtien. On the same day about 3,000 troops of the Japanese 39th Division at Chingmen smashed through the Chinese 30th Corps and reached Yen-chihmiao, 25 miles north of their jumping-off line. Meanwhile, two columns from the 4th Division brigade at Chuchiafu rammed through the Chinese defenses south of Tunglinling with equal ease and reached Liangshuiching and Kuaihuopu, each about 18 miles northwest and north of their original positions. At this juncture, the River West Army got on the move and somewhat tardily "swung into line" from Hengtien to Yenchihmiao and Kuaihuopu. Undeterred by this "swinging into line," troops of the Japanese 39th Division did some swinging of their own. On the twenty-sixth they swept through Yenchihmiao and Hsienchu and on the twenty-seventh reached Liuhouchi, 10 miles farther north. On the same morning, the two columns of the Japanese 4th Division converged on Lichiatang, 10 miles north of Kuaihuopu. At dusk on the twenty-seventh, the Japanese, now confronted by the bulk of the River West Army as well as the Chinese 30th and 77th corps, began to pull back toward their original positions. They had accomplished their mission, to raid and disrupt a 20- to 30-mile belt of Chinese-held territory northwest of their bases at Chingmen and Chuchiachi.

On the Chunghsiang front three Japanese columns totaling about 3,000 men from the 17th and 15th divisions broke through the defenses of the Chinese 44th and 67th corps on November 25. By the twenty-sixth they had sent the Chinese 67th Corps and 149th Division of the 44th Corps scurrying for safety to a line through Wangchiaho, Wulungkuan, and Yunanmen, over 15 miles past their original positions. During this operation the Japanese encircled a Chinese force at Chiangchiachi and Shahotien, overran Sanlikang nearly 30 miles northeast of their jumping-off positions, rolled back a 30-mile section of the line between the Chinese Right Army and Central Army, and with the arrival of about 1,500 reinforcements opened attacks on Wangchiaho and Yunanmen. On November 27 the Chinese 44th and 67th corps counterattacked at Wangchiaho, but in the words of the Chinese history, "the enemy fought on" despite casualties. In other words, the Chinese counterattack was a failure.

On the morning of November 25, about 2,000 troops from the Japanese 3rd Division at Suihsien pushed through the Chinese defense lines at Liangshuikou and struck the 123rd Division of the 45th Corps at Lishan, 10 miles northwest of their jumping-off positions. At the same time, two additional enemy columns, each of battalion strength, broke through the Chinese defense in their front and pressed on for 20 miles toward Hoyuantien and Chingmingpu to the north and northwest. On the twenty-sixth the two enemy battalions attacked the Chinese 124th and 127th divisions at Chingmingpu and nearby Chinchishan, where the Chinese attempted to make a stand 12 miles to the rear of their original positions. Another Japanese battalion struck out from Suihsien through Langhotien to Tangchiafan, a distance of 27 miles. On the twenty-seventh the two Japanese battalions at Chingmingpu and Chinchishan shifted to the vicinity of Hoyuantien to link up with the unit in that area. It had already taken Tangchiafan and had reached a point just east of Huantanchen. By that night the three enemy battalions were in position to launch a dawn attack on the Chinese 125th Division. In the meantime, a fourth Japanese battalion reinforced with cavalry made a fast march to Shangshihtien and Shatien, about 25 miles from Suihsien, and drove a wedge between the Chinese 123rd and 124th divisions.

On November 28, having accomplished their mission to punish the troops of the 5th War Area command and to create a belt of devastation north and northwest of their forward positions, the five Japanese task forces began to return to their base areas. As the enemy withdrew, the Chinese followed at a safe distance in what they labeled a pursuit. But they did not pursue the Japanese beyond the positions they had staked out for themselves. By November 30 the original lines of the Chinese 5th War Area in central

Hupei had been reoccupied, and the Chungking propaganda mills began to bray about another victory in the glorious defense of the homeland. The whole operation was nothing more than a series of coordinated, commando-type raids on a large scale during which far more damage had been done to the Chinese armies and local people than to the Japanese.

Operations in Western Hupei
MARCH 6–21, 1941

Three months later, the last operation in Hupei, which was again billed as a notable Chinese victory in the heroic resistance against totalitarian aggression, turned out to be no more than an eight-day Japanese raid to insure their own security. As before, Japanese impatience at Chinese guerrilla activities had been aroused; this circumstance, coupled with a feeling of contempt for the refusal of the Chinese armies to fight, caused the short spurt of combat west of Ichang on the Yangtze River.

In early March, 1941, the commander of the Japanese 13th Division, General Tanaka, deployed his 65th Regiment and 19th Artillery Regiment on a defense perimeter about 25 miles east of Ichang. The 104th Regiment was sent to the northwest, the 17th Cavalry Regiment to the southwest of the city, and the 58th Regiment to man a bridgehead on the west bank of the river from Chiaochuling to Shangwulungkou, a line that extended for 35 miles.

The Chinese 26th Corps of three divisions from the River Defense Force, with the 32nd Division of the 85th Corps attached, was strung out on a 130-mile "defense line" roughly paralleling the west bank of the Yangtze from Hsiangtzekou on the north to Muchiatang at the southern extremity. The 41st Division was assigned the mission of holding the southern 80 miles of the line, the 32nd Division the northern 50 miles. The 44th Division was to act as the reserve in the vicinity of Tsaochiafan, 100 miles west of the river, in a classic example of "disposition in depth." The 23rd Division was not assigned any specific mission. Since the fall of Ichang in mid-June, troops of the 26th Corps had been comfortably "maintaining surveillance over the enemy" for seven and one-half months. The boredom of this duty had been relieved by intermittent guerrilla raids on the Japanese bridgehead and almost daily raids for food and women on the local Chinese villages. Although he had at his disposal— including the 103rd Division on the southern flank of the line —about seven times the numerical strength of the enemy bridge- head troops, it never occurred to General Hsiao Chih-chu to disturb the status quo in an attempt to clear the west bank of the river. Nor had it occurred to him to place his troops in defensible positions to meet a possible Japanese attack.

At 5:30 A.M. on March 6, 1941, two columns of Japanese infantry, reinforced by cavalry and artillery units, swept through the Chi- nese forward positions at Tanchiataitze and Chaochiatien and pushed on to the main defense line, about 23 miles west of the river. On the same day, a third enemy column attacked and quickly seized Fanchiahu, near the center of the Chinese line and about 40 miles west of the Yangtze. On the seventh the unimpeded Japanese drive reached points over 50 miles west of the river. Meanwhile, the south column continued for another 25 miles to Yutaishan and Chienchiachung. The north enemy force split into two columns. One element pushed on from Fanchiahu, attacked the Chinese 44th Division at Taipingchiao, 18 miles to the west, and forced the lacadaisical defenders of their homeland to fall back in order "to continue the resistance." The second element turned north and captured Hutzeyeh without effort. It then continued on for another 25 miles, bypassed a new Chinese "defense line" at Tuntzechao, swept through Tienwangshih, and finally slowed down on March 11 just south of the next momen- tary pause in the flight of the 32nd Division at Mingchiakung and Hutankou. This Japanese column had driven a wedge between units of the 32nd Division and forced the fleeing northern ele- ments up against the outer works of the fortress of Shihpai, 125 miles from the bridgehead at the Yangtze. During the five-day rout and pursuit, the Japanese had found it necessary to expend only a small quantity of ammunition. They had expected to fight a battle, but had become participants in what amounted to a long-distance game of tag. Describing the state of affairs at this point, the Chinese history stated: "the enemy found himself in a conical position," a military term that defies interpretation.

Nanking, December 11, 1937. Japanese artillery bombarding the south gate of Nanking with direct fire.

Canton in 1937. The Chinese city at the one bridge connecting Canton with the International Settlement of Shameen.

General Wei Li-huang, General Ho Ying-ch'in, respectively Minister of War and Chief of Staff of the Chinese Army, and the author during World War II.

Hankow in April 1938. From left to right: the author; Chinese Communist representative Chou En-lai; Agnes Smedley, correspondent for the *Manchester Guardian;* and U.S. Marine Captain Evans Carlson.

To Mr. Capt. Dorn
E. L. Chow
29/IV 1938

Autographed photograph of Chinese Communist representative Chou En-lai, taken at Hankow in April 1938.

Nanchang Airfield in May 1938. Chinese aircraft lined up on the field before the Hankow campaign.

The occupation of Hankow, October 26, 1938. Japanese troops marching past the French Consulate marine guard.

Japanese artillery forced to retreat ahead of the rampaging waters, after the Chinese blew up the dikes along the Yellow River, June 1938.

Japanese troops pushing through the Mufu Mountains in the first campaign to take Changsha, summer of 1939.

Japanese infantry on the bridge across the Kan River before the final assault on Nanchang, March 26, 1939.

British-guard troops departing Tientsin, 1940.

Bombing of Chungking, 1940.

In the meantime the center of the so-called Chinese defenses had completely collapsed. After routing the Chinese 44th Division and scattered elements of the 32nd Division, the Japanese column from Fanchiahu simply breezed through one location after another until it halted its rapid advance to rest its footsore men about 70 miles west of the Yangtze at Kuankungling, Hutzuchung, and Hsianglingkou.

Twenty-five miles to the south, one of the original enemy columns from the bridgehead took Wuchiapa on March 7, Kaolingpo on the ninth, and on the tenth halted its drive at Lungtanping and Hungshih, 80 miles west of the river. The Chinese 44th Division had melted before its advance.

After routing the Chinese 41st Division at Hsiawulungkou and Chienchiatai on March 7, the Japanese south column drove through Yutaishan and Chienchiachung on the eighth. Unable to catch up with the fleetfooted troops of the Chinese 26th Corps with whom they wanted to fight, this force came to a halt about 85 miles from its jumping-off position at the bridgehead.

In an effort to salvage something from the pusillanimity of the 26th Corps troops and commanders, the Chinese 103rd Division was rushed into positions south of Muchiatang at the southern anchor of the original defense line with orders "to launch a converging attack against the enemy." On March 8, after two abortive attacks by guerrilla forces of the 41st Division, the disorganized and scattered units of the Chinese 26th Corps settled into new positions 90 miles west of the Yangtze "awaiting the opportune time to destroy the enemy and recapture the original positions."

On March 9, elements of the Chinese 103rd, 44th, 32nd, and 41st divisions rallied sufficiently to make a few timid sorties from their respective areas. By nightfall they had retaken a hill or two and an abandoned enemy patrol post and had actually exchanged fire with the Japanese. On the tenth the 103rd Division "recaptured" an undefended area south of Hsiawulungkou.

At dawn on March 11, having completed their punitive maneuver, the Japanese began to return to Ichang. As they marched to the east, elements of the Chinese River Defense Force followed at a safe, unprovocative distance, reoccupying the fire-blackened ruins of scores of villages west of the Yangtze. On March 13 the

Japanese reached their original positions at the bridgehead, or as the Chinese history stated in its usual misleading language: "Unable to sustain our counter attacks, the enemy fell back to his original positions." There had been no determined Chinese counterattacks at any time during the entire operation. The Chinese record then tidied up the whole farce of this phase of resistance with: "The confrontation returned to what it had been," thus ending "the frightened enemy's design to move west."

The Chinese claimed that their troops had "reaped fruitful gains," including 4,000 to 5,000 Japanese casualties. Actually the Japanese had suffered almost no battle casualties. Whatever fruitful gains may have been reaped, they must have been bitter indeed, for the enemy had ravaged over 8,000 square miles of western Hupei and had left four Chinese divisions in shambles. Because of the large number of desertions during the rout of the Chinese, it is impossible to estimate the number of their actual casualties; but the ranks of the 26th Corps and 32nd Division were so badly depleted that their combat effectiveness was wiped out.

16

Chinese Communist Activities in Hopei, Shansi, and Anhwei, November, 1940, to Early 1941

WITH THE ESTABLISHMENT of the United Front for resistance against Japan in July, 1937, the Chinese Communist Party under Mao Tse-tung had agreed to accept Chiang Kai-shek's general authority over its political enclave in northern Shensi province and its two widely separated military forces. The Red Army in the north had been redesignated the 8th Route Army under the overall command of General Chu Teh. Its three divisions were commanded by Generals Ho Lung, Liu Po-cheng, and Lin Piao. Lin Piao was a consumptive who later became Mao's heir apparent. The second military force, in southern Anhwei and Kiangsu south of the Yangtze, had been reorganized as the New 4th Army (Corps) of one division under General Yeh Ting. It had been agreed that both Communist units were to receive financial and logistical support from the Nationalist Government—which they never got. They were to operate under their respective war-area commands, the 2nd and 3rd. Their principal role was to conduct guerrilla activities against the Japanese. Since Chiang Kai-shek would have liked nothing better than to see them both completely wiped out, he never welcomed news of any combat successes by the Communists. He refused to accept the fact that the Communist armies actually wanted to fight the Japanese.

By 1939, Communist political cadres and guerrilla forces had infiltrated into numerous islands of territory abandoned by Chiang's troops and not occupied by the Japanese. They had reorganized large areas of Hopei, Shantung, and northern Kiangsu from the northwest and parts of Anhwei and Kiangsi south of the Yangtze. In the process of moving into these various political vacuums, the Communists had conducted sustained guerrilla-type attacks against the enemy. They had also won over to their side large numbers of local militia units in search of a leader, and even government troops—in one case, according to the official history, 10 newly organized but dissatisfied regiments. In conducting this form of large-scale recruitment, the Communists were accused of "instigating and supporting revolts" and of "launching violent attacks on government forces." At the time, the scattered bands of Communist guerrillas were not capable of launching violent attacks against any organized body of troops.

In January, 1940, the 129th and 115th divisions of the 8th Route Army and government forces in central and southern Hopei clashed frequently—a natural outcome of the proximity and antagonism of the two armed rivals. The nationalist commanders, suddenly bereft of most of their deserting troops, fled to western Shantung and southeast Shansi with the loyal remnants of their commands. By early summer of 1940 the 8th Route Army had extended its control over western Shantung, eastern Honan, and northern Anhwei. Meanwhile, the bulk of the Communist New 4th Corps had crossed the Yangtze without authorization from Chungking and had headed toward the Lunghai Railway area near the borders of Shantung, Kiangsu, Anhwei, and Honan. Nationalist military and civilian authorities in their path did little more than wring their hands and cry for help.

In mid-July, 1940, the Chungking government, helpless in the face of Communist expansion into territory over which it had lost control, accepted the proposals of Chou En-lai, the Communist representative at the capital, for a more practical working arrangement between the two factions. The Shensi-Kansu-Ninghsia border area was to come under the official control of the Shensi Provincial Government (Communist), although in fact it already was. Hopei, Chahar, and that part of Shantung north of the Yellow River were to come under General Yen Hsi-shan's 2nd War Area, in which command General Chu Teh was to be deputy commander. The 8th Route Army and the New 4th Corps were to be moved to the new territory of the 2nd War Area. The 8th Route Army was to consist of three corps, each of two divisions, and five supplementary regiments each with the equivalent strength of one division. The New 4th Corps was to consist of two divisions. Thus Chiang Kai-shek was forced by military necessity to accept an autonomous army of nine divisions within his nationalist forces—not to mention tens of thousands of guerrillas, local militia, and deserters from his own armies, all under Communist control.

Despite some outward signs of cooperation, both sides—probably at the instigations of their high commands—continued to clash at most points of contact. In October, 1940, after elements of the New 4th Corps had joined the 8th Route Army, hostilities between Chinese and Chinese culminated in the Hungchiao incident, during which the nationalists claimed to have lost 5,000 men, including the commander of the 89th Corps who was killed in the action. Intermittent fighting in this confrontation lasted from mid-October until the end of November. During the prolonged clash, nationalist commanders demonstrated that they were as incapable of facing up to the Chinese Communists as they were to the Japanese. "However," in the words of the official history, "in due consideration of the nation's solidarity and conservation of her strength, it [the nationalist government] had to accomodate itself to such Communist actions."

On October 19, General Ho Ying-chin, the smiling chief of the general staff, directed the New 4th Corps to complete its move north of the Yellow River by the end of November. On December 9, since the order had been ignored, the 8th Route Army was directed to move all of its units north of the Yellow River not later than December 31. At the same time the New 4th Corps was ordered to move all of its units, whether north or south of the Yangtze, across the Yellow River by January 30, 1941. Those elements of the New 4th Corps still in the Nanking-Shanghai-Hangchow area south of the Yangtze delayed taking action on the order.

On January 5, near Maolin just south of the Yangtze, the 40th Division of the 3rd War Area attacked the remaining seven regiments (about 7,500 men) of the New 4th Corps without warning. The Communist troops struck back in self-defense and by evening had forced the 40th Division to withdraw from the scene of the engagement. The next day, January 6, 1941, with the approval of Chiang Kai-shek, General Ku Chu-tung, commander of the war area, "took disciplinary action against the Communists." General Ku's discipline consisted of an unprovoked attack by 80,000 of his troops on units of the New 4th Corps as they were moving up to the riverbank to make the crossing. Within two days the Communist rear guard was massacred. Then, pinned down between the river and the 3rd War Area's overwhelming numbers, the bulk of the New 4th Corps troops managed to hold off repeated assaults against their ever-diminishing perimeter for five more days. As the nationalist troops closed in, the battlefield was marked by concentric rings of Communist dead and wounded. On January 14 the survivors of the New 4th Corps ran out of ammunition, and the government troops moved in for the slaughter. When the guns fell silent, over 2,000 killed and 4,000 wounded Communists lay trampled into the muddy riverbank. All but a handful of the defenseless survivors were taken prisoner, as was Yeh Ting, the Communist commander. Most of the wounded were shot, the prisoners executed. After the obliteration of the New 4th Corps, a drumhead military court sentenced Yeh Ting to imprisonment for an indefinite term.

On January 17, Chiang Kai-shek cancelled the designation New 4th Corps and ordered its units north of the Yangtze to disband. His vindictive action against this unit, which for three years had fought valiantly against the Japanese, split the fiction of the United Front wide open. But with the massacre of the New 4th Corps, Chiang could at last savor a vengeful satisfaction that none of his bandit-suppression campaigns had brought him.

To the north, in southern Shansi and northwest Hopei provinces, the Communist 8th Route Army initiated a campaign of widespread guerrilla attacks against the Japanese on November 20, 1940. Called the one-hundred regiment offensive, the operation involved tens of thousands of troops striking at and disrupting every conceivable enemy activity in the areas under attack— railway lines, roads, bridges, depots, and barracks. Caught by surprise, the Japanese suffered heavy losses in manpower, equipment, and face. After being forced to pull in their horns temporarily, enemy reaction was one of extreme brutality and viciousness. The retaliatory campaign inflicted little harm on the elusive guerrilla units who simply faded into the hills when approached by stronger Japanese forces. But to the helpless farmers and villagers of the two provinces it was a systematic program of murder, rape, torture, burning, and deportation to Manchuria. Under a new policy of kill all, burn all, destroy all, the bloody swords and flaming torches of Japanese troops turned loose left county after county reeking with the stench of countless unburied bodies, charred houses, and rotting granaries. The savage punitive operation did not end until December 3, 1940. As at Nanking, Paoting, and other towns and villages, the Japanese had again set aside the chrysanthemum for the sword.

17

Threatening Clouds: World War, 1940-41

As CHINA was being torn apart by Japan, and by her own hapless government, other cataclysmic events on the world stage were to have a far greater influence on the future of those two countries than their conflict in Asia. Though Britain and France had declared war on Germany on September 1, 1939, two days after Hitler's invasion of Poland, neither side undertook active military operations against the other for seven months. But in two lightning moves on April 9, 1940, German sea and air forces descended on Norway without warning, while its army occupied Denmark. On May 10, again without warning, Germany invaded Belgium, The Netherlands, and Luxembourg. Resistance in Norway ceased on April 30, in The Netherlands on May 14; Belgium surrendered on May 26. On May 17, France was invaded. On June 10, Italy declared war on Britain and France. On June 13, Paris was occupied by the German army, which then plunged on to the south and west to occupy about 60 percent of the country. On Marshal Pétain's suit for peace, an armistice between Germany and France was dictated by Hitler on June 22.

On July 20 the United States initiated the construction of a "two-ocean navy." On September 16 the Selective Service and Training Act was adopted by the American government; it provided for the registration of all males between the ages of 21 and 36 and a training program for an army of 1.2 million men with a reserve force of 800,000. On September 28, an embargo was placed on the export of scrap iron and steel from the United

States; this was intended as a blow at Japan, the principal purchaser of the scrap metal.

On September 22, after Germany had pressured the powerless French government at Vichy into acquiescence, the Japanese 25th Corps, consisting of the Guards Division and 21st Independent Mixed Brigade, under Lieutenant General Shojiro Iida, embarked on the complete occupation of Indo-China—a serious threat to Siam and British-owned Burma. American Undersecretary of State Sumner Welles immediately declared that Japanese expansionist moves in Indo-China clearly endangered United States' interests. On July 25, in reprisal for the Japanese action, President Roosevelt ordered the freezing of all Japanese assets in the United States. Great Britain took identical action on July 26. The Netherlands Indies government did the same on July 28, thereby abrogating an agreement concerning oil shipments to Japan. The latter action was a severe blow to the Japanese armed forces, since their oil reserves, unless constantly replenished, had been calculated to last for no more than two years. The eyes of the "go south" advocates in the Japanese cabinet began to look warily across the Pacific toward American shores and south toward the Philippines and the Netherlands Indies with the latter's huge potential for producing oil.

On September 27, 1940, Germany, Italy and Japan concluded a three-power pact pledging total aid of all members to all members for ten years. On October 11th, German military forces began the occupation of Rumania "to protect the oil wells against British designs." Great Britain was in no position to have "designs" on Rumanian oil or anything but her own salvation. Since August 8th, Germany had launched daily, intensive bombing attacks on London, other industrial cities and military installations throughout England. By the end of October, over 14,000 civilians had been killed in London alone. On November 23rd, having no other choice, Rumania joined the Rome-Berlin-Tokyo alliance. On November 30, the United States Government extended a loan of $100,000,000 to China.

On March 11, 1941, the American Congress passed the lend-lease act which empowered the President to provide arms, goods and services to any nation whose defense he deemed vital to the defense of the United States. Fifty destroyers had already been transferred to Great Britain on September 8, 1940. On May 27, 1941, President Roosevelt declared an unlimited state of emergency in the United States. On June 16th, he ordered the closing of all German consulates throughout the country, a move that three days later was reciprocated by the German and Italian Governments.

On April 13, 1941, Russia and Japan concluded a treaty of neutrality—the Russians in order to protect their Far Eastern flank in case war engulfed them in the west, the Japanese in order to win a free hand in the Pacific area. But on June 22, 1941, German armies invaded Russia without warning on a 2,000-mile front. The chancelleries in Tokyo and Chungking were thrown into a bewildered tailspin by this unexpected piece of treachery against an ally. Unanswered questions drifted about the two capitals like noxious vapors from a miasmic swamp. Under the terms of the three-power pact, would Japan be called upon to attack Russia in Siberia? Russia, with whom a neutrality treaty had been concluded only two months before? Would Tokyo's "go south" policy be abruptly switched to a "go north" policy in the midst of an ever-deepening embroilment in China and the south? Would Russia be compelled to cut off aircraft and other war munitions to China? With her ruined economy and shaken military forces, would China be forced to face Japan completely alone? If Germany forced Russia to her knees, which many senior Chinese generals believed could happen, would the then certain occupation of eastern Siberia by the Japanese destroy all hope in north and central China and compel Chiang Kai-shek's government to retire even farther into the south and west?

At the time, there were no answers for either Tokyo or Chungking. The solution of the international disruption and the future course of the worldwide war could now be found only in Washington, and Washington was plainly antagonistic to the aggressive policies of both the Germans and their allies the Japanese. The big question was who would make the next move.

18

Punitive Japanese Operations, January 24 to May 27, 1941

Operations in Southern Honan
JANUARY 24 TO FEBRUARY 10, 1941

DETERMINED TO FURTHER PUNISH the Chinese army and local peasants for guerrilla and bandit activities in Honan north and northwest of the Huai River, General Enbu of the Japanese 11th Corps decided to follow the pattern set by previous punitive operations. By mid-January, 1941, he had assembled a sizable expeditionary force along the Huai River about 15 miles north of Hsinyang on the Pinghan Railway and over 100 miles north of Hankow. For his planned maneuver General Enbu had at his disposal the 3rd, 39th, 40th, and 17th divisions, 18th Composite Brigade, 8th Regiment of the 4th Division, 67th Regiment of the 15th Division, three armored regiments, one heavy artillery regiment, the equivalent of one cavalry brigade, and supporting air force units. Corresponding to five divisions, the infantry units had a strength of about 105,000 men; supporting armored, cavalry, and artillery units close to 15,000; and the air units a few thousand more for a total strength, including 11th Corps troops, of nearly 125,000 men. For the projected operation the bulk of the 11th Corps was organized in three task forces—Left Flank, Central, and Right Flank. The left column was made up of the 3rd Division plus the 8th Regiment of the 4th Division and one armored regiment, the central column of the 17th Division plus the 67th Regiment of the 15th Division and one armored regiment, and the right (east) column of the 40th Division.

In southern Honan at the time, General Li Tsung-jen of the 5th War Area had at his disposal 3 army groups, 1 "army," the 36th Corps, 1 separate brigade, the 14th Artillery Regiment, and a small number of miscellaneous troops. The 2nd Army Group, commanded by General Sun Lien-chung, consisted of 3 corps[1] of 7 divisions; the 33rd Army Group of 2 corps[2] of 4 divisions; the 31st Army Group of 5 corps[3] of 14 divisions; the "2nd Army" of 1 division; and the 36th Corps of 2 divisions. In General Li's command there were 11 corps with the equivalent strength of 29 divisions numbering a total of about 195,000 men.

On January 20 the Japanese 18th Composite Brigade, 8th Regiment, and a regiment of the 39th Division made a preliminary probing attack against the Chinese 29th Corps of the 31st Army Group. At the same time the Japanese 4th Cavalry Brigade and an armored unit from northern Anhwei moved toward Wuyang, 20 miles west of the railway and 75 miles north of Hsinyang; two regiments of the 39th Division with attached engineer, cavalry, artillery, and armored units moved west from Kaifeng on the Yellow River toward Chengchow at the junction of the Lunghai and Pinghan Railways.

After Chiang Kai-shek and the National Military Council arrived at their usual somewhat beclouded assessment of the situation, Chiang ordered the 5th War Area "to avoid decisive frontal action . . . delay the enemy's main strength . . . cut off communications . . . and conduct flank attacks" to destroy the Japanese. Having thus been given an excuse not to put up a fight, General Li Tsung-jen deployed 1 division near Hsiping on the railway 30 miles north of the Japanese advance positions. The other 28 divisions under his command "lay in hiding on both sides of the enemy's anticipated route of advance . . . disposed in depth" to destroy the Japanese. How Li proposed to hide 28 divisions from enemy reconnaissance aircraft on an almost treeless plain devoted to the growth of rice was not disclosed. No doubt the hiding places were a well-kept secret—except to the Japanese.

On the morning of January 25 the three Japanese columns jumped off—the Left Flank Force from Hsaiolintien and Kuchang, the Central Force from Mingkang, and the Right Flank Force from Chengyang, all between 15 and 20 miles north and northwest of Hsinyang. Since the Chinese defense plan "called for the aversion of needless sacrifices"—except of civilian farmlands and villages—their "main force was held in readiness." Translated into plain language, they did not fire a shot. On January 26 the left and central Japanese columns reached Piyang, Kaoyi, Hsingtien, and Chuehshan, 15 to 20 miles beyond their jumping-off positions. On the twenty-seventh, still without meeting any resistance whatever, the three enemy columns advanced another 10 miles to Chunshui, Shahotien, Chumatien, and Junan. Having nothing to do but march along without hindrance, young Japanese soldiers full of boundless energy relieved their boredom by burning farm hamlets, by occasional looting, and by hastily raping females of any age at the hourly halts for 10-minute rests.

At this point the Chinese command decided that the moment of "readiness" had come. The 31st Army Group's 13th Corps of three divisions[4] moved to within about 5 miles of Japanese-occupied Chunshui; the 85th Corps of three divisions,[5] also part of the 31st Army Group, moved toward Shangtsai, 10 miles north of Junan on the right flank; the 2nd Army Group's 68th Corps of three divisions[6] moved to the Hsianghokuan area on the left flank; the 2nd Army Group's 55th Corps of two divisions[7] moved toward Piyang on the left flank; the 2nd Army Group's 59th Corps of two divisions[8] "advanced" toward Nanyang, nearly 30 miles to the rear of all the maneuvering and completely out of the picture. By the twenty-ninth the Japanese left column had brushed aside the Chinese 68th and 13th corps near Hsianghokuan and had pushed on an additional 10 miles to Chiehkuanting. There the 13th Corps launched a halfhearted attack against the Japanese 3rd Division. At the same time the Chinese 85th Corps, after a brief confrontation with the enemy's right column near Junan, turned tail and withdrew hastily to Shangshui, over 20 miles to the north. The enemy's central column continued north along the Pinghan Railway line to Suiping, from where it dispatched its 67th Regiment to take Shangtsai. The Japanese 17th Division pressed on to the north, took Hsiping without a fight, then turned west toward Wuyang to join the Japanese left-flank column. Faced with a linkup of the enemy's 3rd and 17th divisions at Wuyang, the Chinese 13th and 68th corps fled through Wuyang without stopping for breath and finally came to a halt in the area north of Yeh-hsien—a speedy retreat of 30 miles without having made a stand of any kind. The Chinese history describes this bit of defense with "the enemy failed to trap them . . . before [it] completed the encirclement." The Chinese had again demonstrated that they could run faster than their opponents. The Japanese marched unopposed into Wuyang on January 30.

The official Chinese history then states that "failing to find our forces [north] of Wuyang and Shangtsai"—because presumably they were playing hide-and-seek again—"the enemy turned back." Having disrupted and ravaged some 1,500 square miles of farmland and having chased the Chinese armies for 50 miles without being able to catch up to them, the Japanese commander in this area decided that he had accomplished his punitive mission. He had moved his three columns at will. The Chinese had either retreated before giving battle "to avoid needless sacrifices" or had reacted even more strenuously—by running pell-mell—to any move the Japanese chose to make. In the meantime the Chinese 84th Corps recovered Chengyang on the east flank, the town having been abandoned by the Japanese 40th Division when it had marched to the north four days before.

On the left flank, although the Chinese 55th, 59th, and 68th corps of seven divisions fumbled toward Piyang, the Japanese 3rd and 17th divisions did not appear to consider themselves greatly threatened, as reported by the 5th War Area command. They were not. In its own good time the Japanese 3rd Division moved west from Paoanchai and Fangcheng, 13 and 20 miles west of Wuyang, toward Chenping, 30 miles farther west. On the night of February 2 the Japanese 17th Division departed Wuyang on its return to the south. The Chinese 13th Corps "took advantage of this opportunity to recover Wuyang and Paoanchai," since both were now empty of enemy troops. On February 3 the Japanese 3rd Division occupied Chenping and immediately moved toward Nanyang, 20 miles to the southeast; on the fourth it opened an attack on Nanyang from the northwest and the northeast. But before the action got off the ground, the defending 59th Corps of two divisions[9] pulled out rapidly to the southwest. That evening the Japanese moved into the deserted town of Nanyang. The 59th Corps crawled into defensive positions across the Liao River, 8 miles to the west. After burning much of the town that night, the Japanese 3rd Division departed for Tangho, 15 miles to the southeast. On February 6, it then being safe to do so, the Chinese 38th Division "launched the counter offensive" against nothing and "recaptured" the empty town that night "after a fierce battle."

Meanwhile, on February 4 the Japanese 17th Division, with the 8th and 67th regiments, on its march south from Wuyang, reached the Hsianghokuan-Chunshui area. In the mistaken belief that the enemy was retreating after being defeated, the Chinese 68th Corps attacked the west flank of the Japanese columns. After fending off any possibility of a Chinese assault on the main body, the 17th Division continued on its way toward Piyang, 15 miles beyond. Near Piyang, the Chinese 29th Corps of three divisions summoned up enough offensive spirit to go through the preliminary motions of an attack, but not enough to prevent a portion of the Japanese 3rd Division from linking up with the 17th. On February 7 the bulk of the 3rd Division was marching without incident from Tangho toward Tungpo, 25 miles to the southeast. The Chinese 85th Corps of three divisions "trailed the enemy toward the southeast" at a safe distance. Now that it was apparent that the Japanese had completed the southern Honan maneuver and were returning to their base at Hsinyang, a belated form of courage suddenly infected Chinese commanders. Elements of the 13th, 29th, 55th, and 59th corps "pursued the enemy toward Hsinyang and recovered the original positions," without even establishing contact with the Japanese rear guard. But the Chinese Press Bureau in Chungking, under Doctor Hollington T'ong, trumpeted to the world and a bored press the news of another great victory in the unceasing war of resistance.

While these punitive operations were in progress in southern Honan, three regimental columns from the Japanese 21st and 35th divisions and one column consisting of the 4th Cavalry Brigade moved west from the northern Anhwei–eastern Honan border area. Their sectors of activity ranged from the north bank of the Yellow River across from Kaifeng to Pochow and Huaiyang about 75 miles to the south. This area included farmland still flooded from the 1938 opening of the Yellow River dikes. Since their mission was punitive, Japanese aircraft based at Anyang, 75 miles north of the river, indulged in the indiscriminate bombing of Chowchiakou, 40 miles east of the Pinghan Railway; Chengchow at the junction of the Pinghan and Lunghai Railways; Yeh-hsien, northwest of Wuyang; Wuyang; Loyang, 60 miles west of Chengchow; and other cities and towns within easy range.

On January 29 the Japanese 4th Cavalry Brigade galloped into Huaiyang, 40 miles west of their base at Pochow. "To avert needless sacrifices" and a "threat to their left flank," two entire Chinese corps fled in disorder on the approach of the enemy cavalry. Their panic-stricken rout finally came to a halt along a defense line between Taiho and Fuyang, 50 and 70 miles southeast of Huaiyang. Then, having gone beyond their objective and having pillaged the countryside en route, the Japanese cavalry withdrew to the north and northeast. On February 6 the emboldened Chinese corps "recovered" Taiho and Fuyang, neither of which had been anywhere near the limit of the enemy advance. One regiment of the Japanese 35th Division clashed with the Chinese 3rd Division north of Huaiyang and sent it scurrying to the west. The other two Japanese columns, having encountered no Chinese resistance and having visited their wrath on the hapless villages in their paths, returned to their bases on February 10.

For the Japanese units the Honan operations were more in the nature of a training exercise for new replacements from Japan than an offensive campaign. The Chinese propagandists claimed that the enemy suffered over 9,000 casualties during the 17-day field maneuvers and that they themselves has "suffered less casualties than the enemy." Actually the Japanese lost almost no men in combat for the simple reason that there was almost no combat. Due to the continuous long marches, however, many of their replacement troops suffered from fatigue and foot ailments. With few exceptions, Chinese units should have suffered no battle casualties, since they were seldom even in contact with the Japanese.

Operations in Northwestern Kiangsi
MARCH 15 TO APRIL 2, 1941

The scene of the next Japanese punitive effort was south of the Yangtze in the area of Kiangsi province extending 50 to 60 miles west of Nanchang and Poyang Lake. General Tanaki Anan was assigned to conduct the operation with a temporary corps organization consisting of the 33rd and 34th divisions and the 20th Composite Brigade, a force with a strength of about 52,000 men. In preparation for the offensive, General Anan divided his corps into three columns. The north column, the 33rd Division, was concentrated in the vicinity of Anyi, 20 miles northwest of Nanchang; the center column, the 34th Division, between Hsishan and Wanshoukung, about 8 miles southwest of Nanchang; and the south column, the 20th Composite Brigade, near Shihchachieh, on the Kan River 8 miles south of Nanchang. Anan planned to move the three columns to the west and southwest and to converge in the vicinity of Shangkao, about 65 miles from Nanchang.

West and southwest of the initial Japanese troop deployments, the Chinese 19th Army Group commanded by General Lo Choying waited on three successive lines of resistance for the first enemy move. The 19th Army Group consisted of four corps[10] comprised of 11 divisions—a strength of nearly 75,000 men. Despite his numerical superiority, General Lo took no action to interfere with the concentration of the enemy columns. Aggressive attacks by less than half the troops available to him could have knocked out the Japanese south column before it got well started.

Laid out to form roughly parallel right angles 10 to 15 miles apart, the three Chinese lines of resistance invited Japanese attacks at the center of each, thus crumpling the north and east flanks. As might have been expected, Lo Cho-ying's plan was entirely defensive—"to strike the enemy in our first line positions." Then, having struck, to fall back to the second line and "to lure the enemy to our third line positions . . . for decisive actions." The only decisive action in Lo's mind consisted of a decision to retreat before he was attacked.

At dawn on March 15 the Japanese north column attacked Fenghsin on the first line of resistance 13 miles southwest of Anyi, which it captured with little effort. The Chinese 70th Corps of three divisions "made use of high ground on both banks of the Liao River to offer gradual resistance and lure the enemy." The gradual resistance and luring continued through the second line for over 20 miles all the way to the third line at Hualintsai and Shangfutsun. By March 18, two small detachments of the enemy had been lured into being attacked by two divisions of the 70th Corps. On March 19, hopelessly outnumbered, the Japanese units withdrew to Fenghsin to rejoin the main body of the 33rd Division.

At noon on March 15 the Japanese south column[11] attacked the Chinese 107th Division of the 70th Corps and the 51st Division of the 49th Corps south of Shihchachieh at the junction of the Chin and Kan rivers. The Chinese history states that the enemy attack was repulsed. If it was, the repulse must have been of the briefest duration, for by that night the Japanese had knocked aside the two Chinese divisions and had reached a point north of Tucheng, over 20 miles southwest of the scene of their noontime reverse at the river. On the night of March 20 the Japanese brigade crossed the Chin River at Huifu, 5 miles to the rear of the Chinese second line of resistance, and headed for Yangkungyu to link up with the advancing center column, the 34th Division. The official history states that "a portion of the enemy . . . was destroyed by our forces" at this point. In view of the almost unimpeded rate of the Japanese advance of over 50 miles, their destroyed portion must have been very small indeed.

On March 16 the Japanese center column began its drive from southwest of Nanchang along the north bank of the Chin River toward Kaoan. The Chinese 74th Corps of three divisions met this threat by settling down on the third line of resistance from Szehsi to Kuanchiao and Tangu. The 17th Division of the 70th Corps was ordered "to exert pressure on the enemy's flanks in the south," which it did by remaining well south of the Chin River at least 5 miles from the enemy's flanks. Meanwhile, the 26th and 105th divisions of the Chinese 49th Corps, which up to this time had remained east of the Kan River some 40 miles from the combat area, were ordered to attack the enemy south of the Chin River. By the time the foot-dragging 49th Corps arrived south of the Chin River, the enemy was two days' march ahead of it. At this point the 72nd Corps of two divisions "was ordered to operate in the vicinity of Tahsia and Kanfang to respond to the operations." Since the two towns were 20 miles off the route of the Japanese center column, the nature of the corps' response was presumably maintaining surveillance from a distance. On March 20 the combined Japanese center and south columns attacked the Chinese third line of resistance between Kuanchiao and Szehsi. By March 21 they had bulldozed through the Chinese lines and had reached Shangchichia, 5 miles farther south. The Chinese 57th and 58th divisions of the 74th Corps had marched south on March 18 from their positions of surveillance to join the battle. These two divisions stood fast in a determined defense just north of Shangkao, the obvious goal of the Japanese "conical attack." During the three-day fight, a small enemy task force fought its way across the Chin River to outflank the Chinese positions, but it was forced to withdraw.

Between March 22 and 25 the Chinese 70th Corps reached Kuanchiao, 5 miles north of the battle area; the New 15th Division of the 72nd Corps reached Shihkouhsu, 10 miles to the east. Although the Chinese proclaimed these moves constituted a "ring of encirclement," their trap was wide open on the north side. When the Chinese 26th and 105th divisions of the 49th Corps seized Yangkungyu and Lungmenyu on the Japanese center column's route back to Kaoan, the position of the enemy's 34th Division and 20th Composite Brigade could have been seriously endangered—if the Chinese had had enough aggressive spirit to close in on them. On March 25 the 215th Regiment of the Japanese 33rd Division—the north column—broke through the Chinese encirclement at Tsunchienchieh, 15 miles north of the battle area, and joined the 34th Division at Kuanchiao. "The encirclement of the [Chinese] 70th Corps," according to the Chinese history, "was forced to yield making it possible for the enemy forces to link up." Meanwhile, part of the Japanese 20th Brigade rammed its way through the Chinese 49th Corps and reached Huifu, 15 miles northeast of the main battle lines at Shangkao. The three-day struggle was bloody, with considerable hand-to-hand fighting after the Chinese defense had been pulverized by air and artillery attacks. Both sides suffered heavy casualties.

By nightfall on the twenty-fifth the Japanese commander decided that a continuation of the fight could prove to be more costly than the capture of Shangkao was worth. The town had virtually been wiped out by raging fires, air attacks, and artillery barrages. The punitive objective of the operation had already been accomplished, both on the countryside and in the heavy casualties inflicted on Chinese troop units. General Anan ordered his troops to return to their bases. During the night Japanese forward elements broke off the engagement, and the main body of the 34th Division and 20th Brigade started out on the march to the northeast. On the same night a Chinese attempt to effect a second encirclement fizzled out. They were afraid to risk further casualties by closing in on the enemy. On the twenty-sixth, troops of the Chinese 74th Corps and 19th Division of the 70th Corps recovered Szehsi, which by that time had been evacuated by the Japanese 20th Brigade. During the night of the twenty-sixth the Japanese 34th Division launched a heavy counterattack at the boundary between the 107th Division of the 70th Corps and the New 15th Division of the 72nd Corps, "greatly shaking our [the Chinese] positions and effecting the destruction of the enemy." It set the Chinese back on their heels and permitted an orderly Japanese withdrawal—which had been its purpose. During the night of the twenty-seventh the entire Japanese force pulled out and took the road to the northeast. Enroute to Kaoan, Chinese units lay in wait for the column at Tsunchienchieh, 4 miles west of the road; at Yangkungyu; and at Lungmenyu. But since they did not attack, the threat of their presence had little, if any, effect on Japanese troops. On March 28 the Chinese 74th Corps reoccupied the shattered, empty town of Kuanchiao. On the twenty-ninth the Chinese 26th and 105th divisions attacked the Japanese rear guard at Yangkunghsu and Lungtuanhsu. Sharp engagements occurred at each place, but the enemy main body continued on its way in safety. After the Japanese had cleared Kaoan, the Chinese 49th Corps, less the 5th Reserve Division, and the New 15th Division undertook "the pursuit to Tacheng and Niuhsing" at a sensible distance calculated not to raise the ire of the Japanese commander. The Chinese 70th Corps "led the pursuit to Fenghsin" and Anyi—also being careful to "avert needless sacrifices." The 49th Corps recovered Kaoan and Hsiang-fukuan on April 1 and Hsishan, Wanshoukung, and Shihchachieh, between 5 and 10 miles from Nanchang, on the second. The 70th Corps reoccupied Fenghsin on April 2. During the next few days it cautiously moved toward Anyi, occupied a few abandoned outposts southwest of the town "and then halted the attack."

This was as far as the Japanese intended to permit the Chinese to go in what the Chinese press bureau called an "unprecedented [Chinese] tactical victory" that had "dealt a fatal blow against the enemy."

Although the Japanese had paid for their operation with about 3,000 casualties (15,000 according to the Chinese press bureau), the outcome had in no sense been "a fatal blow" to their 34th Division and 20th Composite Brigade. Quite the contrary: again they had beaten a troublesome area into meek submission and had maneuvered more or less at will against a numerically superior Chinese army. The 19th Army Group had suffered at least 10,000 battle casualties and, as usual, considerably more than that number in desertions.

Operations in Southern Shansi

MAY 7–27, 1941

In the spring of 1941 the Japanese North China Front Army turned its attention to that part of southern Shansi just north of the Yellow River between Loyang and Tungkuan at the so-called Big Bend. Still smarting from the Chinese Communist winter guerrilla activities in northern Shansi and Hopei—though the punishment administered to the people of that area had been brutal enough to satisfy even the Japanese—the high command was further enraged by the troublesome presence of General Wei Li-huang's 1st War Area armies in the 20- to 40-mile strip north of the river. For three and one-half years both Chinese nationalist and Communist troops had harassed the Japanese occupying forces in southern Shansi. They had raided roads, railway lines, and river communications constantly, then slipped into the protection of the rugged mountain ranges that terminated at the Big Bend and to the east—the Chungtiao, Luliang, and Taihang mountains.

General Terauchi in Peking decided that the time had come for a drastic mop-up campaign of the area and the establishment of the Yellow River as the barrier between his and the Chinese forces. Though his troops had been drawn into numerous minor actions to quiet his three major provinces of Shansi, Hopei, and

Shantung, his command had not been involved in a major campaign since the summer of 1938. In late March, Terauchi began to concentrate the units he had designated to conduct the projected operation. To the 35th, 36th, 37th, and 41st divisions already in southern Shansi and northern Honan he added the 21st and 33rd divisions, the 4th Cavalry Brigade, and the 9th and 16th composite brigades from Hsuchow, Kaifeng, and western Shansi. The North China Front Army headquarters retained direct command over the 35th, 21st, and 33rd divisions and the 4th Cavalry Brigade. The other units, the 36th, 37th, and 41st divisions and the 9th and 16th brigades, were placed under the command of the 1st Temporary Corps. The six divisions and three brigades had a total strength of about 150,000 men. Units of the 3rd Air Force based at Anyang were assigned to support the operation.

The Japanese 35th and 21st divisions and one regiment of the 4th Cavalry Brigade were assembled in the Hsinyang-Poai area, about 30 miles northeast of Loyang; the 33rd Division and one regiment of the 4th Cavalry Brigade between Yangcheng and Chincheng, about 50 miles due north of Loyang; the 41st Division and the 9th Brigade at Chianghsien, about 40 miles north of the Yellow River and 70 miles northeast of Tungkuan; and the 36th and 37th divisions with the 16th Brigade in the Wenhsi-Hsiahsien-Anyi area, 20 to 45 miles north-northeast of Tungkuan.

General Wei Li-huang's 1st War Area command in southern Shansi north of the Yellow River consisted of the 5th Army Group of 2 corps,[12] each of 2 divisions, and 1 separate division; the 14th Army Group of 2 corps,[13] each of 2 divisions; and 5 corps[14] containing 10 divisions. The 9 corps of 19 divisions had an approximate strength of 135,000 men. In addition, about 18,000 men from the 27th Corps of 3 divisions were available to move west from the Taihang Mountains in the Shansi-Honan border area.

On the afternoon of May 7 the Japanese 35th and 21st divisions with one regiment of the 4th Cavalry Brigade moved from the Hsinyang area in two columns to attack Tsiyuan, 20 miles west of their concentration area, and Menghsien, 20 miles to the southwest. At noon on May 8, after a few hours of disconnected resistance, the three defending divisions of the Chinese 9th Corps abandoned Tsiyuan and Menghsien in a disorderly retreat to prepared positions at Fengmenkou and Lungwanwo, 20 and 13 miles to the west. The Japanese columns caught up with the fleeing Chinese during the night of May 8 and attacked at daybreak on the ninth. The Chinese stood their ground until the morning of May 10, when enemy air strikes induced them to pull out for the west to take up positions "for a converging attack on the enemy." The converging attack never got off the ground; instead, the Japanese converged on the Chinese, drove them out of their defenses, and by May 11 were pressing on to link up with the Japanese 41st Division from the west. The Chinese 47th Division and a part of the 42nd escaped across the Yellow River at Kuangkou, 18 miles west of Loyang. They managed to effect the crossing just in time, for on the morning of May 12 the Japanese south column swept past Kuangkou and that afternoon reached Maotien, 15 miles farther west, in a move that blocked the entire north bank of the river. On the same day the Japanese north column joined elements of the 41st Division at Shaoyuan, 10 miles west of Fengmenkou. The other two divisions of the Chinese 9th Corps[15] were ordered to the mountainous area north of Tsiyuan to take up guerrilla operations, the usual Chinese solution when nothing else could be devised for a unit that was no longer effective. In five days the Japanese had knocked out four Chinese divisions in the eastern sector of the operation.

On May 7, elements of the Japanese 33rd Division moved 15 miles west from Yangcheng. That afternoon they attacked the defense positions of the Chinese 98th Corps of two divisions at Tungfeng. The Chinese held fast against one assault after another for five days. During that time one Japanese battalion broke through the east flank of the defense line and pushed into Hsuehshan, in the rear of Tungfeng and about 10 miles to the southeast; but since this thrust failed to collapse the Chinese positions, the enemy force withdrew. On the thirteenth the entire Japanese 33rd Division and its attached cavalry regiment attacked in a double envelopment. This proved too much for the defending Chinese; the bulk of the 98th Corps fell back about 10 miles to Henghochen. But one regiment of its 42nd Division had had more than enough; it broke and ran for over 35 miles to the Yellow River and crossed to safety before the enemy was able to cut off its escape.

On the afternoon of May 7 the Japanese 41st Division and the 9th Composite Brigade, moving south from Chianghsien and Henglingkuan, struck the Chinese 43rd Corps at Fulochen, 18 miles north of the Yellow River. The force of the enemy attack carried it through the center of the Chinese positions. At 2:00 P.M. on May 8, with the defense line split wide open, the two Chinese divisions fell back to the east and west of the Japanese breakthrough. A strong enemy column poured through the opening and that evening captured Yuanchu on the river. Racing in every direction to escape the Japanese juggernaut, the Chinese "were unable to achieve coordinated shifting [to] the offensive." On May 9 and 10 the Japanese 41st Division dispatched two columns to the east and west of Yuanchu. A few miles from Yuanchu the west column ran into units of the Chinese 5th Army Group's five divisions trying to escape across the river. Part of the Chinese troops managed to make the crossing, but the Japanese forced the bulk of them back into the Chungtiao Mountains, then continued on their way to seize Wufuchien, 12 miles west of Yuanchu, on May 11. The east column brushed aside scattered Chinese resistance and took Shaoyuan on the twelfth. There it linked up with the 35th and 21st divisions from Tsiyuan.

At 4:00 P.M. on May 7 the Japanese 36th and 37th divisions and the 16th Composite Brigade launched a strong attack at the boundary between the Chinese 3rd and 80th corps of four divisions at Chiangtienchen, about 10 miles south of Hsihsien. By evening on the same day the Japanese had penetrated the Chinese lines and forced a wedge of troops through the center. The two Chinese corps fell back to the vicinity of Wangyuan, 14 miles east of Chiangtienchen, "to continue the resistance"—that had hardly begun. On the morning of May 9 the enemy threw its entire weight against the new Chinese positions. By that afternoon the vigor of the assault compelled the Chinese to retreat to Taichaitsun on the river 12 miles southeast of Wangyuan. There, cornered with the river at their backs, the Chinese fought off repeated enemy attacks. Casualties, including the commander of the Chinese 27th Division, the assistant division commander, and the chief of staff, were very heavy in the furious Chinese effort to save their lives; but they stood their ground and prevented the Japanese from taking the small river town.

After their defeat in three of the four sectors, scattered units of the Chinese 5th and 14th army groups attempted to conduct independent guerrilla operations against the Japanese in the Chungtiao Mountains. But since these forces were cut off from any possibility of resupply, General Wei Li-huang ordered the bulk of the units to "break out," slip through gaps in the over-extended Japanese lines, move well to the north and conduct guerrilla operations in enemy rear areas where they could live off the countryside. On May 13 the Chinese began to break out. From the eighteenth to the twentieth the 3rd and 17th corps arrived north of the Fen River, 60 miles to the rear of the most advanced Japanese positions; the 10th Division of the 93rd Corps reached Tuanshih, 70 miles north of the Yellow River; the 98th Corps, less that part of its 42nd Division that had run out on the whole show, north of Hsinshui, about 70 miles from the Yellow River; and the 15th Corps in the mountains north of Tsiyuan. At the same time the 43rd Corps and the 27th Corps from the Shansi-Honan border area somewhat belatedly went through the motions of "responding to the operations"—after they were over—by making a leisurely advance toward Japanese positions north of the river. But by May 27 the operations in southern Shansi had ended over 20 miles from the nearest Japanese outpost. The entire 1st War Area command of organized troop units north of the Yellow River had been broken up into ineffectual guerrilla forces "ready for the counter offensive," which of course never took place. The Japanese had succeeded in wrecking a cohesive force of over 150,000 troops—at least it had had pretensions to cohension before it failed its test in battle.

In October, 1941, the Japanese extended their control of the lower Yellow River in Shansi and Honan provinces by seizing the much bombed railway junction of Chengchow. After an unopposed river crossing, they marched into the battered city against almost no resistance. This made it theoretically possible for the Japanese to open the Pinghan Railway line from Peking to Hankow, but regular train service was frequently interrupted by Chinese Communist troops and guerrilla forces operating from the mountainous Shansi-Hopei border area.

Since there was no bridge at Tungkuan on the south bank of the Big Bend of the Yellow River, the Japanese made no attempt to take it. Later, Chinese and Japanese garrison troops facing each other across the river established rapport. For nearly four years they regularly exchanged wine, liquor, food supplies, and other amenities by boat in order to alleviate the hardships and boredom of a "war situation" that remained static until the end.

With no regular means of supply, most of the 1st War Area troops (five divisions)[16] who had slipped into the Taihang Mountains to be "ready for the counter offensive" soon slipped out of their uniforms to ready themselves for careers of banditry or to disappear into the neighboring farms and villages. Before long the roving bands became as great a curse to the straightlaced Chinese Communists as they were to the peasants of the countryside. The official Chinese history refers to this situation with: "As our isolated force in [the] Taihang Mountains [did] not last long, the Chinese Communists were able to wrest superiority in the Japanese occupied areas. This led to many deep ramifications later." It did indeed.

19

The Second Battle of Changsha, September 7 to October 8, 1941

DURING THE FIVE MONTHS between April and September, 1941, another strange lull in major military operations in China belied the carefully nurtured myth of a heroic nation in daily battle for its very existence. As great events developed in Europe, Chiang Kai-shek saw the flame of hope flare brighter. He welcomed any respite that might relieve him of the necessity of taking positive action. It permitted him to readjust and shift the delicate political balances between himself and his more fractious generals, particularly General Hsueh Yueh, commander of the 9th War Area with headquarters at Changsha. Always suspicious of General Hsueh's intentions and ambitions, for Hsueh had long been outspokenly impatient with the stalling tactics of the national government he served, the generalissimo did not dare to replace his most able and forceful general. Chiang was unwillingly compelled to accept the fact that if it had not been for Hsueh Yueh, Hunan province and the railway from Hankow to Canton would have long since been lost and Chungking seriously endangered.

The Japanese Imperial Headquarters also welcomed the lull in military operations during the summer of 1941. Still uncertain as to Japan's role vis-à-vis Hitler's unexpected invasion of Russia, and deeply embroiled in plans for strategy in the Pacific, the military-dominated cabinet in Tokyo needed a wait-and-see period. But as Japan's ally, Germany, blitzed its way across the steppes of the Soviet Union, confidence and arrogant self-assurance began to return. Before the end of July the Japanese moved south to occupy all of Indo-China; and further dazzling prospects for conquest beckoned—Siam, the British Malayian states, Burma, the Philippines, the Netherlands Indies, the Pacific islands, and even Australia and India. Who could now interfere with Japan's pursuit of her plans? France lay prostrate under the heavy boot of German occupation; after Dunkirk, Britain was driven back to the defense of her own island; The Netherlands had been conquered; the United States seemed too soft and indecisive to offer any resistance other than words. And China was a huge amorphous mass of corruption to be viewed with contempt, a country whose inept armies had been pushed at will across vast expanse of territory, whose people had been terrorized into submission. But there was still one Chinese field commander who, until destroyed, stood as a threat to Japanese freedom of action—General Hsueh Yueh at Changsha. He and his bastion of defense some 350 miles east of Chungking had to be wiped out. At the same time, overall Japanese military strength had to be husbanded for the wider operations that at last promised to raise the Japanese Empire to its desired position of superiority.

General Tadaki Anan was given the honor of putting an end to Hsueh Yueh, his 9th War Area command, and the symbol of resistance that the city of Changsha had become. In mid-August, 1941, General Anan's 11th Corps was augmented for the operation against the Tung Ting Lake area to include the 6th, 40th, 4th, and 3rd divisions, one brigade from each of the 33rd and 13th divisions, the 18th and 14th composite separate brigades, one heavy artillery regiment, and one supporting engineer regiment. In addition, scores of gunboats and armed motor launches were allocated to the corps to operate on the lake and the numerous nearby river channels. About 100 fighter and bomber aircraft would support General Anan's ground forces of over 125,000 men. Shortly after the middle of August the entire corps assembled in the Yochow-Linhsiang-Hsitang-Chungyang area north of the Hsinchiang River that flowed into Tung Ting Lake about 65 miles north of Changsha. During the initial concentration of the corps, two battalions from the 18th and 14th brigades and two regiments, the 115th from the 13th Division and the 235th from

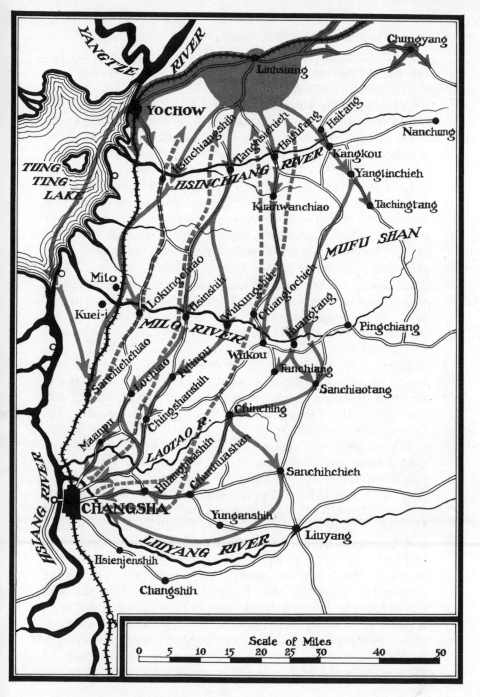

The Second Battle of Changsha (Broken lines
show Japanese withdrawal.)

the 40th Division, had not yet arrived. But this detail in no way lessened the determination of General Anan and his staff to carry out their sublime mission.

Waiting for the Japanese blow to fall, General Hsueh Yueh's 9th War Area command consisted of General Lo Cho-ying's 19th Army Group comprised of the New 3rd Corps of 2 divisions, 2 independent divisions, the Kiangsi Peace Preservation Column with a strength of 1 division, and the 2nd Advance Column of 1 division; the 30th Army Group, which included the 78th Corps of 1 division, and the 3rd, 4th, 5th, and 8th Advance Columns, each with a strength of 1 division; 11 corps[1] with a total of 31 divisions; and two advance columns[2] with a strength of 2 divisions. The entire command included the equivalent of 44 divisions with a strength of close to 300,000 men.

As soon as the Japanese intentions were apparent, Chiang Kai-shek sprang into aggressive activity and ordered the adjacent war areas "to tie down the enemy" and the 9th War Area "to offer gradual resistance and lure the enemy's main force to the bank of the Laotao River," a few miles north of Changsha. Having thus contributed his solution to the military situation, the generalissimo settled down to the more serious business of propaganda and the study of reports from his secret police on the activities of various political combinations seeking power—particularly the Communists.

The 9th War Area disposed the bulk of its troops on four east–west defense lines along the south banks of four more or less parallel rivers flowing into Tung Ting Lake and the Hsiang River—the Hsinchiang, Milo, Laotao, and Liuyang. The 20th, 58th, and 4th corps of 11 divisions manned the northern line along the Hsinchiang River with the equivalent of 3 divisions from the 4th and 20th corps deployed near Nanchung, Mufushan, and north of Pingchiang, 35 to 40 miles east of the Yochow-Changsha railway line, "to attack the enemy's flank and rear." The second defense line along the Milo River, 30 miles south of the first, was manned by the 99th, 72nd, 10th, 79th, and 26th corps of 15 divisions with strong elements between Pingchiang and Liuyang, about 40 miles east of the railway line, "to attack the enemy's flank and rear." The third position along the Laotao River, 25 miles south of the Milo, was not occupied. The fourth along the

Liuyang River, 10 to 15 miles south of the Laotao, was held by the 2nd Provisional, 78th, 37th, and 74th corps of 8 divisions as the last defense line to which the other corps would finally withdraw. The disposition of all units presupposed a gradual retreat—again before the battle was joined. Though the concentration of the Japanese 11th Corps had stretched out over a period of more than two weeks, the Chinese forces made no serious attempt to interfere.

On September 7, 1941, while probing for weak spots in the Chinese defense positions south of Chungfang and Hsitang, 50 and 35 miles east of Yochow, elements of the Japanese 6th Division clashed with Chinese units from the 4th and 58th corps. After skirmishing for half a day, Japanese reconnaissance forces withdrew to the north bank of the Hsinchiang River. For the next ten days, while the Japanese 11th Corps completed its troop dispositions, there was no activity. This situation can only be described as bordering on the absurd. Completely aware of enemy preparations, over 65,000 Chinese troops simply waited in their muddy trenches without firing a shot at the Japanese only a few hundred yards across the river. On September 16 a Japanese flotilla of small craft used as transports for three battalions of the 14th Brigade and a collection of armed motor launches and junks manned by a force of marines cruised about Tung Ting Lake in an area 40 miles north of Changsha. Though this armada "threatened western Hunan," the Chinese made no effort to respond to the threat.

At dawn on September 17, four Japanese columns crossed the Hsinchiang River against slight Chinese opposition at four points 13 to 30 miles south and southwest of Yochow—Hsinchiangshih, Tunghsichieh, Hsilufang, and Kangkou. Although parts of the Chinese 4th, 58th, and 20th corps "offered sustained resistance" along the defense lines, the bulk of the three corps sustained themselves east and northeast of the enemy columns from which vantage points they "attacked the enemy flank and rear" with no effect on its advance to the south. The Japanese dispatched a column to Tachingtang, 12 miles southeast of Kangkou, where they held off the Chinese flank attacks. The four parallel enemy columns[3] proceeded on their way with virtually no impedence. On September 19 they reached the Milo River, over 20 miles south of the Hsinchiang. On the twentieth the Japanese crossed the Milo between Kueiyi and Lokungchiao, about 10 miles from the mouth of the river; at Hsinshih; at Changlochieh-Wukungshih; and between Wukou and Huangtang, 20 miles east of Kueiyi. Again they encountered no serious Chinese resistance. After the enemy crossings had been completed, the Chinese 92nd Division of the 99th Corps and the 10th, 26th, and 37th corps launched feeble counterattacks, then fell back for 10 to 20 miles to defense positions near Tanchiang on the east flank, Fulinpu, Lochiao, and Sanchiehchiao.

The Japanese left-flank column turned eastward at Tanchiang, bypassed the Chinese defenses completely, pushed through San-chiaotang, veered to the south again, and headed for Chinching, 25 miles below the Milo River. Frontal and flank attacks by the Chinese 26th and 4th corps to block the advance of this enemy force failed to do more than slow down its steady progress. The other three Japanese columns struck the Chinese positions at Fulinpu, Lochiao, and Sanchiehchiao and slammed right through them with ease. The Chinese forces fell back rapidly to their third and fourth defense lines along the south banks of the Laotao and Liuyang rivers "to lure the enemy and seek decisive battle." While this luring was going on, the Japanese east column, the 6th Division, divided its forces at Chinching. Its two elements continued their drive between the two rivers, now turning in a westerly direction toward Changsha. One column swept through Sanchihchieh, skirted the north bank of the Liuyang River, and by September 26 had passed Huanghuashih, only 16 miles east of Changsha. The second task force marched through Chunhua-shan on the Chinese third line of defense and, having brushed aside all resistance, reached a point 7 miles southeast of Changsha on the twenty-sixth. On the same day the Japanese 4th and 40th divisions, having crossed the Laotao River and pushed through only slight resistance in their path, came up against the defense works of Changsha, 5 miles east of the city. They attacked in full strength at once.

This was the moment for which Hsueh Yueh had been waiting. With lightning speed he pounced. His first order to his commanders was to hold the Changsha defense positions regardless of cost, not to give one inch of ground to the enemy. This sudden reversal of Chinese tactics and the ferocity of the resulting resistance caught the overconfident Japanese off balance. During the night of the twenty-sixth the defending Chinese stood fast against one assault after another. Daylight revealed stacks of dead and wounded between the lines—this time as many Japanese as Chinese. The Japanese managed to infiltrate detachments of plainclothes troops into the city during the pre-dawn hours on the twenty-seventh. By 4:00 P.M. that day they had all been caught and executed. In a second effort to create panic in Chinese rear areas, Japanese airborne troops were dropped between the positions of the 10th, 78th, and 2nd Provisional corps. Within 24 hours this entire force was picked off one by one and obliterated.

By this time, September 27, General Hsueh had hurled 20 divisions of his 72nd, 26th, 74th, 37th, 10th, 2nd Provisional, 79th, and 78th corps into the raging battle northeast and east of Changsha. At the same time, 11 divisions of the 4th, 20th, and 58th corps were freewheeling against Japanese rear communication and supply lines 40 to 50 miles northeast of Changsha, with the 99th Corps of 3 divisions about 30 miles north of the city. All four enemy routes from the north were completely cut. Nine Chinese divisions of the 74th, 26th, and 72nd corps, having crossed the Liuyang River and pushed on toward Changsha from the east, attacked the main Japanese force[4] of nearly 100,000 men from the rear. Meanwhile, the 3rd, 5th, and 6th war-area commanders launched attacks to the east, west (on Ichang), and north of Hankow to prevent the enemy from shifting units to aid its beleaguered 11th Corps.

General Hsueh Yueh's plan had worked. He had bottled up the Japanese 11th Corps in an area of about 10 by 15 miles between the Laotao and the Liuyang rivers. With no hope of reinforcements or supplies, General Tadaki Anan had no choice but to break off the battle as best he could and fight his way back to Yochow.

At 4:00 P.M. on September 30 the Japanese began to break out of the Chinese encirclement. With no possibility of supplies reaching them, they were in a desperate situation; but, as had happened so many times before, the Chinese failed to exploit their success by closing in before the breakout was completed. The enemy forces managed to fight their way across the Laotao River and headed north in a badly demoralized and disorderly retreat. General Hsueh made them pay for every one of the 60 miles back to Yochow. The Chinese 4th, 20th, and 99th corps intercepted three Japanese columns at Maanpu, Chingshanshih, and Chinching north of the Laotao River and exacted a heavy toll of casualties before the enemy succeeded in battling through its tormenters. The Chinese 79th Corps trailed the Japanese 4th and 40th divisions to Changlochieh and Hsinshih on the Milo River with unceasing attacks on their rear and flanks, shooting all wounded and stragglers. The 72nd and 58th corps raced north to intercept the Japanese 6th Division at Yanglinchieh and Kuanwanchiao south of the Hsinchiang River. Though the routed enemy troops finally struggled across the last river barrier, their wake was strewn with abandoned arms and equipment and numerous dead.

Meanwhile, the 26th, 74th, and 2nd provisional corps mopped up the battlefield area between the Liuyang and Laotao rivers, looting Japanese casualties of shoes and small valuables, putting the wounded out of their misery with a bullet in the head or a knife in the throat, and hunting down half-starved stragglers. As was customary, those taken alive did not endure the ignominious lives of prisoners for long. The victorious Chinese troops crossed the Milo River on October 5, the Hsinchiang on the eighth. As a discomfited General Anan and his 11th Corps crawled back into their original positions near Yochow, the second battle of Changsha came to an end. For once, the Chinese official history correctly stated the case: "our forces scored a major victory in the Second Battle of Changsha."

The last battle in the Sino-Japanese conflict to take place in 1941 was indeed a major victory for the Chinese. It could have been an overwhelming victory had the 9th War Area troops pressed their advantage through Yochow and beyond. They had the Japanese 11th Corps on the ropes and ready to cave in. But even the bold and resourceful Hsueh Yueh could not bring himself to plunge into an offensive campaign that might have destroyed the 11th Corps. As it was, from the Chinese viewpoint, General Hsueh's triumph had been complete; his tactics in drawing the enemy into a trap had proved their worth. But in Chungking, Chiang Kai-shek viewed the victory with mixed feelings, for it had added to Hsueh Yueh's already considerable reputation.

Chiang would rather have seen any of his other generals acclaimed the victor of Changsha, but he was forced to accept the unpalatable fact that the tough, recalcitrant, almost rebellious Hsueh Yueh was the only one who was capable of gaining victory. As for General Hsueh, his arrogant self-confidence and impatience with Chiang's dilatory policies now knew no bounds. Others in high places, equally impatient with Chiang Kai-shek and thirsting for personal power, began to eye Hsueh Yueh as a possible front man should the generalissimo lose his political control or come to an untimely end.

Without organization, effective leadership, motivation, or a national will to fight, the vast human resources of China had proved to be little more than a stumbling block for the determined Japanese. The China of 1937–41 had not been a national entity, for its hundreds of millions of people had lacked any feeling of unity with their government. They had had little to do with the rival military structures that dominated the country.

With few exceptions, Chinese nationalist commanders were not cast in the heroic mold. Nor were they gifted with the strength of character to take great risks to achieve great ends. Their tactics had been confined to delays and stopgaps; their military vision had been myopic. Chiang Kai-shek had elected to stall, to sacrifice land and people, as he waited with the ephemeral hope that America would intervene to save him from the fate that his miscalculations were bringing about—despite America's tradition of isolation. Neither he, the army, nor the people of China had been willing to take victory by their own efforts. Rather, they had chosen to buy time with a ruined countryside, pillaged cities, lost battles, and a few indecisive victories. They had been unable or unwilling to unite.

All this Japan had well known. Despite the empire's numerically inferior population and military forces, Japan had been willing to risk any price for victory, and in this effort had had the national support of a regimented and disciplined people. They had coldly calculated that the advantages of time and territory that China squandered as she waited hopefully for a powerful ally would be negated by the complete paralysis of her fragmented will.

On the other hand, Chinese Communist leaders were imbued

with an implicit faith that time would destroy both her enemies, Japan and nationalist China. By sheer force of will they had inculcated their peasant followers and their ill-equipped army with a burning conviction in the rightness of their cause. Although vastly inferior numerically to its opponents, the Red Army had been thoroughly motivated with a will to win and a determination to make any sacrifice for ultimate victory.

20

The Storm Breaks, December 7, 1941

DURING THE SUMMER AND FALL of 1941, the Wagnerian drama of world conflict was being carried out on stages far from the river valleys of China. While British and Free French forces battled Italian troops for control of Ethiopia, a German and Italian army under General Erwin Rommel attacked the British in Egypt. On April 17 a German army completed the occupation of Yugoslavia; by April 27 Greece fell. On June 22 German armies began "Operation Barborossa"—the invasion of Russia—and by mid-September, they had captured Kiev and had begun the long siege of Leningrad. By mid-October, Odessa had fallen under assault. To meet the staggering German blows, Stalin was compelled to shift troops from eastern Siberia to his crumbling western front, and the Japanese militarists in Tokyo knew that their northern flank was now safe; they could now turn their backs on the north and focus their eyes on the south. The time had come for the initiation of their great plan.

Due to long neglect and a succession of parsimonious congresses, the United States armed forces were ill prepared for war. Nor could the American government meet all the pleas for aid from its allies. After the British disaster at Dunkirk, the American Army had been stripped of its weapons to rearm England. Though war production had greatly increased, neither the army and air corps nor the navy would be ready even for a defensive war until the spring of 1942. In September, Chief of Staff George C. Marshall warned that the nation faced an imminent two-ocean war, that it must immediately embark on a vast production program, and that Germany could not be defeated without massive American participation. He pointed out that when war came, the principal U.S. effort must be geared to the defeat of Hitler first—while maintaining the strongest possible defense against Japan. Both Roosevelt and Churchill agreed.

So Japan had to be fended off, and to that end the defenses of the Philippine Islands had to be built up. On July 26 General Douglas MacArthur was named Commander in Chief Far East and placed in control of all armed forces in the islands. He at once urged that a large force of B-17's be assigned to his command, pointing out that they could stop, or at least deter, any Japanese advance toward Malaya and Singapore, not to mention the Philippines.

On August 9 Japanese Imperial General Headquarters came to the momentous decision which all along had been the lode star of its inflexible thinking. Orders were issued to the army and navy to prepare for a war with the United States and Great Britain that would start by the end of November.

On August 17 Roosevelt warned the Japanese ambassador, Admiral Kichisaburo Nomura, that any further military domination in Asia by Japan would force the United States "to take immediately any and all steps necessary to safeguard American rights and interests."

On August 18 Roosevelt extended the period of draft service in the army by eighteen months.

On August 24 Churchill pledged British aid to the United States if it became involved in a war with Japan.

By the end of August, the Japanese Navy had readied the 6th Fleet, 11th Air Fleet, 3rd Fleet, 1st Air Fleet and the Southern Expeditionary Fleet for war.

At 10:00 A.M. on September 6 an Imperial Conference was held in Room East Number One of the imperial palace in Tokyo. As the emperor listened impassively from his throne chair at the head of the conference tables, various ministers respectfully expounded on the perils the empire faced in the worsening world situation. Minister of War Field Marshal Sugiyama stated forcefully that the time had finally come to decide for peace or war. Then, to the surprise of the participants, the emperor broke with tradition by quoting a short poem written by his grandfather, the emperor Meiji, which asked why the world need be torn by unsettled winds. The stunned ministers bowed in silence. But the military members did not give up their plans.

On September 20th, an alarmed American congress, finally aroused to the danger of the gathering storm, appropriated over $3,500,000,000 for national defense.

To Washington, caught in the vortex of a world hurricane, the problem of China and the loud pleas of Chiang Kai-shek for increased aid began to seem very minor indeed, and near the bottom of a long list of priorities. On July 26, 1940, the United States proclamation placing a limited embargo on the export of scrap metal and aviation fuel had been intended to encourage China in her heroic struggle for freedom. Instead, in October it had encouraged T.V. Soong, Chiang's too-clever brother-in-law, and former U.S. Army Air Corps Captain Claire Chennault to ask for 500 American-piloted airplanes to fly in the service of China. In 1937 Chennault had been hired by Chiang Kai-shek to build up and train his bargain-basement air force. A weather-beaten, square-jawed enthusiast for his own theories of air power, with a limited background of staff and command, Chennault tended to brush aside dull matters like logistics, which he did not understand. To him the words cooperation and loyalty did not exist except in regard to his employer. During his four years in China, he had learned little about the country and its people.

Soong and Chennault were bolstered in their efforts by pleas from Chiang Kai-shek: China's morale and economy were on the verge of collapse; if planes were not delivered on time, China's position was so critical that it might become necessary to make other arrangements. (This was the first of many of Chiang's veiled threats.) Chennault airily stated that 500 planes could destroy the Japanese navy, carry the war to Japan, and forestall a probable Japanese attack on Singapore. In addition to B-17 bombers, he asked for medium bombers and fighters to support a planned counteroffensive to retake Canton and Hankow, an operation about which Chiang Kai-shek had not been informed and which he would not have dreamed of undertaking. But it all sounded hopeful to Washington ears grown weary of China's complaints and lack of offensive action. The list of war materials

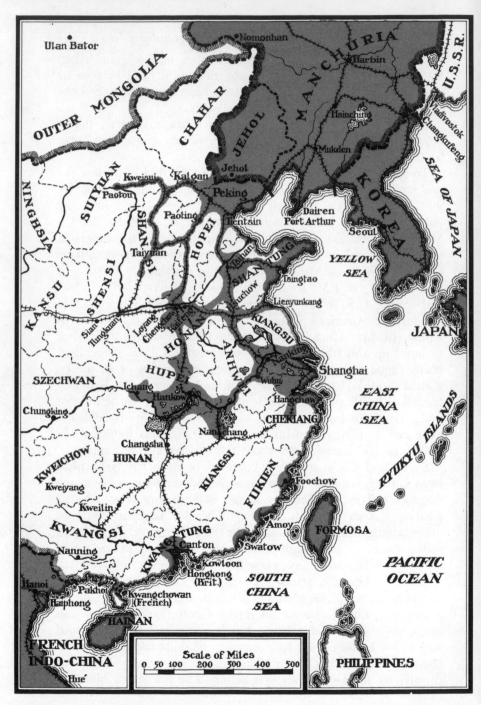

Japanese-occupied Areas in East Asia on December 7, 1941

requested at the same time was as unrealistic as Chennault's daydreams of conquest by air power alone—American ground crews, training planes, an Anglo-American loan of between $200 million and $300 million, credits for the purchase of arms, tanks that were too heavy for Chinese bridges, equipment for which the Chinese had had no training, trucks and heavy machinery for the construction of airfields, since none existed from which B-17s could fly. General Marshall simply labeled the entire Soong-Chennault program as impractical, and that ended it.

But in the spring of 1941, an unconventional compromise was devised through the American Volunteer Group (AVG). Self-designated as supervisor of this unusual unit, Chennault at once assumed the rank of colonel. The 100-man group was recruited from among adventurous American army and navy fliers willing to risk their necks for salaries of $500 to $750 a month and bonuses of $500 for each Japanese plane shot down. Hoping the AVG might delay a Japanese attack on Malaya and Singapore, the British released 100 P-40 fighters that had been allocated to them for the new unit. When the first contingent of pilots arrived by ship at Rangoon in July, it learned that the Chinese government had overlooked making any arrangements for their housing or for a base of operations. The British RAF provided an airfield in Burma. The entire group was not assembled until November, 1941, when it began training at Magwe, about 220 miles north of Rangoon, and later at Loiwing on the China-Burma border north of Lashio.

In March, 1941, when Roosevelt declared that China was eligible to receive aid under the provisions of the Lend-Lease Act, T.V. Soong and his rapacious staff no longer felt it necessary to ask for planes and equipment. They now demanded increased amounts of all items—1,000 planes and scores of 13-ton tanks. Soong also proposed equipping 30 selected Chinese divisions with American weapons and vehicles. After training by American experts, these units would be employed as special assault forces—if the generalissimo could ever get around to settling the delicate political balances involved in their selection. Meanwhile, large quantities of weapons, ammunition, trucks, spare parts, gasoline, and aerial bombs began to pour into the port of Rangoon for shipment on an overloaded, inefficient, narrow-gauge railway to

Lashio, the terminus of the line. From there they were to be transshipped by truck via Loiwing and Paoshan across the treacherous gorges of the Salween and Mekong rivers to Kunming in Yunnan province.

It was soon learned that no more than a trickle of the huge hoard of military supplies was reaching Kunming. China's lifeline to the outside world, the Burma Road, was clogged with staggering corruption, thievery, appalling incompetence, and complete indifference to wartime needs. The docks at Rangoon were piled so high that ships could not unload. An eight-month backlog cluttered the sprawling storage area at Lashio. Chiang Kai-shek had placed a relative, General Yu Fei-p'eng (nicknamed Tu-fei p'ang, meaning fat bandit), in charge of the Lashio depot in order to expedite the movement of supplies into China. As an expediter of munitions, General Yu was totally incompetent. But as an expediter of graft into his own pockets, he was not only extremely efficient but ruthless. In the guise of granting customs clearances, 15 government agencies set up shop at strategic points along the road—Wanting, Paoshan, Yunnanyi, and Kunming itself—to extract their share of "squeeze" in cash, gasoline, or equipment and, of course, to pass on a cut to their ministries in Chungking. Truck drivers dumped precious cargo into roadside ditches to make room for high-paying passengers known as "yellow fish." Their profits were so enormous that one Kunming matron of high position refused to sanction the marriage of her daughter to a major general, preferring instead a truck driver who had "much more money." By early fall of 1941, no more than 6,000 tons per month, out of a road capacity of 30,000 tons per month, were reaching their final destination—an achievement of sorts in view of the grasping Chinese roadblocks.

In order to inject some system into the chaos on the road, to supervise the entire Lend-Lease program to China and the 30-division plan, to support the AVG, and to advise the Chinese government on the practicality of its demands, an American military mission to China (AMMISCA) was sent to Chungking in early October. The headquarters of the mission was equipped with a powerful radio for transmission and reception of messages to and from Washington. Brigadier General John Magruder, the chief of mission, had been military attaché in Peking in the late

1920s and had traveled extensively in China, but he did not speak Chinese. Magruder was inclined to accept the Chinese way of doing things. However, other members of his staff were not. Lieutenant Colonel George W. Sliney bluntly reported that the belief in the United States that "China had fought Japan to a standstill and has had many glorious victories is a delusion" and that "the desire of the Chinese for more modern material was not . . . for the purpose of pressing the war against Japan, but was to make the central government safe against insurrection after . . . other nations had forced Japan out of China."

In Washington, T.V. Soong, never a man to pass up a chance to augment his personal wealth nor one to be deterred by scruples, organized China Defense Supplies to "finance" the procurement of and conduct all business connected with Lend-Lease material for China. He and his associates—both American and Chinese—ladled off fortunes before releasing supplies for shipment to Rangoon.

Meanwhile, in Chungking, Chiang Kai-shek was petulantly sulking over General Marshall's "Europe first" theory. He resented that the United States and Britain planned to put their main effort into defeating Hitler in Europe, while he was expected to defend the Pacific back door by "Chinese offensives against Japanese armies in China." His always touchy feelings were also hurt because he had not been included in the ABDA (American-British-Dutch-Australian) councils and because China was not being treated as an equal by Britain and the United States. The fact that his floundering government and inept generals had done nothing to earn equal status was immaterial. As stated in a report by Owen Lattimore, Chiang believed that since "they [the Chinese] have been fighting our battle for four years, it's about time we started fighting their battle for them." Though Roosevelt worried over Chiang's hysterical complaints, "China hands" in Washington were growing deaf to the repetition and hardened to the baseless assertions of his propaganda machine.

By late September, Japanese intelligence agencies had provided the army and navy general staffs with accurate estimates of the enemy strength their armed forces would have to meet on the outbreak of hostilities. The army was confident that it could overcome British, American, and Dutch forces in its assigned combat zones, particularly since they included a large percentage of native troops. Staff officers were convinced that these "brother Asians" hated their white commanders as much as they themselves did. But the navy was deeply concerned over the frightening power of American naval strength, if combined with that of its allies. This combining of strengths was a possibility that must be prevented at all costs.

The army general staff believed that its mission in southeast Asia could be accomplished by 11 divisions, out of a total of 51; 3 separate brigades; 9 tank regiments; and 2 air groups of 700 planes, out of a total of 1,500. It was estimated that these forces could quickly defeat the following British, American, and Dutch troop strengths in their respective possessions: Malaya and Singapore (about 70,000 British and native troops supported by about 200 planes); Philippine Islands (42,000 American and native troops, about 100,000 poorly equipped and poorly trained men of the Philippine Defense Army, and about 135 bomber and fighter planes); Netherlands East Indies (about 85,000 Dutch and native troops and 300 planes); Burma (35,000 British, Indian, and Burmese troops and about 50 planes); Hongkong (19,000 mostly British troops).

In the projected hostilities, the navy planned to use the Combined Fleet—virtually its entire strength in combat ships—and about 1,600 aircraft, out of a total of 3,300. The admirals felt certain that they could handle without difficulty enemy naval strength in Far East waters, but they worried about the formidable U.S. Pacific Fleet based at Pearl Harbor in the Hawaiian Islands. If it was able to combine with other allied naval forces in the Pacific, it would be more than a match for the Japanese Combined Fleet.

At the time, the entire Japanese Navy consisted of ten battleships, ten aircraft carriers, eighteen heavy cruisers, twenty light cruisers, one hundred and twelve destroyers and sixty-five submarines with a total tonnage of about 1,000,000. Though in general faster than American warships, Japanese naval vessels were more vulnerable in battle because of their lighter armor. The entire U.S. Navy consisted of seventeen battleships, eight aircraft carriers, eighteen heavy cruisers, nineteen light cruisers, one hundred and seventy-two destroyers and one hundred and eleven submarines with a total tonnage of 1,400,000.

The Japanese navy's principal consideration was the problem of the American forces based at Hawaii. Its intelligence agents estimated that the U.S. Pacific Fleet consisted of 11 battleships, 5 aircraft carriers, 16 heavy cruisers, 14 light cruisers, 84 destroyers, and 30 submarines. The actual strength of the U.S. Pacific Fleet in the late summer of 1941 was somewhat less than the Japanese estimate. It consisted of 9 battleships, 1 of which had been converted to a target ship, 3 aircraft carriers, 12 heavy cruisers, 5 light cruisers, 45 destroyers, 30 submarines, 22 minelayers, 14 minesweepers, 6 attack transports, and 27 auxiliary craft—a total of 173 vessels.

The estimate of American, British, Dutch, and Australian naval strength in Far East waters was: U.S. Asiatic Fleet, based at Cavite, Manila Bay: 1 heavy cruiser, 1 light cruiser, 14 destroyers, and 17 submarines. British Far East Fleet, based at Singapore: 2 battleships, Repulse and Prince of Wales; 4 aircraft carriers, 4 heavy cruisers, 4 light cruisers, 6 destroyers, and 7 submarines. Australian Navy: 2 heavy cruisers, 2 light cruisers, 5 destroyers, and 7 submarines. Netherlands East Indies Fleet: 5 cruisers, 3 destroyers, and 19 submarines.

In the early stages of hostilities, the Japanese Imperial General Headquarters planned to employ 2,300 army and navy planes. It was decided that the combined American, British, and Dutch air strength in the Far East and Hawaii—less than 900 aircraft—could be wiped out quickly, but that the United States would soon be able to place as many as 2,600 planes in combat, out of a total of 5,500. However, it was estimated that over the long haul American production capacity might be 10 times that of Japan. Therefore a quick, decisive strike was deemed imperative. The Japanese staffs also considered it essential that the American Pacific bases be destroyed or captured in order to push the American air frontier beyond the range of striking back at Japanese forces.

On October 17 the liberally inclined Prince Konoye and his cabinet were forced to resign by the Japanese militarists. General Hideki Tojo became prime minister and minister of war.

On October 24 the German armies in Russia captured Kharkov. On the thirtieth they began the siege of Moscow.

On November 6 the United States extended $1 billion Lend-Lease credit to the beleaguered Soviet Union. On November 14 President Roosevelt ordered all U.S. Marines to depart from China. Before the end of November, over 750 had embarked at Shanghai for Manila; but a delay in the departure of the *President Harrison*, on which 183 men of the Peking and Tientsin detachments were scheduled to sail, caused it to be captured and the men made prisoners by the Japanese.

On November 15, German troops began the siege of Sevastopol in the Crimea.

On November 17 the American ambassador to Japan, Joseph C. Grew, warned the American government that the Japanese might make a sudden attack on the United States at any time.

The Japanese ambassador to the United States, Admiral Nomura, had been striving since his arrival in April, 1941, to negotiate a settlement of the outstanding problems between Washington and Tokyo, but all his efforts had been blocked by basic differences in the aims and thinking of the two governments. The militarists in Japan had convinced themselves that the establishment of the new order in Greater East Asia would not only benefit all Asians, but would also drive the white nations from the Far East. In order to become the dominant nation in the western Pacific, Japan required oil and scrap metal from the United States, oil and tin from the Netherlands Indies, rice from Indo-China, rubber from Malaya, and access to the limitless markets of China. If Japan were deprived of these imports, the military party felt that they would have three alternatives: collapse, which they refused to accept; negotiation with the United States, which they were willing to attempt on their own terms; war with the United States to enforce their demands. On the other side, the United States, in the person of Secretary of State Cordell Hull, was equally adamant in its position—evacuation of all Japanese troops from China and Indo-China and Japanese acceptance of the Chinese nationalist government (Chiang Kai-shek)— after which a liberal trade treaty could be negotiated between the two countries. During the months of discussions, Hull had a decided advantage over Nomura, for American intelligence agencies had broken the Japanese codes and Hull received messages from Tokyo at the same time as did their ambassador. But Hull was also at a disadvantage because United States' policy was essentially to play for time until the Philippine Islands could be reinforced, to stall in what Hull described as a "rear guard diplomatic action." Although negotiable areas had never really existed on either side, Hull's stubborn disposition and his conviction—with considerable justification—that all Japanese were deceitful did not contribute to a favorable diplomatic climate. Nor had he improved matters in October by describing Prime Minister Tojo of Japan as having a "small bore, straight laced, one track mind" and as being "rather stupid."

On November 1, General Tojo and his new cabinet held a momentous "liaison conference" in the imperial courtroom of the palace in Tokyo. Tojo announced that negotiations in Washington with the stubborn Americans had reached a dead end and time was running out, meaning that the war party had grown impatient for action. A decision on Japan's future course had to be agreed upon. Admiral Osami Nagano, the minister of the navy, advocated starting war with the United States "at once" while Japan still held the advantage. Finance Minister Okinori Kaya was opposed to war: it would ruin the financial and economic structure of the country. Field Marshal Hajime Sugiyama, chief of staff of the army, declared that war should start early in December, but that negotiations with the United States should continue as if sincere in order to give Japan a military advantage. Kaya and Foreign Minister Shigenori Togo heatedly called such a course "diplomatic trickery." After hours of shouting arguments, the army and navy won a unanimous decision to set a deadline for the conclusion of the Washington negotiations—midnight of November 30. If Hull and Nomura could not come to a working agreement by that time, war would be the answer. Though the prime minister professed willingness to compromise, he did nothing to extend the deadline. It was then decided to send an able diplomat, Saburo Kurusu (who was married to an American and fluent in English), to assist the somewhat blundering Admiral Nomura in Washington. The foreign minister hoped rather forlornly that with Kurusu's help, there might still be a chance to engineer peace in spite of the military hotheads. Kurusu left Japan on November 5 and arrived in Washington on the fifteenth.

During the 10-day interval between his departure and arrival, Kurusu's mission was represented to the Japanese people as being America's last chance to take advantage of Japan's preference for peace, on Japan's terms. Even Foreign Minister Kaya, who had argued strenuously for peace, announced truculently that the Japanese aim was to "force Great Britain and the United States to retreat from east Asia." And 300 members of the Diet, though barely noticed by the military, condemned the countries that had tried to strangle Japan. They announced patriotically—if not diplomatically—that "the Japanese people have the grim determination to overcome the national crisis for the independence and honor of east Asia."

At 5:00 P.M. on November 2, Prime Minister Tojo informally reported the decisions of the liaison conference to the emperor. On November 5, 13 members of the cabinet and the privy council assembled in the imperial conference room to await the arrival of the emperor. Tojo informed His Majesty of the near breakdown of negotiations with the United States, and finished by stating: "we must be prepared to go to war, with the time for military action tentatively set for December 1st." Foreign Minister Togo agreed with regret that the chances for success in Washington were dim. General Suzuki pointed out that fighting a long war with Britain, America, and The Netherlands would be "no easy task" due to the critical situation regarding Japan's resources. Therefore, a quick victory in the first few months was the only solution. Admiral Nagano and Field Marshal Sugiyama stressed the importance of secrecy and timing. Sugiyama was confident of an early victory, but warned that fighting America could become a long, drawn-out war. In answer to questions by President Yoshimichi Hara of the privy council, Togo repeated that he saw "little hope of success in the negotiations," and Tojo warned of the dangers of a long war "with a foe like the United States." Then, reminding the conference that since Britain and America threatened the very existence of Japan, Tojo pointed out that moral justification for war had long existed. He silenced further discussion by assuming in a firm voice that all were in agreement. During the one-sided debate, the emperor had remained silent, his unblinking eyes focused on the wall at the end of the room. When Tojo finished speaking, the emperor rose from his chair and stalked out. By his silence he had approved the course of action laid forth by the militarists. He and every man at the conference knew the Washington negotiations would fail because they were intended to fail; they were diversions to catch the Americans off guard.

On November 17 in Washington, conversations began between Secretary of State Hull, Undersecretary Sumner Welles, and Ambassadors Nomura and Kurusu. Neither side budged from its position. On the twentieth the Japanese proposed again that the United States and Japan reopen trade relations and cooperate in procuring oil and other goods from the Netherlands East Indies. The decoded messages from Tokyo delivered to Hull had not been accurately translated. Because of this and because of his instant dislike for Kurusu, Hull came to another of his off-the-cuff decisions: Kurusu was deceitful, he was fully cognizant of his government's trickery, and he was not to be trusted in anything he said. Hull, of course, had no knowledge of the December 1 deadline.

Nonetheless, Hull introduced the two Japanese envoys to President Roosevelt, who after talking with them made an on-the-spot conclusion that negotiations could succeed. Later, the president suggested a modus vivendi for further discussions to the secretary of state. But for two considerations, this temporary compromise might have broken the deadlock—it was never delivered to the Japanese, and a decision for the future had already been made in Tokyo.

On Saturday, November 22, Nomura and Kurusu urged Hull to make an immediate reply to their proposals of a few days before. Hull refused, but he informed them that he would do so as soon as possible. On the twenty-fifth, word of a new Japanese expedition from Shanghai to Indo-China reached Washington. Furious at what he considered "evidence of bad faith . . . while they [the Japanese] were negotiating," Roosevelt approved Hull's recommendation for an entirely new proposal for a peaceful settlement.

On November 26, Nomura and Kurusu were summoned to the State Department. Hull handed them two documents, one of which contained 10 new conditions as a basis for a solution of mutual differences. Included was a peremptory demand for Japan to "withdraw all military, naval, air and police forces from all of China and Indo-China immediately." Also included was a proposal for a nonaggression pact between Japan, China, Great Britain, Soviet Russia, the United States, the Netherlands Indies, and Siam—a complicated bit of diplomatic legerdemain almost impossible of achievement. As bait to win Japanese approval, Hull offered to unfreeze Japanese assets, to conclude a most-favored-nation trade agreement, to link the yen and the dollar firmly together, to reduce trade barriers, and to grant economic concessions. Kurusu saw at once that these economic advantages would be considered a totally unacceptable bribe in Tokyo, and that it would be impossible for the Japanese government to agree to the immediate withdrawal of its troops from China and Indo-China. Shocked at the harshness of the demands, Kurusu asked for further discussions. Hull refused with the reply: "It's as far as we can go." Kurusu departed with the remark that this "practically put an end to negotiations."

On November 27, Hull's answer to the Japanese proposals of November 20 in the form of new demands was received with indignation in Tokyo. When Tojo read it to the cabinet, one outraged general cried out: "This is an ultimatum!" Admiral Shimada declared it to be "unyielding and unbending." Others construed it as a stall for time during which to prepare for the war the United States had already decided upon. The army and navy were enraged at the demand to evacuate all of China. To them, "all of China" included Manchuria. They had no way of knowing that to Hull it had not. This misunderstanding on geographical terms ended any possibility of a postponement of the December 1 deadline. Had Hull sent a conciliatory answer, it seems not impossible that the ensuing holocaust in the Pacific might have been averted—or at least delayed until the United States was better prepared to meet it. But, wooed by China's pleading and deluded by her propaganda, American foreign policy in Asia had for too long been hitched to a dying horse—China. And, imprisoned by *bushido*, the ancient code of death before dishonor and glorification of the emperor, Japan's militaristic policy in east Asia had been set on an unswerving course of conquest. The paths of the two countries, one based on misguided idealism, the other on naked aggrandizement, now met head on. Each side feared the other: the United States because it feared the inherent danger in the German-Japanese-Italian alliance; Japan because it feared isolation and eventual downfall at the hands of Britain and America. In a sense, neither side was to blame; nor were their governments per se. If blame there was, it rested on human frailty, misunderstandings, national ambitions, on the pride and stubbornness of the men in whose hands rested great decisions.

On November 26, Secretary of War Stimson sent a message to General MacArthur in the Philippine Islands warning him of "possible hostile action at any moment." A similar message went to Major General Walter C. Short, commander of the Hawaiian Department, with a caution to do "nothing to alarm the civilian population." Short did nothing, except to set up a sabotage alert. On the same day, Chief of Naval Operations Admiral Stark sent a "war warning" to Admiral Thomas C. Hart in the Philippines and to Admiral Husband E. Kimmel in Hawaii advising them that "negotiations with Japan . . . have ceased and an aggressive move . . . is expected in next few days."

On the twenty-eighth Stimson received another intercepted message regarding Japanese troop movements from Shanghai toward Indo-China. He recommended attacking the convoys at once with Philippine-based B-17s. The president vetoed Stimson's proposal with a dissertation on democratic purposes and the necessity of waiting for the other side to make the first aggressive move.

On November 29, Prime Minister Tojo, four of his cabinet ministers, President Hara of the privy council, and eight former prime ministers, including Prince Konoye, met in the imperial court room for an informal discussion of the situation. Six of the elder statesmen were deeply concerned over the collision course with the United States on which Tojo had set Japan. Two others, both retired generals, supported the prime minister. But Tojo beat down all discussion and questions with: "We can't bow to England and the United States. We've lost 160,000 lives so far in the China Incident. . . . If we go like this [talking] . . . we'll lose our chance to fight. We're already losing valuable time for operations!"

Later that afternoon, Tojo called a conference of the senior members of his cabinet. It was agreed to warn Hitler and Mussolini of the imminent danger of war with the United States. Admiral Nagano reluctantly informed the conferees that zero hour would be on December 8, Tokyo time (December 7, Hawaii time). After further questioning, he admitted that the navy planned to make a surprise attack, but he refused to say where. Vice Admiral Seiichi Ito then blandly announced that in order to ensure complete surprise, negotiations in Washington would have to continue until after the attack had begun. Foreign Minister Togo was indignant at such "unthinkable behavior against the national honor and prestige." But eventually he accepted defeat and sent the warnings to the Japanese ambassadors at Rome and Berlin. The messages ended with: "war may suddenly break out between the Anglo-Saxon nations and Japan . . . and time of breaking out . . . may come quicker than anyone dreams."

The message to Berlin was intercepted and decoded by American intelligence. It was handed to President Roosevelt on the thirtieth. On the same day Prime Minister Tojo declared in a public speech—according to news reports—that "the influence of Britain and the United States must be eliminated from the Far East" and that their "desire to fish in troubled waters" by stirring up Asians against one another "must be purged with a vengeance." (Later, it was denied that Tojo had delivered or even had read the speech.)

Since the mid-1920s, two prophetic books by Hector C. Bywater, the naval correspondent for the London Daily Telegraph, had exercised considerable influence on the thinking of the Japanese navy. Sea Power in the Pacific and The Great Pacific War described in detail a Japanese surprise attack on the American fleet in Pearl Harbor, a simultaneous assault on Guam, and landings at Lingayen Gulf and Lamon Bay on the Philippines' main island of Luzon. The Japanese navy general staff had had the first translated for distribution among senior officers, the second included as required study at the Naval War College. As a historical example of a previous successful surprise attack, instructors at the school could point to Admiral Togo's crushing defeat of the Russian fleet at Tsushima in 1905. However, a majority of Japan's naval tacticians feared the power of the U.S. Navy and discounted the chances for success in such far-ranging operations as those outlined in Bywater's books.

The man who transformed Japan's fear and doubt into resolution and eventual action was Admiral Isoroku Yamamoto. A short man with large shoulders and a heavy torso, Yamamoto had studied at Harvard University and had served as naval attaché in Washington. During his years in America he had developed a healthy respect for the industrial and military potential of his host country. In 1939, Yamamoto was assigned to command the Combined Fleet. On fleet maneuvers in the spring of 1940, deeply impressed by the performance of his carrier-based planes, he decided that a Japanese surprise attack on Hawaii would stand a good chance of success; from that time Yamamoto became the leader of a crusade to win over the navy to his conviction. Although older officers remained cautiously dubious about the proposal, he found many willing converts among the younger admirals, captains, and junior officers.

In February, 1941, Yamamoto wrote to Rear Admiral Onishi of the 11th Fleet asking him to study the feasibility of the plan that was developing in his mind. Onishi and a member of his staff concluded that an attack on the United States Pacific Fleet in Hawaii would involve great risks but would have a reasonable chance of success provided two conditions prevailed: that most of the American capital ships be in Pearl Harbor at the time of the attack, and that a Japanese carrier force be able to move within striking distance of the target without detection. Greatly encouraged, Yamamoto then requested Captain Ogawa of naval intelligence to collect all possible information on the Hawaiian Islands and the habits of the United States Pacific Fleet. It so happened that for the past year Ogawa on his own initiative had been training an unusually intelligent ensign, Takeo Yoshikawa, for espionage in the islands. Now ready for the assignment, Yoshi-kawa departed for Honolulu on March 20. On arrival, he was met by the forewarned Japanese consul general and forthwith went to work.

By April, 1941, the Pearl Harbor project had advanced far enough to be given the code name Operation Z, the designation of Admiral Togo's message to the fleet at the great victory of Tsushima: "on this one battle rests the fate of the nation." The chief of the Operations Bureau assigned Rear Admiral Ryunosuke Kusaka the task of developing a complete, workable operational plan. Despite serious doubts of his own, Kusaka and commanders Oishi and Genda gradually worked out a plan to bring a strike force within air range of Pearl Harbor. They learned that since ships avoided the stormy northern sea lanes during November and December, surprise could be attained by attacking Hawaii from the north during those months. From intelligence reports they discovered that American flying boats patrolled the Pacific for no more than 700 miles north of Hawaii and 700 miles south of the Aleutians. Therefore the strike force could approach Pearl Harbor by following a course between the two patrol zones—a broad no-man's-land of unguarded ocean. It was also concluded that the first wave of the attack should be low-flying torpedo planes, the second high-altitude bombers and dive-bombers. The problems of refueling in midocean, the far from perfect Japanese bombsight, and intensive training for the task force had yet to be worked out.

Meanwhile, the army general staff dispatched highly trained officers to probe the feasibility of assaults on Hongkong and Singapore and invasions of Java, Sumatra, Malaya, Siam, Burma, and the Philippines. With their own hatred of the white races uppermost in mind, army intelligence had convinced themselves that the peoples of southeast Asia would welcome liberation from American, British, and Dutch domination by other Asians, namely the Japanese army. Although army Chief of Staff Sugi-yama was at first dubious about the proposed seizure of all southeast Asia, he, too, gradually became infected by the lure of vast conquests. By mid-August, 1941, he had put the general staff to work on detailed plans.

Training for the naval air attack against Pearl Harbor was accelerated at Saeki and Tominaka air bases on the southern island of Kyushu. Other air units trained at Kagoshima Bay, where nearby steep mountains and high, man-made obstructions close to the harbor had a general similarity to physical conditions at Honolulu and Battleship Row at Pearl Harbor. Admiral Kusaka required his torpedo bomber pilots to fly in over a mountain at 6,000 feet, drop sharply to an altitude of 25 feet, simulate the launching of a torpedo, and then veer off to safety. At Shikoku Island, submariners trained with two midget submarines, slipping in and out of the narrow channel to Mitsukue Bay, a reasonable duplicate of the channel leading to Pearl Harbor. Though all fliers and other participants in these vigorous exercises knew that their training program must presage an important operation, no one except Kusaka, Oishi, and Genda had the slightest inkling of the mission of Operation Z.

On September 2 some 40 key naval commanders and staff officers gathered at the Naval War College outside of Tokyo to work out the final details of the surprise attack on Pearl Harbor. At this time the army was brought in on the secret in order to coordinate the timing for simultaneous attacks and occupations of Malaya, Burma, the Netherlands Indies, the Philippines, the Solomons, and other Pacific island groups. On September 5, a three-sided war game—Britain, America, and Japan—was initiated to determine all possibilities, either favorable or unfavorable. By the time this session concluded, it was decided that Operation Z should go on, even if the strike force were discovered and lost as many as two carriers and one-third of its planes. On September 9 it was decided that the strike force should start on its perilous mission on November 16.

By early November, reconnaissance of the assault areas in Malaya, Siam, Burma, the Netherlands Indies, and the Philippines had been completed and landing sites decided upon. At the same time, all previous problems connected with the Pearl Harbor attack appeared to be solved, including the attachment of wooden fins to torpedoes to prevent them from diving to the bottom in the shallow water of the anchorage. The Japanese army and navy were ready for war with the United States, Great Britain, and The Netherlands nearly a month before the deadline set for the termination of the Washington discussions. Regardless of

Nomura's negotiations with Hull, Yamamoto's dream was about to become a reality, and America was due for a rude awakening. On November 16 the Pearl Harbor strike force, with Vice Admiral Chichi Nagumo in command, assembled in Saeki Bay on the northeast coast of Kyushu at the southern entrance to the Inland Sea. It consisted of the aircraft carriers *Shokaku, Zuikaku, Akagi, Kaga, Soryu,* and *Hiryu;* the battleships *Hiei* and *Kirishima;* the heavy cruisers *Tone* and *Chikuma;* 1 light cruiser; 11 destroyers; 3 submarines; and a number of auxiliary fuel and supply ships. On board the carriers were 382 aircraft—87 fighters, 140 dive-bombers, 109 horizontal bombers, and 46 torpedo bombers. Twenty-seven additional submarines, 5 with special cargoes, were assigned to support the task force with separate missions.

After dark on the seventeenth the flagship *Akagi* and two destroyers slipped out of the bay. The other ships of the strike force followed at irregular intervals, setting different courses as they headed for the rendezvous at Hittokapu Bay in the northern Kurile Islands. All ship captains were ordered to sink any ship of any nationality, including their own, on sight. On November 25, all pilots were assembled on the *Akagi* and were briefed in detail on the mission. This was the first time they knew of their destination, Pearl Harbor.

At 2:00 P.M. on December 1, Prime Minister Tojo called a formal imperial conference to obtain the emperor's approval of the course on which the Japanese army and navy had already embarked. As His Majesty sat silently on the throne chair, Tojo informed him that Japan could not accept the American demands and that the time had come for war with the United States, Great Britain, and The Netherlands "to preserve the empire." Admiral Nagano, privy council president Hara, General Suzuki, and all others present agreed. Tojo concluded the conference with a ringing declaration that a united empire would achieve victory and go on to "greater national purposes" in the service of the emperor. Tojo bowed. The emperor rose and left the room in silence. Shortly after, he affixed his imperial seal to the documents prescribing war. Emperor Hirohito had thus sanctioned Japan's plunge into hostilities.

During the night of the first a Japanese courier plane carrying secret orders for the commanding general of the 23rd Corps at Canton crashed against a mountain in Chinese-held territory. Air reconnaissance on the morning of the second spotted the wreckage of the plane about 50 ,miles north of Canton. It had already been found by the Chinese and was surrounded by troops and local civilians. The Japanese army general staff was alarmed at the prospect of the Chungking government passing on to Washington the secret orders that clearly disclosed its intentions to attack without warning. Their fears proved to be groundless. The Chinese did not even mention finding the orders regarding Japanese plans for war to the United States government or to its mission at Chungking.

On the third, Field Marshal Sugiyama and Admiral Nagano informed the emperor of the date of the simultaneous attacks: December 8, Tokyo time; December 7, Hawaii time. He granted approval at once. That afternoon final orders were dispatched in a new code to General Count Terauchi, commander of the Southern Army, and to Admiral Nagumo, commander of the Pearl Harbor Task Force. Long detailed plans had already been delivered to the components of the Southern Army. The complete plans for the Pearl Harbor force were highly classified and known to only a few.

In Washington, Kurusu was vainly attempting to continue negotiations. He even went so far as to advise President Roosevelt, through Bernard Baruch, to send either a personal representative or a message appealing directly to the emperor for his help in preserving peace.

Meanwhile, intercepted Japanese messages should have warned both Admiral Kimmel in Hawaii and the Navy Department in Washington that a dangerous situation was rapidly developing. One that ordered the Japanese embassy to start burning codes and classified documents was interpreted as "at least a break in diplomatic relations and probably war." But a strange form of lethargic hope, or disbelief, seemed to have gripped American intelligence agencies and higher staffs. They seemed unable to attach any immediate significance to the storm signals. Although the locations of six Japanese carriers were known in late November, the American intelligence services lost track of them completely when the Japanese code was changed. On December 4 the Pearl Harbor strike force was actually less than 1,000 miles northwest of Honolulu.

At dawn on December 4, a convoy of 26 Japanese transports left from the island of Hainan and headed south toward the British-owned Malayan states and Singapore. On the same day, General Terauchi flew to his headquarters at Saigon to direct the operations of his Southern Army. His forces consisted of the 14th Corps of two divisions and one independent brigade, whose mission was to land at Lingayen Gulf and invade the Philippines; the 25th Corps of four divisions and two independent brigades was to seize Malaya and attack Singapore; the 16th Corps of two divisions was to take the Netherlands Indies; the 15th Corps of two divisions was to occupy Siam and invade Burma; three infantry battalions were to seize Guam, Wake Island, and Rabaul in the Bismarck Archipelago. In addition, General Tsukomo Sakai's 23rd Corps of one division from the China Expeditionary Army was poised at Canton ready to launch an attack on Hongkong. In five swift, coordinated moves, Terauchi and Sakai would drive the British, Americans, and Dutch out of southeast Asia forever.

Admiral Sir Tom Phillips, commander of the British Far East Fleet, conferred in Manila with Admiral Hart, commander of the U.S. Asiatic Fleet, and General MacArthur. There was little that any of the three could do but pray. Hart knew only too well that his small, overage fleet could be knocked out of the water in short order. MacArthur's command consisted of less than 40,000 American and Philippine troops, nearly 100,000 Philippine army troops, 35 B-17 bombers, and about 100 P-40 fighter planes. Phillips planned to send the battle cruiser *Repulse* and the battleship *Prince of Wales* up the Malay coast in a show of force. While they were talking, a message was delivered that the southbound Japanese convoy was now off the southern coast of Siam. Manila had been outflanked.

On December 5 in Tokyo, the Japanese reply to Hull's proposals of November 26 was completed. The foreign minister was directed to send the bulk of the long message to arrive in Washington on the morning of December 6, Washington time; the final section breaking off diplomatic relations was to arrive on the morning of the seventh for delivery to Hull at 1:00 P.M. that day. The cables reached the Japanese embassy in Washington as scheduled, but decoding was delayed by a series of petty mishaps, including a farewell party.

On the afternoon of Friday, December 5, the enterprising Japanese spy in Honolulu, Ensign Takeo Yoshikawa, cabled Tokyo that 9 battleships, 3 light cruisers, 19 destroyers, and 3 seaplane tenders had dropped anchor on Battleship Row in Pearl Harbor; that 4 light cruisers and 3 destroyers were tied up at the docks; and that all of the carriers and heavy cruisers were at sea. The message was intercepted and decoded by United States naval intelligence, but it was not passed on for the information of higher authorities.

Yoshikawa's information was not correct. In Pearl Harbor on December 6 and 7 there were 9 battleships, including the target ship *Utah*, 2 heavy cruisers, 6 light cruisers, 30 destroyers, 4 submarines, 9 minelayers, 14 minesweepers, and 27 tenders, storage vessels, and other auxiliary ships.

On Saturday, December 6, President Roosevelt sent a direct appeal to the emperor "to restore traditional amity" between the Japanese and American peoples. It was too late. At that time no one could have stopped the forces already set in motion.

On the same day, Secretary of the Navy Knox was assured by Rear Admiral Kelly Turner that because of the southbound Japanese convoy—now reported as 35 transports, 8 cruisers, and 20 destroyers—the Japanese obviously planned to strike at the British in Malaya. That afternoon several undelivered radio intercepts containing information about the situation in Hawaii came to the attention of a member of the navy Cryptographic Section. After glancing through them, the head of the translation branch set them aside as being of no pressing importance, and thus missed the warning they contained. However, decoding clerks succeeded in deciphering the long intercepted message from the Japanese foreign ministry before Nomura and Kurusu received a complete copy. That evening it was delivered to the president. He recognized at once that its clear import was war. But where?

In Hawaii, neither General Short nor Admiral Kimmel believed that there was any danger of an attack on the islands, either by air or by sea. Nine battleships, 8 cruisers, 30 destroyers, and a number of lesser vessels—101 ships in all—either rode peacefully at anchor, were tied up at the docks, or were in drydock at Pearl Harbor. It was a Saturday night, and normal peacetime liberty had been granted to many of the officers and men. Similarly, weekend passes had been approved for the majority of army personnel.

That night in Manila, the 27th Bombardment Group (B-17s) was giving a welcome party for the new commander of the Far East Air Force, Major General Lewis H. Brereton, in the huge open pavilion of the Manila Hotel. After hearing Admiral Hart and MacArthur's chief of staff on the imminence of hostilities, Brereton ordered all airfields on combat alert. At Clark Field, 60 miles north of Manila, fewer than half of his Flying Fortresses were ready for takeoff. But the base personnel and those of adjacent Fort Stotsenburg were attending the usual Saturday-night dance at the officers' club on acacia-lined Welsh Avenue.

During the night of December 6, a fleet of 27 Japanese submarines stealthily approached the island of Oahu (the location of Pearl Harbor and nearby Honolulu), 12 from the north and 10 from the south. Each of the other 5 carried a midget two-man submarine on its deck. Before midnight, after being launched from their mother ships about eight miles south of Pearl Harbor, the midgets moved slowly toward the target. Their mission was to slip through the narrow channel, wait off Battleship Row until the air attack began, then fire their torpedoes at the nearest large ship.

With the first gray light of dawn on December 7, the Japanese strike force reached its launching area 200 miles north of Honolulu. The first wave of 187 planes—50 horizontal bombers, each carrying a 1,760-pound armor-piercing bomb; 40 torpedo planes, each carrying a 1,760-pound aerial torpedo with an explosive charge of 1,000 pounds; 54 dive-bombers, each carrying a 550-pound land bomb plus heavy machine guns for strafing; and 43 fighters for air cover and strafing—were lined up on the decks of the six carriers in that order. In semidarkness and facing a rough sea, the launching of the planes was accomplished with the loss of but one fighter. The three flights gained altitude quickly and streaked for Pearl Harbor.

At 6:30 A.M. the torpedo net at the entrance to Pearl Harbor was opened for an approaching target ship. As it passed his destroyer, Lieutenant William Outerbridge caught sight of a submarine's conning tower in its wake. He opened fire at once, sank the Japanese midget, and before 7:00 A.M. radioed headquarters at the 14th Naval District that he had attacked and sunk an unidentified submarine. Because of previous false reports, the chief of staff directed that no action be taken until the message was verified.

Just after 7:00 A.M. an army radar station at Kahuku Point, the northern tip of Oahu, picked up a large blip on its screen, apparently a flight of aircraft. After checking their equipment to verify the unusual indication, the two operators located the blip on the plotting board as being less than 150 miles to the north. By the time they had raised an operator at Fort Shafter and the only officer on duty, the blips were plotted as being 90 miles away. The duty officer discounted the report. He knew that a flight of B-17s was expected from the mainland, or that the planes could be from the carriers at sea.

When the first Japanese fighter planes followed by Commander Fuchida's wave of bombers cleared the northern tip of Oahu, they saw at once that all of the American army, navy, and marine planes at Ford Island and Hickam, Bellows, Wheeler, Kaneohe, and Ewa fields were bunched together on the ground like sitting ducks. The air bases would be put out of commission so that air interference with Japanese attacks on the fleet would be minimal.

The torpedo planes circled toward the west coast of the island. Fuchida radioed back to Admiral Nagumo: "Tora! Tora! Tora!" signifying that the Americans had been caught by surprise. Then, like well-aimed arrows, the Japanese bombers headed straight for Battleship Row. The first bomb struck a hangar on Ford Island. It burst into a dense cloud of roiling smoke and flame. The battleship *Oklahoma* was struck by a torpedo, then two more tore into the side of the ship. With shattering explosions the stricken warship listed heavily to port and capsized. Half a dozen Japanese planes converged on the stripped-down *Utah* and tore it apart as roaring fires swept its decks. The blue waters of the bay were suddenly streaked with wide bands of spreading black oil. Other bombers dove toward the *California*, then the *West Virginia* and *Tennessee*. The *Arizona* was hit by five bombs at once from the horizontal bombers. One found the fuel tanks; in seconds, hundreds of tons of smokeless powder were ignited, and the *Arizona* blew into the air in a mass of broken steel and bodies. Two torpedoes struck the *California* on the port side below the water level. The ship began to list heavily. A 1,760-pound bomb landed beside the second stack and penetrated to the protective deck below, where it exploded and set the ship afire. The executive officer, Commander Earl E. Stone, ordered the starboard sea valves opened to counterflood the starboard compartments. This action saved the ship from capsizing. She sank to the muddy bottom on an even keel. The *Nevada*, hit by a torpedo and a 1,760-pound bomb, began to settle into the sand and mud of the harbor, black smoke and white steam spewing out from her torn steel plates. The thickening layer of oil on the surface of the water burst into flames with a swishing roar that quickly enveloped ships in its path. Many of the men who had jumped overboard to swim toward nearby Ford Island were burned alive. The *Utah* keeled over with all on board. Every battleship still afloat was in flames.

In the midst of the holocaust, the destroyer *Helm* got under way and headed for the safety of the open sea. As it dashed through the channel to the harbor entrance, its commander spotted a midget submarine struggling to extricate itself from the sandy coral of the shoreline. The *Helm* opened fire and sank the enemy craft as it slid off into deeper water. The destroyer *Monaghan* rammed and sank another midget just as it discharged its two torpedoes.

Meanwhile, Japanese fighters again strafed Hickam and Ewa fields, leaving most of the closely parked planes in flames. Scofield Barracks, the huge army base that housed the Hawaiian Division, was also strafed.

At 8:55 A.M. the second attack wave of 170 planes—50 horizontal bombers, each carrying one 550-pound and six 130-pound bombs; 84 torpedo planes and dive bombers, each carrying the same bomb load as in the first wave; and 36 fighters—zoomed in from the east. They streaked for the battleship *Pennsylvania*, berthed in drydock, and the already crippled *Nevada*, now trying to make for the open sea. Within minutes six bombs found the *Nevada*. Following a great blast of flames and smoke, the ship was beached.

From photographs and direct ŏbservation, the Japanese believed that the surprise attack had netted 4 battleships sunk, 4 battleships badly damaged and out of action, 1 battleship slightly damaged, 1 cruiser sunk, 4 cruisers out of action, several smaller vessels either sunk or badly damaged, and 250 planes destroyed on the ground. Actually, the final toll in ships was 18 vessels either sunk, capsized, or out of action—battleships *California, West Virginia, Oklahoma, Arizona, Pennsylvania* (in drydock), *Nevada, Maryland, Tennessee,* and *Utah* (converted to a target ship); cruisers *Helena, Raleigh,* and *Honolulu*; 3 destroyers; and 3 miscellaneous craft. One floating drydock was badly damaged and sunk. Of the 166 planes at three navy and marine air bases, 117 were destroyed or badly damaged; the remaining 49, less 6 on patrol, were temporarily put out of action. Of the 113 planes at three army bases, 60 were destroyed or badly damaged and many of the remaining 53 put out of action. A few army planes managed to get into the air and shoot down 11 Japanese aircraft. One bomb landed in the city of Honolulu, killing 68 civilians. There were 3,478 American military casualties—2,335 killed or fatally wounded, 1,143 wounded. The Japanese lost 29 aircraft, 1 fleet submarine, all 5 of their midget submarines and two-man crews, and 49 airmen. Pearl Harbor was the most disastrous single loss in American naval history.

Less than 10 hours later, at 12:35 P.M., Manila time, 54 Japanese bombers and 35 fighters roared over Clark Field in the Philippines and in one blow virtually wiped out the United States Far East Air Force. Presenting easy targets on the field for the Japanese, 32 of 35 B-17s, 30 medium bombers, and all of the fighter planes were destroyed.

On the same day the Japanese moved to attack Guam, Wake Island, and Hongkong. They had landed on the coast of Malaya a few hours before the attack on Pearl Harbor and were already on the march south to attack Singapore from the landward side.

All of the great guns of the Singapore naval base had been emplaced to fight off an attack from the sea. Its rear was nakedly defenseless.

In one day the Japanese had achieved an overwhelming victory. Under the cloak of negotiations, their brilliant plan had accomplished more than Yamamoto and Sugiyama had dared to dream. Though bitterly condemned in England and the United States, the "sneak attack" on Pearl Harbor was a "masterful job of planning, preparing, practicing and executing the attack." In one stroke it had crippled the United States in the Pacific and had given the Japanese free rein for action in southeast Asia, the Philippines, and the Netherlands Indies. Pearl Harbor and the Japanese thrusts to the south were the third time in recent history that Japan had struck without warning, earlier against China in 1895 and against Russia in 1904. Unscrupulous as the action had been, the morality of attacking an adversary without warning can only be judged by the winner or the loser from his point of view—from which side of the fence he happens to be on. Since wars are fought to be won—or they should not be started at all— and since the Japanese navy could not count on defeating the United States fleet in an open confrontation, the Japanese high command had dared to take a great gamble to win a great strategic advantage, one from which the United States was not to recover until the Battle of Midway in June, 1942.

In Chungking, the news of Pearl Harbor was the signal for an outburst of unbridled jubilation. At last, Chiang Kai-shek's problems had been solved. His regime had been saved. Now he would have complete access to the vast reserves of American supplies. His strategy of holding out for allies to win the war he was morally too bankrupt to wage had worked. American, British, and Russian air power could defeat Japan at sea and cut off Japanese armies in China and Manchuria. Chiang could now sit back and indulge himself in matters for which he was more qualified —devious politics and military inaction. He could collect a hoard of equipment and arms with which he would defeat and destroy the hated Communist bandits, and his allies would do all the fighting to defeat Japan. The gods had smiled on him at last. But the smiles of the gods must have been wry, for few but they had known that Chiang Kai-shek had learned about the Japanese plans to attack without warning nearly 36 hours before the debacle at Pearl Harbor, either from the secret papers in the plane that crashed north of Canton or from radio intercepts. Chiang's government had not transmitted the information to Washington nor to the American mission in Chungking. Months later, a very senior Chinese general informed General Stilwell, then commander of the China-Burma-India Theater, that his government had tried repeatedly to communicate by radio with Washington, but "had not been able to get through." Chiang Kai-shek had not bothered to pass on the vital information to the powerful radio station of the American mission. Whether it had been deliberately held back can only be conjectured.

On December 8 the United States declared war on Japan. On the same day Great Britain followed suit. On December 9, after four and one-half years of war, China declared war on Japan. By so doing, Chiang Kai-shek assumed that he had now achieved the status of a full-fledged ally. On December 10 the British battle cruiser *Repulse* and the battleship *Prince of Wales* were sunk by Japanese bombers off Koto Bharu on the east coast of Malaya. The last strong deterrents to Japanese aggression in southeast Asia were now at the bottom of the sea.

Notes

Chapter 3

1. 4th and 89th Divisions
2. 21st and 84th Divisions and 7th Separate Brigade
3. 10th, 83rd, and 85th Divisions
4. 1st, 12th, and 15th Brigades
5. 72nd Division and 7th, 200th, and 211th Separate Brigades

Chapter 4

1. 3rd, 9th, 11th, 13th, 16th and 101st Divisions
2. 6th, 18th and 114th Divisions
3. 51st and 58th Divisions
4. 155th and 156th Divisions
5. 41st, 48th, 159th, 160th, 87th, 103rd, and 112th Divisions
6. 159th and 160th Divisions

Chapter 5

1. 38th, 39th, 105th, and 132nd Divisions
2. 14th and 9th Corps, 85th Division, and 5th Separate Brigade
3. 33rd, 15th, and 17th Corps
4. 19th, 35th, 61st, and 9th Corps
5. 14th Corps and 85th, 66th, and 71st Divisions

Chapter 6

1. 10th, 16th, 110th, 114th, and 5th Divisions
2. 9th and Konoye Divisions
3. of the 2nd Corps
4. 38th and 180th Divisions
5. of General T'ang En-po's 20th Army
6. of the 2nd Army Group
7. 28th, 49th, and 92nd Divisions
8. 4th, 89th, 2nd, and 25th Divisions
9. 10th, 16th, and 5th Divisions
10. 16th, 10th, 5th, and 102nd Divisions

CHAPTER 8

1. 101st, 106th, 6th, 9th, and 27th Divisions
2. 3rd, 13th, 10th, and 16th Divisions
3. 116th, 18th, 17th, 22nd, and 115th Divisions
4. 52nd and 109th Divisions
5. 11th, 16th, and 26th Divisions
6. 159th and 160th Divisions
7. 55th and 185th Divisions
8. 9th and 57th Divisions plus attached "fortress" troops
9. 6th and 13th Divisions plus attached "fortress" troops
10. 72nd and 78th Corps, each of two divisions
11. 13th and 98th Corps, each of two divisions
12. 118th and 143rd Divisions
13. 3rd, 10th, 13th, and 16th Divisions
14. 6th, 9th, 27th, 101st and 106th Divisions and the Taiwan Composite Brigade
15. 11th and 16th Divisions
16. 6th, 9th, 27th, 101st and 106th Divisions
17. 2nd, 53rd, 74th, 66th, 4th, 29th, 8th, 64th, and 70th Corps of 20 divisions
18. 12th, 54th, 6th, 52nd, 53rd, and 92nd Corps of 13 divisions
19. 2nd, 26th, 86th, 55th, 20th, 48th, and 84th Corps of 15 divisions
20. 9th and 57th Divisions
21. 48th and 84th Corps

CHAPTER 10

1. 14th, 93rd, and 98th Corps
2. 38th, 96th, and 47th Corps
3. 3rd, 15th, and 17th Corps
4. New 1st, 22nd, 35th, and Manchuria Corps
5. 100th Corps and New 28th Division
6. 28th and 91st Corps
7. 25th and 29th Corps and 67th Division
8. 21st and 50th Corps
9. 65th and 4th Corps
10. 46th and 64th Corps
11. 62nd, 63rd, 66th, and 83rd Corps
12. 55th, 59th, and 77th Corps
13. 84th and 39th Corps
14. 41st and 45th Corps
15. 44th Corps
16. 7th and 8th Corps

17. 81st Corps and 168th Division (all Mongolian)
18. 80th and New 2nd Corps (Chinese) and 82nd Corps (Mongolian)
19. 5th Cavalry Corps
20. 2nd and 6th Cavalry Corps
21. 79th, 49th, 70th, and 32nd Corps
22. 13th, 18th, 92nd, 37th, and 52nd Corps
23. 8th and 73rd Corps
24. 58th, New 3rd, and 60th Corps
25. 20th Corps
26. 72nd Corps
27. 54th, 53rd, and 87th Corps
28. 27th and 90th Corps
29. 51st, 89th, and 57th Corps
30. 90th, 69th, and New 5th Corps
31. 79th, 49th, 70th, and 32nd Corps
32. 8th and 73rd Corps
33. 58th, New 3rd, and 60th Corps
34. 78th and 72nd Corps
35. 25th and 29th Corps and 67th Division
36. 8th and 72nd Corps
37. 13th, 18th, 92nd, 37th, and 52nd Corps
38. 58th, New 3rd, and 60th Corps

CHAPTER 11

1. 173rd, 174th, and 189th Divisions
2. 89th, 110th, and 193rd Divisions
3. of the 39th Corps

CHAPTER 12

1. 10th and 14th Divisions
2. 139th and 141st Divisions
3. 105th and 9th Reserve Divisions
4. New 13th and New 16th Divisions
5. 133rd and 134th Divisions (27th Army Group)
6. 98th, 82nd, and 140th Divisions (15th Army Group)
7. of the 30th Army Group
8. of the 8th Corps
9. of the 79th Corps
10. 133rd and 134th Divisions
11. of the 79th Corps
12. of the 8th Corps
13. 2nd, 25th, and 195th Divisions with 60th Division of 15th Army Group attached

14. 98th, 82nd, and 140th Divisions
15. 19th and 107th Divisions with 95th Division attached
16. 116th and 130th Divisions
17. 14th, 50th, and 23rd Divisions
18. 59th, 90th, and 102nd Divisions
19. of the 37th Corps
20. of the 37th Corps
21. 19th and 107th Corps
22. of the 52nd Corps
23. 19th and 107th Divisions
24. 90th and 102nd Divisions
25. 43rd and 198th Divisions

CHAPTER 13

1. 170th, 175th, and New 19th Divisions
2. 131st, 135th, and 188th Divisions
3. of the 16th and 26th Army Groups
4. 170th and 135th Divisions
5. 131st and 188th Divisions of the 31st Corps
6. New 19th and 175th Divisions
7. 159th and 160th Divisions
8. 131st and 188th Divisions
9. 46th and 64th Corps
10. 31st and 46th Corps
11. 155th and 156th Divisions of the 64th Corps
12. 159th and 160th Divisions

CHAPTER 15

1. 2nd, 31st, 11th, 29th, 22nd, and 33rd Army Groups
2. 75th, 39th, 2nd, New 12th, and 18th Corps
3. 94th and 26th Corps
4. of the 2nd Army Group
5. of the 11th Army Group
6. of the 2nd Army Group
7. of the 33rd Corps
8. of the 33rd Army Group

CHAPTER 18

1. 55th, 59th, and 68th Corps
2. 77th and 30th Corps
3. 92nd, 85th, 29th, 13th, and 84th Corps
4. of the 31st Army Group
5. of the 31st Army Group

6. of the 2nd Army Group
7. of the 2nd Army Group
8. of the 2nd Army Group
9. 38th and 180th Divisions
10. 49th, 70th, 72nd, and 74th Corps
11. 20th Separate Composite Brigade
12. 3rd and 80th Corps
13. 15th and 98th Corps
14. 9th, 17th, 43rd, 14th, and 93rd Corps
15. 54th and New 24th Divisions
16. of the 98th, 93rd, and 15th Corps

CHAPTER 19

1. 20th, 4th, 58th, 72nd, 26th, 37th, 39th, 10th, 2nd Provisional, 79th, and 74th Corps
2. 6th and 7th Advanced Columns
3. 3rd, 4th, 40th, and 6th Divisions with attachments
4. 4th, 40th, and 6th Divisions, two brigades from 13th and 33rd Divisions, and 14th Brigade

Appendix

THE ORDER OF BATTLE LISTED BY CAMPAIGN

CHAPTER 3

Troop units participating in the occupation of the Peking-Tientsin area:

JAPANESE:
Garrison forces on the Peining Railway—General Kyoji Kotouki
  5th Division—General Itagaki
  20th Division—General Kawakishi
  Kawabe Brigade—General Kawabe
  Sakai Brigade—General Sakai
  Suzuki Brigade—General Suzuki
  East Hopei puppet army
  Air and tank units

CHINESE:
29th Corps (Army)—General Sung Che-yuan
  37th Division—General Feng Chih-an
  38th Division—General Chang Tse-chung
  132nd Division—General Chao Teng-yu
  143rd Division (in Kalgan)—General Liu Ju-ming

Troop units participating in the Japanese drive into Inner Mongolia:

JAPANESE:
Nankow front:
  Garrison forces on the Peining Railway—General Kotouki
    5th Division—General Itagaki
    11th Separate Composite Brigade—General Suzuki
    Air and tank units

Kalgan front:
  Chahar Expeditionary Force—commander of the Kwantung Army
    1st Separate Composite Brigade
    12th Separate Composite Brigade
    15th Separate Composite Brigade

Nine cavalry divisions of the Mongolian puppet army
Senda Mechanized Division (in October)

CHINESE:
Taiyuan Pacification Command—General Yen Hsi-shan
   1st Cavalry Corps—General Chao Cheng-shou
     1st Cavalry Division—General Pen Yu-pin
     2nd Cavalry Division—General Sun Chang-sheng
     6th Cavalry Division—Liu Kwei-wu
     7th Cavalry Division—General Men Ping-yueh
     New 2nd Cavalry Brigade—General Shih Yu-shan
     218 Infantry Brigade—General Tung Chi-wu
     New 5th Infantry Brigade—General An Yung-chan
     New 6th Infantry Brigade—General Wang Tse-hsiu
     New 3rd Infantry Brigade—General Ching Teh-chuan
   7th Army Group—General Fu Tso-yi
     72nd Division—General Chen Chang-chieh
     7th Separate Brigade—General Ma Yen-shou
     200th Brigade—General Liu Tan-fu
     211th Brigade—General Sun Lan-feng
   7th Army Group—General Liu Ju-ming (deputy commander)
     143rd Division—General Liu Ju-ming
     29th Separate Brigade—General Liu Ju-chen
     Two brigades of the Chahar Peace Preservation Corps
   Front Line Command—General T'ang En-po
     13th Corps—General T'ang En-po
       4th Division—General Wang Wan-ling
       89th Division—General Wang Chung-lien
     17th Corps—General Kao Kuei-tse
       21st Division—General Li Hsien-jou
       84th Division—General Kao Kuei-tse
       94th Division—General Chu Huai-ping

1st War Area Command—Generalissimo Chiang Kai-shek
   14th Army Group—General Wei Li-huang
     14th Corps—General Li Mo-yen
       10th Division—General Li Mo-yen
       83rd Division—General Liu Kan
       85th Division—General Chen Tieh

8th Route Army (Communist)—General Chu Teh
   115th Division—General Lin Piao

CHAPTER 4

Troop units participating in the Battle of Shanghai and the Fall of Nanking:

JAPANESE:
Central China Front Army—General Iwane Matsui
    10th Corps—General Yanagawa
      6th Division
      18th Division
      114th Division
      Kunizaki Column
    Shanghai Expeditionary Force—General Iwane Matsui
      3rd Division
      9th Division
      11th Division
      13th Division
      16th Division—General Nakashima
      101st Division
      Taiwan Composite Infantry Brigade
      1st Reserve Infantry Regiment
      Shigito Column
      Three brigades of Chinese puppet troops

CHINESE (after mid-September, 1937):
3rd War Area Command—Generalissimo Chiang Kai-shek, General Ku Chu-tung (deputy commander)
    Right Wing Force—General Chang Fa-kuei
      8th Army Group—General Chang Fa-kuei
        28th Corps—General Tao Kuang
          62nd Division—General Tao Kuang
          63rd Division—General Chen Kuang-chung
        55th Division—General Li Sung-shan
        45th Separate Brigade—General Chang Luan-chi
        2nd Regiment, 2nd Artillery Brigade
        Training Division artillery battalion
      10th Army Group—General Liu Chien-hsu
        11th Reserve Division—General Hu Ta
        128th Division—General Ku Chia-chi
        45th Division—General Tai Min-chuan
        52nd Division—General Lu Hsin-jung
        11th Temporary Brigade—General Chou Hsi-ching
        12th Temporary Brigade—General Li Kuo-chun

37th Separate Brigade—General Chen Teh-fa
Guard regiment
Ningpo Defense Command—General Wang Kao-lan
Central Force—General Chang Chih-chung
  9th Army Group—General Chu Shao-liang
    72nd Corps—General Sun Yuan-liang
      88th Division—General Sun Yuan-liang
      Peace-preservation group
      1st Regiment, 20th Separate Brigade
    78th Corps—General Sung Hsi-lien
      36th Division—General Sung Hsi-lien
    71st Corps—General Wang Ching-chiu
      87th Division—General Wang Ching-chiu
    8th Corps—General Huang Chieh
      61st Division—General Chung Sung
      Salt Gabelle Division—General Huang Chieh
      3rd Division—General Li Yu-tang
      18th Division—General Chu Yao-hua
      1st Battalion, 3rd Artillery Regiment, 2nd Artillery Brigade
      Shanghai Garrison Command—General Yang Hu
  21st Army Group—General Liao Lei
    1st Corps—General Hu Tsung-nan
      1st Division—General Li Tieh-chun
      32nd Division—General Wang Hsiu-shen
      78th Division—General Li Wen
    48th Corps—General Wei Yun-sung
      173rd Division—General Huo Wei-chen
      174th Division—General Wang Tsan-pin
      176th Division—General Ou Shou-nien
    171st Division—General Yang Chun-chang
    19th Division—General Li Chueh
    16th Division—General Peng Sung-ling
Left Wing Force—General Ch'en Ch'eng
  19th Army Group—General Hsueh Yueh
    66th Corps—General Yeh Chao
      195th Division—General Tan Sui
      160th Division—General Yeh Chao
    75th Corps—General Chou Ai
      6th Division—General Chou Ai
    2nd Corps—General Li Yen-nien
      9th Division—General Li Yen-nien
    25th Corps—General Wan Yao-huang

13th Division—General Wan Yao-huang
20th Corps—General Yang Sen
133rd Division—General Yang Han-yu
134th Division—General Yang Han-chung
59th Corps—General Yuan Chao-chang
57th Division—General Yuan Chao-chang
15th Army Group—General Lo Cho-ying
16th Army—General Lo Cho-ying
18th Corps—General Lo Cho-ying
60th Division—General Chen Pei
11th Division—General Peng Shan
67th Division—General Huang Wei
54th Corps—General Huo Kuei-chang
14th Division—General Chen Lieh
98th Division—General Hsia Chu-chung
74th Corps—General Yu Chi-shih
51st Division—General Wang Yao-wu
58th Division—General Yu Chi-shih
39th Corps—General Liu Ho-ting
56th Division—General Liu Shang-chih
34th Separate Brigade—General Lo Chi-chiang
4th Corps—General Wu Chi-wei
90th Division—General Ou Chen
73rd Corps—General Wang Tung-yuan
15th Division—General Wang Chih-pin
15th Army—General Liu Hsing
102nd Division—General Po Hui-chang
103rd Division—General Ho Chih-chung
53rd Division—General Li Yun-heng
23rd Division—General Li Pi-fan
57th Corps—General Miao Cheng-liu
111th Division—General Chang En-tuo
112th Division—General Huo Shou-yi
44th Division—General Chen Yung
16th Artillery Regiment
River Defense Forces—General Liu Hsing
11th Army—General Shang-kuan Yun-hsiang
40th Division—General Liu Pei-hsu
33rd Division—General Ma Hsing-hsien
12th Army—General Chang Fang
76th Division—General Wang Ling-yun
43rd Corps—General Kuo Ju-tung

26th Division—General Liu Yu-ching
Chiangyin Fortress Command—General Hsu Kang
Chenchiang Fortress Command—General Lin Hsien-yang
4th Artillery Regiment
Three separate artillery battalions
Capital Garrison Forces—General Tang Sheng-chih
    72nd Corps—General Sun Yuan-liang
        88th Division
    78th Corps—General Sung Hsi-lien
        36th Division
    74th Corps—General Yu Chi-shih
        51st Division
        58th Division
    71st Corps—General Wang Ching-chiu
        87th Division
    2nd Army—General Hsu Yuan-chuan
        41st Division—General Ting Chih-pan
        48th Division
    83rd Corps
        155th Division—General Chen Kung-hsia
        156th Division—General Li Chiang
        103rd Division
    Capital Garrison—General Ku Cheng-lun
        121st Division—General Wu Chien-ping
        Training Division
        Chiangning Fortress Command—General Shao Pai-chang
23rd Army Group—General Liu Hsiang
    144th Division—General Kuo Hsun-chi
    145th Division
    146th Division
    147th Division
    148th Division

CHAPTER 5

Troop units participating in the three-pronged drive from the Peking-Tientsin-Kalgan area toward the Yellow River:

1. *Operations in the northern sector of the Pinghan Railway corridor:*

JAPANESE:

North China Front Army—General Hisaichi Terauchi
    1st Corps—General Kyoji Kotouki
        5th Division—General Itagaki

14th Division—General Doihara
6th Division
20th Division—General Kawamine
108th Division
2nd Corps—General Juzo Nishio
16th Division—General Nakashima
109th Division
Kwantung Army Expeditionary Force
Five composite infantry brigades
Nine puppet Mongolian cavalry divisions
Kawabe Brigade—General Kawabe

CHINESE (August and September, 1937):
1st War Area—Generalissimo Chiang Kai-shek
  2nd Army Group—General Liu Chih, General Sun Lien-chung
  (deputy commander)
    1st Army—General Sun Lien-chung
      27th Division—General Feng An-pang
      30th Division—General Chang Chin-chao
      31st Division—General Chih Feng-cheng
      44th Separate Brigade—General Chang Hua-tang
    3rd Corps—General Tseng Wan-chung
      7th Division—General Tseng Wan-chung
      12th Division—General Tang Huai-yuan
    52nd Corps—General Kuan Lin-cheng
      2nd Division—General Cheng Tung-kuo
      25th Division—General Kuan Lin-cheng
    14th Army—General Feng Chien-tsai
      42nd Division—General Liu Yen-piao
      169th Division—General Wu Shih-ming
    4th Cavalry Corps—General Tan Tse-hsin
      10th Cavalry Division—General Tan Tse-hsin
    47th Division—General Pei Chang-hui
    17th Division—General Chao Shou-shan
    177th Division—General Li Hsing-chung
    5th Separate Brigade—General Cheng Ting-chen
    46th Separate Brigade—General Pao Kang
    14th Cavalry Brigade—General Chang Chan-kuei
  14th Army Group—General Wei Li-huang
    14th Corps—General Li Mo-yen
      10th Division—General Li Mo-yen
      83rd Division—General Liu Kan

85th Division—General Chen Tieh
20th Army Group—General Shang Chen
　32nd Corps—General Shang Chen
　　139th Division—General Huang Kuang-hua
　　141st Division—General Sung Ken-tang
　　142nd Division—General Lu Chi
53rd Corps—General Wan Fu-lin
　116th Division—General Chou Fu-cheng
　130th Division—General Chu Hung-hsun
　91st Division—General Feng Chan-hai

CHINESE (October, 1937, to January, 1938):
1st War Area—General Cheng Chien
　1st Army Group—General Sung Che-yuan
　　59th Corps—General Chang Tse-chung
　　　38th Division—General Huang Wei-kang
　　　180th Division—General Liu Tse-chen
　　68th Corps—General Liu Ju-ming
　　　119th Division—General Li Chin-tien
　　　143rd Division—General Li Tseng-chih
　　77th Corps—General Feng Chih-an
　　　37th Division—General Chang Ling-yun
　　　179th Division—General Ho Chi-feng
　　　132nd Division—General Wang Chang-hai
　　3rd Corps—General Cheng Ta-chang
　　　139th Division—General Huang Kuang-hua
　　　4th Cavalry Division—General Wang Chi-feng
　　　9th Cavalry Division—General Cheng Ta-chang
　　181st Division—General Shih Yu-san
　20th Army Group—General Shang Chen
　　32nd Corps—General Shang Chen
　　　141st Division—General Sung Ken-tang
　　　142nd Division—General Lu Chi
　　46th Separate Brigade—General Pao Kang
　　14th Cavalry Brigade—General Chang Chan-kuei
　20th Army—General T'ang En-po
　　52nd Corps—General Kuan Lin-chen
　　　2nd Division—General Cheng Tung-kuo
　　　25th Division—General Chang Yao-ming
　　13th Corps—General T'ang En-po
　　　4th Division—General Chen Ta-ching
　　　89th Division—General Wang Chung-lien

53rd Corps—General Wan Fu-lin
  116th Division—General Chou Fu-cheng
  130th Division—General Chu Hung-hsun
  91st Division—General Feng Chan-hai

2. *Operations in the northern sector of the Tsinpu Railway:*

JAPANESE:
2nd Corps—General Hisaichi Terauchi
  10th Division—General Isoya
  16th Division—General Nakashima
  109th Division

CHINESE:
6th War Area—General Feng Yu-hsiang
  1st Army Group—General Sung Che-yuan
    19th Army—General Feng Chih-an
      59th Corps—General Sung Che-yuan
        38th Division—General Huang Wei-kang
        180th Division—General Liu Chen-shan
        Hopei peace-preservation forces
      77th Corps—General Feng Chih-an
        37th Division—General Liu Tse-chen
        132nd Division—General Wang Chang-hai
        179th Division—General Ho Chi-feng
        181st Division—General Shih Yu-san
    3rd Army—General P'ang Ping-hsun
      40th Corps—General P'ang Ping-hsun
        39th Division—General P'ang Ping-hsun
      49th Corps—General Liu Tuo-chuan
        105th Division—General Kao Peng-yun
        109th Division—General Chao Yi
      3rd Cavalry Corps—General Cheng Ta-chang
        4th Cavalry Division—General Wang Chi-feng
        9th Cavalry Division—General Cheng Ta-chang
    67th Corps—General Wu Ke-jen
      107th Division—General Chih Kuei-pi
      108th Division—General Chang Wen-ching
    23rd Division—General Li Pi-fan
    12th Corps—General Sun Tung-hsun
      20th Division—General Sun Tung-hsun
      81st Division—General Chan Shu-tang

3. *Operations in the Kalgan-Taiyuan and Shihkiachuang-Taiyuan railway sectors:*

JAPANESE:

September, 1937:
>   North China Front Army—General Hisaichi Terauchi
>   5th Division—General Itagaki
>   Chahar Expeditionary Force—under Kwantung Army command
>   1st Separate Composite Brigade
>   11th Separate Composite Brigade
>   12th Separate Composite Brigade
>   15th Separate Composite Brigade
>   Nine cavalry divisions of the puppet Mongolian army

October, 1937:
>   North China Front Army—General Hisaichi Terauchi
>   5th Division—General Itagaki
>   11th Separate Composite Brigade—General Suzuki
>   Chahar Expeditionary Force—under Kwantung Army command
>   1st Separate Composite Brigade
>   12th Separate Composite Brigade
>   15th Separate Composite Brigade
>   Nine cavalry divisions of the puppet Mongolian army

November, 1937:
>   North China Front Army—General Hisaichi Terauchi
>   5th Division—General Itagaki
>   20th Division—General Kawakishi
>   109th Division
>   11th Separate Composite Brigade—General Suzuki
>   Chahar Expeditionary Force—under Kwantung Army command
>   1st Separate Composite Brigade
>   12th Separate Composite Brigade
>   15th Separate Composite Brigade
>   Nine cavalry divisions of the puppet Mongolian army

CHINESE:

2nd War Area—General Yen Hsi-shan
>   6th Army Group—General Yang Ai-yuan
>   33rd Corps—General Sun Chu
>   73rd Division—General Liu Feng-pin
>   8th Separate Brigade
>   3rd Separate Brigade—General Chang Chi-yu

34th Corps—General Yang Cheng-yuan
  71st Division—General Kuo Tsung-fen
  196th Separate Brigade—General Chiang Yu-chen
  203rd Separate Brigade—General Liang Chien-tang
New 2nd Division—General Chin Hsien-chang
7th Army Group—General Fu Tso-yi
  35th Corps—General Fu Tso-yi
    218th Separate Brigade—General Tung Chi-wu
    211th Separate Brigade—General Sun Lan-feng
    205th Separate Brigade—General Tien Shu-mei
  61st Corps—General Chen Chang-chieh
    101st Division—General Li Chun-kung
    200th Separate Brigade—General Liu Tan-fu
    7th Separate Brigade—General Ma Yen-shou
  17th Corps—General Kao Kuei-tse
    84th Division—General Kao Kuei-tse
    21st Division—General Li Hsien-chou
  6th Cavalry Corps—General Men Ping-yueh
    7th Cavalry Division—General Men Ping-yueh
    1st Temporary Cavalry Division—General Feng Piao
  New 2nd Brigade—General An Hua-ting
  New 6th Brigade—General Wang Tse-hsiu
  New 2nd Cavalry Brigade—General Shih Yu-shan
14th Army Group—General Wei Li-huang
  14th Corps—General Li Mo-yen
    10th Division—General Li Mo-yen
    83rd Division—General Liu Kan
  9th Corps—General Ho Meng-lin
    47th Division—General Pei Chang-hui
    54th Division—General Liu Chia-chi
  85th Division—General Chen Tieh
  5th Separate Brigade—General Cheng Ting-chen
Deputy Command, 2nd War Area—General Huang Shao-hsiung
  1st Army—General Sun Lien-chung
    27th Division—General Fen An-pang
    30th Division—General Chang Chin-chao
    31st Division—General Chih Feng-cheng
    44th Separate Brigade—General Chang Hua-tang
  3rd Corps—General Tseng Wan-chung
    7th Division—General Li Shih-lung
    12th Division—General Tang Huai-yuan

14th Army—General Feng Chin-tsai
  42nd Division—General Liu Yen-piao
  169th Division—General Wu Shih-ming
  94th Division—General Chu Huai-ping
  17th Division—General Chao Shou-shan
13th Corps—General T'ang En-po
  4th Division—General Wang Wan-ling
  89th Division—General Wang Chung-lien
19th Corps—General Wang Ching-kuo
  2nd Separate Brigade—General Fang Ke-yu
  215th Separate Brigade—General Tu Kun
  72nd Division—General Tuan Shu-hua
1st Cavalry Corps—General Chao Cheng-shou
  1st Cavalry Division—General Pen Yu-pin
  2nd Cavalry Division—General Sun Chang-sheng
15th Corps—General Liu Mao-en
  64th Division—General Wu Ting-lin
  65th Division—General Liu Mao-en
66th Division—General Tu Chun-yi
Advance Force Command—General Ma Chen-shan
  6th Cavalry Division—General Liu Kuei-wu
2nd Cavalry Corps—General Ho Chu-kuo
  3rd Cavalry Division—General Hsu Liang

CHAPTER 6

Troop units participating in the operations in the corridor of the Tsinpu Railway between the Yellow and the Yangtze rivers:

JAPANESE:

North China Front Army—General Hisaichi Terauchi
  Northern Sector Command, Tsinpu Railway—General Nishio
    10th Division—General Isoya
    16th Division, less 30th Brigade—General Nakashima
    110th Division—General Tategawa
    114th Division—General Suematsu
    105th Brigade of the 113th Division—General Motogawa
    One brigade of the 11th Division—General Yamamoto
    5th Division—General Itagaki
    121st Brigade of the 105th Division—General Itada
    Yamashita Brigade—General Yamashita
    Sakai Brigade—General Sakai
    One regiment of the 102nd Division

Central China Expeditionary Force—General Shunroku Hata
   Southern Sector Command, Tsinpu Railway—General Shunroku
   Hata
      9th Division—General Ryosuke
      Konoye Division—General Itada
      111th Brigade of the 106th Division—General Yanagawa
      One brigade of the 3rd Division
      One brigade of the 11th Division
      One brigade of the 101st Division—General Inutsuka
      One brigade of the 116th Division—General Sato
      One brigade of the 13th Division

CHINESE:
5th War Area—General Li Tsung-jen
   2nd Army Group—General Sun Lien-chung
      30th Corps—General Tien Chen-nan
         30th Division—General Chang Chin-chao
         31st Division—General Chih Feng-chen
      42nd Corps—General Feng An-pang
         27th Division—General Huang Chiao-sung
         44th Division—General Wu Peng-chu
   3rd Army Group—General Sun Tung-hsuan
      12th Corps—General Sun Tung-hsuan
         20th Division—General Sun Tung-hsuan
         81st Division—General Chan Shu-tang
      55th Corps—General Tsao Fu-lin
         29th Division—General Tsao Fu-lin
         74th Division—General Li Han-chang
      56th Corps—General Ku Liang-min
         22nd Division—General Ku Liang-min
         Pistol Brigade—General Wu Hua-wen
   11th Army Group—General Li Pin-hsien
      31st Corps—General Wei Yun-sung
         131st Division—General Chin Lien-fang
         135th Division—General Su Tzu-hsing
         138th Division—General Mo Teh-hung
   21st Army Group—General Liao Lei
      7th Corps—General Chou Tsu-huang
         170th Division—General Hsu Chi-ming
         171st Division—General Yang Fu-chang
         172nd Division—General Cheng Shu-fang
      48th Corps—General Liao Lei

174th Division—General Wang Tsan-pin
176th Division—General Ou Shou-nien
22nd Army Group—General Sun Chen (acting)
41st Corps—General Sun Chen
122nd Division—General Wang Ming-chang
124th Division—General Wang Shih-chun
45th Corps—General Chen Ting-hsun
125th Division—General Chen Ting-hsun
127th Division—General Chen Li
24th Army Group—General Han Teh-chin (acting)
57th Corps—General Miao Cheng-liu
111th Division—General Chang En-tuo
112th Division—General Huo Shou-yi
89th Corps—General Han Teh-chin
33rd Division—General Han Teh-chin
117th Division—General Li Shou-wei
Kiangsu peace-preservation units
26th Army Group—General Hsu Yuan-chuan
10th Corps—General Hsu Yuan-chuan
41st Division—General Ting Chih-pan
48th Division—General Hsu Chi-wu
199th Division—General Lo Shu-chia
27th Army Group—General Yang Sen
20th Corps—General Yang Sen
133rd Division—General Yang Han-yu
134th Division—General Yang Han-chung
3rd Army—General P'ang Ping-hsun
40th Corps—General P'ang Ping-hsun
39th Division—General Ma Fa-wu
19th Army—General Feng Chih-an
77th Corps—General Feng Chih-an
37th Division—General Chia Chien-hsi
179th Division—General Ho Chi-feng
132nd Division—General Wang Chang-hai
20th Army—General T'ang En-po
52nd Corps—General Kuan Lin-cheng
2nd Division—General Cheng Tung-kuo
25th Division—General Chang Yao-ming
85th Corps—General Wang Chung-lien
4th Division—General Chen Ta-ching
89th Division—General Chang Hsueh-chung
110th Division—General Chang Chen

27th Army—General Chang Tse-chung
  59th Corps—General Chang Tse-chung
    38th Division—General Huang Wei-kang
    180th Division—General Liu Chen-san
    9th Division—General Chang Teh-shun
    13th Cavalry Brigade—General Yao Ching-chuan
  2nd Corps—General Li Yen-nien
    3rd Division—General Li Yu-tang
    9th Division—General Li Yen-nien
  22nd Corps—General Tan Tao-yuan
    50th Division—General Chen Kuang-yu
  46th Corps—General Fan Sung-pu
    28th Division—General Tung Chao
    49th Division—General Chou Chih-mien
    92nd Division—General Huang Kuo-liang
  51st Corps—General Yu Hsueh-chung
    113th Division—General Chou Kuang-lieh
    114th Division—General Mu Chung-heng
  60th Corps—General Lu Han
    182nd Division—General An En-fu
    183rd Division—General Kao Yin-huai
    184th Division—General Chang Chung
  68th Corps—General Liu Ju-ming
    119th Division—General Li Chin-tien
    143rd Division—General Li Tseng-chih
  69th Corps—General Shih Yu-san
    181st Division—General Shih Yu-san
    New 6th Division—General Kao Shu-hsun
  75th Corps—General Chou Ai
    6th Division—General Chang Chi
    93rd Division—General Kan Li-chu
  92nd Corps—General Li Hsien-chou
    13th Division—General Wu Liang-shen
    21st Division—General Li Hsien-chou
  95th Division—General Lo Chi
  104th Division—General Wang Wen-yen
  1st Regiment, 1st Artillery Brigade
  4th, 5th, 6th, and 7th artillery regiments

CHAPTER 7

Troop units participating in operations in eastern and northern Honan:

JAPANESE:

North China Front Army—General Hisaichi Terauchi
   1st Corps—General Kotouki
      14th Division—General Doihara
      108th Division—General Shimomoto
      Supporting air, tank, and artillery units
   2nd Corps—General Nishio
      16th Division—General Nakashima
      11th Division
      114th Division—General Suematsu
      Supporting air, tank, and artillery units

CHINESE:

1st War Area—General Cheng Chien
   Eastern Honan Army—General Hsueh Yueh
      64th Corps—General Li Han-huen
         155th Division—General Chen Kung-hsia
         187th Division—General Peng Ling-sheng
      74th Corps—General Yu Chi-shih
         51st Division—General Wang Yao-wu
         58th Division—General Feng Sheng-fa
      8th Corps—General Huang Chieh
         40th Division—General Lo Li-jung
         102nd Division—General Po Hui-chang
    27th Corps—General Kuei Yung-ching
         36th Division—General Chiang Fu-sheng
         46th Division—General Li Liang-yung
    17th Army—General Hu Tsung-nan
      1st Corps—General Li Tieh-chun
         1st Division—General Li Tieh-chun
         78th Division—General Li Wen
   3rd Army Group—General Sun Tung-hsuan (acting)
      12th Corps—General Sun Tung-hsuan
         20th Division—General Chang Tse-ming
         22nd Division—General Ku Liang-min
         81st Division—General Chan Shu-tang
    55th Corps—General Tsao Fu-lin
         29th Division—General Tsao Fu-lin
         74th Division—General Li Han-chang

20th Army Group—General Shang Chen
  32nd Corps—General Shang Chen
    139th Division—General Li Chao-ying
    141st Division—General Sung Ken-tang
    142nd Division—General Lu Chi
    Salt Gabelle Brigade—General Chiang Chi-ke
    23rd Division—General Li Pi-fan
  71st Corps—General Sung Hsi-lien
    87th Division—General Shen Fa-tsao
    88th Division—General Lung Mu-han
  39th Corps—General Liu Ho-ting
    34th Division—General Kung Ping-fan
    56th Division—General Liu Shang-chih
1st Army Group—General Sung Che-yuan
  77th Corps—General Feng Chih-an
    37th Division—General Chang Ling-yun
    132nd Division—General Wang Chang-hai
    179th Division—General Ho Chi-feng
  69th Corps—General Shih Yu-san
    181st Division—General Shih Yu-san
    New 9th Division—General Kao Shu-hsun
  53rd Corps—General Wan Fu-lin
    116th Division—General Chou Fu-cheng
    130th Division—General Chu Hung-hsun
  91st Corps—General Kao Tse-chu
    166th Division—General Ma Li-wu
    45th Division—General Liu Chin
  90th Corps—General Peng Chin-chih
    195th Division—General Liang Kai
    196th Division—General Liu Chao-huan
  3rd Cavalry Corps—General Cheng Ta-chang
    9th Cavalry Division—General Chang Teh-hsun
    4th Cavalry Division—General Wang Chi-feng
  New 8th Division—General Chiang Tsai-chen
  95th Division—General Lo Chi
  91st Division—General Feng Chan-hsi
  New 35th Division—General Wang Ching-tsai
  61st Division—General Chung Sung
  106th Division—General Shen Ke
  109th Division—General Li Shu-sen
  94th Division—General Chu Huai-ping
  24th Division—General Lin Ying

9th Reserve Division—General Chu Huai-ping
8th Reserve Division—General Ling Chao-yao
28th Separate Brigade—General Wu Hua-wen
Hopei militia forces—General Chang Yin-wu
Hopei-Chahar Guerrilla Forces—General Sun Tien-ying
14th Separate Cavalry Brigade—General Chang Chan-kuei
2nd Brigade, New 1st Cavalry Division—General Ma Lu
13th Cavalry Brigade—General Yao Ching-chuan
6th Artillery Brigade—General Huang Yung-an
10th Separate Artillery Regiment—Colonel Peng Meng-chi
5th Regiment, 1st Artillery Brigade—Colonel Li Kang-yen
7th Separate Artillery Regiment—Colonel Chang Kuang-hou
9th Separate Artillery Regiment—Colonel Kuang Yu-ai

CHAPTER 8

Troop units participating in the Hankow (Wuhan) campaign:

JAPANESE:

Central China Expeditionary Force—General Shunroku Hata
    11th Corps—General Okamura
        101st Division—General Inutsuka
        106th Division—General Yanagawa
        6th Division—General Inaba
        9th Division
        27th Division
        Taiwan Infantry Brigade
    2nd Corps—General Prince Naruhito
        3rd Division
        13th Division
        10th Division—General Isoya
        16th Division—General Nakashima
    Army Troops—General Hata
        116th Division—General Sato
        18th Division
        17th Division
        15th Division
    Three air regiments—General Tokugawa

CHINESE:

9th War Area—General Ch'en Ch'eng
    1st Army Corps—General Hsueh Yueh
        20th Army Group—General Shang Chen
            32nd Corps—General Shang Chen

139th Division—General Li Chao-ying
141st Division—General Tang Yung-liang
142nd Division—General Fu Li-ping
Salt Gabelle Brigade—General Chiang Yung-ke
18th Corps—General Huang Wei
11th Division—General Peng Shan
16th Division—General Ho Ping
60th Division—General Chen Pei
9th Army Group—General Wu Chi-wei
29th Army—General Li Han-huen
64th Corps—General Li Han-huen
155th Division—General Chen Kung-hsia
187th Division—General Kung Ke-chuan
9th Reserve Division—General Chang Yen-chuan
70th Corps—General Li Chueh
19th Division—General Li Chueh
91st Division—General Feng Chan-hai
6th Reserve Division—General Chi Chang-chien
37th Army—General Wang Ching-chiu
25th Corps—General Wang Ching-chiu
52nd Division
109th Division—General Liang Hua-sheng
4th Corps—General Ou Chen
59th Division—General Chang Teh-neng
90th Division—General Chen Yung-chi
8th Corps—General Li Yu-tang
3rd Division—General Chao Hsi-tien
15th Division—General Wang Chih-pin
66th Corps—General Yeh Chao
159th Division—General Tan Sui
160th Division—General Hua Chen-chung
74th Corps—General Yu Chi-shih
51st Division—General Wang Yao-wu
58th Division—General Feng Shang-fa
29th Corps—General Chen An-pao
40th Division—General Li Tien-hsia
79th Division—General Chen An-pao
167th Division—General Chao Hsia-kuang
Poyang Lake Garrison
2nd Army Corps—General Chang Fa-kuei
30th Army Group—General Wang Ling-chi
72nd Corps—General Wang Ling-chi

New 13th Division—General Liu Juo-pi
New 14th Division—General Fan Nan-hsuan
78th Corps—General Chang Tsai
New 15th Division—General Teng Kuo-chang
New 16th Division—General Chen Liang-chi
3rd Army Group—General Sun Tung-hsuan
12th Corps—General Sun Tung-hsuan
20th Division—General Chang Tse-min
22nd Division—General Shih Tung-jan
81st Division—General Chan Shu-tang
31st Army Group—General T'ang En-po
13th Corps—General Chang Chen
23rd Division—General Ouyang Fen
89th Division—General Chang Hsueh-chung
35th Division—General Wang Ching-tsai
98th Corps—General Chang Kang
82nd Division—General Lo Chi-chiang
193rd Division—General Li Tsung-chien
195th Division—General Liang Kai
32nd Army—General Kuan Lin-cheng
52nd Corps—General Kuan Lin-cheng
2nd Division—General Chao Kung-wu
25th Division—General Chang Yao-ming
92nd Corps—General Li Hsien-chou
21st Division—General Hou Ching-ju
95th Division—General Lo Chi
11th Army—General Li Yen-nien
2nd Corps—General Li Yen-nien
9th Division—General Cheng Tso-min
57th Division—General Shih Chung-cheng
Tienchiachen fortress units
Tiennan Fortress Command—General Hou Kuei-chang
54th Corps—General Hou Kuei-chang
14th Division—General Chen Lieh
18th Division—General Li Fang-pin
Wuhan Garrison Command—General Lo Cho-ying
Yangtze River South Region—General Wan Yao-huang
6th Corps—General Kan Li-chu
93rd Division—General Kan Li-chu
16th Corps—General Tung Chao
28th Division—General Tung Chao

Yangtze River North Region—General Chou Ai
 75th Corps—General Chou Ai
  6th Division—General Chang Ying
  13th Division—General Fang Ching
  Fortress units
Wuhan Garrison—General Kuo Chan
 94th Corps—General Kuo Chan
  55th Division—General Li Chi-lan
  185th Division—General Fang Tien
 37th Corps—General Huang Kuo-liang
  92nd Division—General Huang Kuo-liang
30th Army—General Lu Han
 60th Corps—General Lu Han
  184th Division—General Chang Chung
  49th Division—General Li Ching-yi
  102nd Division—General Po Hui-chang
26th Army—General Wan Fu-lin
 53rd Corps—General Wan Fu-lin
  130th Division—General Chu Hung-hsun
  116th Division—General Chou Fu-cheng

5th War Area—General Li Tsung-jen, General Pai Ch'ung-hsi (acting
commander)
 3rd Army Corps—General Sun Lien-chung
  2nd Army Group—General Sun Lien-chung
   30th Corps—General Tien Chen-nan
    30th Division—General Chang Chin-lieh
    31st Division—General Chih Feng-cheng
   42nd Corps—General Feng An-pang
    27th Division—General Huang Chiao-sung
    44th Separate Brigade—General Wu Peng-chu
  26th Corps—General Hsiao Chi-chu
   32nd Division—General Wang Hsiu-shen
   44th Division—General Chen Yung
  55th Corps—General Tsao Fu-lin
   29th Division—General Tsao Fu-lin
   74th Division—General Li Han-chang
  87th Corps—General Liu Yin-ku
   198th Division—General Wang Yu-ying
 4th Army Corps—General Li Pin-hsien
  29th Army Group—General Wang Tsan-hua
   44th Corps—General Peng Cheng-fu

149th Division—General Wang Tse-chun
162nd Division—General Chang Chieh-cheng
67th Corps—General Hsu Shao-tsung
150th Division—General Liao Chen
161st Division—General Hsu Shao-tsung
11th Army Group—General Li Pin-hsien
84th Corps—General Chin Lien-fang
188th Division—General Liu Jen
189th Division—General Lin Ya-hsi
48th Corps—General Chang Yi-shun
173rd Division—General Huo Wei-chen
174th Division—General Chang Kuang-wei
176th Division—General Ou Shou-nien
68th Corps—General Liu Ju-ming
119th Division—General Li Chin-tien
143rd Division—General Li Tseng-chih
86th Corps—General Ho Chih-chung
103rd Division—General Ho Shao-chou
121st Division—General Mo Ting-fang
26th Army Group—General Hsu Yuan-chuan
10th Corps—General Hsu Yuan-chuan
41st Division—General Ting Chih-pan
48th Division—General Hsu Chi-wu
199th Division—General Lo Shu-chia
21st Army Group—General Liao Lei
31st Corps—General Wei Yun-sung
131st Division—General Lin Tse-hsi
135th Division—General Su Tsu-hsing
138th Division—General Mo Teh-hung
7th Corps—General Chang Kan
171st Division—General Chi Tao-chung
172nd Division—General Cheng Shu-fen
19th Army—General Feng Chih-an
77th Corps—General Feng Chih-an
37th Division—General Chang Ling-yun
132nd Division—General Wang Chang-hai
51st Corps—General Yu Hsueh-chung
113th Division—General Chou Kuang-lieh
114th Division—General Mo Chung-heng
71st Corps—General Sung Hsi-lien
61st Division—General Chung Sung
88th Division—General Chung Pin

36th Division—General Chiang Fu-sheng
27th Army—General Chang Tse-chung
   59th Corps—General Chang Tse-chung
      38th Division—General Huang Wei-kang
      180th Division—General Liu Chen-san
      13th Cavalry Brigade—General Yao Ching-chuan
      One cavalry regiment
   45th Corps—General Chen Ting-hsun
      125th Division—General Wang Shih-chun
      127th Division—General Chen Li
24th Army Group—General Han Teh-chin
   57th Corps—General Miao Cheng-liu
      111th Division—General Chang En-tou
      112th Division—General Huo Shou-yi
   89th Corps—General Han Teh-chin
      33rd Division—General Chia Yun-shan
      117th Division—General Li Shou-wei
27th Army Group—General Yang Sen
   30th Corps—General Yang Sen
      133rd Division—General Yang Han-yu
      134th Division—General Yang Han-chung
17th Army—General Hu Tsung-nan
   1st Corps—General Hu Tsung-nan
      1st Division—General Li Cheng-hsien
      78th Division—General Li Wen

CHAPTER 9

Troop units participating in the fall of Canton:

JAPANESE:
21st Corps—General Mikio
   11th Division
   18th Division
   104th Division
   Supporting air and naval units

CHINESE:
12th Army Group—General Yu Han-mou
   62nd Corps—General Chang Ta
      151st Division—General Mo Hsi-teh
      152nd Division—General Chen Chang

63rd Corps—General Chang Jui-kuei
   153rd Division—General Chang Jui-kuei
   154th Division—General Liang Shih-chi
65th Corps—General Li Chen-chiu
   156th Division—General Li Chiang
   157th Division—General Huang Tao
   158th Division—General Tseng Yu-chiang
9th Separate Brigade—General Li Chen-liang
20th Separate Brigade—General Chen Mien-wu
Humen Fortress Command—General Chen Tse

CHAPTER 10

Troop units participating in the battles for Nanchang:

JAPANESE:

11th Corps—General Okamura
   6th Division—General Inaba
   101st Division—General Saito
   106th Division—General Matsuura
   One brigade of the 116th Division—General Sato
   120th Cavalry Regiment—Colonel Hasekawa
   22nd Artillery Regiment—Colonel Nakahira
   One battalion of marines
   Supporting air and naval craft

CHINESE:

9th War Area—General Ch'en Ch'eng, General Hsueh Yueh (acting commander)
   19th Army Group—General Lo Cho-ying
     79th Corps—General Hsia Chu-chung
      118th Division—General Wang Ling-yun
      76th Division—General Wang Ling-yun
      98th Division—General Wang Chia-pen
     49th Corps—General Liu Tuo-chuan
      105th Division—General Wang Tieh-han
      9th Reserve Division—General Chang Yen-chuan
     70th Corps—General Li Chueh
      19th Division—General Li Chueh
      107th Division—General Tuan Heng
     32nd Corps—General Sung Ken-tang
      139th Division—General Li Chao-ying
      141st Division—General Tang Yung-liang
      142nd Division—General Fu Li-ping

5th Reserve Division—General Tseng Chia-chu
Poyang Lake Garrison—General Tseng Chia-chu
 (three regiments of Kiangsi peace-preservation forces)
Lu Shan Guerrilla Command—General Yang Yu-chen
 (two peace-preservation regiments)
74th Corps—General Yu Chi-shih
 51st Division—General Wang Yao-wu
 58th Division—General Feng Sheng-fa
 60th Division—General Chen Pei
Hunan-Hupei-Kiangsi Border Guerrilla Command—General Fan
Sung-pu
 8th Corps—General Li Yu-tang
  3rd Division—General Chao Hsi-tien
  197th Division—General Ting Ping-chuan
 73rd Corps—General Peng Wei-jen
  15th Division—General Wang Chih-pin
  77th Division—General Liu Chi-ming
 128th Division—General Wang Ching-tsai
1st Guerrilla Command—General Kung Ho-chung
1st Army Group—General Lung Yun, Generals Lu Han and Kao
Yin-huai (acting commanders)
 58th Corps—General Sun Tu
  New 10th Division—General Liu Cheng-fu
  183rd Division—General Yang Hung-kuang
 3rd Corps—General Chang Chung
  184th Division—General Chang Chung
  New 12th Division—General Kung Hsun-pi
 60th Corps—General An En-pu
  182nd Division—General An En-pu
  New 11th Division—General Lu Tao-yuan
30th Army Group—General Wang Ling-chi
 78th Corps—General Hsia Shou-hsun
  New 13th Division—General Liu Juo-pi
  One brigade of the New 16th Division
 72nd Corps—General Han Hsien-pu
  New 14th Division—General Fan Nan-hsuan
  New 15th Division—General Teng Kuo-chang
Three divisions of the 32nd Army Group were committed during
the counteroffensive to recapture Nanchang.

CHAPTER 11

Troop units participating in operations in north Hupei west of the Pinghan Railway line:

JAPANESE:

11th Corps—General Okamura
   3rd Division—General Yamawaki
   13th Division—General Tanaka
   16th Division—General Nakashima
   4th Cavalry Brigade

CHINESE:

5th War Area—General Li Tsung-jen
  Right Flank Army—General Chang Tse-chung
    33rd Army Group—General Chang Tse-chung
      55th Corps—General Tsao Fu-lin
        29th Division—General Tsao Fu-lin
        74th Division—General Li Han-chang
      59th Corps—General Chang Tse-chung
        38th Division—General Huang Wei-kang
        180th Division—General Liu Chen-san
        13th Cavalry Brigade—General Yao Ching-chuan
      77th Corps—General Feng Chih-an
        37th Division—General Chia Chien-hsi
        132nd Division—General Wang Chang-hai
        179th Division—General Ho Chi-feng
        9th Cavalry Division—General Chang Teh-hsun
    29th Army Group—General Wang Tsan-hsu
      44th Corps—General Liao Chen
        149th Division—General Wang Tse-chun
        150th Division—General Liao Chen
      67th Corps—General Hsu Shao-tsung
        161st Division—General Hsu Shao-tsung
        162nd Division—General Chang Chieh-cheng
      122nd Division—General Wang Chih-yuan
  Left Flank Army—General Li Pin-hsien
    11th Army Group—General Li Pin-hsien
      39th Corps—General Liu Ho-ting
        34th Division—General Kung Ping-fan
        56th Division—General Liu Shang-chih
      84th Corps—General Chin Lien-fang
        173rd Division—General Huo Wei-chen
        174th Division—General Chang Kuang-wei

189th Division—General Lin Ya-hsi
125th Division—General Wang Shih-chun
River Defense Force—General Kuo Chan
26th Corps—General Hsiao Chih-chu
41st Division—General Ting Chih-pan
32nd Division—General Wang Hsou-shen
185th Division—General Fang Tien
128th Division—General Wang Ching-tsai
9th Peace Preservation Regiment
31st Army Group—General T'ang En-po
85th Corps—General Wang Chung-lien
4th Division—General Chen Ta-ching
23rd Division—General Li Pi-fan
91st Division—General Feng Chan-hsi
13th Corps—General Chang Chen
89th Division—General Chang Hsueh-chung
110th Division—General Chang Chen
193rd Division—General Li Tsung-chien
21st Army Group—General Liao Lei
7th Corps—General Chang Kan
171st Division—General Yang Fu-chang
172nd Division—General Cheng Shu-fang
48th Corps—General Chang Yi-chun
138th Division—General Mo Teh-hung
176th Division—General Ou Shou-nien
2nd Army Group—General Sun Lien-chung
68th Corps—General Liu Ju-ming
119th Division—General Li Chin-tien
143rd Division—General Li Tseng-chih
30th Corps—General Tien Chen-nan
27th Division—General Huang Chiao-sung
44th Separate Brigade
22nd Army Group—General Sun Cheng
45th Corps—General Chen Ting-hsun
127th Division—General Chen Li
41st Corps—General Sun Cheng
124th Division—General Wang Shih-chun

CHAPTER 12

Troop units participating in the first Battle of Changsha:

JAPANESE:

11th Corps—General Okamura

6th Division—General Inaba
106th Division—General Nakai
33rd Division—General Amagasu
3rd Division—General Fujita
101st Division—General Saito
One brigade of the 13th Division—General Tanaka (Nara Column)
Supporting air, naval, and river craft

CHINESE:
9th War Area—General Ch'en Ch'eng
  19th Army Group—General Lo Cho-ying
    32nd Corps—General Sun Ken-tang
      139th Division—General Li Chao-ying
      141st Division—General Tang Yung-liang
    49th Corps—General Liu Tuo-chuan
      105th Division—General Wang Tieh-han
      9th Reserve Division—General Chang Yen-chuan
  1st Army Group—General Lu Han
    58th Corps—General Sun Tu
      New 10th Division—General Liu Cheng-fu
      New 11th Division—General Lu Tao-yuan
    60th Corps—General An En-pu
      183rd Division—General Yang Hung-kuang
      184th Division—General Wan Pao-pang
    Second Advance Column
      6th Kiangsi Peace Preservation Regiment
  30th Army Group—General Wang Ling-chi
    78th Corps—General Hsia Shou-hsun
      New 13th Division—General Liu Juo-pi
      New 16th Division—General Wu Shou-chuan
    72nd Corps—General Han Chuan-pu
      New 14th Division—General Chen Liang-chi
      New 15th Division—General Fu Yi
    Hupei-Hunan Border Area Advance Force—General Fan Sung-pu
      8th Corps—General Li Yu-tang
        3rd Division—General Chao Hsi-tien
        197th Division—General Ting Ping-chun
      Third Advance Column—General Chung Shih-pan
        4th Kiangsi Peace Preservation Regt.—Col. Cheng Chih-chung

5th Kiangsi Peace Preservation Regt.—Col. Chung Shih-
pan
9th Kiangsi Peace Preservation Regt.—Col. Hsu Pu-chih
First Advance Column—General Kung Ho-chung
Hupei Peace Preservation Regiment—Col. Pi Tsung-yun
27th Army Group—General Yang Sen
20th Corps—General Yang Han-yu
133rd Division—General Hsia Chun
134th Division—General Yang Kan-tsai
15th Army Group—General Kuan Lin-cheng
52nd Corps—General Chang Yao-ming
2nd Division—General Chao Kung-wu
25th Division—General Chang Han-chu
195th Division—General Chin Yi-chih
37th Corps—General Chen Pei
60th Division—General Liang Chung-chiang
95th Division—General Lo Chi
79th Corps—General Hsia Chu-chung
98th Division—General Wang Chia-pen
82nd Division—General Lo Chi-chiang
140th Division—General Li Tang
20th Army Group—General Shang Chen
Tung Ting Lake Garrison Command—General Huo Kuei-
chang
53rd Corps—General Chou Fu-cheng
116th Division—General Chao Shao-tsung
130th Division—General Chu Hung-hsun
54th Corps—General Chen Lieh
14th Division—General Chueh Han-chien
50th Division—General Chang Chun
23rd Division—General Sheng Feng-yao
87th Corps—General Chou Hsiang-chu
43rd Division—General Chin Teh-yang
198th Division—General Wang Yu-ying
73rd Corps—General Peng Wei-jen
15th Division—General Wang Chih-pin
77th Division—General Liu Chi-ming
4th Corps—General Ou Chen
59th Division—General Chang Teh-neng
90th Division—General Chen Yung-chi
102nd Division—General Po Hui-chang

70th Corps—General Li Chueh
    19th Division—General Tang Po-yin
    107th Division—General Tuan Heng
New 6th Corps—General Chen Chiu-cheng
    5th Provisional Division—General Tai Chi-tao
    6th Provisional Division—General Lung Yun-fei
74th Corps—General Wang Yao-wu
    51st Division—General Li Tien-hsia
    57th Division—General Shih Chung-cheng
    58th Division—General Chen Shih-chen
5th Corps—General Tu Yu-(Li)ming
    1st Honor Division—General Cheng Tung-kuo
    200th Division—General Tai An-lan
    New 12th Division—General Chiu Ching-chuan
99th Corps—General Fu Chang-fang
    92nd Division—General Liang Han-ming
    76th Division—General Wang Ling-yun
    11th Division—General Yeh Pei-kao

CHAPTER 13

Troop units participating in the campaign in southern Kwangsi:

JAPANESE:
21st Corps—General Seiichi Kuno
    5th Division—General Imamura
    One brigade of the 18th Division
    Taiwan Composite Brigade
    Konoye Division—General Itado
    Supporting air, marine, and naval units of the 4th Fleet

CHINESE:
Generalissimo's Kweilin Headquarters—General Pai Ch'ung-hsi (director)
    16th Army Group—General Hsia Wei
        31st Corps—General Wei Yun-sun
            131st Division—General Chin Lien-fang
            135th Division—General Su Tzu-hsing
            188th Division—General Mo Teh-hung
        46th Corps—General Ho Hsuan
            170th Division—General Hsu Chi-ming
            175th Division
            New 19th Division

26th Army Group—General Tsai Ting-kai
  1st, 2nd, 3rd, and 4th separate infantry regiments
35th Army Group—General Teng Lung-kuang
  64th Corps—General Chen Kung-hsia
    155th Division—General Chen Kung-hsia
    156th Division—General Hua Chen-chung
37th Army Group—General Yeh Chao
  66th Corps—General Yeh Chao
    159th Division—General Tan Sui
    160th Division—General Hua Chen-chung
38th Army Group—General Hsu Ting-yao
  2nd Corps—General Li Yen-nien
    9th Division—General Li Yen-nien
    76th Division—General Wang Ling-yun
  5th Corps—General Tu Yu-(Li)ming
    200th Division—General Tai An-lan
    New 12th Division—General Chiu Ching-chuan
    1st Honor Division—General Cheng Tung-kuo
  9th Corps—General Kan Li-chu
    49th Division—General Li Ching-yi
    93rd Division—General Kan Li-chu
    2nd Reserve Division
  99th Corps—General Fu Chung-fang
    92nd Division—General Liang Han-ming
    99th Division
    118th Division
  36th Corps—General Yao Chuan
    5th Division
    96th Division
43rd Division
New 33rd Division
Kwangsi Pacification Training Division
Supporting air and artillery units

CHAPTER 15

Troop units participating in operations in Hupei from April, 1940, to March, 1941:

JAPANESE:
11th Corps—General Katsuichiro Enbu
  3rd Division—General Yamawaki
  4th Division—General Kenzo Kitano

13th Division—General Tanaka
30th Division—General Muragami
6th Division, less one brigade—General Norimoto Kitano
40th Division, less one brigade—General Amaya
20th Separate Brigade
185th Separate Brigade—General Kayashima

CHINESE:
5th War Area—General Li Tsung-jen
  2nd Army Group—General Sun Lien-chung
    68th Corps—General Liu Ju-ming
      119th Division—General Li Chin-tien
      143rd Division—General Li Tseng-chih
      27th Separate Brigade
    30th Corps—General Chih Feng-cheng
      27th Division—General Huang Chiao-sung
      30th Division—General Chang Chin-lieh
      31st Division—General Chih Feng-cheng
  31st Army Group—General T'ang En-po
    13th Corps—General Chang Hsueh-chung
      89th Division—General Chang Hsueh-chung
      110th Division—General Chang Chen
      New 1st Division
    85th Corps—General Wang Chung-lien
      4th Division—General Chen Ta-ching
      32nd Division—General Wang Hsiu-shen
      11th Separate Brigade
  11th Army Group—General Huang Chi-hsiang
    92nd Corps—General Li Hsien-chou
      21st Division—General Hou Ching-ju
      47th Division
    84th Corps—General Mo Shu-chieh
      178th Division
      188th Division—General Mo Teh-hung
  29th Army Group—General Wang Tsan-hsu
    44th Corps—General Liao Chen
      149th Division—General Wang Tse-chen
      150th Division—General Liao Chen
    67th Corps—General Hsu Shao-tsung
      161st Division—General Hsu Shao-tsung
      162nd Division—General Chang Chieh-cheng
    New 14th Brigade

22nd Army Group—General Sun Chen
    45th Corps—General Chen Ting-hsun
        125th Division—General Wang Shih-chun
        127th Division—General Chen Li
    41st Corps—General Sun Chen
        123rd Division
        124th Division
    1st Guerrilla Division
33rd Army Group—General Chang Tse-chung
    55th Corps—General Tsao Fu-lin
        29th Division—General Tsao Fu-lin
        74th Division—General Li Han-chang
    77th Corps—General Feng Chih-an
        37th Division—General Chia Chien-hsi
        132nd Division—General Wang Chang-hai
        179th Division—General Ho Chi-fang
    59th Corps—General Huang Wei-kang
        38th Division—General Huang Wei-kang
        180th Division—General Liu Chen-san
        9th Cavalry Division—General Chang Teh-shun
75th Corps—General Chou Ai
    6th Division—General Chang Ying
    13th Division—General Fang Ching
    4th Cavalry Division
39th Corps—General Liu Ho-ting
    56th Division—General Liu Shang-chih
River Defense Force—General Kuo Chan
    94th Corps—General Li Chi-lan
        12th Division
        185th Division—General Fang Tien
        55th Division—General Li Chi-lan
    26th Corps—General Hsiao Chih-chu
        23rd Division—General Sheng Feng-yao
        41st Division—General Ting Chih-pan
        44th Division—General Chen Yung
    128th Division—General Wang Ching-tsai
2nd Corps—General Li Yen-nien
    76th Division—General Wang Ling-yun
    33rd Division—General Chia Yun-shan
New 12th Corps—General Cheng Tung-kuo
    1st Honor Division—General Cheng Tung-kuo
    5th Division

18th Corps—General Peng Shan
    18th Division—General Li Fang-pin
    77th Division
    199th Division
Eastern Hupei Guerrilla Force
    7th Corps—General Wang Tsan-pin
        171st Division (one brigade)—General Yang Fu-chang
        172nd Division (one brigade)—General Cheng Shu-fang
        3rd Guerrilla Division
        4th Guerrilla Division
    Guerrilla Corps—General Cheng Ju-huai
        16th Guerrilla Division
        19th Guerrilla Division
        11th Guerrilla Division

CHAPTER 18

Troop units participating in Japanese punitive operations from January 27 to May 27, 1941:

1. *Operations in southern Honan from January 24 to February 10, 1941:*

JAPANESE:
11th Corps—General Enbu
    3rd Division—General Yamawaki
    39th Division
    40th Division—General Amaya
    17th Division
    One regiment of the 4th Division—General Kenzo Kitano (division commander)
    One regiment of the 15th Division
    18th Separate Brigade
    Three tank regiments
    One heavy artillery regiment
    Supporting air units

CHINESE:
5th War Area—General Li Tsung-jen
    2nd Army Group—General Sun Lien-chung
        55th Corps—General Tsao Fu-lin
            74th Division—General Tsao Fu-lin
            29th Division—General Li Tseng-chih
        59th Corps—General Huang Wei-kang

38th Division—General Li Chou-sze
180th Division—General Liu Chen-shan
68th Corps—General Liu Ju-ming
    143rd Division—General Huang Chao-sung
    119th Division—General Chen Hsin-chi
    36th Provisional Division—General Liu Ju-chen
33rd Army Group—General Feng Chih-an
  77th Corps—General Feng Chih-an
    37th Division—General Chi Hsing-wen
    179th Division—General Ho Chi-feng
  30th Corps—General Chih Feng-cheng
    27th Division—General Hsu Wen-yao
    30th Division—General Chang Hua-tang
2nd Army—General Ho Chu-kuo
  3rd Division—General Kuo Hsi-peng
  One separate infantry brigade
31st Army Group—General T'ang En-po
  92nd Corps—General Li Hsien-chou
    21st Division—General Hou Ching-ju
    142nd Division—General Fu Li-ping
    14th Provisional Division—General Liao Yun-tse
  85th Corps—General Li Chu-ying
    4th Division—General Shih Chueh
    25th Division—General Ni Tzu-huei
    11th Reserve Division—General Chang Tang-hsiang
  29th Corps—General Chen Ta-ching
    19th Division—General Lai Ju-hsiung
    91st Division—General Wang Yu-wen
    16th Provisional Division—General Li Chiang
  13th Corps—General Chang Hsueh-chung
    89th Division—General Shu Yung
    110th Division—General Wu Shao-chou
    New 1st Division—General Tsai Chi
  84th Corps—General Mo Chu-chieh
15th Separate Brigade—General Huang Tze-hua
Supporting artillery, engineer, and antitank units

2. *Operations in northwestern Kiangsi from March 15 to April 2, 1941:*

JAPANESE:
11th Corps—General Tadaki Anan
  33rd Division—General Sakurai

34th Division—General Okamo
20th Separate Composite Brigade—General Ikeda

CHINESE:
9th War Area—General Lo Cho-ying, acting commander
    19th Army Group—General Lo Cho-ying
        49th Corps—General Liu Tuao-chuan
            26th Division—General Wang Ke-chun
            105th Division—General Wang Tieh-han
            5th Reserve Division—General Tseng Yu-chu
        70th Corps—General Li Chueh
            19th Division—General Tang Ying-po
            107th Division—General Sung Ying-chung
            9th Reserve Division—General Chang Ying-chung
        72nd Corps—General Han Chuan-pu
            New 14th Division—General Chen Liang-chi
            New 15th Division—General Fu Yi
        74th Corps—General Wang Yao-wu
            51st Division—General Li Tien-hsia
            57th Division—General Yu Cheng-wan
            58th Division—General Liao Ling-chi
        2nd Advance Column—General Kang Ching-lien

3. *Operations in southern Shansi from May 7 to 27, 1941:*
JAPANESE:
North China Front Army—General Terauchi
    1st Corps
        36th Division
        37th Division
        41st Division
        16th Separate Composite Brigade
        9th Separate Composite Brigade
        35th Division
        21st Division
        33rd Division
        One regiment of the 4th Cavalry Brigade

CHINESE:
1st War Area—General Wei Li-huang
    5th Army Group—General Tseng Wan-chung
        3rd Corps—General Tang Huai-yuan
            7th Division—General Tseng Wan-chung
            12th Division—General Tang Huai-yuan

80th Corps—General Kung Ling-hsun
  165th Division
  New 27th Division
  34th Division—General Kung Ping-fan
14th Army Group—General Liu Mao-en
  15th Corps—General Wu Ting-lin
    64th Division—General Wu Ting-lin
    65th Division—General Liu Mao-en
  98th Corps—General Wu Shih-ming
    42nd Division—General Liu Yen-piao
    169th Division—General Wu Shih-ming
  9th Corps—General Pei Chang-hui
    47th Division—General Pei Chang-hui
    54th Division—General Liu Chia-chi
    New 24th Division
  17th Corps—General Kao Kuei-tze
    84th Division—General Kao Kuei-tze
    New 2nd Division
  43rd Corps—General Chao Shih-ling
    70th Division
    New 47th Division
  14th Corps—General Chen Tien
    85th Division
    94th Division—General Chu Huai-ping
  93rd Corps—General Liu Kan
    10th Division—General Li Mo-yen

CHAPTER 19

Troop units participating in the second Battle of Changsha from September 7 to October 8, 1941:

JAPANESE:
11th Corps—General Tadaki Anan
  6th Division—General Kanda
  40th Division—General Aoki
  4th Division—General Kenzo Kitano
  3rd Division
  One brigade of the 33rd Division
  One brigade of the 13th Division
  18th Separate Brigade
  14th Separate Brigade
  Supporting artillery and engineer regiments

CHINESE:

9th War Area—General Hsueh Yueh

    19th Army Group—General Lo Cho-ying

        New 3rd Corps—General Yang Hung-kuang

            183rd Division—General Li Wen-pin

            12th Division—General Chang Yu-jen

        5th Reserve Division—General Tseng Yu-chu

        195th Division—General Kuo Po-li

        Kiangsi Peace Preservation Column—General Hsiung Pin

        2nd Advance Column—General Kang Ching-lien

    30th Army Group—General Wang Ling-chi

        Hunan-Hupei-Kiangsi Border Area Advance Force—General Li Mo-yen

            Southern Hupei Command—General Wang Ching-hsiu

                4th Advance Column—General Hsu Shu-nan

                5th Advance Column—General Huang Tao-nan

                8th Advance Column—General Fang Pu-chou

            3rd Advance Column

          78th Corps—General Hsia Shou-hsun

            13th Division—General Tang Chu-po

        20th Corps—General Yang Han-yu

          133rd Division—General Hsia Chun

          134th Division—General Yang Kan-tsai

          54th Provisional Division—General Kung Ho-chung

        4th Corps—General Ou Chen

          60th Division—General Tung Yu

          59th Division—General Chang Teh-neng

          90th Division—General Chen Kai

          102nd Division—General Po Hui-chang

          7th Advance Column—General Li Tse-liang

        58th Corps—General Sun Tu

          New 10th Division—General Lu Tao-yuan

          New 11th Division—General Liang Teh-kuei

          6th Advance Column—General Li Ching-yi

        72nd Corps—General Han Chuan-pu

          New 16th Division—General Wu Shou-chuan

          New 14th Division—General Chen Liang-chi

          New 15th Division—General Fu Yi

        26th Corps—General Hsiao Chih-chu

          22nd Division—General Wang Hsiu-shen

          41st Division—General Ting Chih-pan

          44th Division—General Chen Yung

37th Corps—General Chen Pei
  140th Division—General Li Tang
  95th Division—General Lo Chi
99th Corps—General Fu Chung-fang
  92nd Division—General Liang Han-ming
  99th Division—General Kao Kuei-yuan
  197th Division—General Wan Yi-wu
10th Corps—General Li Yu-tang
  3rd Division—General Chou Ching-hsiang
  10th Reserve Division—General Fang Hsien-chueh
  19th Division—General Chu Yu
2nd Provisional Corps—General Tsou Hung
  7th Provisional Division—General Wang Tso-chang
  8th Provisional Division—General Chang Chun-yu
79th Corps—General Hsia Chu-chung
  6th Provisional Division—General Chao Chi-ping
  98th Division—General Wang Chia-pen
  82nd Division—General Ou Pai-chuan
74th Corps—General Wang Yao-wu
  51st Division—General Li Tien-hsia
  57th Division—General Yu Cheng-wang
  58th Division—General Liao Ling-chi
Engineer Command—General Chu Huan-ting

Bibliography

Abend, Hallett. *My Life in China, 1926–41*. New York: Harcourt, Brace, 1943.

Arlington, C. L., and Lewishohn, W. *In Search of Old Peking*. Peking: Henry Vetch, 1935.

Axtell, James. *The Scholastic Philosophy of the Wilderness*. Williamsburg: William and Mary Quarterly, Third Series, Volume XXIX, No. 3, July, 1972.

Bisson, T. A. *Japan in China*. New York: Macmillan, 1938.

Bredon, Juliet. *Peking*. Shanghai: Kelly and Walsh, 1933.

Bywater, Hector C. *The Great War in the Pacific*. New York: 1928.

Carlson, Evans F. *The Chinese Army*. New York: American Council, Institute of Pacific Relations, 1940.

———. *Twin Stars over China*. New York: Dodd Mead, 1940.

Clubb, O. Edmund. *20th Century China*. New York: Columbia University Press, 1964.

Collier, Price. *The West in the East*. New York: Charles Scribner's Sons, 1911.

Crow, Carl. *Handbook for China*. Shanghai: Kelly and Walsh, 1933.

Curtis, Lionel. *The Capital Question of China*. London: Macmillan, 1932.

Davies, John Paton, Jr. *Dragon by the Tail*. New York: W. W. Norton, 1972.

Dorn, Frank. *The Forbidden City*. New York: Charles Scribner's Sons, 1970.

———. *Walkout*. New York: Thomas Y. Crowell, 1971.

Fairbank, John K. *The United States and China*. Cambridge: Harvard University Press, 1948.

Gernet, Jacques. *Ancient China*. Berkeley: University of California Press, 1968.

Goette, John. *Japan Fights for Asia*. New York: Harcourt, Brace, 1943.

Griswold, A. Whitney. *The Far Eastern Policy of the United States*. New York: Harcourt, Brace, 1938.

Hahn, Emily. *The Soong Sisters*. New York: Doubleday, 1943.

Hattori, Takushiro. *The Complete History of the Greater East Asia War*. Vol. 1. Tokyo: Hara Shobo Publishing Company, 1948.

450   *Bibliography*

Hsu Long-hsuen and Chang Ming-kai. *History of the Sino-Japanese War, 1937–45.* Taipei, Taiwan: Chung Wu Publishing Company, 1971.

Isaacs, Harold R. *The Tragedy of the Chinese Revolution.* London: Secker and Warburg, 1938.

Joint Committee of Congress. *Investigation of the Pearl Harbor Attack on December 7, 1941.* Washington, D.C. U.S. Government Printing Office, 1946.

Japanese Government. "Japanese Monographs and Studies." Manuscript compiled in Tokyo, Japan, from 1945 to 1960.

————. "Political Strategy prior to the Outbreak of War." Manuscript compiled in Tokyo, Japan, from 1945 to 1949.

Keenan, Joseph B., and Brown, Brendan F. *Crimes against International Law.* Washington, D.C.: Public Affairs Press, 1950.

Lamb, Gene. *A Tabloid History of China.* Tientsin, China: Peiyang Press, 1938.

Langer, William L. *An Encyclopedia of World History.* Boston: Houghton Mifflin, 1948.

Latourette, Kenneth Scott. *The Chinese, Their History and Culture.* New York: Macmillan, 1946.

Lattimore, Owen. *Manchuria, Cradle of Conflict.* New York: Macmillan, 1936.

Linebarger, Paul M. A. *The China of Chiang Kai-shek.* Boston: World Peace Foundation, 1941.

Liu, F. F. *A Military History of Modern China.* Princeton: Princeton University Press, 1956.

Malraux, André. *Man's Fate.* New York: Smith and Haas, 1934.

Miliukov, Paul N. *Russia, Today and Tomorrow.* New York: Macmillan, 1922.

Peck, Graham. *Two Kinds of Time.* Boston: Houghton Mifflin, 1950.

Peffer, Nathaniel. *The Far East, A Modern History.* Ann Arbor: University of Michigan Press, 1958.

Pelissier, Roger, ed. *The Awakening of China, 1783–1949.* New York: Putnam's, 1967.

Powell, John B. *My 25 Years in China.* New York: Macmillan, 1945.

Quigley, Harold S. *The Far Eastern War, 1937–41.* Boston: World Peace Foundation, 1942.

Smedley, Agnes. *Battle Hymn of China.* New York: Alfred A. Knopf, 1943.

Smith, Arthur H. *Chinese Characteristics.* London: Fleming H. Revell Company, 1894.

———. *China in Convulsion.* 2 Vols. New York and Toronto: Fleming H. Revell, 1901.

Snow, Edgar. *Red Star over China.* New York: Random House, 1938.

———. *The Battle for Asia.* New York: Random House, 1941.

Stimson, Henry L. *The Far Eastern Crisis.* New York: Harper Brothers, 1936.

Stuart, John Leighton. *Fifty Years in China.* New York: Random House, 1946.

Toland, John. *The Rising Sun: The Decline and Fall of the Japanese Empire: 1936–1945.* New York: Random House, 1970.

Tong, Hollington K. *Chiang Kai-shek, Soldier and Statesman.* Shanghai: China Publishing Company, 1937.

Treistman, Judith M. *The Pre-history of China.* New York: Doubleday, 1972.

Tuchman, Barbara W. *Stilwell and the American Experience in China, 1911–45.* New York: Macmillan, 1970.

Utley, Freda. *China at War.* New York: John Day, 1939.

Wallin, Homer N. *Pearl Harbor, Why, How, Fleet Salvage and Final Appraisal.* Washington, D.C.: U.S. Naval History Division, 1968.

INDEX

Index

455